The Ancestor, Volume 4

Ancestor
HRA

THE ANCESTOR

A Quarterly Review of County and
Family History, Heraldry
and Antiquities

NUMBER IV
JANUARY 1903

ARCHIBALD CONSTABLE & CO LTD
2 WHITEHALL GARDENS
WESTMINSTER S.W

CONTENTS

                                                                        PAGE
THE KNIGHTS OF CHAWTON (*Illustrated*)   1
NOTES ON THE LORD GREAT CHAMBERLAIN CASE
                          By J. Horace Round   7
THE HUGUENOT FAMILIES IN ENGLAND :
                          III. The Vandeputs   29
THE STORY OF A KEY. By the Lord Hylton   44
THE VALUE OF WELSH PEDIGREES. By H. J. T. Wood   47
THE BONNY HOUSE OF COULTHART
                          By Oswald Barron, F.S.A.   61
THE EARLS OF MENTEITH. By F. A. Blaydes   81
SOME EXTINCT CUMBERLAND FAMILIES : III. The Tilliols
                          By the Rev. James Wilson   88
NORTH COUNTRY WILLS. By W. Paley Baildon, F.S.A. .   101
OUR OLDEST FAMILIES : V. The Leightons   115
NOTES ON SOME ARMORIAL GLASS IN SALISBURY
    CATHEDRAL. By the Rev. E. E. Dorling (*Illustrated*). .   120
A GENEALOGIST'S KALENDAR   127
A FAMILY OF LAWYERS . . . . *facing* 142
THE ARMS OF THE KING-MAKER. By J. Horace Round
                          (*Illustrated*)   143
FAMILY HISTORY IN THE PUBLIC RECORDS   148
REVIEWS :
    The Records of Colchester   149
    Early Lancashire Records   151
    The Oriel Register   159
    Armorial Kalendars   161
    The Swordsman and the Sword   166
    Sussex Marriage Licenses, 1586–1643   170
    A Little Peerage   171
    Scrope of Danby   173
    The Beginning of the Bewleys   176
WHAT IS BELIEVED   183
SOME PORTRAITS AT THE SOCIETY OF ANTIQUARIES
                          By Mrs. G. E. Nathan (*Illustrated*)   190
WHICKLESWICK : A LOST TOWNSHIP. By W. H. B. Bird   205
A FIFTEENTH CENTURY BOOK OF ARMS (*Illustrated*) .   225
LETTERS TO THE EDITOR   251
EDITORIAL NOTES.   258

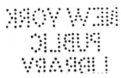

THE pages of THE ANCESTOR will be open
to correspondence dealing with matters
within the scope of the review.

Questions will be answered, and advice
will be given, as far as may be possible,
upon all points relating to the subjects
with which THE ANCESTOR is concerned.

While the greatest care will be taken
of any MSS. which may be submitted for
publication, the Editor cannot make himself responsible for their accidental loss.

All literary communications should be
addressed to

THE EDITOR OF THE ANCESTOR
2 WHITEHALL GARDENS
WESTMINSTER S.W

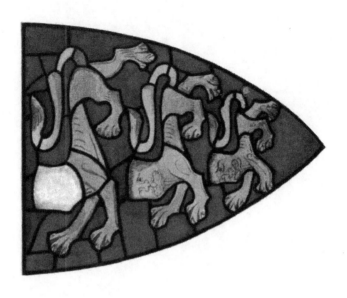

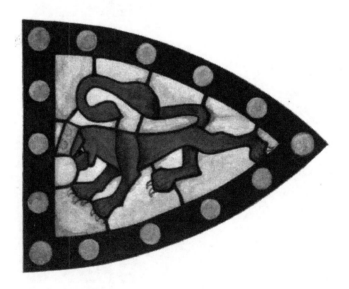

THE KNIGHTS OF CHAWTON

THE little village of Chawton lies some two miles from
Alton along the London road. At this end Alton
straggles, unlovely with gasworks and a modern church, but
ends suddenly without villa outposts, and Chawton, a pretty
village with cottages of the old fashion, is well reached by a
road bordered with trees. Chawton House is an ancient one
lying on the hillside beyond the village, the chief house of a
manor, with a little church upon the slope below it.

For some seven generations Chawton House was the seat
of a Hampshire family of the name of Knight, which came to
an end in 1679. Every succeeding owner has borne their
name, and the continual failure of heirs and the appearance
again and many times again of a new kinsman of the original
stock to make his home in Chawton and to carry on the old
name and shield is one of the most interesting stories to the
genealogist and antiquary.

The Knights were possibly men of the Hampshire lands.
The name recurs at early dates amongst the witnesses to deeds,
but it is frequent in many parts of the country. The arms as
borne by the old house of Chawton were a green shield with a
golden bend engrailed or ' bend lozengy ' as the later heralds
came to style it ; but the evidence of the shield is of little value,
as the same or like arms were assumed by different families of
the name after the haphazard fashion of Tudor armory. They
were borne by an Edmund Knight who was Norroy King of
Arms in the reign of Elizabeth, and they were also credited
during the herald's visitation of London in 1634 to a family
of Knights in Kent, London and Essex who had come from
Calais, together with a crest of a demi-monk or friar with his
hood pulled over his head and a lantern in his hand, a crest
evidently standing for a figure of Night. Between the family
of Norroy, the family from Calais and the family at Chawton
no known connection exists.

At Chawton we begin surely with one William Knight, who
on 19 November, 1524, had a grant of the site of the manor,
with its demesne lands, and from that date the name is settled

at Chawton, which was formerly a manor of the St. Johns.
William Knight is succeeded by his son John Knight, the
builder of what is now the oldest part of Chawton House.
The hall of his building remains, and his building date of 1533
is still to be seen over the old stables before the house.

John Knight is followed by his son, another John, who in
1551 purchased the site of the manor and the demesne lands
which had been leased to his grandfather. The son of this
John the younger, one Nicholas Knight who died in 1585,
completed the purchase of the manor in 1578, by which time
we may assume that the family had come to the condition of
squires or gentry.

The growing fortunes of the house are marked by the
shrievalty of Nicholas's son John Knight, who serves as High
Sheriff of Hampshire in 1609. He dies without issue, and
Chawton passes to a younger son, Stephen Knight, High
Sheriff in 1622. John Knight, Stephen's son and heir, dies
childless, and Richard his brother succeeds, leaving another
Richard his son, seventh in descent from our William of 1524,
and last of his house.

The family ends at its highest point of prosperity. Richard
is knighted and marries with a knight's daughter. Little is
known of his life, but we may believe that he was a known
'malignant,' for his name figures in the list of those chosen
out of Hampshire for the honour of that cavalier order of the
Royal Oak, which he who had hidden in the oak planned but
never brought to be. In this list Richard Knight's name is
followed by an estimate of his income at £1,000 yearly. In
1679 he was one of six knights, all members at one time of the
proud corporation of Winchester, and in that year he dies
without a child to succeed him at Chawton, where his portrait
still hangs, of which portrait we are enabled by the kindness of
the now Knight of Chawton to give an illustration.

If we may trust the painters of that day we English were
in the seventeenth century a handsome race and a dignified.
Richard Knight makes no exception to the rule. His is the
easy face of one who would have been styled a good liver and
an honest householder, and it is fairly set off by his peruke and
laced cravat and the breastplate and pauldrons in which our
ancestors of the Restoration loved to be painted, although the
plates themselves were passing to the lumber room and the
blacksmith's scrap heap.

SIR RICHARD KNIGHT.

THE LEWKENOR CARPET.

SIR CHRISTOPHER LEWKENOR.

MARY, DAUGHTER OF THOMAS BENNETT, ALDERMAN OF LONDON.
WIFE OF RICHARD LEWKENOR. OB. 1648.

Now begins from the death of Sir Richard Knight the curious story of Chawton and its many heirs of many names.

Sir Richard's aunt, Mary Knight, had been married to an Oxfordshire man, Richard Martin of Ensham, and when Sir Richard casts about for a heir he chooses Richard Martin, a grandson of this marriage, to be his devisee of Chawton with its manor and lands.   With Richard Martin a great old family, that of the Lewkenors of Sussex, comes to be associated with Chawton.   Richard Martin's father, Michael Martin, had married Frances, elder daughter and coheir of St. Christopher Lewkenor, knight, the recorder of Chichester, by Mary daughter of John May of Rawmere.

Sir Christopher was a stout cavalier who had been in arms for the king, and had been knighted in 1644, being then a colonel in the king's service. A known malignant, he was declared a traitor by the Commonwealth, which ordered his lands to be sold. He was son of a distinguished lawyer, Sir Richard Lewkenor, Chief Justice of Chester. His grandfather was Chief Justice of Wales and a cadet of the historic house of the Lewkenors, descendants of Roger Lewkenor of Horsted Keynes, sheriff of Surrey under Edward I. The Lewkenor pedigree, a pedigree upon which expert research is sadly needed, shows a long line of knights, sheriffs of Surrey and Sussex and parliament members. They were a soldierly race, casting themselves freely in the strife of the Roses and fighting for King Henry at Bosworth. Their matches were with the noblest of their shire. Sir Thomas Lewkenor married with the daughter and heir of Sir Edward Dalyngruge, founder of Bodyam Castle, by his wife the heir of the Wardeuxs and the Bodyams of that ilk. His son, Sir Roger Lewkenor, matched himself with Eleanor, the sister and coheir of Hugh the last Lord Camoys. From Roger, a younger son of this marriage, came, by four descents, our Sir Christopher Lewkenor. Sir Christopher's picture by Vandyke is at Chawton, but the most important relic there of the Lewkenors is the wonderful carpet hanging upon the wall made for them in 1564 and enriched with shields of the great Lewkenor alliances. When a hundred years old this carpet was sent by a lady of the dying family of Lewkenor to the Knights of Chawton as to the nearest of her blood, to be kept as an heirloom at Chawton.

The strange fate of the house has now fastened upon Chawton, which does not remain for a second generation with

these new lords. Richard Martin takes the name of Knight
and dies unmarried in 1687. His brother and heir, Charles
Martin, takes the name of Knight and dies unmarried in 1702.
Elizabeth their sister and heir succeeds them, and with her the
Lewkenors come again into the story, for her husband, William
Woodward, was son of Sir Christopher's younger daughter by
Edward Woodward of Fosters in Surrey. Her husband, by
whom she had no issue, took the name of Knight. So also
did Bulstrode Peachey, an uncle of the first Lord Selsey, who
was her second husband, by whom in 1735 she was again left
a childless widow. At the last died Elizabeth Knight in 1737,
leaving Chawton away to Thomas May of Godmersham Park,
with whom begins a fourth family of Knight of Chawton.

With Elizabeth Knight in 1737, Knights of Chawton
who could show a descent from the family's first founder come
to an end. Thomas May is a cousin after the broad Scottish
sense. He is not a May. No one in this remarkable pedigree bears their own name for long. Sir Christopher Lewkenor's wife had been a daughter of John May of Rawmere.
Her brother Christopher May left a daughter and heir, Anne,
who married William Brodnax of Godmersham in Kent, whose
son is our Thomas May, whose name of Brodnax became May
in 1727 and Knight in 1738.

The Brodnax family was an old one in that fifth division
of the world—Romney Marsh. At an early date we find
them at Hythe and Burmarsh, and they were matching themselves with families of knightly rank in the sixteenth century.
Thomas Brodnax, afterwards Thomas May and at the last
Thomas Knight, was grandson to William Brodnax of Godmersham, who had married a daughter of the Digges family of
Chilham. William Brodnax was knighted soon after the
restoration, and was fourth in descent from Thomas Brodnax,
the first of Godmersham.

Thomas Brodnax alias May alias Knight was High Sheriff
of Kent in 1729 and rebuilt his ancestral house of Godmersham,
about 1732. He lived on until 1781, leaving one surviving
son Thomas Knight of Chawton and Godmersham. In him the
curse of Chawton was once again fulfilled, for he died without
issue in 1794.

This last Knight, with his pedigree before him, had to seek
out a kinsman who should follow him in the lands and name.
For this purpose a long journey from bough to bough of this

A MEMORIAL OF KING CHARLES I.

THE LEWKENOR JEWEL OF THE BATH.

RICHARD (MARTIN) KNIGHT.
1667-1687.

DAME PRISCILLA KNIGHT.
By Lely.

banyan tree of allied families was necessary. His mother, Jane Monk, was eldest daughter and coheir of William Monk of Shoreham by Hannah his wife, daughter and coheir of Stephen Stringer of Goudhurst in Kent. Stephen Stringer's wife Jane was daughter to John Austen of Grovehurst and of Broadford in Horsmonden, who died in 1705, and sister to another John Austen, whose son William Austen was father of the Reverend George Austen, whose third son Edward Austen, third cousin to Thomas Knight of Chawton, was chosen by him to succeed him at Chawton.

With this Edward Austen begins the last dynasty of Knight of Chawton. He was born of a Kentish family of the same class from which all his predecessors had been drawn, the now all but vanished class of the small squires and gentlemen and yeomen living on and by their estates. The Austen pedigree begins in Horsmonden where John Austen of Broadford died in 1620, leaving eight sons to the founding of the family. His fifth son Francis Austen, who afterwards lived at Grovehurst, was grandfather to Jane Austen, the wife of Stephen Stringer, and to John Austen, great-grandfather to the new owner of Chawton. Under James I. the family bought of the Whetenhalls the manors of Grovehurst, Hoathe, Smeethes and Capell, together with a seat called Broadford, where they lived for several generations.

The Austens were a naval family at the time in our history when a career at sea offered the most glorious of possibilities, but it is not their sea-captains who carry them to the Valhalla of the *Dictionary of National Biography*. Fame has come to their name through the doings of a home-keeping lady of the house, for Edward Knight's sister was no less a Jane Austen than the Jane of Pride and Prejudice, to whose memory our publishers offer a yearly sacrifice of a new edition. She wrote of the life she lived amongst, and in her pages we may imagine ourselves in a picture gallery without a catalogue, hung with nameless Austens, Bridgeses, Brodnaxes and Knights.

Edward Austen became thus Edward Knight of Godmersham and Chawton. He was High Sheriff of Hampshire in 1801 and died at a good old age in 1852. His miniature portrait is amongst our illustrations. His wife, a daughter of Sir Brook Bridges of Goodnestone, died forty-four years before him, leaving behind for a delicate and sufficient memorial her beautiful miniature by Cosway. His eldest son Edward succeeded

him at Chawton, served as High Sheriff in 1822, reached his
father's great age, and died leaving his eldest surviving son by
his second marriage to follow him at Chawton.   This son is
Montagu George Knight, the present lord of Chawton, by
whose kindness we are enabled to give our readers yet another
row of pictures from the walls of an English country house.

Floreat domus, but with the memory before him of the dead
and gone Knights, Martins, Woodwards, Peacheys, Mays and
Brodnaxes who have passed away in fulfilling the hungry fate
which has followed this house, one who bears the name of
Knight of Chawton must needs carry a memorial that the life
of a family is but a fleeting and uncertain thing.

EDWARD KNIGHT, SON OF REV. GEORGE AUSTEN.
OB. 1852, ÆT. 85.

ELIZABETH, DAUGHTER OF MICHAEL MARTIN
OF ENSHAM, OXFORDSHIRE. SHE TOOK THE
NAME OF KNIGHT ON THE DEATH OF HER
BROTHER CHRISTOPHER, IN 1702. OB. 1737,
ÆT. 64.

ELIZABETH, DAUGHTER OF SIR BROOKE
BRIDGES, BART., WIFE OF EDWARD AUSTEN,
AFTERWARDS KNIGHT. OB. 1808, ÆT. 35.
(COSWAY.)

NOTES ON THE LORD GREAT CHAMBERLAIN CASE

IT is probably no exaggeration to say that the contest for
the high office of Lord Great Chamberlain before the
Committee for Privileges in 1902 was, so far as antiquarian
learning and feudal law are concerned, the most remarkable
case of our time. That this solitary survival of the court of
our Norman kings should have for its root of title a charter
of Henry I. is of itself notable enough ; but that descendants
of the original grantee should dispute among themselves,
before the House of Lords, the right to hold the office under
Charles I., George III., and Edward VII., is an even more
striking instance of historical continuity. For the rival
claimants before the Committee in 1902 stood in the shoes of
rival claimants in 1626. The judges of three centuries ago
were summoned, as it were, from their graves, and addressed
once more the House of Lords through the mouths of the
counsel of to-day. Their law on such a matter as this is not
wholly ours ; their facts, in the light of our fuller knowledge,
require much correction ; yet every word that fell from the
lips of Mr. Justice Doddridge, arguing, as against his brother
Crewe, that no private entail could affect the descent of an
office akin to an earldom, was read to the Committee by
Mr. Cripps. And the reasoning of that great antiquarian
lawyer, whose massive features are seen in the frontispiece to
the last volume of *The Ancestor*, was deemed as sound by
counsel for the Crown as it was when it turned the scale in
the days of Charles I.

I do not propose to discuss here the decision arrived at
last spring, having already given a sketch of the case in the
pages of the *Monthly Review*.[1] But, apart from the direct
issue at stake, the question as to which of the claimants was
entitled to this great office—if indeed it had not reverted to
the Crown,—the arguments before the Committee, and the

[1] June, 1902, pp. 42–58. (There are a few printer's errors in the
article, due to the proof having miscarried.)

researches on which they were based, had a bearing on several matters of historical importance or antiquarian interest, and, above all, on certain questions, as yet unsettled, of peerage law, such as the doctrine of abeyance and its development, and the value of the recognition by the Crown of dignities or styles assumed in error or, at least, on no apparent ground.

Having volunteered to act as expert for the Crown in the case, it fell to my lot to prepare memoranda on some of the special points involved and to study the remarkable collection of proofs brought together for the claimants and for the Crown. Of a copy of this collection I am the fortunate possessor, and from it I propose to make some extracts for the benefit of the readers of this Review, commenting on the evidence which they afford.

I.

One of the most important discoveries resulting from the printing of these documents appears, I think I may safely say, to have been detected by no one but myself. Nor, I think, has any mention of it yet appeared. This is the more remarkable because it strongly supports the contention I advanced on behalf of the Crown, a contention which also, as among the claimants, may be said to have favoured the Duke of Atholl against the other competitors. This contention is that the Crown has often recognized in error titles wrongly assumed. The question is one of practical and indeed present importance, not only in view of claims to dignities on the strength of such recognition in the past, but also for its bearing on the *status* of dignities of which the assumption is at present recognized in various ways by the Crown.

It was the Mowbray and Segrave case that definitely raised the issue as to what recognition of a title by the Crown was needed to prove that an abeyance had been 'somehow or other'[1] determined. I need not here repeat my criticism of the amazing decision on this point of the Committee for Privileges on that occasion (1877);[2] the law lords seemed to vie with one another in their eagerness to accept as conclusive evidence recognition by the Crown, in any form, of the titles

---

[1] The expression is the then Lord Chancellor's (*Studies in Peerage and Family History*, p. 439).
[2] Ibid. pp. 435–57.

in question. Their acceptance of such recognition as valid could only be explained by their ignorance of the fact that, as I have already said, the Crown has frequently recognized quite formally, but in error, titles wrongfully assumed ; and unfortunately the fact that it had done so, a fact fatal to the claimant's contention, was not brought to their notice by the representatives of the Crown.

I have elsewhere given abundant proof of this erroneous recognition of peerage titles by the Crown,[1] but the evidence in the Great Chamberlain case has enabled me to add to it by bringing to light the formal recognition by the Crown, in Letters Patent of Creation, of no fewer than five baronies, every one of which must have been wrongfully assumed.

John (Dudley) Earl of Warwick and Viscount Lisle was created Great Chamberlain for life February 17, 1546–7, by Letters Patent of Edward VI. On examining this grant for life—one of the proofs on which the Crown relied—I observed at once that the earl is styled ' Comes Warwici Vicecomes Lisle *Baro de Somerey et Tyas Dominus Dudley*.' Although his use of these styles appears to be quite unknown—it is ignored even in the *Complete Peerage*, which is well informed on these matters—the evidence of these Letters Patent does not stand alone. When this trusted officer of Henry VIII. was raised to the peerage as Viscount Lisle (March 12, 1541–2), he was styled only Sir John Dudley, Kt., in the patent, and no baronies were named ; but at dinner, after his creation, in the Lord Great Chamberlain's chamber, formal proclamation was made of the king's style and of his own, the latter being given as ' du noble et puissant Monsʳ John Duddelley, Visconte Lysley, baron de Malpas, seigneur de Basset de Drayton et de Tiasse.'[2] The new viscount was not satisfied even with this collection of honours. On August 4, 1543, he issued a patent under the great seal of his office of High Admiral as ' Viscount Lisle, baron of Malpas and Somerey, K.G., Lord Bassett and Tyasse,'[3] thus adding to his styles that of ' Baron of Somerey,' which we have seen assigned to him by the Crown three or four years later (February 17, 1546–7).

To account for his use of these styles we must roughly

---

[1] *Studies in Peerage and Family History*, pp. 100, 447–8, 450–6.
[2] *Letters and Papers, Henry VIII.* (1542), xvii. 72, citing Add. MS. 6113, fo. 89.
[3] Ibid. xviii. (ii.), 3, from original at Public Record Office.

grasp his descent. The son of the extortionate and detested minister of Henry VII., John Dudley, as he rose higher and higher in the world, afforded a remarkable illustration of two conflicting tendencies. On the one hand he was eager himself to show that he was no mere upstart, but a member of a house entitled to ancient feudal honours. On the other, the men who envied his rise, and the 'ancient nobility' doubtless as well, were busy spreading the tale that he was really of plebeian origin. For we must not forget that if the 'new man' has been apt at all periods to seek for himself a pedigree, malice and jealousy have been apt also to detract from the origin of those who have risen greatly in the world. I was recently sent a precise narrative of the origin of a certain ducal house less than two centuries ago. It was utterly irreconcilable, of course, with all the peerage books, but appeared to be a straightforward story with no malice about it. Yet a short examination convinced me that its facts were sheer invention, and that the whole tale sprang from the tendency of which I have spoken. The alleged humble origin of the two families in question had no foundation in fact. And this appears to have been the case with Dudley's origin also. Mr. Sidney Lee, who has investigated the matter with his usual care, holds, in his 'Life of Edmund Dudley' for the *Dictionary of National Biography*, that John's grandfather was a younger son, as John himself formally certified, of a Lord Sutton de Dudley, and was not, as the spiteful story ran, a mere carpenter of Dudley. In the *Complete Peerage* this view is accepted by G. E. C., but those who may wish to learn more of a matter hotly discussed when Dudleys were high in favour may refer to Twamley's *History of Dudley Castle and Priory*, where they will find discussed at some length (pp. 25–6, 118–21) the views that have been held on the subject.[1]

What is absolutely certain is that John Dudley took advantage of the impoverished condition of the head of the house to purchase from him Dudley Castle, the ancient seat of his Someri ancestors. Twamley held that he did this before 1543, and even, probably, not later than 1538. Canon Dixon, on the other hand, though actually citing Twamley, places the

---

[1] 'This ambitious nobleman was extremely anxious that it should be believed that he was connected with the Sutton family, though he was probably descended from a Dudley carpenter' (p. 25).

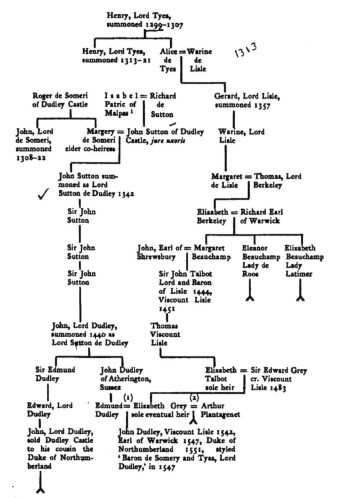

¹ She had a moiety of the barony of Malpas in right of her father and another quarter in right of her mother.

purchase apparently in 1552 or 1553.[1] The importance of the date lies in the fact that John Dudley's assumption of styles which could only be claimed (whether rightly or wrongly) by the head of his house must have been based on his acquisition of the old *caput baroniæ*, Dudley Castle. It will be seen from the pedigree on preceding page that the styles of Malpas, Somerey and Dudley were all derived from this source ; and as he had already, when created a viscount (March 12, 1541–2), assumed the first of the three, his acquisition of the castle may be placed before that date.

Malpas, of course, was the title not of a peerage dignity, or even of a pre-peerage baron *in capite*, but of one of the Earl of Chester's barons in his palatinate. Someri (' Somerey '), as will be seen from the pedigree, must have been assumed in right, not of a direct, but of a collateral ancestor (summoned from 1308 to 1321), of whom the Suttons of Dudley moreover were only the senior co-heirs. There were thus three objections to that assumption of this title by Dudley which received the formal sanction of the patent of 1547 : (1) it would now be recognized as extinct ; (2) if it was not extinct it was vested in co-heirs ; (3) Dudley was not, in any case, one of such co-heirs. As for the barony of Dudley itself, attributed to John, Earl of Warwick in the patent of February 17, 1546–7, it was clearly that which was then vested in his grievously impoverished cousin, the head of the house.

On the other hand the barony of ' Tyas ' or ' Tyasse ' was one which (the pedigree shows) the earl must have claimed through his mother. But if its attainder in 1321 was, as alleged, reversed some years later, John Dudley was, even so, only its senior co-heir, and the title apparently had not been heard of for more than two centuries. The Beauchamp coheiress through whom he derived his share in its representation gave him an excuse for adopting Warwick as the title of his earldom, for using as a badge the bear and ragged staff of its earls, and for powdering his guidon ' with ragged stayffes of silver.' By a singular coincidence the barony of Tyas, Tyes, or Teyes,[2] after thus fitfully emerging in its assumption by John Dudley, one of its co-heirs, made its appearance anew in 1660, when George Monck was created Duke of

---

[1] *Dictionary of National Biography*.
[2] The latinized form of the name in early days, viz. ' Teutonicus,' has sometimes puzzled antiquaries.

Albemarle and Baron Monck of Potheridge, Beauchamp and *Teyes*. George Monck, like John Dudley, was a man of gentle birth, but wished, on rising rapidly in rank, to accentuate the fact by selecting titles indicating ancient descent. His ancestor Thomas Monck of Potheridge had married a half sister (*ex parte materna*) of John Dudley, and though he could not take, like him, Warwick for a title—that earldom being then held by the Rich family—he obtained Albemarle, a Beauchamp title, and added to his baronial styles Beauchamp and Teyes. These of course were new creations, for he was not even a co-heir of Beauchamp or of Teyes. In October 1688 his titles became extinct, and six months later a barony of Teyes was among the peerage dignities bestowed by William III. on Marshal Schomberg. This barony is described by Courthope and by G. E. C. as 'Teyes, co. Middlesex,'[1] but I think that this is a misapprehension, and that it was merely a revival of one of Monck's titles, senselessly bestowed on Schomberg after the fashion of the time.

Dudley's reason for not assuming his mother's barony of Lisle was doubtless, as suggested by Courthope and others, followed by G. E. C., that he had alienated the manor of Kingston Lisle, the possession of which was then necessary to a claimant of that title. Moreover it was virtually represented among his peerage dignities by the Viscountcy of Lisle. For his assumption of the barony of Basset of Drayton it is not easy to account. The heirship to the last baron is a matter of some difficulty ; indeed, in the last volume of *The Ancestor* two contradictory versions of that heirship are, apparently, given (pp. 166, 217). It is, in any case, an interesting addition to the history of that title, which was also assumed by the family of Shirley, and to such good purpose that when their heir-general was created Earl of Leicester (1784), his possession of the barony was formally recognized in the patent ! Here was a case precisely parallel to the recognition, by the patent of 1547, of John Dudley's assumptions, and on it Courthope thus comments :—

An instrument has thus been allowed to issue under the Great Seal, in which *three* Baronies are recognized to be vested in an individual, to *neither* of which he was *legally entitled* ; and what is no less extraordinary, one of the

---

[1] *Complete Peerage*, vii. 380. 'County Middlesex' should apply only, I think, to the accompanying earldom of Brentford.

said dignities has never existed since the reign of Edward I., and another was at that moment entirely vested in other persons.[1]

Yet this is the sort of evidence that will have to be accepted as decisive if the Mowbray and Segrave judgment is allowed to have any weight.

When the Earl of Warwick surrendered in his turn the Lord Great Chamberlainship it was bestowed for life on William (Parr), Marquis of Northampton, by Letters Patent of February 4, 1550. In this patent I at once detected the recognition by the Crown of two more assumptions. For in it the grantee is styled 'Marchio Northampton' comes Essex' dominus Parre *dominus Mermyon dominus Seintquintin* et de Kendall.'[2] Here again we have two assumptions of no small interest, both of them unknown to the compiler of the *Complete Peerage*. The pedigree which I have constructed opposite will show that Sir William Parr was a junior co-heir of the Lords FitzHugh, who were junior co-heirs of the Lords Marmion and sole heirs of the barony of St. Quintin, if such a barony existed.

It is a singular fact that the barony bestowed on Sir William Parr was at first actually believed to be that of FitzHugh. John Hussey wrote that he heard that Sir William Parr 'shall be Lord Fytzhyw,'[3] and on the very day of his creation (March 9, 1538–9[4]) the same correspondent actually asserts that he has been made 'Lord Fytzhywe.'[5] His assumption of the Marmion barony presents no difficulty, but that of the St. Quintin title is very curious. For a Committee for Privileges to-day would certainly not consider that he had any right to it, even as a co-heir. There was in the first place but one summons, with no proof, it would seem, of sitting ; and in the second this summons was to a Parlia-

---

[1] Compare *Complete Peerage*, i. 258.

[2] I do not lay stress on Kendal being here entered as if it were a separate title. The Parrs had for some generations been 'of Kendal,' and William Parr is usually stated to have been originally created Lord Parr *of Kendal.* It is pointed out however by G. E. C. (vi. 69, note *b*) that he seems to have been created Lord 'Parr' simply. I would suggest that, when his uncle was created Lord Parr 'of Horton' (23 Dec. 1543), it became necessary to distinguish his own barony of Parr as that of Parr 'of Kendal.'

[3] *Letters and Papers, Henry VIII.* (1539), xiv. (i.), 179.

[4] This has hitherto been undetermined.

[5] *Letters and Papers, Henry VIII.* (1539), xiv. (i.), 187.

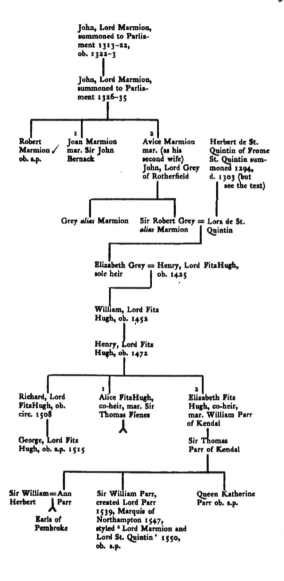

John, Lord Marmion, summoned to Parliament 1313–22, ob. 1322–3

John, Lord Marmion, summoned to Parliament 1326–35

Robert Marmion ob. s.p.

1 Joan Marmion mar. Sir John Bernack

2 Avice Marmion mar. (as his second wife) John, Lord Grey of Rotherfield

Herbert de St. Quintin of Frome St. Quintin summoned 1294, d. 1303 (but see the text)

Grey *alias* Marmion

Sir Robert Grey = Lora de St. *alias* Marmion Quintin

Elizabeth Grey = Henry, Lord FitzHugh, sole heir ob. 1425

William, Lord Fitz Hugh, ob. 1452

Henry, Lord Fitz Hugh, ob. 1472

Richard, Lord FitzHugh, ob. circ. 1508

1 Alice FitzHugh, co-heir, mar. Sir Thomas Fienes

2 Elizabeth Fitz Hugh, co-heir, mar. William Parr of Kendal

George, Lord Fitz Hugh, ob. s.p. 1515

Sir Thomas Parr of Kendal

Sir William = Ann Herbert Parr

Earls of Pembroke

Sir William Parr, created Lord Parr 1539, Marquis of Northampton 1547, styled 'Lord Marmion and Lord St. Quintin' 1550, ob. s.p.

Queen Katherine Parr ob. s.p.

ment recognized as of very doubtful validity, namely that of
22 Edward I. (1294).[1] Moreover the descent, as it stands,
appears to be clearly erroneous when compared with that of
Marmion. One or more generations seem to be omitted,
but the pedigree as I give it is that which is accepted in the
Complete Peerage and elsewhere. Although the assumption of
this title by William Parr has been overlooked, Courthope,
followed by G. E. C., mentions that the Earls of Pembroke
(his sister's heirs) assumed it. The singular question now
arises whether the present Earl of Pembroke could not claim
the barony, urging that, according to the judgment in the
Mowbray and Segrave case, the patent of 1550 is proof that
the abeyance of the barony had 'somehow or other' been
determined in favour of the Parr co-heir, and that such determination involved the existence of this barony, and, in consequence, the validity of the writ of 1294 and the absence of
any necessity for proving a sitting under it. Would not
that be a pretty question for the Committee for Privileges
to decide ?

Attention may be drawn to another case, not indeed of
formal recognition in error by the Crown, but of the formal
use of the style of a barony by a peer who would be only
recognized as one of its co-heirs. John Beke of Eresby,
Lincs, was summoned to Parliament in 1295 and 1296. Any
right to a barony under these summonses fell into abeyance
(by the modern doctrine) between his two daughters at his
death.[2] These were Alice, wife of Sir William Willoughby of
Willoughby (whose son and heir obtained all Eresby), and
Margaret, wife of Sir Richard Harcourt of Stanton Harcourt.[3]

---

[1] See the observations under ' Clyvedon ' in Courthope's *Historic Peerage*.
It may be useful to add that there was some discussion on writs of summons
to this Parliament in the Wahull case (1892). I am indebted to Mr. Lindsay, K.C., one of the counsel in the case, for the loan of the Minutes of
Evidence, in which I noted this (pp. 64 et seq.).

[2] See *Complete Peerage*, i. 304 ; viii. 141, 306.

[3] See *Coll. Top. et Gen.* iv. 344–5, where nothing is said of Margaret's
heirs. In the *Complete Peerage* (i. 304) she is styled ' ancestress of the Earls
Harcourt.' It may be worth noting, therefore, that her representation soon
passed, with an heiress, from the Harcourts to the Astleys of Pateshull, Staffs.,
with whom it remained till some century and a half ago, when it fell among
co-heiresses, of whom the eldest has since been represented by the Earls ot
Tankerville.

No assumption of 'Beke' as a title is mentioned, it would seem, in the *Complete Peerage*, but the evidence in the Great Chamberlain case brings to our knowledge the fact that at the Coronations of James II., William and Mary, and Anne, Robert Earl of Lindsey (then Great Chamberlain) styled himself 'Baron de Willoughby *Beke* et Eresby,'[1] in his petitions to the Court of Claims, and that his son Peregrine, Duke of Ancaster, used the same styles, before the Court of Claims, at the Coronation of George II.[2] Doubtless some document could be found proving that the Crown took him or his father at their own valuation in the matter, and that the abeyance of the barony of Beke had, consequently, 'somehow or other' been determined. The point has an interest of its own, because the Willoughby barony dates only from 1313, while that of Beke would be assigned to 1295 or 1296. This has a direct bearing on G. E. C.'s suggestion that 'it is very possible that the precedence of the Barony of Beke (1295) was allowed to that of Willoughby, and that the summons of 1313 may be looked on in the light of a termination of the abeyance[3] of the Barony of Beke in favour of the Willoughby co-heir.'[4]

But nothing is so surprising as the petition of the Earl of Oxford to the Court of Claims of Charles II. (similarly printed among the proofs from the Coronation Roll), in which he is allowed to style himself 'Seigneur Bolebeck Stanford [i.e. Sandford] Badlesmere et Scales grand Chamberlaine d'Angleterre,' although his right to the whole of these titles had been notoriously disallowed in 1626 ![5]

Law, we must remember, is not always equivalent, as alleged, to common sense, and although the historian would at once recognize the importance of the fact that the Crown has recognized the assumption of dignities in error, the lawyer, it would seem, does not. So, at least, I gathered when pre-

---

[1] This curious combination seems to be parallel to William Parr's 'dominus Mermyon, dominus Seintquintin et de Kendall.'

[2] Coronation Rolls of these Sovereigns.

[3] This is dangerously modern language.

[4] *Complete Peerage*, viii. 141, note (b). Compare the suggestion as to the Barony of Teyes being really the origin of that of Lisle (these dignities have been dealt with above) in vol. vii. p. 381, note (a).

[5] 'Scales' was not expressly named on that occasion, but any right to it (as senior co-heir) had passed away from the Veres, with the other baronies named, in 1526, according to that decision.

paring the evidence for the Crown in the Lord Great
Chamberlain case. Not much stress, I learnt, could be laid
on the evidence of such recognition as bearing on the recognition, undoubtedly in error, by Queen Mary and Queen
Elizabeth of the hereditary right of the Earls of Oxford to
the Lord Great Chamberlainship. Yet, as I have said, the
value of Queen Elizabeth's acceptation of their claim to that
office is shown by the fact that she had recognized in no less
formal a manner their right to a viscountcy and two baronies,
all of which they had assumed in error, as was duly decided
by the judges in their opinions delivered to the House of
Lords (1626).[1] In a great indenture of entail (1575) the
parties thereto are styled

Edward de Veer, Erle of Oxenforde, Lord Great Chamberlaine of
England, *Viscount Bulbeck and Lord of Badlesmere and Scales*, of thone partie,
and the right honorable Thomas Erle of Suffolk, Viscount Fitzwater, *Lord
Egremonde and Burnell* . . . Sir William Cordell knight master of the Rolls,
and Thomas Bromley Esquier the Quenes majesties Solicitor Generall of
thother partie.

The whole of the titles here italicized in a formal indenture
to which the Master of the Rolls and the Solicitor-General
were parties were mere wrongful assumptions ; and if it be
urged that here at least they were not formally recognized by
the Crown, I reply that by a writ of Privy Seal (June 8, 1588)
Queen Elizabeth granted Earls Colne Priory 'Edwardo de
Veere comiti Oxon *vicecomiti Bulbeck* magno Camerario Anglie
domino de Badlesmere et de Scales.'[2] We have only to italicize
also the words 'magno camerario Anglie' to solve the whole
problem of the Lord Great Chamberlain case. This the
historian certainly would do ; the lawyer, it seems, would not.
Here as elsewhere, in my own experience of this historic case,
I could only say with good reason : 'If this is law, give me
history.'

II

The grants for life only of the Great Chamberlainship of
England, made in the reigns of Henry VIII. and of Edward VI.,
were among the most keenly discussed documents in the case.
For the whole history of its descent was upset by the discovery,

---

[1] See *Monthly Review* (as above), pp. 52–3, and compare p. 17, note 5, above.
[2] These documents are in the possession of the Rt. Hon. James Round, M.P.

established on this occasion, that the Earl of Oxford who was known to have held it from 1526 to 1540 had done so, not by hereditary right, but only under a grant for life. Thus was solved the great difficulty which had always surrounded the descent, for this earl, though heir-male of his predecessor in the earldom, was not, as the earls had been till then, heir-general under the charter by which Henry I. granted the Great Chamberlainship, and had, therefore, no hereditary right to that great office.[1] This discovery was frankly admitted in Lord Ancaster's 'case,' where we read, 'It has now been ascertained that the King in the first instance granted this office *for life* to John, Earl of Oxford, who died 1540.'

Before this fact had been discovered it was difficult to account for the circumstance that this earl had not been succeeded by his son and heir in the office of Great Chamberlain. When the right to the office was disputed in 1660, some rough notes were compiled for the use of Montagu, Earl of Lindsey, then Great Chamberlain, and in these the above difficulty was thus accounted for :—

John the 6th of that name was Earle of Oxford and Lo. Great Chamberlaine of England and lived till 7th Eliz., and by reason he was not so wise as his ancestors and came seldom to co(u)rt the office of Great Chamberlaine was granted to John, Earl of Warwick, Viscount Lisle, for life, etc., etc.

I have seen the absurd document from which this quotation is taken, but it will probably be enough to say that it places the life grant of the office to Robert, Earl of Sussex in 32 Henry VIII. *before* what is known as the Award, which famous and hotly discussed record it assigns to ' 33 H. VIII.', though its date is well known to be ten years earlier (23 Henry VIII.). This alone will be sufficient to show the worthlessness of such a document, of which the writer was obviously at sea. Yet this amazing document was actually printed in full among the proofs of Lord Ancaster's case.

That I have not, in so describing it, spoken too strongly will be evident from this extract from *Speeches delivered by Counsel* (pp. 183–4) :—

Attorney-General. My Lords, there is only one other document, that is of much later date, on which I ought to say a word or two in this connexion ; it is a document which was read by my learned friend, Mr. Haldane,—it is at page 188 of this same volume. . . . [reads extracts].

[1] See chart pedigree of the Earls of Oxford on next page.

Lord Davey. What has that reference to ?
Attorney-General. I do not know, my Lord.
Lord Davey. Does anybody know ?
The Lord Chancellor. It purports to refer to an Act of Parliament ?
Attorney-General. Yes, my Lord, the year of which is not given [!] . . .
Lord James of Hereford. What evidence is there for this document ?
Attorney-General. No evidence whatever.
Lord Chancellor. I take it that it would not be evidence at all. If you look at it, it does not purport to be the original document at all. . . .
Attorney-General. Yes, my Lord. I called attention to the fact that this was not evidence when my learned friend, Mr. Haldane, began to read it, but your Lordship said that it might be taken for what it is worth, and I submit it is worth nothing ; so far as it goes the assertions are so wild that they rather turn the case the other way.

Nevertheless, as was pointed out by the Attorney-General—

it seems to have started the idea, which was exploited by some of my learned friends, that the sixteenth Earl was not so wise as some of his ancestors, and that that accounts for these life grants that were made by Henry VIII. and Edward VI.

The argument of Lord Ancaster's counsel to this effect was unlucky, for its baseless character was easily shown. But it had the effect of introducing the most diverting evidence by which the case was enlivened. And, oddly enough, not content with disparaging the intelligence of the earl (1540–65), who was 'not so wise as his ancestors,' counsel—'by mistake,' perhaps, as the Attorney-General suggested—disparaged that of his predecessor and kinsman, the fourteenth Earl ! A chart pedigree is needed to make the kinship clear.

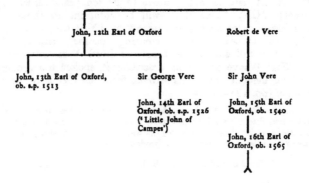

To quote from another part of the Attorney-General's speech :—

> My Lords, it has been suggested in the course of this case that the sixteenth Earl, who succeeded to the Earldom in 1540, was not so wise as his ancestors, I think, it has been put . . . Three successive earls have been disparaged, one, I think, by mistake—the fifteenth for the sixteenth ; but the real intention was to disparage the sixteenth Earl, and to suggest that he was not quite so wise as some of his ancestors had been. And your Lordships remember that my learned friend, Mr. Haldane, read a good deal of matter evidently with that object. I would only refer your Lordships, if I may, to such a source of information as the *Dictionary of National Biography* . . . and I really do not know what is the ground for suggesting that the sixteenth Earl was so incapable that it would give some sort of colour to the idea that these grants were made on account of his particular incapacity.[1]

The first document cited in this connection by Mr. Haldane was the grant to the Duke of Norfolk (May 29, 1514) of the wardship of the fourteenth earl—known as ' Little John of Campes' (from his Cambridgeshire seat at Castle Camps)— who had succeeded his uncle in 1513, being then a boy of about thirteen. After the manner of the time he had already been betrothed, but the document recites that, though this was done ' according to the law of the Church,' the king, on the boy becoming his ward, rejected the betrothal as invalid on the ground that the young earl had been under fourteen at the time, ' whereby it appertained to us by reason of our prerogative to offer and propose to the same now Earl another woman as his wife . . . to which same Earl . . . we offered Margaret Courteney that he should take her as his wife . . . which he utterly refused.'[2] For this the youth had to pay a heavy fine to the king, who, however, bestowed the amount on the Duke of Norfolk, by whom the young earl was secured as a son-in-law.

Ten years later the young earl and his wife, who had attended, in due splendour, the Field of the Cloth of Gold (1520), were the subject of the following wonderful ' Order,' framed by no less great a person than Cardinal Wolsey himself.[3]

> An order made by the reverend Father in God Thomas Woolsey Cardinall of England by direcčon from the Kinge to Lymitt John Earle of Oxenford in the orderinge of his expences of houshold and other his affaires in his yonger yeares as allsoe for his demeanor towarde the Countesse his wief in the xv^th yeare of Kinge H. 8.

[1] *Speeches delivered by Counsel*, p. 175.   [2] Ibid. p. 19.
[3] Quoted by Mr. Haldane (ibid.). The authority cited is the Hargrave MS. 249 (p. 223), and the date of the document is February 16, 1523–4.

ffirste it is ordered by the most reverend Father in God, Thatt to th' intent the said Earle yett beinge younge and nott att anie fordele to maintaine a great and ordinarie house maie not onelie by example of other have better experience and knowledge here after of such thinges as bee requisite for him to knowe in that behalfe but alsoe by spareinge and moderate expences in the beginninge of his youth bee more aboundantlie furnished beforehand for the supportacon and maintenance of those and other charges when the Cause shall require, and in the meane time bee the better able to serve the Kinges grace as shall appertaine, The same Earle shall incontinentlie dissolve discharge and breake his houshold, Soejourninge hee and the Ladie his wief theire familie and servantes hereafter to be menčiond wth His ffath^r in Lawe the duke of Norffolke at such convenientt prizes for theire boardes as betweene the same duke and the Ladie Dutchesse his wief and the said Earle of Oxford by mediacon of his ffreindes can be accorded Covenanted and agreed.

Item it is further Ordered thatt for good Councell to bee givenn and due service to bee done vnto the said Earle and the Countesse his wief as well in orderinge of his landes as otherwise they shall have the number of officers and servants vnder written (vizt) for his landes John Josselin to bee his Audito^r And Surveio^r and Receiver of the same and for the said service of them both one Chaplyn, twoe gent[lemen], sixe yeomen, three Groomes, and three horsekeepers wch a page, Twoe Gentle Woemen and one Chamberer to attend vppon the Ladie his wief, Of wch said menn and women servantes nowe to be deputed chosen and assigned the said Earle of Oxenford shall wth all diligence certifie the names in writeinge vnto the said moste Reverend Father to the intentt thatt vppon inquirie and knowledge had of theire sadnes good demean' and fidelity they maie bee by him approved or not beinge found of such quality reiected and accepted And semblablie from time to time the said moste reverend Fath^r in God shall approve such officers and servantes as hee shall thinke good to bee about the said Earle and Countesse his wief for theire most Weale Hono^r and proffitte, And them vppon theire merittes or demerites to accepte or expell att his pleasure, Wherevnto the said Earle shall at all seasons bee conformable Nott admitteinge or takeinge into his service anie person but such as shalbee by the said most reverend Fath^r soe allowed and approved (as aforsaid).

Item the said officers and servauntes and everie of them from time to time being shalbee takenn vsed and ordered as officers and servantes indifferentlie to the said Earle and Ladie his wief beinge obedientt to theire service and good comandem^{tes} wthoutt anie speciall Lymitacon, of anie of the said officers or menn servauntes to bee either the said Earles or the said Countesses servauntes onelie, whereby there should appere or arise anie particuler or partiall distincčon some of them to belonge vnto the said Earle and some to the said Countesse.

Item the said Earle of Oxford shall sadlie moderatelie and wth temperance and discretionn vse himselfe from time to time as well in his expences as in his diett, and other his dailie conversačons forbearing to make or passe anie Graunte of Annuite office or otherwise but by the advise and consentt of the said most reverend Fath^r in escheweinge the greate decaie of his Landes and hindrance in his substance, semblably for conservacon of healthe and avoidinge sundrie inconveniences hee shall have vigilant regard thatt hee vse not much to drink hott wines, ne to drinke or sitte up Late or accustome himself wth hotte or vnwholsome meates contrary to his complection whereby hee may bee broughte into infirmitie and disease.

Item the said Earle shall alsoe moderate his hunteinge or other Disporte or haunteinge or vseinge the same excessiuely daily or customably But onely at such tymes and seasons as maie bee convenientt for the Weale and recreačon of his Bodie and as by the saddest and moste discreeteste of his servauntes shalbee advised and thought expedientt.

Item in all oth^re the gestures and behaviours of the said Earle he shall vse himselfe hono^bly prudently and sadlie forbearinge all riotous and wild companies excessiue and superfluous apparell, And namely hee shall as to a nobleman apperteigneth Loveingly familiarlie and kindlye intreat and demeane himself towarde the said Countesse his wief as there may bee perfecte Love Concord and vnitie engendered nourished and continewed betweene them as to the lawes of God, and for bringeinge forth fruite and childrenn betweene them to Gods pleasure doth apperteigne, wherein the said Earle shall speciallie see thatt hee give not eare and harkeninge vnto simple or euill tongued personns wch ffor particuler malice or to attaine ffavor thankes or otherwise shall contrive sedičous and slanderous reporte betweene them, But like a Nobleman shall cherishe Loue and entertaine the said Countesse his wief wth all gentlenes and kindnes to bee vsed eith^r to oth^r And generallie the said Earle shall discreetly substantially and sadly Governe vse behave and order himself in all his actes demeanores gestures and proceedings as to such a Nobleman doth and shall appertaine, ffor observačon of wch premisses deuised by the Kinge speciall comandem^t : for the politiq' orderinge weale and increase of the said Earle (as aforsaid) Nott onely hee standeth Bound wth sufficientt suretes to the said most reuerend Fath^r (Thatt is to saie) hee himselfe in the sofñe of Twoe Thousand Powndes and sixe suretes everie of them in ffive Hundred markes.[1] But alsoe theise presente Articles in papers indented Tripartite the one remayneinge wth the same most reuerend Fath', anoth^r wth the said Earle, and the Third wth the Executores of the Laste Will and Testam^t of the Late Earle of Oxford signed wth all theire Handes bee alternately and interchangeably deliuered eith 'to oth', The 16th day of ffebruarie the 15th yeare of the Kinges raigne [16 Feb. 1524].

JOHN OXENFORD.[2]

F. CARKIS.
EBOR.[2]

After this document, or the bulk thereof, had been read, the chancellor not unnaturally observed :—

It is very interesting, but I do not know that it seems to reflect any light upon the Chamberlainship.[3]

For, as the accompanying pedigree shows, the earl in question (1513–26) had nothing to do with the earl (1540–65) whose intelligence was impugned.[4]

[1] They would thus be sureties for £2,000 in addition to the earl's own £2,000.
[2] These represent the signatures of the earl and the cardinal.
[3] *Speeches delivered by Counsel*, p. 20.
[4] At a later stage the chancellor, with equal justice, remarked : 'But it was only in respect of Little John that I heard any imputation upon the intelligence of any of them' (ibid. p. 175).

The allusions in this document to Little John's 'hunteinge' tempt me to quote from another source an allusion to that of his successor, the more especially as any reference to fox-hunting as an aristocratic sport at so early a date as this is of great rarity and interest.

Father, I besetch you whan ye meet wyth the ryght honorable lorde ot Oxforth, to geve thanks unto hys Lorchyp, for whan he came to a towne callyd Yeldam,[1] to the parsons there of to hunte the foxe, he sente for me and my cossyns, and mad us good schere ; and lett us see schuch game and plesure as I never saye in my lyfe.[2]

This delightful schoolboy letter was written to 'Master Crumwell' by his son Gregory, then being taught, with his cousins, by the rector of Toppesfield, Essex, from which place it is written. One would like to know the name of the jolly parson of Yeldham, the parish adjoining Toppesfield, who seems to have given Gregory many a 'good time.' The letter[3] is the more interesting because Mr. Asquith seems to have suggested that Cromwell had sinister designs in the matter of the Great Chamberlainship and played the earl false in drafting 'the Award.'[4] Yet he and Mr. Haldane had both quoted the interesting letter of the earl to Cromwell some two years after 'the Award, which is addressed 'To his loving friend Mr. Cromwell,' and in which he styles him 'My especial friend as always you have been.'[5]

We may now pass at last to the sixteenth earl (1540–65), the one who, we are asked to believe, was 'not so wise as his ancestors.' It is to him that the following letter of his brother-in-law Sir Thomas Darcy of Chiche (now St. Osyth) relates.

(27 *June*, 1547)

Sir Thomas Darcy to William Cecil.

After right harte comendacõ(ns) these shalbe to advertyse you y⁺ accordynge to my late cõicacyon had w⁺ yow in my lords graces galerye at Westmynster, I have by all means y⁺ I can inqryd of ye mater, betwen my lorde of Oxenford and the gentillwoman w⁺ whom hee is in Love namyd Mⁿ Dorothe late

---

[1] Doubtless Great Yeldham, of which the living seems to have been then in the earls' gift. The parish adjoined Castle Hedingham, in which was their ancestral seat.

[2] Ellis' *Original Letters*, 3rd ser. i. 339 (No. cxxi.).

[3] It is dated October 15, and assigned to 1531 in *Letters and Papers, Henry VIII.* v. 227.

[4] *Speeches delivered by Counsel*, pp. 150–1.

[5] Ibid. pp. 31–2.

woman to my Ladie Katheryn his doughter, And uppon cõicacyon had wᵗ them bothe, I have founde and doe perceyve them to bee in the same case yᵗ they wer in when my said lorde of Oxenforde was befor my lordes grace And non other, savynge that the bannes of matrimonye between them were twyse proclaymed in on daye, other treatyse or solempne cõicacyon hathe not ben before wytnesse but onlye be in secrett between them twayn. Syr yf yt shall stande wᵗ my lordes graces pleasure to have this mater further steyd [stayed], As my lorde of Oxenfords honor welthe and preservacyon consideryd, I thynke yt very expedyent And maye righte well be, Then I beseche you I maye bee therof advertysed, And yt yee will move his grace to dyrecte his lettres to Mr. Edward Grene of Sampford in whose house the said Dorothe dothe now contynewe commaundinge hym by the same neyther to suffre my said lorde of Oxenford to have accesse to hyr ne shee unto hym, And that noo prevey messengers maye goo between them whyche as I suppose wilbee yᵉ surest wey to stey them. And upon further adv'tysement to be had from hys grace yf yt shall so stande wᵗ his pleasure I will entre in cõicacyon w my lorde Wentworthe for a maryage to bee hadd between my said lorde of Oxenford and on of his doughters, And as they uppon sighte wᵗ other treatyce may agree soo to procede in the same, Syr uppon yoʳ mocyon to bee made unto my lordes grace concernynge the premysses I praye yow I maye bee advertysed by this berer of his pleasure in the same, whyche knowen I shall ryghte gladlye indevor my syllff to accomplysshe by thayd of the blessed Trynytie who have you in his contynewall preservacyon From Hedingham Castell the xxvij daie of June [1547]

By yoʳ louynge frynde
THOMAS DARCY.

[Endorsed] From Sir Thomas Darcy, Knight.[1]

The reading of this letter by Lord Ancaster's counsel was followed by this conversation :—

The Lord Chancellor. I do not quite understand what the meaning of that is. In the first place Lord Oxford was not at that time a minor.
Mr. Haldane. . . . He cannot have been a very sensible person, I think.
The Lord Chancellor. He was making love to his daughter's maid.
Mr. Haldane. Yes, he was certainly doing that.
The Lord Chancellor. That is a new proof of lunacy.[2]

The student of our old social life will feel grave doubt whether 'Mistress Dorothe' was a 'maid' in the modern sense of the word. The 'woman' of a great lady, such as the Lady Katheryn, only child of the Earl of Oxford, was herself, probably, of gentle birth, and, indeed, is styled a 'gentillwoman' in this very letter. I cannot but think that she was a relative, if not indeed a daughter, of the Mr. Green of

[1] *State Papers* (Domestic), Edward VI. vol. i. No. 45.
[2] *Speeches delivered by Counsel,* p. 37.

Sampford, at whose house she is described as residing. The Greens of Sampford were of good position and at this period received knighthood.[1]

When the earl did marry again he chose for his wife an Essex woman who was probably little, if at all, superior to 'Mistress Dorothe' in position. For Margery Golding was the daughter of a Halsted man, who, although he is entered as bearing arms in the 1552 visitation of the county, was spoken of by the Duke of Somerset as his 'servant.' This, we learn from another document printed in the Great Chamberlain case, a letter of October 5, 1549, addressed 'to our loving servant Golding esquyer' by the duke, who signs himself 'your lovinge Lord and Master.' In this letter he commits to Golding, 'for the confidence we have in your being our servant,' the ordering of the Earl of Oxford's 'things, servants, and ordynarie power' for the king's service, a precaution probably inspired by the duke's critical position as Protector at the time, and his doubts as to the earl's support of his policy. In any case it seems to have led to the earl's marriage with Golding's daughter before the visitation of 1552, when we find Golding entered as the earl's father-in-law. Enough has now been said of the very mistaken idea that those who were spoken of as 'servants' or 'women' then and long afterwards could not be of gentle birth.[2]

When Sir Thomas Darcy wrote the letter printed above, his true motive was one which only a genealogist would detect. The 'Lord Wentworth,' for one of whose daughters he proposed to secure the earl as a husband, was no other than his own cousin! The accompanying chart pedigree will show quite clearly the relationship of all the parties. It is of some importance to do this, because in the *Complete Peerage* (iii. 22) the first Lord Darcy of Chiche is entered only as son 'of Roger Darcy (Esquire of the body to Henry VII.) by Elizabeth,' his mother's origin being thus ignored, together with the very interesting connection that it involved.

---

[1] See Morant's *Essex* (ed. 1816), ii. 525.

[2] In Wolsey's 'Order' (above), it is provided that 'Twoe Gentle woemen' shall wait upon the Countess, but these are spoken of in the next line as 'women servantes,' just as the 'twoe gentlemen' are included, apparently, among the men servants. We have an interesting survival of this practice in the name of the Queen's 'women of the bedchamber,' who are selected from the aristocracy (see, for instance, Mr. Lindsay's *The Royal Household*, p. 217).

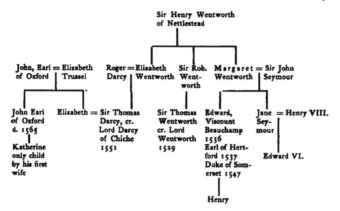

On the other hand it is no new discovery that Sir Thomas Darcy had married the earl's sister. Yet this fact, which explains some of the documents in the case, does not appear to have been mentioned. Sir Thomas had obtained for life (1541) the custody of Colchester Castle, which had previously been held by his father-in-law, and an extract from the Acts of the Privy Council, actually printed among the proofs in the case, shows Sir Thomas acting in conjunction with his brother-in-law, the Earl of Oxford, and his cousin, Lord Wentworth, for the defence of the east coast. Sir Thomas and the earl were to have 'thordre of the Kinges Majesties subjects of the Countie of Essex,' and—in what might be thought a modern colloquialism—the earl was 'to back him with the power of the shire,'[1] a responsibility which seems to imply that he was in no way deemed by the government a fool. Indeed, a year later he was 'thanked for his diligence' by the council in sending soldiers 'to Brykelsey [Brightlingsea] to serve in the greate barke.'[2]

The Duke of Somerset, who, it will be seen, was also a cousin of Sir Thomas Darcy, had his own game to play. He had himself been created Lord Great Chamberlain for life in 1543, but had resigned that high office in February 1546-7 on his nephew's accession to the throne. A year later he completed

---

[1] *Acts of the Privy Council*, May 12, 1545 (cited in volume of proofs, fo. 108).

[2] Ibid. May 31, 1546 (proofs, fo. 109).

an arrangement by which he secured for his son Henry the hand of the Earl of Oxford's heiress with all her father's possessions. This arrangement took the form of an indenture between the duke and earl (Feb. 1, 1547–8), which was voided after the duke's fall by a special Act of Parliament (Jan. 1551–2). This Act (with certain omissions) was printed at great length among the proofs in the recent case, with the object of showing that the earl 'had been frightened into executing' the conveyances of his estates by the threats of the duke,[1] but no mention was made of the all-important point that the whole arrangement was based upon a marriage between the duke's son and the earl's only child (see chart pedigree), in addition to which I have seen evidence that the earl was to receive for his consent a sum of money, which, although he was not paid, he subsequently claimed. Modern historians are well aware that recitals in Tudor Acts of Parliament cannot be accepted as evidence, though Froude would have liked to treat them as such, and an Act passed, as this was, after the duke's fall, was not likely to speak in favourable terms of his conduct. While voiding the rights, under the arrangement, of 'Lord Henry sonne to the saide late Duke, Ladye Katheryn dowghter of the saide now Earle,' the Act contains this proviso :—

Provided allso and be it enacted by thauctoritie aforesaide that yf the saide Ladye Katheryn doughter of the saide nowe Earle shall affye her self and shalbe maryed by the advyce and Counsaile of the saide now Earle her father in his Lieftyme, And yf she shall fortune not to be marryed by the advyce and Councell of the saide now Earle in his Lief tyme, yf then the saide Ladye Kateryn shall fortune to marrye her self by the advyce and Cowncell of the Executors that the saide now Earle shall make and constitute in and by his Last will and Testament, or of the more parte of them, That then the saide Ladye Katheryn her executors or administrators shall have and perceive by auctoritie of this Acte to her owne use towardes her advauncement in her maryage the somme of one thowsande powndes.[2]

J. HORACE ROUND.

[1] See Mr. Haldane's speech (*Speeches delivered by Counsel*, p. 39).

[2] She married Edward Lord Windsor, whose descendant Thomas Lord Windsor petitioned the Crown in 1660 for the office of Lord Great Chamberlain on the singular ground that the earl's second wife (*née* Golding) had not been lawfully married to him, so that he had left 'Katherine his only Doughter and Heir (by Dorothy, Doughter of the Earl of Westm[or]land, his only lawful Wife) who was married to Edward Lord Windsor, Great Grandfather of the Petitioner' (*Lords' Journals*, cited in 'Supplemental Documents' on the case, fo. 45).

III. THE VANDEPUTS

I. GILLIS VAN DER PUTTE, or Giles Vandeput, the founder in England of the family of Vandeput, was born at Antwerp about 1576, his tombstone in the church of St. Margaret Pattens describing him as aged 70 at the time of his death. Truly an evil year for a baby to be born in Antwerp. On the fifth of November in 1576 the marble town hall of Antwerp was a gutted ruin with five hundred palaces burning around it. The margrave, the burgomaster, the magistrates and senators had met, fighting like the stout Flemings they were, a death which eight thousand of their neighbours had shared. Antwerp, the richest and most luxurious city in Christendom, in the day of wrath which is called the Spanish Fury, fell to utter wretchedness. Six millions of her hoarded wealth was taken by the fire which ran amongst her tall houses, and six millions fell into the hands of those children of the devil, the Spanish soldiery. For that age at least it was all over with the city to which our own days have seen trade and wealth returning ; and Antwerp must have been a place of nightmares to those survivors who had seen the kennels swilled with citizens' blood. A house whose splintered door had once let in those who sought and found that vast plunder could be no longer a pleasant abiding place for the merchant who was left in it with a burnt out warehouse and a broken strong box, and with a memory of what, as the estates of Brabant testified, ' shall be abominable so long as the world stands.'

The father of Gillis Vandeput is said to have fled from

Antwerp to London, but as yet nothing is known concerning his movements. The good estate to which his son came would point to something of the Vandeput treasures having been saved from the burning. Those great houses, a single one of which is said to have yielded three hundred thousand gulden to the plunderers, must have covered even in ruins many a money chest which escaped the seekers. It is certain that a bag of money came with the Vandeputs, but the rising prosperity of Gillis Vandeput is the first news of the family which we gain on this side of the water. His father, if he came with his son, must have died before obtaining naturalization. This father is said in the pedigree set down by Morgan in the *Sphere of Gentry* to have been one Henry Vandeput, who was twice married, first to Elizabeth Hustard, and secondly to Mary the daughter of one Napier or Navagheer of Ypres, by whom he had our Gillis Vandeput. In Le Neve's book of knights Giles Vandeput is described as 'naturalized in parl[t] 21 Jacobi I[mi].' It is at least worthy of note that, amongst the long list of strangers made denizens in that year, the Patent Roll includes the name of one 'Egidius Adriance,' or Gillis Adriaanzoon, which makes it possible that Master Morgan, with his mind woolgathering over Joseph's Coat or Honour Dative, has blundered over an unfamiliar name, making a Henry of an Adrian.[1] Some of the Vandeput pedigrees allege that the father of Giles fled to England in 1567 or 1568, when a hundred thousand of his countrymen fled abroad with their money and goods ; but this at least is contradicted by the monument of the son.

On the fourth of February 161⅔ Anna, the daughter or Giles Vandeput, was christened at the Dutch Church in the Austin Friars, the first of Giles's children of whom we have record. In 1618 Giles learns that the Vandeput money bag, although safe from the furious Spaniard, has enemies to menace it even in the parish of St. Margaret Pattens, where he had taken up his abode. The 'strangers,' who are now a flourishing colony in London, are slandered by envious tongues, and the British Solomon upon his throne is seeking his Ophir in all likely corners. A vexatious complaint is begun in Hilary term of 1618 in the court of Star Chamber, and no less than

---

[1] Henry Vandeput, however, heads the pedigree registered in the last Heralds' Visitation of London.

forty of the outlandish merchants are arraigned by the evidence of desperate and bankrupt witnesses on a string of vague charges, chief amongst which was a charge of impoverishing the country by sending bullion out of it. Amongst these forty victims we find our Giles Vandeput—evidence enough that he is a plump citizen and forward in his world. Better evidence of his condition is in the fact that he is fined the vast sum of 3,000*l.*, and is glad to escape in 1620 with a payment of 1,000*l.*

Giles Vandeput died in London 24 March 1646, aged 70, according to the evidence of the monument over his tomb in the church of St. Margaret Pattens. He made a will 6 Feb. 164⅚. By it he gives 25*l.* each to his three children, Peter Vandeput, Sarah, the wife of Nathaniel Parkhurst ; and Giles Vandeput. He gives 40*l.* to the poor of the Dutch Church, and 5*l.* to the poor pensioners of St. Margaret Pattens. The residue of his estate he gives to his wife Sarah, his executrix, who proved the will 13 April 1647 [*P.C.C.* 68 *Fines*].

The wife of Giles Vandeput was Sarah Jaupin, daughter, according to the pedigrees, of John Jaupin of Ypres in Flanders. Her surname is proved by the christening entries of her children at the church of the Austin Friars, three of them being christened as children of Gillis van der Putte by Sarah Jaupin his wife. The arms of her family were *vert with three golden pineapples*, a shield which Rietstap gives to the name of Jaupin of Flanders. She was buried with her husband in the church of St. Margaret Pattens, and the monument sets forth that she was a very learned woman of Ypres, and that she died 13 March 165⅚, aged 67. She made a will 2 Sept. 1656, being then a widow and of St. Margaret's parish. She gave to the poor of the Dutch Church 10*l.*, to the poor of 'Rood Church' (a name of St. Margaret Pattens) 5*l.*, and to the poor of Woodford in Essex, 2*l.* To her grandchild Sarah Parkhurst, daughter of Nathaniel and Sarah, she gave 400*l.*, to be paid her at marriage ; and the residue of her estate she gave to her sons Peter Vandeput and Giles Vandeput, merchants, whom she made her executors. Peter Vandeput proved the will 9 July 1657 [*P.C.C.* 227 *Ruthen*], his brother Giles being then also dead.

Giles Vandeput had five children by Sarah Jaupin his wife :—

    i. Peter Vandeput, of whom presently (II.).

ii. Giles Vandeput, christened 11 March 161⅘ at the Dutch Church in the Austin Friars, and died young.

iii. Giles Vandeput, christened 7 July 1614 at the Dutch Church in the Austin Friars. He married 14 Dec. 1648, at St. Dionis Backchurch, Elizabeth Parkhurst, daughter of Sir Robert Parkhurst of Purford in Surrey, knight. He was named as an executor in his mother's will, but died soon after her in September or November 1656. He made a will 1 Feb. 165½, wherein he describes himself as of the parish of St. Martin Orgars and a merchant of London. He desired to be buried in Rood Church, otherwise called St. Margaret Pattens, close by the east wall on the north end of the commandments, where lay the body of his father 'of blessed memory.' He gave legacies to his sister Parkhurst and her husband, Nathaniel Parkhurst. To his wife, who had a jointure of his lands in Essex, he gave his lease in St. Martin's Lane, with plate and household stuff and half his other personal estate. The other half he gave to Peter Vandeput his brother, to whom he gave the reversion of the Essex lands, making him his executor. On 9 Feb. 165⅝ he added a codicil, giving to his wife and her heirs the reversion of the manors and lands of Mashbury and Chicknall, which he had lately purchased of John Pete, esquire. Administration with the will annexed was granted 8 Nov. 1656 [*P.C.C.* 257 *Berkeley*] to Rowland St. John, one of his men, a legatee under his will, for that the executor refused to prove the will. On 5 May 1662 administration *d.b.n.* was granted to Thomas Ewster, exor. of the said Rowland St. John; and on the death of Thomas Ewster further administration was granted 31 March 1666 to Benjamin St. John, brother of the said Rowland. Elizabeth Vandeput, his widow, was married soon after her husband's death to Francis Finch, second son of Sir Heneage Finch, Baronet. By Giles Vandeput she had no issue.

1. Anne Vandeput, christened 4 Feb. 161⅔ at the Dutch Church in the Austin Friars. She probably died young.
2. Sarah Vandeput, christened 5 March 162⅔ at the Dutch Church in the Austin Friars. In 1643

she was married to Nathaniel Parkhurst of Woodford in Essex, gent. The allegation for the marriage licence bears date 28 Sep. 1643 [*Bp. of Lond.*], he being aged about 24. She was a legatee, with her daughter Sarah Clifton, in the will of her brother Peter Vandeput, 31 Jan. 166$\frac{8}{9}$.

II. Peter Vandeput of College Hill in the parish of St. Margaret Pattens, merchant, son and heir of Giles Vandeput, was christened 25 Aug. 1611 at the Dutch Church in the Austin Friars. He is described as a rich man, speaking many tongues, the knowledge of which he may have gained from the 'learned lady' his mother. He married Jane Hoste, daughter of Dierick Hoste of London and of Sandringham in Norfolk, a merchant, who like his son-in-law was of the 'strangers,' being son of Jacques Hoste of Middleburg in Zeeland, who was born at Oudenaarde in Flanders. He was buried by his parents in the church of St. Margaret Pattens, and from his monument we learn that he died 9 Feb. 166$\frac{8}{9}$, aged 57. He made a will 31 Jan. 166$\frac{8}{9}$, describing himself therein as a merchant of London. He directed that lands to the value of 10,000*l.* should be purchased by his brother-in-law Theodore Hoste, and his friends Mr. John Colvile, goldsmith, and Mr. Robert Clayton, scrivener, which lands were to be settled upon Jane his wife for her life, with remainder to his son Peter. He gave to his wife his messuage on College Hill, which had descended to him from his father Giles Vandeput. To his daughter Jane Vandeput he gave 4000*l.* at her full age or marriage. He gave a legacy to his cousin Bartholomew Hamey, M.D., whose position in the pedigree is uncertain. This will was proved 1 March 166$\frac{8}{9}$ [*P.C.C.* 27 *Coke*] by Jane Vandeput, the relict and executrix. She died 4 Feb. 167$\frac{2}{3}$, aged 53, and was buried by her husband in St. Margaret's Church. Her will is dated 13 Oct. 1670, and it was proved 18 Feb. 167$\frac{2}{3}$ [*P.C.C.* 28 *Pye*] by her son Peter Vandeput the exor. To this son she gave the messuage on College Hill, given her by her husband. She gave 2,000*l.* more towards the portion of her daughter Jane Vandeput, and names her brother Theodore Hoste, esq., and her friend Robert Clayton, the scrivener, who writes out the will. This Robert Clayton is now an alderman of London. He died a knight, 'vastly rich,' having, according to Peter le

Neve, come up to London as a poor boy, the son of a joiner at Bulwick in Northamptonshire.

Peter Vandeput had issue by Jane Hoste his wife, according to their monumental inscription, seven children, of whom two only survived their parent :—

    i. Sir Peter Vandeput of whom presently (III.).

    ii. Sarah Vandeput, who is named as the eldest daughter in Morgan's pedigree.

    ii. Jane Vandeput, who was born about 1654. She was married 6 May 1674, at St. Olave's in Hart Street, to Edward Smith of Hill Hall in Essex, the allegation for the license being dated 4 May 1644 [*Vicar Genl.*]. She died 28 July 1720, and was buried at Theydon Mount. Her husband, who was christened 28 Sep. 1637 at Thaxted, succeeded his father as second baronet of his family, and was High Sheriff of Essex in 1680. He died 24 June 1713, and was buried at Theydon Mount 1 July 1713. His will, dated 24 July 1712 was proved 1 July 1713. From the issue of this marriage spring the Smiths, baronets of Essex, who have added Bowyer to their name of Smith, which name a grotesque misapprehension of the ancient written character has urged them to write of late years as 'Smijth.'

III. Sir Peter Vandeput of London and of Richmond in Surrey, knight. He was a minor at the death of his father, but must have been of full age at the date when he proved his mother's will, and was probably so at the date of its making in 1670. He was therefore born about 1649 or 1650. He was Sheriff of London in 1684, holding the office jointly with Sir William Gosselin, and being knighted at Whitehall 26 Sep. 1684 [*Le Neve*]. He married Margaret Buckworth, daughter of Sir John Buckworth of West Sheen in Richmond, knight, an alderman of London, who brought 800*l.* a year into jointure. He died in 1708, and was buried in St. Margaret's Church, leaving a will dated 10 May 1707, wherein he is described as of Richmond. He gave 4,000*l.* each to his son and daughters, Peter, Hester, Anne and Sarah Vandeput, all being minors. He also named his daughters Jane, wife of Mr. Philip Jackson, and Elizabeth, wife of Mr. Robert van Sittart. He gave to his wife Margaret his leases in Long Acre, his share in the New River Company, his messuages and lands in Tower Street, his leases in Gracechurch Street and in St. James's, Westminster, and his messuages and barge-houses in Lambeth. This will was proved 30 April 1708 [*P.C.C.* 102 *Barrett*] by Margaret, the relict and executrix. In 1720 she set forth a bill of complaint in Chancery against one William Taylor [*C.P. before* 1714, *Sewell* 35] concerning her leasehold house in St. James's Street, of which she had lately had Sir Richard Steele for a tenant. She made her will 6 Jan. 173$\frac{4}{7}$, being then of St. Giles's-in-the-Fields. She desired to be buried by her husband in St. Margaret's Church. She gave legacies to her son Sir Peter Vandeput, baronet, and to his lady and children ; to Dame Jane Jackson and her children at home, and to her daughter Jane, wife of Anthony Corbiere, esq. ; to her grandsons Philip and John Jackson ; to her son-in-law George Baker, esq., and his wife (Elizabeth) ; to her son-in-law Henry Ewer, esq., and his children (excluding his son's wife) ; to her son-in-law Mr. William Dunster [who was a merchant of St. Mary-at-Hill parish in 1724] ; and to her son-in-law Robert Holford, esq., and his wife and children. She gave her leasehold estate in Leadenhall Market and Gracechurch Street to her son Peter, he paying 250*l.* yearly to her daughter Elizabeth Baker for life ; and she gave him also her leaseholds in St. James's, Westminster. She names her sister Elizabeth Hartopp. She made her son Sir Peter Vandeput her residuary legatee and executor, who proved the will 15 Jan. 173$\frac{8}{9}$ [*P.C.C.* 23 *Henchman*].

Sir Peter Vandeput and Margaret Buckworth his wife are said to have had no less than twenty-two children, a fertility which boded, as in other like cases, the coming extinction of the family. Of these children we can reckon some eleven, four sons and seven daughters.

 i. Sir Peter Vandeput, first baronet, of whom presently (IV.).

 ii. Edward Vandeput, christened at Richmond 2 June 1690 and buried there 4 June 1690 as ' Mr. Edward Vandeput, a child.'

 iii. Thomas Vandeput, christened at Richmond 15 Dec. 1694 and buried there 4 Nov. 1695.

 iv. Thomas Vandeput, christened at Richmond 25 July 1696 and buried there 29 July 1696.

i. Jane Vandeput, wrongly called Mary in most of the
pedigrees. She is said to have been born in 1679.
She was married at Richmond 2 March 169⅞ to Sir
Philip Jackson of Richmond, knight, a Turkey merchant, by whom she had issue five sons and five
daughters, the 'Richmond beauties,' of whom Mary
married Roger Morris, esq., by whom she was mother
of Colonel Roger Morris, husband of Mary Philipse
daughter of the Patroon of Philipsburg, and ancestor
of the family of Morris of York. His will, dated
27 May 1717 (at which date he was not yet a knight),
with codicils 6 Nov. 1722 and 18 Dec. 1724, was
proved by her 18 Dec. 1724 [*P.C.C.* 273 *Bolton*].
She died 14 Aug. 1731. Her will, dated 3 July
1731, was proved 17 Aug. 1731 [*P.C.C.* 211 *Isham*]
by William Dunster, her brother-in-law, power being
reserved, *etc.*, to Anthony Corbiere, esq., the son-in-
law (who had married her daughter Jane in 1722), the
other executor.

ii. Elizabeth Vandeput. She is said in the pedigrees to
have been born in 1683. She is named in her father's
will of 1707 as wife of Mr. Robert van Sittart. He
was son of Peter van Sittart, who came to London
from Danzig at the latter end of the seventeenth century, the ancestor of Lord Bexley. He was born 26 June
1679, and married Elizabeth Vandeput 15 April 1707.
He died 20 Dec. 1719, s.p. His will, dated 29 March
1717, was proved 12 Jan. 17⅟₆ [*P.C.C.* 20 *Shaller*], he
being then of Shottisbrooke, co. Berks. His widow
was married at Richmond 1 Aug. 1728 to George
Baker of Richmond, afterwards of Brockenhurst House,
co. Hants, who died in 1770, s.p.

iii. Hester Vandeput, a minor at date of her father's will.
She married Henry Ewer of Bushey Hall, co. Herts,
and of Richmond, esquire. Allegation for marriage
licence 4 July 1709 [*Fac. Off.*]. Their son Anthony
was christened at Richmond 1 June 1710.

iv. Anne Vandeput, who was christened at Richmond 16
March 169¼ and died young.

v. Anne Vandeput, christened at Richmond 28 June 1693.
Wife of William Dunster of St. Mary-at-Hill, London,
merchant.

vi. Sarah Vandeput, christened 28 Dec. 1697 at Richmond. She was wife of Robert Holford, esq., a Master in Chancery, son of Sir Richard Holford, by whom she had five children. She was married to him in 1717, the allegation for the marriage licence being dated 25 April 1717 [*Fac. Off.*] he being then aged about thirty, a bachelor, and of Lincoln's Inn. His will, dated 11 Nov. 1752, gave her his house in Bedford Row. She proved the will 22 Jan. 1753 [*P.C.C.* 22 *Searle*].

vii. Margaret Vandeput, christened at Richmond 20 July 1699 and buried there 16 July [*sic*] 1699.

IV. Sir Peter Vandeput of Twickenham, co. Middlesex, and afterwards of Standlynch, co. Wilts, first baronet. He was a minor in 1707 at the date of his father's will, and was created a baronet 7 Nov. 1723. He married in 1712 Frances Matthew, one of the daughters of Sir George Matthew, of Southwark and Twickenham, knight. The indenture of settlement before marriage was dated 25 July 1712, whereby she brought a marriage portion of 6,000*l.* On 3 Dec. 1725 she set forward a bill in Chancery (by Edward Partheriche of Ely, esq., her next friend) on behalf of herself and of Peter, George and Frances, her only surviving children, against her husband and others, concerning the provisions of this marriage settlement, and the settlement of the Vandeput leaseholds in 'Elme Field *alias* Long Acre' [*Chan. pro. ante* 1714 *Sewell* 1310]. Sir Peter Vandeput bought the estate at Standlynch 1 July 1726 of the trustees of the Bocklands of Standlynch. He died 25 August 1748 at Mayence in Germany, and was probably buried in his chapel at Standlynch, as he had desired in his will, which is dated 8 May 1747. He gave his old capital messuage and lands and houses at Standlynch, which were not comprised in his marriage settlement, with his new capital messuage there, and his interest in the land in the said settlement, to Henry Godde of St. Martin's-in-the-Fields, saddler, and Josias Depouthe of Friday Street, merchant, in trust to pay to George, the natural son of his son George Vandeput, 1,000*l.*, and after that payment to hold the said messuages and lands in trust for the testator's said son George, with remainder in tail to his heirs male, with remainder to his heirs female, and with further remainder to John Jackson of St. Anne's, Westminster, oilman, whom the testator made his residuary legatee and executor, and to whom the testator gave his leaseholds in Long Acre and elsewhere in St. Martin's and St. Giles's, subject to the payment of 250*l*. yearly to the testator's son George during his mother's life. Administration, with this will annexed, was granted 10 Jan. 174⅞ [*P.C.C.* 28 *Lisle*] to George Vandeput the son, the executor renouncing.

Dame Frances Vandeput, the widow of Sir Peter, died 3 March 1764, as we learn from a coffin-plate inscription quoted by Hoare in his *History of Wiltshire*. She was buried at Standlynch. She made a will 25 March 1757, which, with a codicil dated 22 Feb. 17⅞⅜, was proved 11 April 1764 [*P.C.C.* 158 *Simpson*] by John Upton of Lincoln's Inn, the executor. She gave to her son Sir George Vandeput her plate, pictures and household goods. To her granddaughter Frances Vandeput she gave her gold watch with its seals and her fine Japan cabinet with the china upon it. The residue of her estate she gave to her executor, John Upton, esq., in trust for the education of her said granddaughter, to whom the principal was to be paid on her coming of age. If the said Frances should die a minor, the testatrix willed the principal to her son Sir George. If he were dead the principal was to remain equally to Master George Vandeput, Sir George's natural son, and to Miss Philadelphia Geary, the said Sir George's natural daughter, both of which children were minors in 1757.

The said Sir Peter Vandeput and Frances Matthew his wife had issue, besides other children who died young :—

    i. Peter Vandeput, who died in 1734. Admon. of his goods was granted 21 June 1734 [*P.C.C.*] to Sir Peter Vandeput, the father. He is described as late of Groningen in Holland and a bachelor.

    ii. Sir George Vandeput, second and last baronet, of whom presently (V.).

    i. Frances Vandeput, christened at Twickenham 6 Jan. 17⅞⅜. She died 14 Dec. 1739 as appears by her coffin plate at Standlynch, where she was buried.

V. Sir George Vandeput, the second and last baronet, was born about 1717. He matriculated at Wadham College, Oxford, 31 July 1734, as eldest son of Sir Peter Vandeput of Twickenham, baronet, his elder brother Peter being then lately dead. He rendered his name famous in its generation by fighting a Westminster election in 1749 against Lord

Trentham, and great store of the hoarded Vandeput guineas disappeared amongst the free and independent electors of Westminster. From this time forward we hear no more of the great Vandeput fortune. The election began 22 Nov. 1749, the poll closing 8 Dec. 1749, with Trentham leading by 4,811 to Sir George's 4,654. Sir George demanded a scrutiny, but on 15 May 1750, Lord Trentham was declared the elected of Westminster by a majority of 170. The Vandeput pedigree was unrolled in the midst of the contest, Lord Trentham's supporters professing themselves anxious to know whence came this 'Englishman with a Dutch name.' The Vandeput faction hastened to produce their evidences of nationality, and Sir George was declared to be no hungry foreigner, but a man whose ancestor had come here in Queen Elizabeth's time with a full money bag. Sir George Vandeput married at St. George's Chapel, Hyde Park Corner, 20 April 1747, Mary Judith Schutz or Schûtz, daughter of Augustus Schutz of Shotover House near Oxford, and granddaughter of Baron Schûtz, a Hanoverian favourite of George I., whom he followed to England. Augustus Schutz, the baron's eldest son, was Master of the Robes and Keeper of the Privy Purse to George II., whom he had formerly served as equerry. The Schutz family are familiar to us through the eighteenth-century memoirs and letters. Of Lady Vandeput's younger sister, an attendant upon one of the princesses, it is written :—

> Charlotte and Schutz like angry monkeys chatter,
> None guessing what's the language or the matter.

Augustus Schutz, sometimes called Baron Schutz and some-times Augustus Schutz, esquire, was esteemed by some ot his contemporaries as a maker of puns, but the verdict of a a wider circle pronounced him German dulness in the flesh. He died 26 May 1757, and the next day Mr. Horace Walpole writes to George Montagu: 'I wish your brother and all heirs to estates joy, for old Schutz is dead and cannot wriggle him-self into any more wills!' His daughter, Lady Vandeput, died 21 May 1771, at Chelmsford, and on 19 August 1772, Sir George Vandeput married at Kelvedon in Essex his second wife, Philadelphia Geary, youngest daughter of Lieut.-Colonel Geary of Long Melford in Suffolk, and the mother of Sir George's natural daughter Philadelphia. Sir

George Vandeput died at Kensington 17 June 1784. His will is dated 1 July 1782, at which time he was living in Wigmore Street in the parish of Marylebone. He gave to his daughter Frances Drury 50*l.* for mourning, and for the like purpose he gave legacies of 20*l.* to [his natural son] Captain Vandeput of H.M.S. *Atlas*, and 50*l.* to [his natural daughter] Mrs. Philadelphia Smyth. The residue of his estate, together with the houses in St. James's Street, Little Roper Street and Fox Alley or Court, all in St. James's, Westminster, he gave to his wife, Dame Philadelphia, who proved the will [*P.C.C.* 357 *Rockingham*]. His widow survived him two-and-twenty years, dying 3 Jan. 1806, at Stanhope Street in Mayfair. She made a will 8 March 1804, being then of Nottingham Street in Marylebone, which was proved 3 Jan. 1806 [*P.C.C.* 89 *Pitt*], by John Woods, esq., one of the exors., power being reserved, *etc.*, to Richard Very Drury, the other exor., who also proved the will 11 Mar. 1826. She gave legacies to Philadelphia Smyth of Warren Street, Fitzroy Square, widow, whom however she does not name as her daughter ; to George Vandeput, a clerk in the War Office ; and to Emily Camell of Bungay, the widow of Admiral Vandeput.

By his first wife Mary Judith Schutz, Sir George Vandeput had issue :—

i. A son who was born 19 Sep. 1754 and died young.
ii. Frances Vandeput, born about 1750, who became sole heir of the Vandeputs. She was a legatee under the will of her grandmother, Frances Vandeput, in 1757. She married 13 June 1776 [*Gent.'s Mag.*] Richard Vere Drury, a lieutenant in the navy, the youngest son of the Rev. George Drury, rector of Claydon and Akenham, co. Suffolk, who came of a cadet branch of the Drurys of Rougham. Richard Vere Drury was of Kingston near Portsmouth. His wife Frances Vandeput, by whom he had three sons and a daughter, died 23 Feb. 1787, and was buried at Claydon. He married secondly, in June 1788, Susan Gibson, daughter of John Gibson, rector of St. Magnus by London Bridge, which Susan survived him and died at Kingston in Nov. 1835, aged 82. Richard Vere Drury died 6 April, leaving issue by both wives.

Sir George Vandeput left two natural children :—

George Vandeput, of whom presently (VI.), and

Philadelphia Vandeput, the first mention of whom occurs in the will of her grandmother, Dame Frances Vandeput in 1757, which will speaks of her as Miss Philadelphia Geary, natural daughter of Sir George Vandeput. Her christian name and surname show that she was the daughter of Philadelphia Geary, whose *liaison* with Sir George must therefore have begun long before her marriage to him in 1772. In the wills of her father and mother she is spoken of as Mrs. Philadelphia Smyth, and no relationship is stated. She was married at Ipswich 14 Dec. 1779 to Charles Smyth, a captain in the West Essex regiment of Militia, who was born at Lynn Regis in April 1752. He was great-grandson of Sir Edward Smith of Hill Hall, co. Essex, by his wife Jane Vandeput, daughter of Peter Vandeput (II.). He died in May 1792, and was buried at Camberwell, his wife surviving him.

VI. George Vandeput, natural son of Sir George Vandeput, is the first of his line to find his way into the pages of the biographical dictionaries, a measure of fame which even the great Westminster election failed to bring to his father. His mother's name is uncertain, but as the will of his grandmother, Dame Frances Vandeput, in 1757 names him as her son's natural son, Master George *Vandeput*, whilst the natural daughter of Sir George is called in the same will Miss Philadelphia *Geary*. In spite of this difference, and in spite of the fact that the statement has appeared in print that the boy and girl were children of Sir George by different mothers, it is at least possible that both were children of Philadelphia Geary. His grandfather who gave him 1,000*l*. by his will dated 8 May 1747, and the recognition by his grandmother's will in 1757 of both children, would favour the suggestion that they were the children of a *ménage* known to, and at the least tolerated, by the respectable Sir Peter and Dame Frances. His widow and his natural son George are given legacies under the will of Dame Philadelphia Vandeput, and he himself in giving a legacy to Philadelphia Smyth, styles her his 'dear sister.' His naval career was a long one, and like many of the captains of his age, most of his life was spent at sea. He became lieutenant on 24 Sep. 1759 under Captain Hugh

Palliser of the *Shrewsbury*. On 17 April 1764 he was given
the command of the *Goree* sloop, and on 20 June 1765 that
of the *Surprize* of 20 guns. In June 1767 he was given the
Carysport, a 28-gun frigate, on the Mediterranean station, and
in Dec. 1773 he commissioned the *Asia* line of battleship for
the North American station. Whilst lying off New York
in 1776 he came by an adventure which has made welcome
material for the biographers of his useful and honourable but
monotonous career. A powder ship was taken by a tender of
the *Asia*, and Captain Vandeput, instead of transhipping her
war material on the spot, was moved by some impression of
suspicion to order her to lay off for the night. The order
brought a sudden confession from one of the powder ship's
men, who would have been doomed to pass the night aboard
her, that a certain barrel held a musket lock actuated by a
piece of clockwork, which was even then at work and ticking
its way towards an explosion. So Captain Vandeput brought
the *Asia* home in 1777 with sound timbers, and took her to
the East Indies. In 1782 he did his duty at the relief of
Gibraltar, being then in the *Atlas* of 98 guns, and in the same
year he was in the action off Cape Spartel. Flag-rank came
to him at last : rear-admiral in 1793 and vice-admiral in
1794. In the *St. Albans* he commanded the squadron off
North America in 1797, removing his flag to the *Asia* in
1798. Admiral of the blue 14 Feb. 1799, he died suddenly
on board the *Asia* at sea on the 14 March 1800, and his body
was carried in the *Cleopatra* to Providence, where it was buried
on shore. He made a will, dated at Halifax 11 Nov. 1799,
making his wife Emily his principal legatee. He gave legacies
to his dear sister Philadelphia Smyth, widow, and to his nephew
Augustus Vere Drury, then his lieutenant in the *Asia*. Of this
will he made his wife Emily his executrix, naming his 'particular friends' the Rt. Hon. William Windham, Secretary of War,
and the Hon. George Nassau as executors with her. The will
was proved 19 Aug. 1800 by the relict alone [*P.C.C.* 631
Adderley]. His wife's surname is uncertain ; but a niece of
hers named in the Admiral's will is called Sarah Walls. In
October or November 1801 she married as her second husband
Robert Camell, M.D. of Bungay in Suffolk, the descendant
of a Scots Campbell who had come southward in the time of
Elizabeth. She was given a legacy by the will of Dame
Philadelphia Vandeput in 1804. She died at Bungay 2 Dec.

1827 in her 69th year, and her husband, who survived her, died at Ditchingham 5 July 1837.

By his wife Emily, Admiral Vandeput left no issue, but he is said to have left a natural son George. This George is without doubt the George Henry Vandeput named in the will of his father as 'George Henry Vandeput, now a clerk in the office of the Secretary of War.' Dame Philadelphia Vandeput in her will of 1804 gives a legacy to this 'George Vandeput, a clerk in the War Office,' in which office a place must have been found for him by his father's 'particular friend,' the Rt. Hon. William Windham.

Admiral Vandeput is said to have assumed the title of baronet, but of this we have no trace. He certainly made no attempt to insist upon his title being used officially by the Admiralty. The story must have originated in the circumstance that *Betham's Baronetage* accepted without question the legitimacy of the recognized son of Sir George Vandeput. George Vandeput, whose life and death were at sea, was not at hand to suggest corrections in the baronetage, and Dame Philadelphia Vandeput could hardly have wished to make clear the last generations of the Vandeput pedigree. The Admiral's son George, the War Office clerk, is also stated to have styled himself a baronet, but this still more vague claim must have contented itself with modest and private assertion.

O. B.

THE STORY OF A KEY

NASH'S *History of Worcestershire* (i. 251), in the account of the parish of Cofton Hackett, after stating that about the year 1637 the manor came into the possession of Thomas Jolliffe of the county of Stafford, through his marriage with an heiress, Margaret Skinner, further narrates that the dining parlour of the manor house, 'a large convenient building,' contains a portrait of this gentleman 'with a key in his hand, which the tradition of the family says was given him by King Charles I. when in prison, that he might have access to him when he pleased. It is probable that this picture was painted when the king's affairs were quite desperate, as Mr. Jolliffe is represented with a melancholy, desponding countenance, his pistols and sword hanging upon a pillar before him as if he were saying "Hic arma cestumque repono." He continued faithful to his sovereign till the last and attended his execution.'

The portrait thus described is now the property of Mr. Michael Biddulph of Ledbury, formerly member for Herefordshire, the Cofton estate having been entailed by the will of a second Thomas Jolliffe, who died in 1758, on the descendants of his sister Anne, wife of Robert Biddulph of Ledbury ; but I consider myself fortunate in being the owner of an exact replica of Mr. Biddulph's picture, which appears to have been ordered by, or given to, a younger brother of the original, viz. William Jolliffe of Caverswall Castle, Staffordshire, who, dying in 1711, left two daughters—coheiresses—Anne, wife of Philip Papillon, of Acrise, Kent, and Lucy, Viscountess Vane. The Papillon family must have inherited the picture which is now in my house, and the Mr. Papillon of 1760 gave it to his kinsman, John Jolliffe, from whom I descend, and whose letter of grateful thanks for the gift of the portrait of his 'respected ancestor' (in reality his grandfather) is preserve . at Crowhurst Park, the residence of the present head of the Papillon family.

The canvas of my picture measures 25 inches wide and 28 high ; the face is turned three-quarters to the spectator, the dress is black, and a short black cape, trimmed with gold lace and surmounted by a white lace collar, covers the shoulders. The figure is visible to the waist, and the right hand is holding the key, of which Nash speaks. To the left of the head a sword and heavy silver-mounted pistol are seen hanging by leather straps to a hook on the wall.

The problem of which I venture to seek the solution from the readers of *The Ancestor* is the meaning of the key aforesaid. Nash's explanation thereof, founded only on a ' family tradition,' which, when he wrote his account of Cofton in 1779, had, I fear, been dimmed by the lapse of 130 years, is quite inadmissible. It is not usual to allow to prisoners the privilege of handing the key of their gaol to friends, however attached, and in the case of a captive like Charles I. Nash's story seems absurd. Before, however, making my own humble suggestion as to the real significance of the key in question, I ought to recite in due sequence the few and meagre facts which I have been able to glean respecting the subject of these portraits.

Thomas Jolliffe was baptized in Leek Church, Staffordshire, 12 April, 1617, being the eldest son of William Jolliffe of Leek and his wife Ann, daughter of Benedict Webb of Kingswood, Gloucestershire. He married in or before 1638 Margaret Skinner, the Cofton register for that year recording the interment of ' a son of Mr. Thomas Jolliffe and Margaret his wife, buried the 1 day of . . . dying a few . . . after birth.' Other children were baptized at Cofton in 1639 and 1641, and in all probability the squire was living at home when Charles I. ' lay at Cofton Hall ' on 14 May, 1645 (Nash, i. 152). As to this event Nash can hardly be in error, for he quotes from a circumstantial *Journal of the King's Army* by Mr. Richard Symonds in the Harleian Library. King Charles was thus apparently the guest of Thomas Jolliffe, leaving Cofton the following day, continues Symonds' journal, for Himley Hall, when so far as *facts* are known to me the brief connexion between the unhappy king and his loyal subject ceased for ever. The loyalty of the master of Cofton seems to have been unquestioned, because in the first list of justices of the peace for Worcestershire promulgated 10 July, 1660, only six weeks after the ' happy Restoration,' the name of Thomas Jolliffe appears (Nash, i.), whilst in 1672 and 1673 he served successively as high sheriff for Worcestershire and Staffordshire. Moreover, in 1684 his

D

eldest surviving son John married into a very loyal family, taking to wife Anne, eldest daughter of Thomas, second Lord Crewe of Steane.

I have read the will of Thomas Jolliffe, dated 13 August, 1684, and the inscription on his monument in Cofton Church recording his death 23 Oct. 1693, aged 76, but no word or phrase in either will or epitaph afford the slightest clue to the history of the key ; nor is the name of Jolliffe to be found in any list of Charles I.'s attendants known to me.

My only conjecture is that on the May-day in 1645, when Charles slept at Cofton Hall, its owner was made happy by some temporary permission to wait upon the king, and to retain the key of the sovereign's chamber. The vision of Lady Margaret Bellenden and the royal 'disjune' at Tillietudlem flits across one's memory. One room and key at Cofton Hall were doubtless looked on as sacred from that 14th of May onwards, and the cavalier squire may have determined to transmit to posterity the honours conferred on his house by being depicted holding in his hand the emblem of his king's trust and his own loyalty.

I need not add that any communications with which I may be favoured on this subject will be very gratefully received.

HYLTON.

AMMERDOWN, RADSTOCK.

THE VALUE OF WELSH PEDIGREES

A WELSHMAN whose family was of any position in the sixteenth century can, as a rule, without much trouble find a pedigree thence to Adam : an Englishman who is unable to do the same has a natural tendency to regard all Welsh pedigrees with distrust, not to say contempt. At first sight it is undoubtedly an astounding proposition that an eighteenth century MS. such as *The Golden Grove* should be a good authority for eleventh and twelfth century pedigrees, yet that there are good *prima facie* reasons for such being the case I hope to show in the present article ; that such *is* the case can only be proved by showing that with certain exceptions Welsh pedigrees will stand all tests applied to them, and then arguing that if portions of a pedigree derived from one source or common set of sources be proved to be true, the remainder is so.

Genealogists as a rule fail to recognize that a Welshman regards a pedigree from a totally different point of view to an Englishman. To fulfil modern requirements an English pedigree must be a family history in brief ; the individuals named in it must 'live,' the important dates in their lives must be mentioned, and all facts known about them must be recorded. It is not so and has never been so with a Welsh pedigree ; a Welshman is satisfied with the mere names of his ancestors, and would rather know his female descents than his collateral relations. At the present time tradition in Wales is very highly esteemed,[1] and ordinary individuals are content with the traditional pedigrees, the result being that as a rule the Welsh genealogist is content to compare the various traditional pedigrees and to endeavour to reconcile conflicting statements, so that little has been done to test these pedigrees on modern lines.

After some experience in dealing with the ordinary collections of Welsh pedigrees, I have come to the conclusion that such mistakes as occur in them, apart from those

---

[1] I recently investigated a traditional relationship between two existing families, and found the common ancestor had died more than 300 years ago.

incidental to frequent copying and compilation, are due to one or other of the following causes, which I will state in the form of axioms :—

I. Generations are frequently omitted.

II. An individual occasionally is affiliated to his wife's parents, or to one of his wife's parents or one of his own.

III. An individual is sometimes affiliated to a step-parent, but only in cases where such step-parent has had issue by the real parent.

IV. Little attention is paid to the Christian names of women.

V. Previously to 1560 or thereabouts the dates assigned to and facts stated about individuals are not contemporary with the pedigrees, but late and generally quite untrustworthy additions.

VI. Legitimacy must be considered in regard to the Welsh law on the subject, which differs from the English.

It will be convenient to consider a concrete instance, and I will select the earlier part of the Geraldine pedigree from *The Golden Grove*, l. 1783, etc.

This pedigree is not strictly speaking a Welsh one, and it must be borne in mind that the arguments hereafter adduced in favour of the genuineness of Welsh pedigrees only apply to the descendants of Gerald de Windsor and Nest daughter of Rees ap Tewdur ; the remainder of the pedigree must be taken as representing a tradition, probably a very early one. I have selected this example chiefly in order to have the advantage of comparing it with the results of recent research, as appearing in *The Ancestor*, by Mr. Round ; he gives the same pedigree thus :—

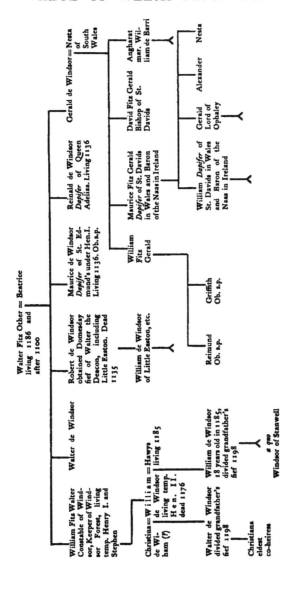

It will be seen at once that the two pedigrees agree in many points, in particular with regard to the father and grandfather of Gerald de Windsor ; and bearing in mind that the one is really a pedigree of the Irish branch, the other of the Welsh, the discrepancies are not more than might be expected. I will venture, however rashly and with all the deference due to Mr. Round, to make a few criticisms on his pedigree, feeling sure that so keen a critic and ardent searcher after truth must be conscious of its weakness at certain points. After careful study of Mr. Round's second article the only evidence I can find given by him for the paternity of Gerald de Windsor[1] is that Giraldus Cambrensis[2] 'styles him on one occasion Geraldus de Windesora.' Surely this by itself would hardly be sufficient even for the most careless herald, whose laxity our author has so often justly exposed. But when backed up as it is by the pedigree in the Harleian Roll and that in *The Golden Grove*, the connection would seem to be sufficiently shown. This being the case, the argument that Gerald had a brother Maurice,[3] because Maurice de Windsor is more frequently mentioned than Gerald de Windsor, must fall to the ground, since it is based on insufficient premises. The case for Reinald is little better. They would both appear to belong to the family, but their true place in the pedigree is, in my opinion at all events, not at present ascertained. That there were two marriages between the Hastings and Windsor families does not appear in the Hastings pedigree given by Mr. Round[4] owing to an unfortunate misprint ; it should read Robert de Hastings married the daughter and heir of William de Windsor. And here Mr. Round seems for once to have fallen into a trap, the like of which fortunately for genealogists is rarely set. The facts are these: In Domesday we find under Essex—'Terra Witti de Warenna. Hundred de Dommauua. Estanes tenuit Duua liva femina, etc.'[5] 'Terra Galteri diaconi. Hund de Witbrictesherna. Eistanes ten & Galt in dnio qd tenuit Dodinc, etc.'[6] 'Robert de Windsor obtained Estanes in the days of Henry I.' William son of Robert obtained a

<hr>

[1] p. 95.
[2] It must be noted that he was not the Gerald, Lord of Ophaley, of the pedigree, but a son of William de Barri.
[3] p. 92.
[4] *The Ancestor*, No. 2, p. 91.   [5] f. 36.   [6] f. 36*b*.

fresh confirmation of it from Henry II.'[1] Robert de Hastings held Eistanes at the time of the Liber Niger, his son William also holding there ; and it has been shown by Mr. Clark that this Robert de Hastings was a son of Walter the Deacon.[2] So that we have two contemporary Williams, sons of two Roberts, sons of two Walters, both Domesday tenants, holding two manors of practically the same name in the same county. What could seem more reasonable than to identify the two men and the two places as Mr. Round has done, though Mr. Clark has not ?[3] Yet the daughter and heiress of the one William married the son and heir of the other, and the places are far apart. 'One could not desire a better illustration of the mischief in county history that may follow from identifying wrongly a single Domesday manor.'

Turning to *The Golden Grove* pedigree it is evidently not derived from the same source as O'Daly's *History of the Geraldines*[4] or *The Earls of Kildare*[5] and is not based on Geraldius' history ; this is accordingly available for comparison, the results of which seem worth noting. The place of Giraldus Cambrensis in the pedigree is wrong ; his mother has been omitted (note Axiom I. ante), and it seems probable in view of the Harleian Roll pedigree that Alexander is also placed a generation too high. (Incidentally I may mention that Gladys daughter of Rhiwallon ap Cynfyn, who is stated in *Burke's Peerage* to have been Gerald the steward's mother, was his wife's mother. Axiom II.) As Nest had children by four (?) husbands, Gerald the Steward, King Henry, Stephen the Constable and Owen ap Cadwgan, it is difficult to decide (Axioms III. and VI.) whether the individuals alluded to by Giraldus as his relations were descendants of Gerald the Steward or not, but of the individuals occurring in *The Golden Grove* pedigree (exclusive of those noticed by Mr. Round) Giraldus names his ' consobrinos' Odo de Kerreu,[6] who married a daughter of Ricardus filius Tancardi and Reimund, 'tam Stephanidæ quam Mauricii ex fratre primævo nepos . . . vir amplæ quantitatis staturæque paulo plus quam mediocris . . . who married Basilia sister to Earl Richard,' evidently

---

[1] *The Ancestor*, No. 2, p. 92. [2] *Arch. Journal*, xxvi. 123–4, etc.
[3] See *Arch. Journal*, xxvi. 122, 130.
[4] *The Ancestor*, No. 1, p. 119. [5] Ibid. p. 120.
[6] He witnesses the charter of Peter, Bishop of St. Davids (*The Ancestor*, No. 2, p. 94).

Raymond Crassus or le Gros. We also read of another Gerald, 'frater Odonis primævus,' who was killed by the men of Ros, probably one of the two sons of William who are stated in the Harleian Roll pedigree to have died s.p.[1] William son of Gerald and his brothers are mentioned in the Brut in 1146 in conjunction with Cadell son of Griffith (i.e. Griffith ap Rhys ap Tewdwr), and his brothers Maredudd and Rhys—brothers-in-law of William if his wife is correctly given in the pedigree.

I have taken my example of a pedigree from *The Golden Grove*. This is the latest and most accessible of the general collections of Welsh pedigrees; it appears to have been compiled in the years 1752–65 and contains some later additions, chiefly in the handwriting of Theophilus Jones, who used it for his *History of Breconshire*, published in 1805, and states in effect that it is the book of the Arwydd-feirdd (chief bard), taken by command of the Earl of Carberry.[2] Mr. Pym Yeatman names Evan Evans as the compiler.[3] It is certainly not by Hugh Thomas, as stated by Mr. Horwood,[4] for he died in 1720, but it is possible that some of his MSS. are now bound up with it. On going through the pedigrees it will be seen that certain dates in the seventeenth century constantly occur; in the case of Breconshire these are 1644 and 1686, the dates at which the collections of pedigrees of Richard Williams of Llywel, sometimes known as Dick Howell William, and David Edwards of Rhydygors are known to have been made, so that it would seem that the immediate source of *The Golden Grove* was, as regards Breconshire, the works of these two genealogists. A similar state of affairs is found in regard to the other counties, the conclusion being that *The Golden Grove* is a copy and continuation of pedigrees drawn up in the seventeenth century. Going further back references will be found to various other pedigree writers under their initials (a list of thirty has been inserted by Jones at the beginning of the first volume), so that it would appear that the book in its present form contains a

---

[1] The entry is 'Willimus fillius Giraldi de Penbrook (his father is styled Giraldus de Windsor Castelanus de Penbrook) genuit duos fillios sine sobole extinctos.'

[2] Vol. ii. 140, and cp. p. 139 with *The Golden Grove*, G. 1030.

[3] *Notes and Queries*, ser. 9, v. 359.

[4] *2nd Rep. Hist. MSS. Comm.* app. p. 31.

continuous series of additions made to existing pedigrees, each addition being within the reasonable knowledge of its author, and is not a collection of pedigrees made at a late date and therefore of little value.   This is of course a deduction from the internal evidence—the external evidence will appear later.

Mr. Vaughan, writing from the Welsh point of view in an interesting article in *Y Cymmrodor* (vol. ix.), shows that the various pedigrees of the royal line in their earliest part are inconsistent, but concludes that 'they are not entire fictions but are founded on truth though overlaid with much that is false.'   He divides the existing collections of pedigrees into three classes—

I. Those compiled before Henry VII.

II. Collections compiled temp. Henry VII.

III. Collections compiled subsequently to the last mentioned date.

The earliest collection of pedigrees I have come across are those appended to the oldest known Welsh annals, the Annales Cambriæ, in Harleian MS. No. 3859.   They are discussed at length by Mr. Egerton Phillimore,[1] who concludes that in their present form they were composed in the last half of the tenth century, the date of the MS. being upwards of a century later, and 'that up to the date when all Welsh records necessarily became more or less fabulous, these genealogies have every claim to rank beside the Annales and the Saxon Genealogies as a valuable historical authority.   The late Mr. G. T. Clark and Mr. Alewyn Evans have left collections of pedigrees brought down to the present time, and the work is still being carried on in Wales.

Welsh pedigrees are to be found in two forms, and as one of them is, so far as I am aware, peculiar to Welsh genealogy, I give an instance of the pedigree of Pryse of Gogerddan in each form, taken from the printed edition of *Lewys Dwnn* (i. 44; ii. 23).   The earlier collections are as a rule in the second form or a modified version of it.

---

[1] *Y Cymmrodor*, ix. 141.

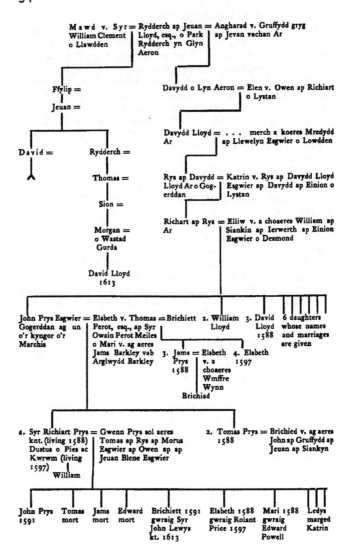

Mawd v. Syr = Rydderch ap Jeuan = Angharad v. Gruffydd gryg
William Clement | Lloyd, esq., o Park | ap Jevan vachan Ar
o Llawdden | Rydderch yn Glyn
| Aeron

Ffylip =

Jeuan =

Davydd o Lyn Aeron = Elen v. Owen ap Richiart
o Lystan

David =   Rydderch =

Davydd Lloyd = . . . merch a koeres Mredydd
Ar   ap Llewelyn Esgwier o Lowdden

Thomas =

Rys ap Davydd = Katrin v. Rys ap Davydd Lloyd
Lloyd Ar o Gog- Esgwier ap Davydd ap Einion o
erddan   Lystan

Sion =

Morgan =
o Wastad
Gurda

Richart ap Rys = Elliw v. a choaeres William ap
Ar   Siankin ap Ierwerth ap Einion
Esgwier o Desmond

David Lloyd
1613

John Prys Esgwier = Elsbeth v. Thomas = Brichiett 2. William 3. David 6 daughters
Gogerddan ag un Perot, esq., ap Syr   Lloyd   Lloyd   whose names
o'r kyngor o'r   Owain Perot Meiles   1588   and marriages
Marchis   o Mari v. ag aeres   are given
                 Jams Barkley vab   3. Jams = Elsbeth 4. Elsbeth
                 Arglwydd Barkley   Prys   v. a   1597
                                       1588   choaeres
                                              Wmffre
                                              Wynn
                                       Brichiad

1. Syr Richiart Prys = Gwenn Prys sol aeres   2. Tomas Prys = Brichied v. ag aeres
knt. (living 1588)   Tomas ap Rys ap Morus   1588   John ap Gruffydd ap
Dustus o Pies ac   Esgwier ap Owen ap ap   Jeuan ap Siankyn
Kwrwm (living   Jeuan Blene Esgwier
1597)
        William

John Prys Tomas Jams Edward Brichiett 1591   Elsbeth 1588   Mari 1588 Ledys
1591   mort   mort mort   gwraig Syr   gwraig Rolant gwraig   marged
                                John Lewys   Price 1597   Edward   Katrin
                                kt. 1613   Powell

Then follow the children and marriages of William Lloyd
ap Rishiart ap Rys and David Lloyd ap Richart ap Rys in
narrative form, the arms of Richiart Prys Sgwier (a coat of
six quarters impaling another coat with the same number of
quarters), and the date 29 December, 1588; and the whole
ends—

Receved off Richd Pryse x^s
By me booke
Thomas Jones of ffowntaen gat.

Gogerdden yn Swydd Abertify

Tad Sr Ric^d ab Pric o Sir Abertiwy. Sion ap Ric^d ab R^s Dd lloid ab
D^d ab Rudd^h ab Jeun. lloid ab Jeun. Gr^h voel ab Gr^h ab Yeroth ab Kadifor
ab Gwaith.

Mam Richard ab R^s oedd Kattrin v^h Rs. Dd lloid ab D^d ab Eiginon ap
Holl ab Tydir ab Einon vychan ab Einon ab Mirig ab Jeun. ab Gronw ab
Ivor ab Idnerth ap Kydogan ab Elistan Glodrydd.

Mam R^s oedd v^h Owein ab Richard ab Gr^h ap Llnn ab Mdd^h bengoch
ap Llnn. ab Hoell ab Seissyllt ap Llnn. ab Kodogan ab Elistan Glodrydd.

Mam Kattrin v^h R^s ab D^d oedd Varged verch Jeun. ab Owein ab Mdd^h ab
D^d vachan ab Gr^h ab Einion ab Ednyfed ab Sulien ab Kyradog ab Gollwyn.

Mam Varged v^h Jeun. ab Owein oedd Oleybryd v^h Mdd^h ab Jeun. ab Llnn.
ab Tydir ab Gronwy ab Eignion ab Seysyllt ab Ednyowein synydd ab Brochwel
ab Walder ab Ydris arw ab Klydno ab Ynir varfdruch ab Gwyddno garnir.

Mam Oleibryd v^h Mdd^h oedd Vallt v^h Rhys gethin o byellt ab Owein ab
Ric^t ab Gr^h ab Llnn. ab Mdd^h bengoch ab Llnn. ab Hoell ab Seisyllt at Llnn.
ab Kydogan ab Elistan Glodrydd.

Mam Owein ab Mdd^h ab D^d oedd Llyky v^h Jeun. ab Kydogan weithwas
ab Gr^h ab Gr^h ab Beli ab Selif ab Brochwel ab Aeddan ab Kyngen ab Elisse
ab Gwylawg ab Beli ab Mael myngein ab Selyf varf. Kadav ab Kynan gar-
rwyn ab Brochwel Ysgethrog.

Mam Llyky v^h Jeun. ab Dodogan oedd Wenhwyfar v^h Ryffry ab Alo ab
Rywallon vichan ab Rywallon llwyd ab Ithel ab R^s ab Ivor ab Hoell ab
Morgan vichan o Evas ab Morgan ab Jestyn ab Gwrgan twysog Morganwg.

Mam Riffri ab Alo oedd v^h Eynon ab Destaen ab Ioreth ab Gurgenv ab
Yeroth vchdryd ab Edwin vrenin.

Mam R^s D^d lloid ab D^d ab Eignion oedd Wenllyan v^h Owein arglwydd y
Towyn.

Mam D^d Lloid ab D^d ab Eignion oedd Wladys v^h Mdd^h ab Gwin. ab
Madog lloyd ab Llnn. ab Meilyr gryg ab Gr^h ab Yeroth ab Owein ab Rodri
ab Hoell ab Enathan ab Brochwel ab Aeddna ab Kyngen ab Elisse ab
Gwylawg.

Mam R^s D^d lloid ab D^d ab Rudd^h oedd v^h Owein ab Rickard ab Gr^h ab
Llnn. ab Mdd^h bengoch ab Llnn. ab Hoel ab Seissyllt.

Mam D^d Lloyd ab D^d ab Rudd^h oedd Varged v^h Griffith Jeun. vichan ab
Jeun. ab R^s ab Llawdden.

Mam Jeun. Gr^h voel oedd Ethlyw v^h Mdd^h ab Kydogan yantach ab
Kydogan ab Llnn. ab Gr ab Mdd^h ab Edelfrich ab Predyr ab Peisroyn ab
Einion envydd ab Pyll ab Sandde ab Gwyddno Garanhir.

Mam Rudd[h] ab Jeun. Lloid oedd Yngharad v[h] Rickard ab Eynon ab Kynfrig ab Morgan ab Phe. ab Seisyllt ab Llnn. ab Kydogan ab Elistan Glodrydd.

Mam Ellilyw v[h] Mdd[h] ab Kydogan vantach oedd Wenllian v[h] Mdd[h] ab Owein ab yr arglwydd R[s] Gr. ab R[s] ab Tewdwr.

Mam D[d] ab Rudd[h] oedd v[h] Varred v[h] Gruff[h] ab Jeun. ychan ab Jeun. ab R[s] ab Llawdden.

Mam John ab Richard ap R[s] oedd Ethlyw v[h] Gllm. ab Jenkin ab Yeroth ab Eiginon ab Gr[h] ab Llnn. ab Kynfrig ab Osbuan ab Wyddeb ab Gwydd laces.

Mam Gllm. ab Jenkin ab Yeroth oedd Wenllyan v[h] Kynfrig ab Ropert ab Yeroth ab Ryryd ab Yeroth ab Madog ab Ednywiein.

Mam Wenllyan oedd Yngharad v[h] Gruf[h] vichan ab Gruf[h] ab D[d] goch ab D[d] ab Gr[h] ab Llnn. ab Ieroth drwyndwn ab Owein Gwynedd.

Mam Ethlyw v[h] Gllm oedd Lawry v[h]—ab R[s] ab D[d] ab Hoell ab Gr[h] ab Owein ab Bleddyn ab Owen Brogyntn.

Mam Lowri oedd Varged v[h] Rowland ab Gr[h] goch ab Madog ab Mirig ab D[d] ab Llwarch ab Jeun. gann ab Kynddelw ab R[s] ab Edryd ab Methan ab Iasseth ab Korwed ab Marchaidd.

Mam Varged oedd Lawri v[h] Tydyr ab Gr. vichan ab Madog gripl ab Gr. varwn gwin ab Gr[h] arglwydd Dinas Brân ab Madog ab Gr. Maylor ab Madog ab Mdd[h] ab Bleiddyn ab Kynfyn arglwydd Powys a Iarll Caerlleon.

Sion ab Styfyn ab Jeun. gwin ab Siames ab R[s] ab D[d] ab Howel ab Vain ab Llnn ab Hoell ab Madog ab Trahayarn ab Gr[h] goch ab Gr[h] voel ab Gronwy ab Gwirgene ab Kydogan ab Elystan Glodrydd.[1]

For the benefit of English readers I will add a translation of the beginning of the second version and show the whole of it in pedigree form. The words in brackets are omitted by Lewis Dwnn :—

The father of Sr. Richard Pryse of co. Cardigan was John son of Richard son of Rees [son of] David Lloyd son of David son of Rhydderch son of Jevan Lloid son of Jevan [son of] Griffith voel son of Griffith son of Iorwerth son of Kadivor son of Gwaithvoed.

The mother of Richard son of Rees was Katherine daughter of Rees [son of] David Lloyd son of David son of Einon son of Howell son of Tudor son of Einon vychan son of Einon son of Merick son of Jevan son of Gronow son of Ivor son of Idnerth son of Cadogan son of Elistan Glodrydd. [The rest of this genealogy will be made clear by the great chart pedigree of Pryse, which accompanies this article.]

It is more convenient to consider the actual pedigrees as apart from the collections of pedigrees in different divisions to those given by Mr. Vaughan—

    I. From the earliest times to circa A.D. 942.

    II. From that period to A.D. 1536.

    III. From that period to the present time.

---

[1] This last has no connection with what goes before, but is the paternal descent of John Price of Pilleth, co. Radnor (*Lewys Dwnn*, i. 252).

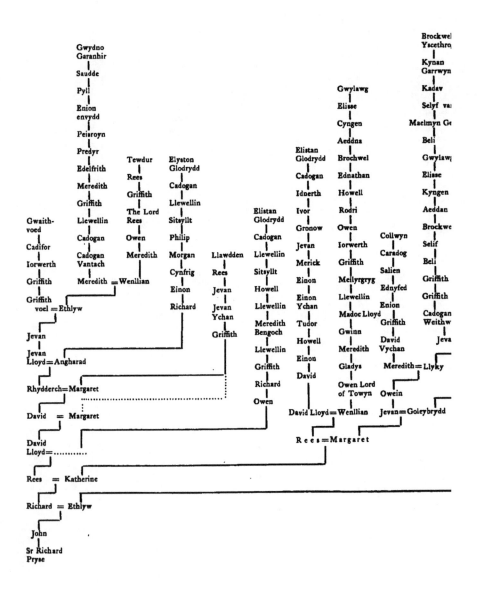

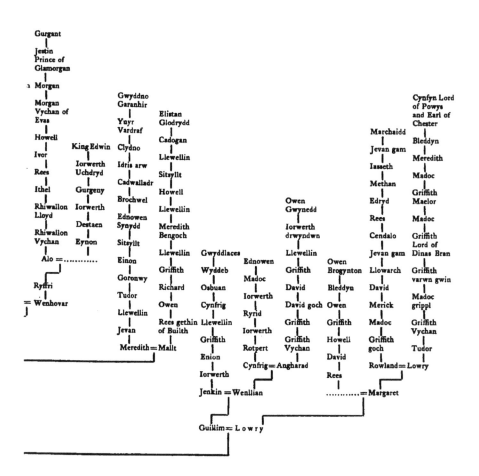

The second division covers the period from the passing of the laws of Howell Dda to the year in which the laws of Wales were made identical with those of England by the Statute of 27 Henry VIII. c. 26, entitled 'An Act for Laws and Justice to be ministered in Wales in like form as it is in this realm,' which enacted—

That all persons inheritable to lands which shall descend after the Feast of All Saints next coming within the Principality of Wales shall forever after the said Feast inherit and be inheritable to the same lands after the English tenure without division or partition and after the form of the Laws of this Realm of England, and not after the form of the Laws of this Realm of England and not after any (Welsh) tenure nor after the form of any Welsh Laws or Customs : And that the Laws, Ordinances and Statutes of this Realm of England forever and none other Laws, Ordinances, or Statutes from and after the said Feast shall be had, used, practised and executed in the said Dominion of Wales.

This statute contained the proviso—

That lands in Wales which have been used time out of mind by the laudable customs of the said Country to be departed and departable among issues and heirs male shall still so continue and be used, in like form, fashion and condition as if this Act had never been had nor made.

And towards the close of the sixteenth century we find actions for land based on the claim that it was held by Welsh tenure and therefore descended equally to all the male children.

Of the pedigrees earlier than A.D. 942 I do not propose to treat. It is possible that the arguments advanced with respect to the later ones are applicable to them at all events for some time previous to this date, since the laws of Howell Dda are known to have been founded on those of Dyfnwal Moelmud, who probably flourished about 400 A.D., though there was another chieftain of the same name who is said to have lived about 800 years earlier, but whether the provisions in Howell's laws as to the kindred are taken from the earlier laws must be considered an open question.

I have already shortly noticed the later pedigrees, and need only now say that with the exception of parish registers there are plenty of Welsh records in existence by which a pedigree may be proved. As a matter of fact I consider it considerably easier to trace a Welsh pedigree than an English one.

The basis of Welsh pedigrees I believe to be the Welsh laws, and the basis of the Welsh laws may be said to be the kindred. We find three groups of kindred—those within the

fourth degree; those within the seventh degree and those within the ninth degree; there is however some confusion as to how
these degrees are reckoned, and it would seem that the above
description of the groups is not strictly accurate. As to the
first group however there is no doubt, it consists of the
descendants of a common great grandparent; as to the other
groups the difficulty is shortly whether 'degree' means intermediate degree, or degree in an ascending line, e.g. whether
David Lloyd, 1613, in the above pedigree of Pryse, is related to
Sir Richard Pryse in the thirteenth or seventh degree. For my
present purpose it is unnecessary to go into the question. I will
adopt Professor Rhys' 'conjecture'[1] (though I consider that
his argument is convincing, and that the objections to it will
probably disappear on more accurate study of the laws), that
degree means intermediate degree, so that David Lloyd would
be related to Sir Richard Pryse in the thirteenth degree, as
should this view be incorrect my present argument would be
strengthened.

We have to consider the kindred from two points of view :
I. The relations of the individuals composing it *inter se*.
II. Their relations to those outside the kindred.

I. Here we are only concerned with the first group of
kindred, the descendants of a common great-grandfather,
and principally with regard to land tenure. The provisions of
the laws as to this shortly were as follows : On the death of
an original holder his sons divided his lands equally between
them, but the family holding was not broken up, because the
division was not final. The sons of the brothers did not claim
per stirpes. They were first cousins and had the right to claim
an equality of shares *per capita*; but still the family holding
was not broken up : another division is provided for, to take
place, presumably, when all the grandchildren are dead. Then
the great-grandchildren or second cousins finally divide equally
between them ; after this third division each of the great-grandchildren is regarded as an original holder.[2]

The group of kindred to the fourth degree was also responsible for the marriage of daughters, who were entitled to
a marriage portion and to be married to a free tribesman so

---

[1] *Celtic Folk-lore*, p. 421.
[2] This is practically quoted from Mr. Seebohm's *Tribal System in Wales*.
I have also made great use of Rhys and Jones' *History of the Welsh People*.

that their sons might have full tribal rights [1]—in this case the group is extended to the descendants (possibly only the male descendants) of the eight great-grandparents.

We are therefore led to conclude that official pedigrees must have been kept, as it would be practically impossible for a man to know all his second cousins accurately.

II. This conclusion becomes almost irresistible when we consider the relations of the kindred to outsiders. Here the group of second cousins, apparently *all* the descendants of the eight great-grandparents, were jointly responsible for ' saraad,' i.e. the payment for insult or injury short of homicide ; the group of third cousins (accepting Professor Rhys' conjecture above mentioned, otherwise fifth cousins), descendants of the sixteen great-great-grandparents through females as well as males are responsible for galanas—payment for homicide. Should there be a deficiency in this, ' the spear penny ' was to be gathered from the sixth (or ninth) cousins, though these are regarded as outside the kindred and there is a special provision for its collection.

> The murderer is to take a servant of the Lord, carrying with him a relic, and wherever he shall meet with a person beyond the seventh degree of kindred, let such person take his oath that he is not descended from any of the four kindreds from which the other is descended and unless he take that oath, let him pay a spear penny, and if he take the oath he is to be exempted.

Supposing these pedigrees to have been kept, the question arises, Who kept them ? The answer is clearly given in the following extracts from the so-called ' anomalous laws,' which are not of the same importance as the ' codes,' from which what goes before has been taken, but still of an early date and considerable authority :—

> Three branches of the Art of Bardism. First, the primitive bard, or a bard licensed by privilege, having his degree and his privilege, by discipleship, from an authorized teacher who is a presiding bard ; and upon him depends . . . every memorial and record of country and kindred, in respect to marriages and kins and arms and territorial divisions, and the privileges of the country and kindred of the Cymry.[2]

---

[1] It would seem that the residence in Wales of a foreigner and his descendants till the ninth generation conferred these rights, and that intermarriages with the daughters of full tribesmen generation after generation made the descendants of a foreigner tribesmen in the fourth generation.

[2] *Ancient Laws and Institutions of Wales* (ed. 1841), p. 511.

There are three branches of literature : . . . thirdly, one who is informed in book and letter . . . and in preserving a literary record in respect to the three records of the bards of the isle of Britain ; and these are, the genealogy of descent by marriages, territorial divisions, and praiseworthy actions and sciences.[1]

There are three errors of law : an uncertain claim ; an imperfect answer ; and an unsupported record.

There are three means of relief from the three errors : keeping and maintaining a systematic record of kin and descent by legitimate marriages . . . it was on account of the uncertainty of claims that it has been regulated and established for bards, qualified by the privilege and degree of session, specially to have the custody of kin and descent.[2]

There are three functions pertaining to the teachers of the country and kindred as being clergymen : . . . second, keeping authentic record of privileges and customs and tribestocks, and genealogy of descents, with legitimate marriages and of honourable actions, and of all excellencies of a country and kindred.[3]

There are three records of a kindred : the record of a court of law ; the record of a chief of kindred conjointly with his seven elders ; and the record of bardism : the record of a court of law depends upon the judges ; the record of a chief of kindred depends upon his seven elders, to wit the privileges and events of their kindred, and the seven elders are to transfer it to the chief of kindred who succeeds the one who may die ; and the record of bardism depends upon bards authorized as teachers, and by the privilege of session. These three records are called the three authenticated records of country and kindred ; and upon them depends the authenticating of every degree of descent, and every privilege of arms ; for from the privilege of land originates the privilege of arms ; and when the privilege of arms shall be found authenticated by record and symbol, that becomes a testimony in every suit as to land and soil.[4]

To sum up very briefly : the ancient laws of Wales practically necessitated the keeping of official records of pedigrees ; the bards were entrusted with the keeping of them ; we have a continuous series of collections of pedigrees dating from very early times. Is it likely that with authentic material at hand, the later pedigrees should be inventions ?

'Therfore (to quote an old writer) let such disdainefull heads, as scant knowe their owne Grandfathers, leave their scoffing and tawnting of Welshmen, for that thing that all other nations in the world doo glorie in ; and let them read the ancient writer Berosus . . . and if they beleeve him, let them not denie our origin ; and if they credit not him, let them beleeve no more but what they see with their eies, or what pleaseth their fond fantasies.'

H. J. T. WOOD.

[1] *Ancient Laws and Institutions of Wales* (ed. 1841), p. 513.
[2] Ibid. p. 521.   [3] Ibid. p. 547.   [4] Ibid. p. 559.

THE BONNY HOUSE OF COULTHART

AN OLD STORY RE-TOLD

'Oblivion the cancard enemie to fame and renoune, the suckyng serpent to auncient memorie.'—*Hall's Chronicle*.

THE genealogical tree, like the aloe, bursts into full flower only after long intervals. Two such flowering periods in England were the Elizabethan and the early Victorian ages. The Elizabethan heralds, at home in their new house, with a charter of incorporation and other braveries, found themselves attendant upon a new nobility, and heard a new gentry knocking at their doors. The wars of the Roses had been a very murrain amongst the ancient earls and barons of the land, who were all but exterminated by axe and sword and forfeiture. The creatures of the house of Tudor sat in the high places of the house of lords, and the country manor houses were filled with men of new names made rich by the new woollen trade or by lawyers who fattened upon the extravagances of Tudor litigation.

With such a market for their wares the heralds and pedigree makers fell joyfully to work. For the new gentleman were found arms and crest, which hinted at near kinship to the most illustrious bearer of his name or of a name in any way resembling it, whilst for the new lord were traced out and emblazoned in gold and many colours those marvellous pedigree rolls which are our wonder to-day when we see them brought out of their leather cases and pulled out along the hall floor or the hall table. Over the shields at the head sit the ancient kings of the earth from whose loins derives the Elizabethan lord whose name and style thirty feet below are engrossed above his great shield of many quarters. If we turn the pages of a peerage of to-day we find it still fragrant with the family legends and ancestral chronicles which flowed so easily from Elizabethan quills.

After the Elizabethan age, genealogy has its period of repose. Now and again an artist arises to find ancestral legend for the house of some new peer. The story of the Feilding descent from the house of Habsburg is one which a Cooke or

Dethick might have been proud to father, and the great duke's Churchill pedigree is a seemly fiction. But for the most part the Elizabethan legends are copied and re-copied, mumbled and mis-quoted, until the coming of the great Victorian period.

A great romancer had then filled the minds of the English with dreams of crumbling castle and haunted abbey, of tourneys and jousts, of errant knights and moss troopers until our people became mad with the madness of La Mancha. Armour which had cankered in wood-sheds and back-kitchens was brought forth and scoured, helmets which had for generations held the shepherd's tar and raddle and the groom's liniments were rescued from their vile offices and honourably cleansed by their happy finders. Ancient furniture was sought out, and books printed in the black letter, whilst the curiosity-monger's back-room became a workshop of Gothic oddments conceived and fashioned after a style which makes the epithet of forgery too harsh a word to use concerning such innocent devisings.

In the north country many a cattle-grazing bonnet-laird was sought out upon his hillside to be greeted as high chief of his clan, and to be persuaded to quit his comfortable breeches for plaid petticoats whose colour and pattern were vouched to him by Edinburgh tradesmen as those belonging to his name and blood. Further to the south infatuated gentlemen gathered in Drury Lane armour, and for three rainy August days solemnly pushed at each other with painted lances.

Such was the time of the renaissance of family legend. The old English landed gentry, dissatisfied with the neatly engrossed succession of John to Robert and of Richard to John, which was all that their pedigrees would afford them, sought impatiently for ancestral tales which should plump out these wizened facts, and ancestral tales were soon forthcoming in great plenty. Beside the landed gentry, and amongst them, a new class had arisen. Bankers, ironmasters and manufacturers had prospered in the fat years which followed Waterloo, and these were not slow to demand a wedding garment of pedigree woven with legend. Above others this class was the natural prey of the pedigree maker, and amongst this class Mr. John Ross Coulthart stands for a tall obelisk of warning example.

The facts of Mr. Coulthart's biography are simple and massive. The *Banker's Magazine* for January 1858 published

his portrait and with it an abridgement of his life and achievements. He had been a schoolboy at Buittle in the stewartry of
Kirkcudbright, and left school to become clerk to a banker and
attorney at Castle Douglas. In 1834 we find him a principal
clerk at a branch bank in Halifax, and from 1836 he was
manager of the Ashton, Staleybridge, Hyde and Glossop Bank
at Ashton-under-Lyne. In 1855 he was looking upon his
lesser townsmen from the mayoral chair of Ashton-under-
Lyne. There was a baker in the *Hunting of the Snark* who
only baked bridecake. With the bridecake of such a specialist
we might fairly compare the rich style of the writer to whom
we owe this sketch of a career, a writer, doubtless, who wrote
no biographies but those of bankers. In a sentence we are
given our man : 'Though in some respects Mr. Coulthart
may be said to be engaged in an arduous and exacting profes-
sion, yet he has not neglected to cultivate general literature,
nor to employ his time in the acquisition of information which
has been deemed useful by his fellow townsmen and the public.'
In fact, the muse of literature jogged Mr. Coulthart's elbow
until he consented to publish, in 1838, an octavo volume of
Decimal Interest Tables.

Needless to add that the intellectual brow, the upturned
collars, the flashing eye, the large black silk bow and respectable whiskers of the accompanying portrait from a steel plate
do nothing to injure the impression which a reader would
derive from the biography of Mr. Coulthart.

But biography and portrait help us nothing in our search
for the most important events in Mr. Coulthart's moving story,
events which will keep the name of Coulthart green, when the
glowing periods of his *Decimal Interest Tables* sleep in the library
of forgotten books. We say that these events were his meeting
with Mr. Alexander Cheyne and with Mr. Geo. Parker Knowles.

At some unknown date in the forties Mr. Coulthart met
with Alexander Cheyne, esquire, a barrister-at-law, and bachelor
of arts of Trinity College. Little is known of Mr. Cheyne.
He was admitted to Grays Inn in 1833. He was the author of
a work on the familiar subject of *Justice to Ireland,* and in 1853
he died at Broughton near Manchester, mourned with unctuous
sentences in the work of Mr. George Parker Knowles, genealogist and heraldic artist, who is found in 1854 in possession
of the confidence and intimacy of Mr. Cheyne's friend and
patron Mr. Coulthart.

In 1846 appeared the *Dictionary of the Commoners*, and Mr. Coulthart, throwing aside the bank manager and the computer of decimal interest, revealed himself to the world and to Ashton-under-Lyne as the eldest born of the most splendid line of north Britain, the house of Coulthart of Coulthart and Collyn. At the same time he beckoned forth from the press a pedigree—a pedigree which will remain for an enduring monument of human impudence and credulity. For some nineteen years this pedigree waxed and flourished, the wonder and delight of popular genealogists, and although the axe was laid smartly to its root in 1865, it were hazardous to suggest that this great trunk of imposture is now dead and sapless.

The pedigree cannot be better introduced than in the words of Mr. George Parker Knowles, written in 1855, at which date an edition of the family history of the Coultharts appeared sumptuously printed upon vellum, and printed, as a footnote vainly stipulates, for private circulation only. Its title is :—

A
Genealogical and Heraldic account of the
Coultharts of Coulthart and Collyn
Chiefs of the name
from their first settlement in Scotland in the reign of Conanus
to the year of our Lord 1854,
by
George Parker Knowles
Genealogist and Heraldic Artist.

Derived from the family muniments.

The preface by Mr. George Parker Knowles opens modestly enough. He cannot affect ignorance of the fact that fame and merit will wait upon the compilers of this work, but of that fame he will ask for no more than his share, his humble share. The 'transcribing and translating of the old deeds, wills, charters, pedigrees, marriage settlements, genealogical notices, etc.,' had been accomplished by the departed Cheyne, to whom Mr. George Parker Knowles renders a tribute probably as heartfelt as one artist might yield to another. 'Judging,' he says, 'of that gentleman's learning and research by the memoranda which he left behind him, it is deeply to be regretted that he did not live to bring the undertaking to a conclusion.' 'Divine Providence,' as Mr. George Parker Knowles admits with resignation, 'ordered it otherwise,' and Alexander Cheyne, esquire, was in Dethick's bosom.

But Cheyne was at least happy in his literary executor, and we have few regrets for his sake when we are once embarked upon the Genealogical and Heraldic Account.

Few families can justly claim so ancient and honourable a descent as the Coultharts of Coulthart and Collyn, and fewer still can establish their lineage by such unerring documentary evidence. Deriving an uninterrupted male succession from the era of Julius Agricola, the genealogy is clearly traceable by means of monkish chronicles, historical achievements, marriage alliances, royal charters, baronial leases, sepulchral inscriptions, sasine precepts, judicial decreets, and fragmentary pedigree, to the present lineal representative, who has furnished me with such an extensive collection of ancestral muniments, partly arranged by domestic annalists and antiquaries, that I am enabled to compile from the family archives the following brief record of The COULTHARTS OF COULTHART AND COLLYN, chiefs of the name, and also to annex thereto heraldic and genealogical accounts of The ROSSES of Renfrew, The MACKNYGHTES of Macknyghte, The GLENDONYNS of Glendonyn, The CARMICHAELS of Carspherne, The FORBESES of Pitscottie, The MACKENZIES of Craighall, and The GORDONS of Sorbie; who have all, through heiresses, become incorporated with the house of Coulthart, as successive generations meandered down the stream of time.

It is possible that a higher antiquity might have been claimed for this illustrious house had the chief of his name and family, as Mr. Knowles invariably styles his patron, fallen into the hands of a less scrupulous genealogist. But Mr. Knowles, pushing aside untrustworthy documents and evidence which might perchance have taken the line of Coulthart back to the earlier stone age, insists upon 'confining' his 'details to the evidence of documents obviously authentic.'

He finds, therefore, 'the family name and descent to be derived from COULTHARTUS, a Roman lieutenant, who fought under Julius Agricola, at the foot of the Grampian mountains, when that victorious general was opposed by the confederated forces of the Scots, Picts and Danes, under Corbredus Galdus. Peace having been restored soon after that decisive engagement, COULTHARTUS, instead of returning to Rome, married Marsa, daughter of Kadalyne, chief of the Novantes, by whom he acquired large territorial possessions near the present Whithorn in the county of Wigtown.' Coulthartus, it would appear, was a subaltern of whom even Mr. Spenser Wilkinson would approve, being 'versed in all the wisdom and learning of the Romans'—a meet ancestor for his remote descendant who penned the famous *Decimal Interest Tables*. He was content however to live his retired life as a simple 'Caledonian chieftain' at Leucaphibia, where he died 'beloved and lamented' in the twelfth year of King Conanus. As a Roman soldier he had done his duty : such a man could have done no less as a Caledonian chieftain. He dies all unconscious that he has founded the most wondrous pedigree on earth, or that such distant bards as Alexander Cheyne, B.A., and George Parker Knowles will wake the string in praise of the line of Coulthartus.

His son JULIUS, the hope of the house, is famous as the builder of several strong castles near Adrian's Wall. He died as became the son of COULTHARTUS in routing a band of Irish robbers which infested the Western Islands of Scotland, and is succeeded by his brother, whom COULTHARTUS had quaintly named ACKALINE.

It is not in length only that the line of Coulthart is to excel all other houses. Ancient families whose scanty chronicles yield but that fact that John follows James, to be followed by another John, will marvel, and marvelling will envy, when they see how virtue, courage, piety and muscular development bring forth their due fruit in each generation of the Roman subaltern's children.

ACKALINE fights heroically under King Ethodius, and that against the Romans themselves, which speaks well for that sovereign's wise policy towards the families of uitlanders, and he brings up a son, DORALDUS I. This DORALDUS loses his life whilst suppressing another rebellion in those troublesome Western Islands, and begets MORADUS his son and heir.

By this time the house of Coulthart is one which kings delight to honour. Of MORADUS we are told that such was the esteem in which he was held by King Donaldus I. that he was present at that monarch's funeral by special invitation. This courtesy is well repaid by THORWALDUS, son of MORADUS, who 'exerts himself greatly' in deposing the usurper NATHALOCUS, placing upon the Scottish throne the true lineal successor of Ethodius II.

Of COULTHARTUS II., son of Thorwaldus, we are told that he 'surpassed most men of his time in the manly exercises of running, riding, shooting arrows, throwing the dart, and wielding the battle-axe.' Of his golfing record nothing seems to be known, but the prowess of his remote descendants with the long bow is here traced to its source. His son DIORTHACA, husband of Amica, daughter of Bathircus, embraced the Christian religion, and here has its spring the traditional piety of the Coultharts. We may note that his representative the banker and author insists, before putting his family history into type, that Mr. George Parker Knowles shall solemnly sign and attest his work in the presence of the Lord Bishop of Manchester and of the incumbent of St. Matthew's, Manchester. Thenceforward the chronicle goes gallantly on, and no Coulthart is found wanting in the family qualities. The throne of Scotland, in those ages which would be dark enough but for the lantern light of the Coulthart pedigree, was of a truth propped and shored up by the reckless loyalty of the Coultharts.

CORNELIUS son of Diorthaca is slain in battle with the Picts. It is by the aid of MORALINTHUS his son that Picts, Romans and Britons are routed by Eugenius II. at the memorable battle on the banks of the Cree, perishing himself with his elder sons Galdus and Halinthus in the equally memorable battle on the banks of the Dee. Our grief for these fallen heroes is chastened by the thought that ORPHEUS, the youngest born of Moralinthus, is forced 'to fly with other religious men to Icolmkill.' To this breathing space we owe the early history of the line of Coulthartus, for 'in learned seclusion, ORPHEUS wrote a chronicle of the times in which he lived, including the preceding annals of his ancestors,' the accumulations of which must by this time have cried aloud for a fitting chronicler. In such wise did Orpheus begin what George Parker Knowles was to complete. In the case of TYRUS his son the Venerable Bede comes to the assistance of Mr. Knowles, relating in his chronicle that Tyrus dwelt in his days at Coulthart, an estate which we now hear of for the first time. Coulthart, which must have taken its name from Agricola's lieutenant, is described by Bede (teste Mr. Knowles) as near Epiacum in Galloway. Tyrus was present at the ratification of the treaty of peace between Fergus II. and Placidus, and was slain in the general engagement between the allied Scots, Picts and Welsh and the Roman forces. By this time death for the fatherland had become for the Coultharts something more than a sweet and decorous thing. It was a passion, a fascination and a habit.

CONANETH son of Tyrus routs Britons for Eugenius II. and spends 'the evening of his life in the exercise of charity, devotion and other Christian virtues.' Doubtless in this pious leisure he found time to post up the family chronicle, which must have been again neglected by the stirring generations which followed Orpheus. He begets PAULUS, 'also an exceedingly religious man,' who drives from the Scottish border the Saxons under Hengist and Octa. His grandson COULTHARTUS III., moved to emulation by the deeds of his namesake Coulthartus II., is famous in his age for his skill 'in the military exercises of the age in which he lived,' his taste therein shaming our own War Office, whose interest is ever fixed upon the military exercises of earlier ages than our own. EUTACUS son of Coulthartus revives a family custom, and is killed fighting under King Aidanus, leaving a younger son MORALDUS, a monk famed for his miracles, and an heir KENTYRUS, who achieved one of those records which have been of late so popular, being present at four coronations. We pass DORALDUS II., a famous warrior, GOLFRIDUS, who made peace for Scotland by 'a lengthy interview' with St. Cuthbert, and KINOTELLUS, killed under King Amberkelethus, to arrive at COULTHARTUS IV. The recurrence of the famous name brings new honours to the house of Coulthart, and Coulthartus IV. would seem to have been pious to a degree notable even in his family. In such wise generation follows generation, and chief succeeds chief. Ever the records grow of deeds of war and piety, ever the sons of Coulthartus are the right hand of their sovereign. DONATUS wins glory in the wars, CORNELIUS II. meets the family fate at Haddington, and DUNSTANE his son is 'basely beheaded' with Alpinus his king.

With MORDACHUS son of Dunstane we get another glimpse of the pride of place of the family. It would appear that only a few Scottish noblemen 'anxiously desired to punish without delay the Picts for their unparalleled baseness and barbarity,' but Mordachus was one of those few, and by his counsel and influence the punitive expedition was raised which was to blot out the very name of Pict. As Mordachus dies full of years and honour at Coulthart Castle we see that the old *stammhaus* mentioned by Bede is rising with the family in importance. FERGUS and CUTHBERTUS are succeeded by COULTHARTUS V., a great builder and, alas! a restorer of churches. CORNELIUS III. is created Thane of Galloway, and we may note that up to this point the family services had not even earned a baronetcy from the ungrateful men who owed their thrones to the line. The Thane is killed in battle near Buchan, and his grandson OSBERTUS, son of Jowethus, fights at Loncarty. WALUAIN son of Osbertus is killed at Murthlack, and DONALDUS his son, 'though scarcely arrived at man's estate when the responsibilities of the chiefship of his family devolved upon him, was almost immediately called to the councils of his sovereign.' Old or young a Coulthart must be forthcoming. His son COULTHARTUS VI., baron or lord of Coulthart, is tempted by Macbeth, but a usurper can hope for no aid in war or council from a Coulthart, and Coulthartus VI. ' joyfully joined, with all his retainers, the standard of Malcolm Kianmore when that prince returned to his native land.'

ALFRED son of Coulthart was summoned by King Malcolm ' to a conference at Forfar, to determine as to the best means of placing the kingdom of Scotland in a posture of defence against the anticipated invasion of William Duke of Normandy, commonly called WILLIAM THE CONQUEROR.' By reason of his sage counsels William, Duke of Normandy, was forced to abandon his schemes, and to this Alfred some further acknowledgments are made by the grudging sovereign. King Malcolm grants him a confirmation charter of the barony of Coulthart with a condition that the chief of Coulthart should furnish three horses to the king of Scotland in war time, for which reason *three colts courant* have ever since been borne by the family of Coulthart as an armorial ensign. The distinction was no doubt the more prized by the family for its singularity, the invention of heraldic bearings belonging to a later age. Unique as was the honour the grateful Coultharts soon paid their debt in full. The name of THEOBALD, a second son, 'occurs as being one of Macduff's followers in keeping Macbeth's rebellious party in subjection.' GODOFREDUS, lord of Coulthart, ' actively opposed the usurpations of Donald Bane and Duncan,' whilst REGINALDUS his brother distinguishes himself at the battle of Lothian.

Sir RADULPHUS DE COULTHART claims our attention as ' the first laird on record that used the territorial designation as a surname,' and hearing this we feel that we are at last on the home track towards our banker-mayor. His heir Sir PETER DE COULTHART, ' chief of his name and family,' contributes ' to the relief of the Christians in Jerusalem,' and the younger brothers of Sir Peter add their swords to their brother's subscription and are killed together at Acre. In WILLIAM DE COULTHART, the famous piety of the family is honoured by Pope Innocent III., who speaks of him, of course in a bull, as 'chief of his name.' Sir ROGER DE COULTHART 'was invested with the knightly girdle by Alexander II. at the Royal Haddington tournament in 1240.' It must have been his prowess at Haddington which won him the white hand of Isabella, a daughter of Walter Stewart, hereditary High Steward of Scotland. The jealousy of her kinsmen may account for the omission of this lady from all the pedigrees of Stewart. The knightly girdle was not all that Sir Roger was invested with at Haddington. The king 'heraldically added to the three black colts courant on his silver shield a fess sable, which armorial ensigns have ever since, without alteration, been borne by the chiefs of the family.' The arms are borne upon the seal, with which another Sir Roger seals a grant of lands in 1443. The seal, of which many illustrations exist, is as notable as aught else Coulthartian. The legend SIGILLVM COVLTHARTI is unique. The helm above the shield is the barrel helm of the thirteenth century, the supporters of the *colt* and the *bart* suggest the fifteenth century, whilst the colt's head crest is borne sidelong on the helm in the manner of the nineteenth century.

Alexander de Coulthart, son of the valiant jouster, commands 'a battalion of the Scottish army at the battle of Largs,' and marries a lady mysteriously described as 'Helen, daughter of the De Roberton, co. Lanark,' but we must hurry by four generations illustrated by piety and learning, and by the deaths of two brothers Coulthart at Nevill's Cross, to Gilbert de Coulthart, in whom we see the first trace of dissatisfaction in this generous race, the most ancient house in Scotland, warriors who marked every notable battle by falling in it covered with glorious wounds, territorial magnates who matched with Stewarts, Crawfords, Montgomerys, Hays and St. Clairs. The peerage which nowadays rewards the enterprise of our brewers was denied to them, and they remain, like Coulthartus their founder, simple 'Caledonian chieftains.' What wonder is it that Gilbert de Coulthart carries his mighty sword oversea and rebukes his country by dying at Dantzic in the service of Prussia against the Turks.

But his sons forgive. For the next four generations the Coultharts resume their ancestral customs, and each chief dies in the field against Scotland's enemies. The first of these doomed warriors was Sir Roger, who rushed upon his fate at Roxburgh Castle in 1460. The warlike spirit of another Roger is released at Sauchyburn. Flodden with its hecatomb of Scottish nobles, demands its Coulthart, and Richard de Coulthart, 'chief of the name' obeys. Cuthbert son of Richard, a man 'of extraordinary physical powers'—a true Coulthart in short—finds that even his strength cannot retrieve the fortunes of Flodden, and saves his life on that day. If he had not so escaped there might have been no Coulthart corpse decorating the field of Solway Moss, where he falls 'commanding a division of the Scottish army with admirable courage and discretion.'

After the death of Cuthbert the family hangs up the sword of Coulthartus—the military career is henceforward for its cadets. The heads of the house, who are now 'of Coulthart and Largmore,' stay at home, enlarge their mansions and cultivate their fields, producing at last one Richard Coulthart of Coulthart and Largmore, 'an eminent practical agriculturalist and author of the once celebrated work entitled *The Economy of Agriculture*. He died in 1717 leaving issue a son, James Coulthart of Coulthart and Largmore,' chief of his name and family, great-grandfather of our John Ross Coulthart, bank manager and *litterateur*, of Coulthart, Collyn and Ashton-under-Lyne. Fifty-eighth in descent from the lieutenant of Agricola, he was in lonely splendour the last of his line. His only sister had bestowed her hand upon one James MacGuffie, surely a *mésalliance* for one of her race, since even Mr. George Parker Knowles could only trace the MacGuffies to a John MacGuffie, who had fallen at Flodden beside, it may be, the valiant Richard de Coulthart. But as the Coultharts were alone amongst the Scottish nobles in their use of arms before the invention of those distinctions even so the ancestral MacGuffie served his country as a colonel in her army before that rank had become recognized by the Scottish War Office.

The pedigree of the bonny house of Coulthart of Coulthart was drunk in greedily by the hungry wastes of the Landed Gentry books which were then in their high noon. It was the great day of fantastic legends of ancestry, but no matter in what collection of imaginative chronicles it was welcomed as a guest the history of the Coultharts stood, even as its chiefs were described by their admiring sovereigns in charter and deed, *facile primarius*. For twenty years it ran its course unchallenged and unquestioned, a fact which vouches for our fathers' hearty appetite for wonders. It was 'the stoup, the pride, the ornament' of Dictionaries of Commoners and Landed Gentry, of Illuminated Visitations, of County Family books, of Anecdotes of Heraldry. The arms of Coulthart with its noble quarterings, its historic crest and supporters as borne upon Sir Roger's seal, were illustrated in all the armories and books of heraldric illustration.

Such books as Lower's *Patronymica Britannica* and Anderson's *Genealogy and Surnames* took the story of Coulthartus to their bosoms, whilst the latter author's *Scottish Nation*, a work whose three volumes still cumber the shelves of reference libraries and trip up the antiquarian neophyte, enrolled the whole tale amongst the glories of Scottish history. The very name of Coulthart was made the text for the wildest etymologies of bewildered guessers, bogged by the fact that the descendants of Coulthartus, having used no surname for thirty-four generations, assumed the surname at the time of the first crusade, not from the memory of their Roman forbear, but from their land called Coulthart. Mr. Anderson wrote :—

It would be useless to speculate on its original signification beyond what is supplied in giving the name of its first recorded possessor in Scotland, though we may add that all the earliest traditions and etymologies regarding it, and also all the armorial bearings belonging to it, refer the derivation to the prowess and valour of a Roman horse-soldier.

Mr. Anderson is not an easy author to follow upon his speculative journeys into philology, but it seems fairly plain that, in his opinion at least, Coulthartus is a name akin to Lionheartus or the like familiar names in Latin. Coulthartus being 'a Roman horse-soldier' was imbued with the courage of the mettled colt he bestrode. Hence we arrive with ease at the origin of his name.

Mr. Lower, esteemed in his day an antiquary of some weight, decorated his paragraph concerning the Coulthart name with the famous Coulthart seal, and added to Mr. Anderson's etymology the illuminating remark that—

the name of the Scottish locality is probably synonymous with that of Coudhard, a village in the department of Orne, a few miles N.E. of Argentan.

Time having made his ravenous meal of all the ancient monuments of the house, the extreme magnificence of which, as vouched for in the Coulthart history, had doubtless tempted the spoiler and iconoclast, altar-tombs to the illustrious dead sprang up mysteriously by the churches of Kells and Kirkpatrick Fleming, and a window by Willement, in the Gothic taste of Great Exhibition days, glazed a gable in the church of Bolton-le-Gate, bearing the arms, crest, quarterings and supporters of the Coultharts and the shield of the MacGuffies. Dr. James Prince Lee, Bishop of Manchester, the same obliging prelate who had witnessed Mr. Knowles' solemn declaration of good faith attached to the pedigree, wrote the inscription for another altar-tomb in Bolton church when in 1847 Mr. John Ross Coulthart succeeded to the chieftaincy of his name. Of course Mr. William Coulthart is described by the good bishop in the quaint language of the Coulthart charters as Gulielmus Coulthart de Coulthart et Collyn arm. gentis nominisque sue facile primarius.

The paper boat, or parchment boat to be exact, sailed down stream with favouring winds until 1865.

In 1866 copies of the Coulthart publications were forwarded to Mr. John Gough Nichols, F.S.A., for notice in his *Herald and Genealogist*. The review which followed was an amazing one when we consider the credit which Mr. Nichols enjoyed as an antiquary. The story of Coulthartus, of Ackaline, of Moraldus, Orpheus and Theodore was swallowed whole after a little preliminary gaping and wondering. The grant of arms by Malcolm Kianmore was boggled at, Mr. Nichols considering 'the epoch too early for the origin of armorial bearings,' and questioning whether arms punning upon the surname would have been assumed two generations before the surname was assumed. But Mr. Nichols allowed nothing for the memory which such an ancestor as Coulthartus I. must have left behind. The seal of Roger de Coulthart was accepted meekly enough, the reviewer contenting himself with the remark that the inscription SIGILLVM COVLTHARTI was 'unusual in form.' After the death of Sir Gilbert at Dantzic Mr. Nichols was of opinion that 'for some generations after, the fate of each successive head of the family is remarkable.' A picture of the seal, another of the Bolton window, and nine more of the Coulthart arms and quarters were gratefully accepted by Mr. Nichols for the decoration of his pages, and the Coulthart bookplate was made frontispiece for the year's volume.

But before this review was in type the storm has broken from a clear sky. A pamphlet no bigger than a man's hand

had been already put about in Edinburgh, the anonymous
work of the learned George Burnett, and within a few months
'all' as Mr. John Evelyn of Wotton would have put it,' was
dust.'

After fifty-eight generations woe came upon the house of
Coulthartus, the like of which had not been in all the glorious
and checkered record. When Moralinthus fell upon the banks
of the Dee and with him Galdus and Halinthus ; when Orpheus,
taking with him little but writing materials, was in full flight
for Icolmkill, the fortunes of the house must have seemed gloomy
and unpromising. But worse was here. The house which
rolled back in turn Pict, Roman, Saxon, Dane and Englishman
took Mr. Burnett's quill between the joints of the harness.
Like that of the Yorkshire house of Squeers the coat of arms
of the Coultharts 'was tore', and the great cloud of ancestors
had flown into the air like startled pigeons. Coulthartus,
Ackaline, Orpheus, Roger of the tournament, Gilbert the
wanderer, Cuthbert the huge and valiant, all were gone.
In the ear of Mr. John Ross Coulthart, where he sat gloomy
and alone, chief of his name and last of his race in every sense
of the word, the boding voice of the family banshee must
have grown to a positive shriek.

Mr. Burnett triumphed with a cruel triumph. Mr. John
Gough Nichols made such hurried amends as might be made
for the unfortunate hospitality which the *Herald and Genealogist* had shown towards Mr. Knowles's chronicle, and the
County Families and Landed Gentries made haste to straiten
the space which they had afforded so lavishly to the house
of Coulthart of Coulthart, Collyn, Largmore and Ashton-
under-Lyne.

The family estates followed the ancestors, disappearing
from the face of the map. Coulthart and its castle were
sought vainly in atlas and gazetteer. According to Mr.
Burnett no such lands as those of Coulthart existed or had
ever existed in Wigtownshire.

No family of Coulthart had been known in Scotland or
elsewhere. As freeholders they were sought for in the
register of retours at Edinburgh, and not a single name was
forthcoming in that great record of the Scottish landed houses.
They were sought as feuars or leaseholders, but the sasine
register was silent as was the register of retours. History
and record alike failed to yield a single Coulthart of the line,

and the pedigree was again examined for its abounding references to chronicle and charter. Ptolemy and Tacitus, who had commemorated the earlier heads of the house, were searched at first hand, but the passages had been wiped from their pages. The Venerable Bede had vouched for the descendants of Coulthartus as living in his day at the foot of the Grampians, but set in the box and questioned by Mr. Burnett this treacherous father denied his statement made to Mr. Knowles and Mr. Cheyne.

The few Coulthart charters printed by Mr. Knowles were tracked down by the enemies of imaginative genealogy, and they at least were forthcoming in the Great Seal Register, but certain peculiarities could not escape notice. Where the name Coulthart occurred in the muniments gathered by Mr. Cheyne other names were found in the charters in the register. A grant to *Johanni de Coulthart militi* appeared as to *Alexandro de Meynies militi*. The famous royal charter to *Willielmo de Coulthart gentis nominisque sui facile primario* appeared as to *Gilberto de Glencharny*, whose name was followed by no such subtle royal compliment, and the barony of Coulthart was changed to the barony of Glencharny. It was pointed out that Mr. Coulthart's ancient charters followed, oddly enough, the form of the charters in the abbreviated form afforded by the printed volume of the Great Seal Register, rather than the fuller form which original charters had taken. When we consider the carping spirit, the malicious distrustfulness, which now characterized the inquiry into the Coulthart pedigree it will be readily understood that attention was directed to such details as these.

Other Coulthart documents were examined with much cruel mirth. It was not the fault of the chief of Coulthart that he possessed a family marriage settlement dated in the twenty-first year of King Kennethus III., who only reigned from 997 to 1005. Yet much was made of this singularity of the date, and more of the fact that the national collections of Scotland contained no written legal documents before the close of the eleventh century. Still more matter for laughter was found in the fact that the settlement was made upon the marriage of William de Coulthart with *Angus* de Cumin, and it was freely suggested that the well learned Mr. Cheyne had considered Angus nothing but an earlier version of the name Agnes.

The houses whose representation had passed into the broad stream of Coulthart, adding quarterings to its great shield, were next raked over in the same ungenerous humour. One and all were declared fabulous as Coulthart. Glendonyn of Glendonyn, perhaps suggested by a passage in the *Monastery*, came first to the handling. These Coulthart Glendonyns were of Glendonyn in Ayrshire, and the fact that the only known family and lands of Glendonyn were in Roxburgh-shire was held to be evidence against Mr. Coulthart's quar-tering. Macknyghte of Macknyghte was sought through chronicles, pedigree books and records and was not found, although the arms of this house were forthcoming in the shape of a shield recorded as that of Macnaught of Kilquharity. Carmichael of Carspherne, according to Mr. Knowles, was a quiet living family which had made little history. Needless to say, the shyness of the lairds of Carspherne became still more pronounced when Mr. Burnett came to seek traces of them. The family of Ross of Renfrew would have succeeded to a peerage had the Scottish house of lords been aware of their descent, but the pedigree of the Lords Ross had ignored this famous branch. Forbes of Pitscottie and Gordon of Sorbie were cried for in vain by genealogists, and no ancestral voice replied from either house. When the armorial bearings of these families were demanded of the Lyon Office, the Lyon Office confessed its inability to exemplify them, and the armories from Davy Lindsay to Nisbet were drawn in vain for the shields figuring as Mr. Coulthart's quarterings.

The later chroniclers quoted by Mr. Cheyne were sifted to Mr. Cheyne's discredit as an accurate note-taker. Of Gilbert de Coulthart, who went in the train of Earl Douglas to Rome in 1449, we read in the chronicle :—

Thair were utheris of lower estates, as *Coulthart*, Urquhart, Campbell, Forester and Lowther, all knightis and gentlemen whose convoy maid the Earle so proud and insolent.

With a Coulthart in his train the intolerable pride of Earl Douglas might be pardoned, but Mr. Cheyne, by some strange error, had read *Coulthart* in the chronicle where *Calder* was, and the passage in the original can hardly be said to illustrate the foreign adventures of the valiant Gilbert.

Leaving chronicles and heraldry the critics fell to trivialities. Here on the pedigree was a captain of the Royal Artillery under James I., who must have been at that time the only commissioned officer of a corps which was raised long after his death. To an Admiral Coulthart of the royal navy who flourished in the early sixteenth century the like objection was raised.

Criticism having done its fell work, constructive genealogy set up its scaffolding and attempted to rebuild the pedigree upon new evidences. But here, where the ancient methods of the Elizabethans, of Cheyne and of Knowles, had been followed with such success, modern inquiry met failure only.

When Pip, the Pip of *Great Expectations*, had confessed to Joe Gargery that his tale of the wonders of Miss Havisham's household as told to his sister and Uncle Pumblechook had not its base upon fact, it will be remembered how the good Joe pleaded for a single marvel to remain as a truth. If there was no black velvet coach ' at least there was dogs, Pip ? Come, Pip,' said Joe persuasively, ' if there warn't no weal cutlets, at least there was dogs ? A dog,' said Joe, ' a puppy ? Come ! '

If there be one name in the pedigree of Coulthart upon which the genealogist might set his finger and say, ' Surely here be truths,' it is the name of ' Richard Coulthart of Coulthart and Largmore, an eminent agriculturist, and author of the once celebrated work entitled the *Economy of Agriculture*.' The words carry conviction, and when we are told that he too is as shadowy as Moralinthus or Kentyrus, and that the once celebrated work entitled the *Economy of Agriculture* has disappeared not only from the farmer's table, but also from all libraries and catalogues of libraries, we sympathize with Joe Gargery's demand for a single puppy.

No pedigree however short ever took the place of the great work of Messrs. Cheyne and Knowles. But the Coulthart estate of Largmore furnished some slight clue. The barony of Largmore shrunk, it is true, upon examination, to a little farm in Kells, but that at least remained upon the map when Coulthart and Collyn had faded from sight. This farm had been purchased by a shrewd, although half-witted farm labourer named James Coulthart, playfully entitled 'Laird Cowtart,' and commemorated in a dozen Galloway folk tales as the obstinate man who sat all night in his field because the good wife had called him indoors to his broth a second time when he had warned her to call him once only. It is probable at least that he was the grandfather of William Coulthart, father of the last chief.

F

When all else had gone one does not look for the arms of Coulthart of Coulthart to survive the fate of the land and pedigree. But they remained ! The supporters of the colt and the hart trotted back together to their twelfth century deviser, but the shield remained.

A glance at an ordinary of arms revealed the fact that Mr. Coulthart had begun his career as a Scottish chieftain by assuming, doubtless under the advice of Mr. Cheyne, the shield of arms appertaining to his name. Or rather, as no such shield was forthcoming, Mr. Cheyne braced upon his client's arm the nearest and handiest shield of a family whose name might be considered as remotely resembling the chieftain's own. This happened to be the shield of arms of the well known family of the Colts of Essex and Suffolk, created baronets in 1692. It will amaze even those who are acquainted with the methods of dead and gone heralds to learn that Mr. Coulthart was allowed by the Lyon Office at Edinburgh the stolen coat of the Colts. The nature and impudence of his assumption can hardly have escaped notice, yet the shield was officially recorded as his property in November, 1846, the grant being made out in the name of Mr. Coulthart's father, who was then living. Ten years afterwards, on the strength of the Lord Lyon's complacent venality, Mr. Coulthart attempted to record the same shield at the English College of Arms. Here he failed. A line must be drawn somewhere, and the College of Arms drew it at recording the undifferenced coat of a living baronet to a Lancashire bank-manager who derived from Scotland his dissimilar surname.

A compromise however was arrived at, and the chief of his name and race suffered himself to be persuaded to take out in England a second grant of arms, possibly for use at Ashton-under-Lyne, whereby his undeniably commercial pursuits might not tarnish the ancient shield derived from the eleventh century Alfred and on record at the Lyon Office. The new shield is Colt with a difference. The colours remain, and one of the two colts above the fesse ; but below the fesse, in place of the third colt is a black water-bouget taken from the Shield of Ross and speaking of the chieftain's descent from the Lords Ross of Renfrew. In this curious document the grantee was, as we understand, described with all his territorial titles, as 'John Ross Coulthart of Coulthart, Collyn and Ashton, esquire.'

Mr. Burnett's mingled criticism and satire were slow to leaven the genealogical bookshelf. But by degrees the Coulthart legend faded and grew less. The pedigrees shortened and disappeared, the armories gave the shield of Coulthart with less and less of commentary on the antiquity of the house, and the peerages were slowly purged from the matches which the daughters of peers had been allowed to contract with fifteenth and sixteenth century chiefs of Coulthart and Largmore. At last the shield itself disappeared from all modern works but the semi-official list of recorded Scottish arms issued by the present Lord Lyon King of Arms, from which, indeed, it can hardly be expunged without affecting the value of the book as a record.

Yet such a pedigree sleeps but to wake. The new scrap-books of heraldry and genealogy have need of its stately proportions, and we shall not look in vain for a reference to it amongst those genealogical paragraphs in newspapers and, magazines which add gaiety to our column of ‘What is Believed.’

It was never discredited by those who love such things in sincerity. An often exposed medium may be deserted at last by the most faithful listeners for table raps, but an exposed pedigree never wants for friends.

The Coulthart pedigree found its last loyal friend in Mr. Joseph Foster, who is still making us our popular books of arms and pedigrees. Many years after the Coulthart exposure Mr. Foster found the neglected pedigree of Coulthart, smoothed out its creases and printed it entire—from Coulthartus I. to his fifty-eighth descendant—in a great volume of *Lancashire Pedigrees*. The only detail we can find which struck Mr. Foster as an unlikely one and needing an editor's hand was the title of the early sixteenth-century Admiral R.N., and this officer's exact rank is therefore left unindicated by his last chronicler. The record of a still more notable officer, the major who, although safe in the army of King Charles II., fled abroad for dread of the wrath of Oliver Cromwell and never returned, is left with its early bloom upon it by the unsuspicious Mr. Foster! The grant of arms in the eleventh century is solemnly recited, although the pictured arms in the margin are those of the more modern grant of 1859.

To add salt to the performance Mr. Foster's preface to *Lancashire Pedigrees* tells us that ‘The day is past, except for the day, to publish apochryphal pedigrees. Ingenuity cannot hide an obscure origin, nor a distinguished descent be concealed. Truth is sought for ingenuously and successfully.'

With Mr. Foster in the ascendant, still seeking truth ingenuously and successfully, crabbed Archæology has no reason to grudge Romance her Corelli.

OSWALD BARRON.

THE EARLS OF MENTEITH

A PAGE FROM THE PAST

IN my book-hunting days I acquired, some years ago, a copy of *The Book of Common Prayer* according to the use of the Church of Ireland printed in the year 1721. It was a nice copy bound in black morocco with silver corners and clasps, and originally there had been a silver monogram 'H.R.' in the centre of each cover ; on the title page is written 'E.M.H. etc.' The fly-leaves are all covered with writing in a neat feminine hand signed at the end in a bold hand 'E. Moira Hastings.' This signature is evidently that of Lady Elizabeth Hastings, eldest daughter of Theophilus ninth Earl of Huntingdon, who inherited the baronies of Hastings de Hastings and Hastings de Hungerford on her brother's death in 1789, which proves that the notes in this volume must have been made between that date and the writer's death in 1808. This lady was the third wife of Sir John Rawdon, 4th Bart., who was elevated to the peerage of Ireland as Baron Rawdon of Moira, co. Down, and created Earl of Moira 30 Jan. 1762. As this marriage took place in 1752, it may be assumed that the interesting account of the ancestry of Helena Graham, which forms the subject of this writing was committed to paper towards the close of the eighteenth century. I was much interested in perusing these pages of MS. written so long since, and though the genealogical information therein set forth may be well known to students of Scotch genealogies, still it seemed to me sufficiently interesting to entitle it to find a nook in the pages of *The Ancestor*. The dry bones of genealogies are *caviare* to the multitude, but in this case, being clothed with a touch of romance, they have an additional interest which I trust will render this article interesting to the general reader.

One cannot help being struck with the keen spirit with which the writer carefully tabulated the descent of the honours—the loss of which she so pathetically bewails—as well as with the gentle touch of irony when she writes, 'The Scotch claim conveyed honor — the Conway conveyed (if gained) profit & the gratification of resentment.' Not the least interesting portion of the MS. is, perhaps, the descriptive account given of 'the various trifles belonging to the family esteemed as consequential appendages,' and her grief at the modernization of the watch given by King Charles II. to the last Earl of Menteith will appeal to the sympathies of many, whilst one's mirth will be provoked at the mention of the 'wedding night-cap' of the last Earl of Menteith, especially when one tries to picture the renowned Earl's appearance clothed in such an article of head-gear! The Rawdons were an old West Riding family seated at Rawdon near Leeds, and several of them—in successive generations—entered the army and rendered a good account of themselves fighting for their king. One of them, George Rawdon, attached to Lord Conway's regiment of foot, distinguished himself in the 'Irish Rebellion' of 1641, and as a reward for his services was by King Charles II. in 1665 created a Baronet of Ulster, by letters patent dated 20th May, and presumably had a grant of land, as thereafter Moira in County Down became their chief place of residence and the source of their subsequent title of Earl Moira. This George Rawdon was previously secretary to Edward, Lord Conway, principal Secretary of State, whose eldest daughter Dorothy he married in 1654 ; she died in 1676 leaving three sons surviving, whereof Edward, born in 1655, and John, born in 1656, both fell fighting in France some years later, so that Arthur the youngest, born 17 Oct. 1671, became the heir of the family and was the husband of Helen or Helena Graham the heiress of this MS. Sir Arthur died 17 Oct. 1695, aged 33, and his widow Lady Helena died a few years later in 1709, leaving issue one son, Sir John Rawdon, Bart., who succeeded to the family estate, and a daughter Isabella, who was married in 1719 to Sir Richard Levinge, Bart. This Sir John married in 1717 Dorothy, second daughter of Sir Richard Levinge, Bart., Speaker of the House of Commons, and was succeeded by his son Sir John, who was elevated as above stated to the peerage of Ireland as Baron Rawdon of Moira, co. Down, and whose third wife was Lady Elizabeth Hastings the writer of the following MS.

F. A. BLAYDES.

PEDIGREE OF HELENA GRAHAM, LADY RAWDON

King Robert the 1st   Marjory Bruce = Walter Ld. High Steward

Walter Ld. High Steward 2d. son   King Robert 2d. = Euphemia Ross
    2d. wife

Sir John Stewart of Railston 2d. son   David Earl of =
Strathern

Sr. Patrick Graham = Euphemia Stewart
by his first wife ances- | Heiress 2d. wife
tor to the Dukes of
Montrose

Sr. Patrick Graham Earl = Lady Euphemia Stewart
of Strathern in Jur. Uxor. | Heiress & Countess of Strathern

Malise Earl of Strathern.   King James the 5th
reannexed Strathern to the Crown & gave him
in lieu of it the Earldom of Menteith

Alexander Ld. Kinpont ob. v.p.

Alexander 2d. Earl of Menteith

Wm. 3d. Earl of Menteith   Walter Ancestor of the Grahams of Gartur mentioned
as the present male Representatives of this line

John 4th Earl of Menteith

William 5th Earl of Menteith

John 6th Earl of Menteith

William 7th Earl of Menteith had the title of = Agnes daughter
Earl of Strathern restored to him by Charles | of Lord Gray
the 1st. It was afterwards revoked & there | the 7th of that
was again a creation or Restoration to him of | title
the titles of Airth and Menteith

John Ld. Kinpont murdered   Sr. James Graham = Helen a daughter   Sr. Charles Graham
in Montrose's Camp in his   2d. son   of Primate Bram-   3d. son died unm.
Father's lifetime   hall & a coheiress
to his Br. Sr.
Thos. Bramhall

William 8th Earl of Airth & Menteith
died unmarried Sept. 24th, 1694, & left   Sr. Arthur Rawdon Bt. = Helen Graham
his estate to the Montrose family. This | heiress
Ld. had 2 sisters—Mary wife of George
Allardice & Elizabeth wife of Sr.   Sir John Rawdon Bart. =
William Graham of Gartmore—these
certainly did not leave issue

John Rawdon Earl of =
Moira

Francis Hastings Rawdon
Earl of Moira

It seems that there has appeared Claimants to the title of Airth and
Menteith, from the families of Allardice and Graham of Gartmore.   No
person would be more averse to claiming the Ancient Hereditary Honors of
another family, than I should be, holding such adventitious gifts of Fortune in
a sacred degree of estimation.   But I am persuaded from the proofs that have
fallen beneath my inspection that in the lineal line *direct* that the claims
(whatever they may be) rest with the present Lord Moira.

The Family Letters from Scotland to Helen Graham all treat her as
Heiress of the Family.   Lord Kinpont was murdered in the Marquis of
Montrose's Camp in 1644, he married Lady Mary Keith Daughter of Wᵐ
Earl Mareschal, by whom he left three children Wᵐ Earl of Airth and
Menteith, and Mary and Elizabeth both styled Honᵇˡᵉ·   This Earl died the
12ᵗʰ of Sepʳ 1694—the younger of the family must therefore be 50 years of
age at his death, some of them more, & it was impossible that if the sisters
had had issue by their respective marriages it should not have been known by
their family, & allied as they were, & descended from the greatest families,
& the 'reddest Blood' in Scotland that their claims wᵈ not have been
supported is improbable.   One particular relation & Correspondent I place
much dependance on—Lord Gray married Lady Mary Stewart daughter of
Robᵗ Stewart, Earl of Orkney by her he had an only son Andrew his
successor & 7 daughters who all married & left issue, two of these daughters
were

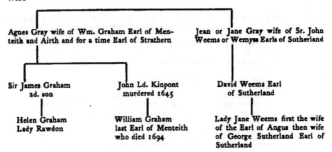

Agnes Gray wife of Wm. Graham Earl of Men-   Jean or Jane Gray wife of Sr. John
teith and Airth and for a time Earl of Strathern   Weems or Wemyss Earls of Sutherland

Sir James Graham   John Ld. Kinpont   David Weems Earl
2d. son   murdered 1645   of Sutherland

Helen Graham   William Graham   Lady Jane Weems first the wife
Lady Rawdon   last Earl of Menteith   of the Earl of Angus then wife
          who died 1694   of George Sutherland Earl of
          Sutherland

This Jane Lady Sutherland resident in Scotland & yet writes to Helen
Lady Rawden as Heiress of the Graham Menteith family ; that she was that
Lady Sutherland is proved by her lamentation for the death of her daughter
Lady Arbuthnot, & the mention of her having taken the 7 children of her
deceased daughter Lady Arbuthnot to her house.   The letters of this Lady,
show her to have been both a sensible and well-educated personage—there are
also letters from the last Earl of Menteith and Airth to his niece, and from
the Blackadder Family.   Lady Christian sister to Wᵐ (for a time Earl of
Stratherne) Earl of Menteith & Airth was Aunt to S James Graham &
Great Aunt to Lady Rawdon ; Lord Kinpont's connections by marriage are
also to be considered—

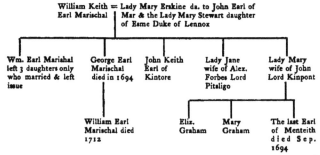

It seems impossible that so numerous a kindred of such a high rank and station should be ignorant of the claims of their neices & that so far from the acknowledgement of the Rights of them & their descendants that their Cousin Germain their Father's youngest brother's daughter should be allowed to be the heiress ; some of these—Lady Jane or Jean Keith Lord Kintore's daughter was the wife of Sʳ Wᵐ Forbes of Monimusk, and Lady Kinpont's sister the wife of Alexander Forbes Lord Pitsligo ; the sister of Sʳ Arthur Rawdon, Mary Rawdon was then the wife of Arthur Forbes Lord Forbes eldest son of the Earl of Granard & thro' that connection S Arthur Rawdon must have learnt when his wife was addressed by part of the family as the Heiress of her Cousin Germain's prior Right had it existed. The various trifles belonging to the family esteemed as consequential appendages were transmitted to Helen Graham Lady Rawdon. Charles the 2 during his illness gave to the last Earl of Menteith the watch which belonged to his Father Charles the 1ˢᵗ which watch is now in the possession of the present Lord Moira. I was grieved at beholding it in my time modernized, the dial plate was of silver coarsely engraved with the hours and minutes ; the inward workmanship coarse & instead of a chain a piece of catgut was the material by which it was wound up, there was a clumsy Repeater in it distinct from the main work & the ribbon which was the same the King wore it with was brown brocaded with silver. It ought I thought to have remained in its first state as a sample of the progress of mechanism in that article. The Ring also was the gift of Charles the 2ᵈ to the Earl of Menteith, it was a mourning one he had made for his Father's memory ; the enamel is bad. It represents King Charles the 1ˢᵗ his Queen Henrietta of France & Charles the Second, the blue enamel on the back is marked by black enamel wᵗʰ a Death's Head and Crown, & the letters C.R.—a small enamelled miniature of Charles the 2ᵈ in a Ring which I gave to Lord Moira was also a gift to Lord Menteith from that King.

I have likewise in my possession the once Earl of Strathern's then the Earl of Menteith's wedding nightcap & his Countesse's Pin-Cushion, and some old Japan & China once belonging to her. It may be asked wherefore the claim of Helen Graham Lady Rawdon was not immediately stated & pursued. The answer is that S Arthur Rawdon died at the same time that Lord Menteith bid adieu to life, & that the great lawsuit was going on for the Conway property. Earl Conway had brought up & educated Sr. Arthur Rawdon when a third son, his Brothers dying he became head of the

Family & Lord Conway declared that he should be his heir & made the marriage for him with the Heiress of Graham. When Earl Conway's will was divulged it appeared to be one which left nothing to his only nephew whom he had educated as his Heir, but that the property was bequeathed to the brother of his Lord Conway's wife. The consequence of this it was said caused Lord Menteith to leave also his property in the manner in which he did. Lady Rawdon sold as much of her fortune as was within her power to carry on the Conway lawsuit. The Scotch claim conveyed Honor, the Conway conveyed (if gained) profit, and the gratification of resentment, & Helen Graham Lady Rawdon was left a widow with an extensive lawsuit to carry on, & thereby involved in narrow circumstances, as she supported it from her own income, had not the ability to exert herself for mere Honorary acquisitions however antient & desirable.

She had only one son surviving—a sickly infant—whom she left a minor, and in a few years a second long minority took place—a state which is ever ruinous to the claims of a family & usually to their property is as destructive a course.

Thro' the elapse of time, & omission of early claim, it is probable that these hereditary rights will hereafter remain solely as honorable pretentions, but as such the family should ever proudly bear them in remembrance.

I have collected as many of the old letters as I could find from papers esteemed in a later day rubbish ; but the wch from their having been docketed, appear to have been regarded formerly with a degree of respect.

This Helen Graham is said to have been once on the point of marriage with the noted Lord Dundee at that period Laird of Claverhouse, a circumstance that seems to announce that she had at that juncture a slain [1] ? prospect of some essential rights—she died 1709 having survived her husband Sr Arthur above 15 years. She was a well educated & a learned woman, but superstitious in some respects (at least) to excess. Loving Sr Arthur passionately she dreamt her husband appeared to her immediately after his death, & being convinced that it was an apparition not a dream she —during the remainder of her life—always had a person to sleep with her, & a woman servant who sat all night within the curtains of her bed holding her hand.

In the same work of Sr John Scot's at Scarvy, there is the best printed acc^t I have met with (tho' short) of Sr James Stewart the eldest son of Lord Blantyre, by oral tradition asserted to have had equal abilities to the admirable Crichton, & in moral character to have been much his superior. He was the first husband of Lady Dorothy Hastings (she became afterwards 2^d wife to Dillon Earl of Roscommon, but left no surviving issue by either).

Sr John Scot gives a concise account of the duel between S James Stewart & the eldest son of Lord Wharton in which both combatants fell. Sr James Stewart was a friend of the unfortunate & basely wronged & scandalously vilified Robert Car, Earl of Somerset.

E. MOIRA HASTINGS, etc.

---

[1] This word is an interlineation written very small, but under a magnifying glass I can make nothing out of it but 'slain'—possibly 'strong' may have been intended.

In another hand is the following note :—

This Prayer Book belonged to Helen Graham Daughter & Heiress to Sr James Graham K^{nt} 2^d son of William Earl of Menteith & Airth who by the grant of Charles the first had ratified to him the title of Earl of Strathern the which title being again revoked, he was styled Earl of Airth & Menteith. There is a curious small book in Lord Moira's Library (the title) the ' Staggering Statesman ' written by Sr John Scot of Scarvy—therein it is related that this William Earl of Menteith was banished to the Isles he possessed for having declared that he had the ' reddest Blood in Scotland ' & one of the Earl's Law Counsellors (who is named in the course of the recital of this audacious declaration as having assisted him in the proof of it) was involved in punishment for so *heinous* a procedure. For the nature of the redness, or richness of his Blood, I refer to the work of George Crawford Esqr·

[NOTE.—The above memoranda are of much interest, but afford a curious illustration of the beliefs held in families as to their ' rights ' to peerage dignities, especially, perhaps, Scottish ones. For the claims to these earldoms and the work of Sir Harris Nicolas dealing with them have clearly shown that the sisters of the last earl left issue, though the writer here states that they ' certainly did not.' The descendants of Mary, wife of Sir John (not of George) Allardice, have more than once claimed the dignities, while William Graham, the heir of the other sister, not only assumed the earldom of Menteith, but actually voted in right of it from 1742 to 1761.

It will be observed that the writer does not quote from the letters on which she relies. If they are now in the possession of Lord Moira's representatives their contents would be of interest and possibly of importance in case of a renewed claim to the honours.—J. H. R.]

SOME EXTINCT CUMBERLAND FAMILIES

III. THE TILLIOLS

THE Tilliols were a family of distinction who lived at
Scaleby, a manor on the north side of the river Eden
about six miles from Carlisle, and took a prominent part in
local affairs for more than three centuries.   Scaleby Castle, the
head of the manor, is one of the most interesting feudal sites
in Cumberland, inasmuch as its history is written chapter by
chapter in the architectural remains within its own precincts
from the palisaded enclosure to the medieval fortress.   Its
proximity to the Border gave it an important strategic position
for stopping the inroads of the Scots, and made it a defensive
outpost of considerable consequence to the city of Carlisle.
In the troublesome days of international feuds, the Tilliols
were employed in many difficult operations against the
hereditary enemy and it was little wonder that the family
became conspicuous as a fighting race and displayed qualities
which one would expect from the nature of their position and
the employments on which they were engaged.   Like several
of the great magnates of the neighbourhood, they had a town
house or residence within the strong walls of Carlisle either for
the sake of safety in times of special danger or perhaps, as it is
more likely, for their own convenience when in attendance on
the *curia comitatus* or Court of the County.

None of the name of Tilliol has left so permanent a
record on the district in which he lived as the first of the
family, Richard Ridere,[1] or Richard the Knight as he was more
usually called, who was enfeoffed with the manor by Henry I.
The grant was made before 1130 when Richard the Knight
accounted for 20s. for the farm of his own land.   For some
years before that date he held a confidential office under the
Crown as the collector of the Noutgeld or tribute of cattle, the

---

[1] Richard is surnamed Ridere only in the great inquest of 1212 (*Victoria
Hist. Cumberland*, i. 422).   It must be an early English form of *miles*, the
knight, the equestrian, or the rider, and not a prophetic symptom of the
name given to men who dwelt on the borders of the Debatable Land and were
afterwards known as Border riders.   Compare the High and Low Dutch
ritter and *ridder*.

tenurial rent due to the king from tenants by cornage at that
time passing into a money payment. His services must have
been acceptable to his employer, for he had a grant of Etard's
land by such a service as any freeman ought to render.[1] This
property appears afterwards among the possessions of his
descendants as Etardby,[2] from its former owner, now cor-
rupted into Etterby, a vill on the Eden in the parish of
Stanwix overlooking Carlisle. Though he witnessed charters
as Richard the Knight,[3] the name by which he was probably
known among his contemporaries, his grandson had adopted
the surname of Tilliol, perhaps from Teilliol or Telliole in
Lower Normandy from which the family may have originated.[4]
He has left his name in Rickerby or Richardby, an estate his
family held of the priory of Carlisle, and in Rickergate or gate
of Richard, a municipal ward of modern Carlisle, where they
owned burgages and had a residence from an early period.[5]

During the period of the usurpation of Stephen and the
Scottish domination of Cumberland, we lose sight of many of

[1] *Pipe Roll*, 31 Henry I. ff. 141–2, ed. Hunter.

[2] *Inq. p.m.* 31 Hen. III. No. 46.

[3] Bain, *Calendar of Documents*, ii. 1606 (11).

[4] Round, *Calendar of Documents in France*, p. 221 ; *Rotuli Normanniæ*, i. 337,
ed. Hardy ; *Charter Rolls*, 1 John, p. 16b, ed. Hardy.

[5] Robert de Stutevill granted to Guy, a merchant and burgess of Carlisle,
the messuage in Richard Street (*in vico Ricardi*) next to the 'barony' (*baronia*)
of Peter de Tyllol in the same street, and John de Bothilton confirmed to the
said merchant for life the same messuage next the land of the 'barony' of
Symon de Tyllol. From another deed about the same property we learn that
Richard Street was within the city walls (*Reg. of Holmcultram*, MS. ff. 28–30),
and is now known as Scotch Street. St. Alban's Church abutted on Richard
Street. There can be little doubt, as Denton suggested so long ago as 1610,
that 'the gate, port and street in Carliell' took its name from 'Richard the
Ryder,' the first ancestor of the Tilliols to settle in the district (*Cumberland*, p.
155). It is worthy of observation, said Mr. Charles Brooke, Somerset Herald,
that the magnates or tenants *in capite* in the reign of the Conqueror had most
of them houses in the capital city or town of the county where their
possessions lay, which we may conclude were town residences for them during
the winter or to be near the *curia comitatus*. Of the twenty-four tenants *in
capite*, mentioned in Domesday Book, twelve of them had houses in the city of
York (*Archæologia*, vi. 48). Several of the county families of Cumberland had
town houses in Carlisle, which they occupied on special occasions like
assizes, quarter sessions, and parliamentary elections, up to a comparatively
recent period. Rickerby or Ricardeby, which almost faces Rickergate on the
opposite bank of the river, was held by the Tilliols of the prior of Carlisle for
one mark yearly (*Inq. p.m.* 31 Hen. III. No. 46), and at a later period from
the Bishop of Carlisle when that property was allotted to the See.

our county families and know little of what took place between
the cession of the district to David I., and its recovery in 1157
by Henry II. It would be mere conjecture to say that there
was or was not a displacement of Crown tenants during that
period. David's court at Carlisle swarmed with Scotsmen of
the name of Brus, Morvill, Heriz, Sumervill, and Lindesay,
some of whom at that time held lands in Cumberland. It is
rarely that we meet with the old names of the Norman settlement in attendance on him, except in cases where they were of
Scottish descent, like Waldeve and Alan, or the sons of Suan.[1]
It is very suspicious, as far as the Tilliols are concerned, that
in the year when the county was recovered, Peter de Tilliol
obtained possession of the land of his grandfather and was
debited in 1158 with a sum of 50s. owing to the Crown for
his admission thereto.[2] There seems to be only one inference
from this circumstance, that his father, whose name has not
been revealed, was never in possession of Scaleby and that the
sheriff depended on the title of Richard the Knight and the
claimant's relationship to him as the lawful heir, as his
authority for giving him seizin. Henry II. gave him Holm
Werri, now variously called Weary, Willow, or Willy Holm,[3] outside the city of Carlisle south of the Eden opposite Etardby, at
an annual rent of 20s., but the property did not remain
long in possession of the family.

Simon de Tilliol, son of the aforementioned Peter, was the
next owner of the manor and succeeded his father in 1183[4]
He confirmed to the priory of Lanercost certain land in Scaleby
which his father gave, and added as his own gift several acres
within the same manor.[5] In 1201 he paid a fine of 100s. that

---

[1] One charter only may be cited in illustration ; whereby David, King of
Scots, sent greeting to all his approved men of Coupland and confirmed the
alms which Maud, wife of Godard, gave to the priory of St. Bees. The
charter was witnessed at Lamplou, now Lamplugh, in the western part of the
county, by Walter the Chancellor, Robert de Brus, Hugh de Morvill, Adam
son of Swen, William Sumervill, Alan son of Waldef, Henry son of Swan,
William de Heriz, Gospatric son of Orm, Ranulf de Lindesey, and Durand the
Knight (*Reg. of St. Bees*, M.S. i. 16.)

[2] *Pipe Roll,* 4 Hen. II.

[3] There seems little doubt that Holm Werri or Weary Holm took its name
from Guerus or Werricus, a Fleming, who held land and houses in Carlisle
before 1130 (*Pipe Roll,* p. 142). Richard son of Werricus was amerced for a
false claim in 1198 (ibid. 9 Ric. I.)

[4] *Pipe Roll,* 29 Hen. II. [5] *Reg. of Lanercost,* MS. vi. 4.

he might not be compelled to serve abroad, but he must have died soon after, as his land was in the hands of the sheriff in the following year.[1]   Geoffrey de Lucy had custody of Peter his son and heir with his widow and lands in 1204, and paid a fine of 20 marks and one palfrey for having the marriage of the widow with her assent and that of her friends.[2]   The heir was still a minor in 1212 and in ward of Geoffrey de Lucy, and his lands, consisting of one vill, were valued at £15 a year.[3]

Peter de Tilliol succeeded his father when he came of age. He was on the king's service with his former guardian, Geoffrey de Lucy, in the Isle of Wight (*in Insula*) in 1225,[4] but he must have returned to the north within a year or two, for in 1227 he had a plea in the courts with his neighbour, Richard de Levinton, about the bounds of the adjoining manors of Scaleby and Kirklinton, a quarrel which seems to have arisen over the diversion of a watercourse.[5]   This member of the family, who was often employed in the public affairs of the county,[6] died in 1246, when Mary his wife gave security that she should not marry without the king's leave, and had a dower assigned her out of her late husband's lands.   In the ' extent ' of his lands made on December 5, 1246, under writ dated on the previous November 18, the jurors stated that in the demesne of Scaleby there were 233 acres of arable land, each acre worth 7*d*. yearly, 20 acres of meadow each worth 12*d*., and a mill worth 7 marks ; also 4 acres of arable land and 1 acre of meadow in demesne, worth 5*s*., which David the singer and Gilbert son of Beatrice held. There were in the manor 20 bondmen and 6 cottars.   Various freeholders were in possession of Etardby, Houghton, Ricardby, and the house, with curtilages, in the suburb of Carlisle.   The total issues of the estates in demesnes, homages and rents were valued at £28 10*s*. 9*d*. yearly.   The verdict of the inquest was that the heir of the said Peter de Tilliol, Geoffrey by name, was sixteen years of age in the first week of Lent in the 30th year of the king's reign.   Concerning his

---

[1] *Pipe Rolls*, 3 & 4 John.
[2] Ibid. 6 John ; *Rotuli de Oblatis et Finibus*, p. 201, ed. Hardy.
[3] *Victoria Hist. Cumberland*, i. 422, 425.
[4] *Pat. Roll*, 9 Hen. III. m. 4.
[5] Bain, *Calendar*, i. 971.
[6] *Pat. Roll*, 20 Hen. III. m. 2*d*. ; Bain, *Calendar*, i. 1289, 1296.

marriage the jurors had known nothing at that time as the heir
was lying ill at Cambridge and it was said that his . . . was
broken.[1] Geoffrey was delivered to the wardship of Robert de
Acre till he came of age.[2]

Geoffrey de Tilliol lived the quiet life of a country gentleman and took little part in public affairs. In 1261 William
son of Robert arraigned an assize of novel disseisin against
him and Robert de Tilliol for common of pasture in Scaleby,
and in 1266 he and the said Robert had a safe conduct to come
to the king's court about their business.[3] Geoffrey was the
lessee of a farm in Torpenhow, belonging to John de Kirkpatrick
and Margery his wife, of the heritage of Richard le Brun. In
1292 the farm in Geoffrey's hands was distrained at the assizes
of Carlisle, as John lived in Scotland and had no other property
in the county.[4] Though it was certified that he held the
manor of Scaleby and the barony of Houghton of the king by
cornage, he was allowed a respite of becoming a knight in
1278.[5] On his death in 1295 the jurors found that Robert
was the son and heir and thirty years of age.[6]

Robert de Tilliol succeeded to the property in 1295[7] on
the eve of the great rupture between the two kingdoms which
spread havoc and devastation throughout the northern counties
and which lasted with little cessation till the union of the
Crowns three centuries later. In a short time John Balliol
revolted and Edward I. took the field. For many years
Robert de Tilliol, then in the prime of life, was actively
employed in the king's service raising levies, summoning
knights and enforcing musters for the army against Scotland.[8]
In 1299, when affairs on the Border were looking dark and

---

[1] *Inq. p.m.* 30 Hen. III. No. 46 ; *Calend. Geneal.* i. 18. It is very
disappointing that the record is deficient at the critical word, as we should
have liked to know whether the young Tilliol had met with his accident among
'the flannelled fools at the wicket' or 'the muddy oafs at the goal'!
Cambridge was fully equipped as an educational institution at this period. Mr.
Gladstone has told us that 'it is first in the year 1209 that a trustworthy
notice of it is found' (*Romanes Lecture*, 1892, p. 14).

[2] *Fine Rolls*, ii. 18, ed. Hardy.

[3] *Bain*, i. 2249, 2398.

[4] Ibid. ii. 645.

[5] *Close Roll*, 6 Edw. I. m. 13 ; *Bain*, ii. 146, p. 37.

[6] *Inq. p.m.* 23 Edw. I. No. 10 ; *Cal. Geneal.* ii. 495.

[7] *Originalia*, 23 Edw. I. m. 7.

[8] Palgrave, *Parliamentary Writs*, i. 325–6 et passim.

menacing, he was ordered to raise 2,000 footmen in Cumberland, and Hugh de Multon had a similar command to raise 1,500 footmen in Westmorland 'to repress the increasing malice of the Scots.' In the following year when King Edward arrived on the scene on his way to Carlaverock, he joined him in a commission with Sir John of Wigton to raise 2,000 men in Cumberland for that expedition.[1] Rural life in some parts of the county at that period may have been interesting, but in the district north of the Eden it was decidedly dangerous. The old defences at Scaleby were not strong enough to protect its redoubtable owner. A man occupying his conspicuous military position could not help but be a mark for Scottish vengeance as often as the opportunity presented itself. His manor-house lay close to the frontier. The great Edward had breathed his last at Burgh-by-Sands and the Border magnates were soon left to shift for their own safety. As Tilliol could not wait, he was one of the first to apply for and to obtain licence to crenellate his mansion of Scaleby in the marches of Scotland.[2] From the year 1307 the manor-house had become entitled to be called Scaleby Castle. The busy soldier, however, had found time to increase his possessions in his own neighbourhood. In 1304 he purchased without the King's leave a messuage, 14 acres of land, and a sixth part of the manor of Kirklinton from Patrick Trompe, a tenant in chief, which got him into trouble and of which he was disseised, but as it was found after inquisition that the King was in no way injured by the transaction, and as Robert had done the state some service in Scotland, he was pardoned and confirmed in the purchase.[3] Robert de Tilliol was fortunate enough to win the appreciation of his countrymen as well as the recognition of his sovereign, for he was elected a knight of the shire to serve in the parliaments of

---

[1] *Pat. Rolls*, 27 Edw. I. m. 11, 28 Edw. I. m. 16 : *Fœdera*, i. 915. Robert was beleaguered in the Castle of Lochmaben in 1301, when his position was hazardous. He appealed to the king for more troops for Sir John Soulis and Sir Ingram de Umframville, at the head of four banerets, twelve score men-at-arms and 7,000 footmen or more, 'burnt for us our town and assailed our peel from the middle of prime until the hour of nones,' but by the help of God he was not afraid of them (Stevenson, *Documents*, ii. 432–3). See also *Letters from the Northern Registers*, pp. 246–7.

[2] *Pat. Roll*, 1 Edw. II. pt. i. m. 18.

[3] *Inq. ad q. d.* 32 Edw. I. No. 113 ; *Cal. Geneal.* ii. 671 ; Bain, *Calendar of Documents*, ii. 1609.

1301 and 1315,[1] and Edward II. not only granted him the privilege of free warren in his manor of Scaleby in 1307, but also committed to him during pleasure in 1313 the lands of Walter de Corry, a rebel Scotsman, in Kirklinton and Kirkandrews.[2] A large property in Yorkshire came to the family by Robert's marriage with Maud second daughter and coheiress of Roger and Isabel de Lauceles of Ellerton in that county.[3] His lands were taken into the king's hand after his death in 1321 till the heir was declared.[4] The widow survived till 1344.[5]

Peter or Piers de Tilliol, the eldest son and heir, was of the age of twenty-two at his father's death. The son like his father was an active agent in Border affairs, serving on many commissions of both peace and war with the Scots. Immediately after succeeding to the estates he was chosen knight of the shire in 1322, and was returned by the sheriff in 1324 to attend a great council of the realm. In the latter year he was nominated one of the commissioners with power to select and array the knights of the county required for military service in Gascony, and in 1326 he was commanded to certify the names of persons in Cumberland eligible for the degree of knighthood.[6] Owing to his position as a Border chieftain, he was mixed up in the multitudinous quarrels and disputes of the March laws. In 1333 he was commissioned to make strict inquiry into the abduction of Sir Roger de Kirkpatrick, a knight of Scotland, who had fled to England to save his life,[7] and in 1337 he was joined with others in finding out, by juries of the men of the shires of Roxburgh and Dumfries, the names of people in Eskdale, Liddesdale, and other places who were suspected of assisting the enemy.[8] With Hugh de Moriceby, he raised 100 hobelars in 1337 for the Border service, and in 1340 he was joined with Thomas Wake, lord of Liddel, and Antony de Lucy to put down thieving within

1 Palgrave, *Parl. Writs*, ii. pt. ii. 141, 150; *Parliaments of England*, i. 13, 48, Blue Book.
2 *Charter Roll*, 1 Edw. II. pt. i. m. 33; *Originalia*, 6 Edw. II. m. 16; *Inq. ad. q. d.* 6 Edw. II. No. 43; *Pat. Roll*, 10 Edw. II. pt. i. m. 24.
3 *Close Rolls*, 16 Edw. II. m. 23, 17 Edw. II. m. 33.
4 *Inq. p.m.* 14 Edw. II. No. 42; *Originalia*, 14 Edw. II. m. 7.
5 Ibid. 17 Edw. III. No. 34; *Originalia*, 17 Edw. III. m. 12.
6 *Parliamentary Writs*, ii. pt. ii. 258, 650, 682, 736, 739.
7 *Pat. Roll*, 7 Edw. III. pt. i. m. 25*d*.
8 Ibid. 11 Edw. III. pt. i. m. 33*d*; *Fœdera*, ii. 960.

their commission.[1] This member of the family acted as sheriff
for some years after 1326 and was summoned to Parliament
no less than eleven times between the years 1322 and 1348.[2]

It would be futile to attempt an enumeration of the
services which Peter de Tilliol had rendered to his country
during his comparatively short life. Some indication of their
nature and variety has been already given. But two other
events in which he had borne a part may be mentioned, as they
caused no small stir in the neighbourhood of Carlisle and may
be said to possess some points of interest at the present time.
The citizens of Carlisle were becoming restive at this date and
were manifesting an inclination to press their chartered liberties
beyond legitimate bounds. In 1341 William de Bohun, Earl
of Northampton and Constable of England, complained that
his men of Annandale, coming as of old by the Solway to sell
their goods at the fairs and markets of the city, were hindered
and unduly taxed by John de Stretford, keeper of the Solway,
to their great loss and damage, a complaint which Peter de
Tilliol was instructed to inquire into and redress.[3] But
matters of graver moment arose in 1345, when the citizens
were eager for the exercise of an inordinate slice of local self-
government. Complaint was made to the king that the mayor
and bailiffs, usurping the royal warrant, had sentenced certain
persons for sedition in the city to be drawn and hanged, and
actually carried out the sentence, whereas the Scotsmen implicated in the same disturbances were harboured and maintained
by them. But a more serious indiscretion had been committed, inasmuch as Peter de Tilliol, the most eminent of the
citizens, with the mayor, the bailiffs, the Scots, and the
commonalty, tumultuously attacked the castle, entering the
outer ward, besieging it in warlike fashion, wounding many
of the garrison with arrows and darts, and endeavouring to
seize the castle, till at last they were driven out helter-
skelter by the bishop and the king's men. It was a famous
row to be made, as the record says, 'on pretence of an old
grant to the city by one of the king's progenitors.' The
citizens evidently had an exaggerated opinion of their own
importance. They also claimed on this occasion to appropriate

---

[1] *Close Roll,* 11 Edw. III. pt. i. m. 9; *Pat. Roll,* 14 Edw. III. pt. ii. m. 42d.
[2] *List of Sheriffs,* p. 26, Rolls series; *Parliaments of England,* i. 64, 80, 85, 91,
etc., Blue Book.
[3] Bain, *Calendar of Documents,* iii. 1372.

from the wastes in the city a 'long street' in the king's highway, to build on the foss of the castle, thus touching the
king's prerogative, and to be owners of two parts of the *solum*
of the castle, and many other such enormities.[1] Though
Tilliol must have regretted the escapade, his misdemeanour
cannot have been viewed seriously in high quarters, for in the
following year he was included in a commission to punish
evil doers who broke out of the bounds of Cumberland and
plundered the vill of Blamyre in the barony of Kirkandrews
in Scotland, carrying off the goods of the king's lieges there.[2]
He died on October 30, 1349, and Robert his son and heir,
being of full age, reigned in his stead.[3]

Sir Robert Tilliol succeeded to the belligerent tempera-
ment of his father as well as to the family estates. Though
he was often employed in the king's service both as escheator
in the northern counties and as sheriff of Cumberland for
several years,[4] it seemed more to his taste to be harrassing the
enemy at every opportunity. The Scots called him Tuylliyoll.
In 1357 he accomplished some very successful expeditions, or
'drives' as we should call them according to the nomenclature of modern warfare. In company with Sir Thomas de
Lucy, the great lord of Cockermouth, he forayed the lands of
William, lord of Douglas, in Eskdale with a great force raised
in the two counties, and robbed the poor people there in open
day of 1,000 oxen, cows, and other young beasts, 1,000 sheep
and horses, and plundered all the houses. It was complained
that Lucy lay in ambush and seized the people who tried to
rescue their goods. The crime was bad enough when committed in time of war, but the raiders, starting from Lochmaben Castle, which was nothing but a den of thieves, ravaged
the land in open day with banners displayed in time of truce,
and had set to ransom many of the people to their damage of
£5,000 sterling.[5] There is little doubt that the authorities
looked through their fingers at Tilliol's depredations in
Eskdale. In the next year, on the unrepentant culprit's
application, the king made him a grant for life of the herbage

[1] Bain, *Calendar of Documents*, iii. 1448.
[2] *Close Roll*, 20 Edw. III. pt. 1. m. 15*d*.
[3] *Inq. p.m.* 23 Edw. III. pt. i. No. 51.
[4] *Originalia*, 30 Edw. III. m. 5 ; *List of Sheriffs*, p. 26. About this time
the conjunctive particle 'de' began to be omitted from the family name.
[5] Bain, *Calendar of Documents*, iii. 1664.

of Morton and Mortonscough in the forest of Inglewood. Sir Robert was chosen knight of the shire[1] six times at various dates between 1352 and 1365 and died at Ireby between cock-crowing and dawn on April 6, 1367. His will was proved at Rose Castle on April 16 following.[2] He bequeathed all his goods to his wife Felice and to his children ; his body he wished to be buried in the church of the Friar Preachers in Carlisle. From a deed drawn up by his executors two months later, we learn that all his lands and tenements in Ireby, except the site of the manor within the water ditches, the park of Torpenhow, and other tenements in Newbiggin, were bequeathed to Felice for life with re-mainder to Peter his eldest son and heir, and that his other sons Geoffrey and Roger were also provided for.[3] Peter the heir was only eleven years of age and became a ward of the Crown. The widow survived her husband only two years.[4]

When Peter de Tilliol came of age he was chosen knight of the shire of Cumberland in 1378 and served in Parliament from time to time from that date till 1426.[5] Meanwhile he filled the office of sheriff three times[6] and often acted as escheator for Cumberland and Northumberland.[7] His avoca-tions were more peaceful than those of many of his ancestors. It is only now and then that we meet with him in connection with Border troubles. As sheriff, in 1387, he was obliged to levy fines for March offences, and in 1390, having failed in his capacity as escheator to report the traitors who were supplying grain to the Scots, he was attached by the officers of the Exchequer, but he was pardoned in making oath in the king's presence that the mandatory letters never reached him.[8] In 1398 he was appointed with his brother Geoffrey among the arbitrators to determine international disputes.[9] As a justice of the peace he administered the law with becoming clemency, though on several occasions those who failed to pay Sir Peter

---

[1] *Parliaments of England,* i. 150, 159, 161, etc.
[2] *Testamenta Karleolensia,* p. 82, ed. R. S. Ferguson.
[3] *Catalogue of Ancient Deeds,* iii. 444–5.
[4] *Inq. p.m.* 41 Edw. III. pt. i. No. 58 ; 43 Edw. III. pt. ii. No. 31.
[5] *Parliaments of England,* i. 199, 206, 241, 255, etc.
[6] *List of Sheriffs,* p. 27 ; *Pat. Roll,* 11 Ric. II. pt. ii. m. 30.
[7] *Pat. Rolls,* 10 Ric. II. pt. ii. m. 13*d,* 11 Ric. II. pt. ii. m. 34.
[8] Ibid. 11 Ric. II. pt. ii. m. 30; *Close Roll,* 14 Ric. II. m. 9*d.*
[9] *Fædera,* viii. 58, old edition.

the debts due to him got into serious trouble.[1] As the citizens of Carlisle, always pugnacious in their relations with the county, in which encounters they usually came out in the second place, were grievously injured in 1427 by certain 'malefactors' who broke the banks of their watercourse at Blackhall and diverted the stream so that 'le Castelmylne' could not grind and the king could not get his rent owing to the depreciation in its value,[2] Tilliol was commissioned with other knights of the county to hold an inquest on the dispute and report on its merits to the Crown. Sir Peter Tilliol died on Sunday, January 2, 1435, after having enjoyed the estates, if we include the time of his minority, for the long period of sixty-seven years. It was declared by the inquest after his death, taken in the following May at Penrith, that Robert his first begotten son was the heir of all his manors and thirty years of age and more, but that the said Robert was an incurable lunatic (*qui quidem Robertus omnimodo est fatuus ideotus et fatuetate detentus.*)[3] Thus ended one of the proudest of our Cumbrian houses, a family which had rendered conspicuous service to the county for three centuries, occupying prominent positions in time of peace and performing brave deeds in time of war.

Robert the last male heir of the family did not long survive his father, for he died on Thursday before Martinmas in the same year, leaving his two sisters as his heirs, viz. Isabel, wife of John Colvell, thirty years of age, and Margaret wife of Christopher Moresby, twenty-six years of age.[4] The great Tilliol property, which consisted of over ten manors in Cumberland, was not divided for over a century after! Sir Peter's death, the two daughters and their heirs holding it in moiety.[5] On the death of Isabel Colvell's son

---

[1] *Pat. Rolls*, 12 Ric. II. pt. i. m. 36 ; 3 Hen. VI. pt. i. m. 20 ; 6 Hen. VI. pt. i. m. 26. Peter Tilliole was put in the commission of the peace in 1380 (*Pat. Roll*, 3 Ric. II. pt. iii. m. 13*d.*)

[2] *Pat. Roll*, 5 Hen. VI. pt. i. m. 14*d.*

[3] *Inq. p.m.* 13 Hen. VI. No. 24.

[4] Ibid. 14 Hen. VI. No. 23.

[5] Isabel Colvell died possessed of half the Tilliol estates in 1438 (*Inq. p.m.* 17 Hen. VI. No. 37). William Colvell her son and heir died in 1479 (ibid. 19 Edw. IV. No. 59). Margaret Moresby, late the wife of Thomas de Crakanthorpe, died in possession of the other half in 1458 (ibid. 37 Hen. VI. No. 30), her first husband Christopher Moresby having predeceased her in 1442 (ibid. 21 Hen. VI. No. 61.) Their son Christopher Moresby, who

William, which took place in 1479, her portion passed to the Musgraves by marriage with the heiress of the Colvells, and Margaret Moresby's moiety having been held for two descents passed in a similar manner to the Pickerings and then to the Westons.

William Gilpin, recorder of Carlisle and owner of the manor of Scaleby, who died in 1724, has related a remarkable story of attempted fraud in relation to the Tilliol property which is deserving of mention by reason of its apparent authenticity. It is said that after the death of William Colvell in 1479, Robert his brother pretended a title to the estates of his grandfather, Sir Peter Tilliol, alleging that he had made a will by which he devised that William Colvell his grandson should change his name to Tilliol and have the manors of Houghton, Rickerby, Ireby, Solport, a moiety of Newbiggin, and a third part of Kirklinton, together with the castle of Scaleby, to him and to his heirs male, with remainder to Robert, the second son of Isabel his elder daughter, in like manner and upon the same condition that he should assume the name of Tilliol. But Robert, though he had complied with the conditions of the will, never succeeded in getting possession of the estates. 'There is yet extant,' said Mr. Gilpin 'an authentic instrument under the seal of the Commissary General of York, dated September 27, 1481 (which I have in my custody), which testifies that one William Martindale, Knt., did in the court of York for the discharging of his conscience swear that he saw the will and that it pur ported an entail as aforesaid, and that he and others in the favour of Margaret, second daughter of the said Peter de Tilliol, had destroyed it.'[1] It may be noted that Gilpin had a personal interest in the truth or falsehood of the story of the will, for it was from Sir Edward Musgrave that his father purchased Scaleby Castle a portion of the Colvell moiety of the Tilliol estates.

held his mother's moiety, died in 1461 (ibid. 1 Edw. IV. No. 35). In the rentals of the bishops of Carlisle, from whom the reputed manor of Rickerby was held, the succession of Robert Tilliol, or 'Robert the fool' as J. Denton called him (*Cumberland*, p. 154), was not recognized, inasmuch as the 'heredes Petri Tilliol chivaler' continued to account to the bishops for rent and service till the close of the fifteenth century.

[1] John Denton, *Cumberland*, p. 154.

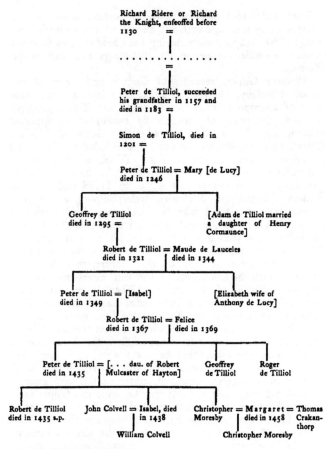

Richard Ridere or Richard
the Knight, enfeoffed before
1130   =

. . . .
=

Peter de Tilliol, succeeded
his grandfather in 1157 and
died in 1183 =

Simon de Tilliol, died in
1201 =

Peter de Tilliol = Mary [de Lucy]
died in 1246

Geoffrey de Tilliol   [Adam de Tilliol married
died in 1295 =   a daughter of Henry
                                        Cormaunce]

Robert de Tilliol = Maude de Lauceles
died in 1321   died in 1344

Peter de Tilliol = [Isabel]   [Elizabeth wife of
died in 1349   Anthony de Lucy]

Robert de Tilliol = Felice
died in 1367   died in 1369

Peter de Tilliol = [. . . dau. of Robert   Geoffrey   Roger
died in 1435   Mulcaster of Hayton]   de Tilliol   de Tilliol

Robert de Tilliol   John Colvell = Isabel, died   Christopher = Margaret = Thomas
died in 1435 s.p.   in 1438   Moresby   died in 1458 Crakan-
                                                                              thorp
                       William Colvell   Christopher Moresby

In the roll of fourteenth century arms
called Jenyns's Ordinary (of which a
copy exists in the Cotton MS. *Tiberius
E. ix.*) the arms of Monsire Piers
Tyllioll are recorded as *de goules a une
eon rampant dargent et une baston dazure*

JAMES WILSON.

NORTH COUNTRY WILLS

THE northern counties are exceptionally well served by their archæological societies. The Surtees Society in particular is one of the best in England, as it is one of the earliest. Two of its latest volumes, issued this year, deal with wills, a subject of the greatest interest to all genealogical students.

A will is such an intensely human document that its value, apart from mere questions of pedigree, cannot be overestimated. We find a testator dealing in his last moments with the final distribution of his property, we learn who are his favourite children, what are his most treasured belongings, his plate and jewels, his clothes, his horses and dogs. It is to be regretted that the attention of publishing societies is not more directed to this class of document.

The Surtees Society has already done a great deal in this direction. The first of the volumes alluded to is a collection of wills and administrations enrolled in the records of the Manor of Knaresborough, and is edited by Dr. Collins, who has done so much to earn the gratitude of the northern genealogist. It contains full abstracts of all enrolled wills, grants of administration and of tuition, from 2 Henry VIII. to 3 and 4 James I., 'no matter how insignificant in life the testator may have been or how uninteresting the will' (*Introduction*).

There is a fair sprinkling of Visitation families, but the bulk of the wills are those of yeomen, farmers, tradesmen and the like. This exhaustive plan opens out quite a new field ; we see not only the castle, the hall and the manor-house, but we are introduced to the farm, the shop and the cottage as well.

One of the most interesting wills in this volume is that of Sir William Ingilby of Ripley Castle and Padsidehead, 1578 ; this is accompanied by a very complete inventory, from which a few extracts may be made. Let us take first the bill for the funeral expenses.

Imprimus, in blacks for murning gownes and cottes, iiij^{xx} xvj*li*. ; to the paynter for armes and other suche like, xvj*li*. ; his mortuarie, xx*s*. ; his heriott, xl*s*. ; charges to the poore in redie money, viij*li*. ; charges of the funerall dinner, xiij*li*. vj*s*. viij*d*. Probacion of the testament, regestring, and the obligacion, xij*s*. Sum, cxxxvj*li*. vij*s*. viij*d*.

Next the plate. Sir William kept in a chest

in his owne bedd chambre three pounced peces of silver, with one cover, a bolle of silver with a cover parcele gylte, two silver cuppes double gilte with covers, a dussan silver spones with thappels upon the endes, five gylted spones, x new silver spones,

valued at £33 6*s*. 8*d*. Besides this there were in the buttery ' seaven silver tunnels, eight silver spones, and one silver salt duble gilte with a cover,' valued at £9.

His owne apparell—one velvett gowne, v*li*. ; one long damaske gowne, xl*s*. ; one long chamlett gowne, xiij*s*. iiij*d*. ; one long cloth gowne, x*s*. ; one long blacke frese gowne, vj*s*. viij*d*. ; a blacke cloth coote, a black frese coote, a blacke frese jerking, and a blacke spanishe jerkinge, xx*s*. ; a sattan dublet, xx*s*. ; two paire of blacke hoose, a paire of frese sloppes, and fower lynne shirtes, xiij*s*. iiij*d*. ; two felt hattes, one velvett capp, and one litle round cloth capp, xiij*s*. iiij*d*. ; thre paire of bootes, a paire of spurres, two paire of shoes, two sadles and two bridles, xx*s*. ; his girdle, sword and dagger, xiij*s*. iiij*d*. ; his purse and money in it, xx*li*.

In his own bedchamber were two stand-beds, one having a ' teaster of blew and yallow velvett' and ' thre hanginges of grene saie ' ; the other had a ' teaster of redd and yallow saie.' Other beds in the house are mentioned. One had a ' teaster with the honginges of red saie ' ; another (' in the chambre over my ladies chambre ') had a ' teaster of blacke and yallow damaske, and two hanginges of redd and yallow saie.' Total of inventory, £700 18*s*.

The references to pre-Reformation affairs are neither numerous nor important. Thomas Benson, 1511, leaves ' unam vaccam capitatam albam ad fabricacionem le Roode lofte ' ; Miles Gill, 1512, bequeathes ' unto th' abbot and convente of Fontaunce for to be assolled of harmes agaynes thaym doon ijs.'

We should perhaps hardly expect, so late as 1591, to find Richard Burnand of Knaresborough, esquire, directing,—

First, I geue and bequeith my soulle unto the handes and mercye of my Saviour and Redemer Jesus Christe, most hartelye prainge our blissid mother Marye and all the holye company of heaven to praye unto Him that He will forgeue me, before I departe this transsitorye lyef, my innumerable synnes commytted against Him.

Of funeral directions the following from the same will is the best example :—

> Item, I will thatt within one holle yeare after my departure, two holle large and stronge brasse pictures be maid, resemblinge my brother Fraunces stature and myne, and thatt the same pictures, soe beinge maide and ingraven, be faste wrought into and nailed above the marble stone where my brother lyeth, with a subscribtion written under therein, likewise in brasse, declaringe our names and parentes, and parentes by father and mother, and thatt we bothe died unmaried, beinge the laste males of the full bloode of that name.

Thomas Lightfoot, 1559, directs that 'everie persone beinge att the daye off my buriall shall have one farthing loyff' (loaf); John Sporett, 1559, 'I will that my neybors shall have breyde and aill att the daye of my buriall'; Christopher Bank, 1566—

> I will that my neighbours shall have a dynner at Fuiston the day of my buriall, and the powre people to be served the daye of my buriall at the discrecion of my supervisors, as they shall thinke good ;

John Thorpe, 1571—

> I will that ther be halpeny dole delt for me at my parishe churche at Fuiston, and that all honest folkes that gooes to yᵉ churche with me have ther dinners.

Perhaps we may add here an extract showing that 'ancestors' were not confined to the landed gentry : Edward Spence of Fewston, laborer, directs that he shall be buried ' in the church yeard there emongst my auncestors.'

The kindly charity of Robert Turner (1551) deserves a note. He bequeaths—

> to Thomas Thorpe, my nevey, all my lether and all maner of stuff belonging to the occupacion within my shoppe. Allso, I will yᵗ he make thirteyn pair of shoys, which shalbe geven to thirteyn pooer folkes within the paryshe of Fuyston.

Richard Burnand's will, already quoted, contains some further items of interest :—

> I geue unto my lovinge cossynes and faithfull freindes, for soe in my lief time I have alweis founde theim, Sir Richard Mauleverer of Allerton Maleverer, Knight, Richard Hudson, Doctor of the Lawe, Richard Goodriche of Ribston, esquier, everye one of theim an ounce of golde a pece, to maike theim rynges, beinge engraven withe theire armes and myne togither, upon two severall scutchions, well hopynge of there faithefull love and favors towardes those who shall succede me.
>
> Item, I geue unto my frend, Mr. Edward Wythes, the picture I promised him yf I died before him, and unto his wief I geve an other picture, which ys maid like unto the other, savinge they dyffer in personages.

Item, I geue to my cossyn Dynnys Baynebrigge and his wief, two sylver goblettes, worthe in valewe xl*s*. a pece, with my armes and name upon theim, and they to have the use of theim duringe theire lyves ; and after theire deceases, I geve the same goblettes unto Anne Faux and Elizabethe Faux.

Mrs. Bainbrigg was the widow of Edward Fawkes of York, and mother of the celebrated Guy ; Anne and Elizabeth were her daughters.

Guy himself was not forgotten :—

Item, I geue unto Guy Faux awo angells, to maike him a rynge.

Richard Barroby of Pannal (1539) thus quaintly records his dissatisfaction with his sons :—

And in casse my ij sonnes John and Henrye doo demande or clame anye parte of my goodes in the name of their childes portions, I wull yem noo parte of my goodes, by reasone I had greate charges off theym bothe, fyndynge theym att scolle, and afterwords I dyd lowsse John my sonne furthe his apprentyschyppe, which was no lytill coste ; as for Henrye, I dyd lene (loan) hym xxvj*s*. viij*d*. which he never payd me agayne, thoughte y* he saithe he paied me.

He bequeaths all his goods to his daughter Janet.

John Yeadon of Killinghall (1590) is equally outspoken. He gives the residue of his goods to four friends—

only upon trust that whereas I have a brother called John Yeadon, and a nece called Dorotie, his daughter, and whereas my sayd brother is a lame man and soone distempered, and so unfytt eyther to governe himselfe or anything I shall gyve him,

the trustees are to provide for them at their discretion. This affords a late example of the singularly inconvenient custom of christening two brothers by the same Christian name.

Henry Shaw of Clint, clerk (1595) bequeaths

his short gowne and a typpytt ot black silke which he had lent to Tho. Atkinson for iij dayes to ride on woweinge with.

Let us hope that the lady of Mr. Atkinson's choice was duly impressed by his borrowed plumes, and that the 'woweinge' was brought to a satisfactory ending.

Here is a charming touch of favouritism :—

And the reste remaynynge [of my goods] I geue unto my doughter Dorothye. I geve to my said children sex silver spones, to everye of them two, but Dorothye to have two of the beste.

Mrs. Katherine Roundell of Scriven (1522) boldly asserts :

I awe no dettes to no man y* I knawe of, bot x*d*. to Wylliam Dakar, nor none is awynge to me.

Some bequests read very strangely :—

I give, if God send my doughter a childe and a christen soule, vj*s.* viij*d.* (William Shutt, 1579).

I give to my sonn Thomas, half a mare and half a sadle, and a cart whele (John Bates, 1580).

To my doughter Elizabethe the greateste ketle, soe that she paye everie ot her children iij*s.* iiij*d.* (Joan Lodge, 1591).

I will that if anye person or persons shall nott be contente with such gyftes as given to them by vertue of this my will and testament, shall be clearlie and utterlie voyded out of the same, and they shall haue no comodytie or profyte by vertue of the same (George Spence, 1587).

A most interesting list of articles of attire might be compiled from these wills. We find coats of various materials : frieze, buckskin, fustian ; doublets are made of ' worsett ' (? worsted), buckskin, say, or leather ; jackets are generally described by their colours : grey, blue, tawney, marble, black ; one is made of say, without sleeves, and another is described as ' my greatest kelter jackett ' ; gowns are ' fox furred,' ' lyned with saye,' ' tawnie,' ' violett,' damask, ' reversed wythe velvett ' ; a ' Spanyshe jerkyn ' occurs, ' my best over hose or sloppes,' ' my best understockinges,' ' my best blacke britches,' ' one paire of fustian sleves ' and ' one smokke redie maide.'

Head gear is represented by ' my best sylke hatt,' a ' black button bonnet,' a white cap, ' one velvett bonett eged w' gold, ij frountlettes and one patlett of velvett.' Mistress Beckwith of Clint possessed a ' gould bellyment,' whatever that may have been.

Arms and armour are not often referred to, but the following are mentioned : jack, ' stele cote,' ' steill bonette,' ' stele cappe,' ' salletts,' one buckler, several bills and swords, one ' Carlille axe ' and one ' calever.' In Thomas Coghill's inventory (1585) are ' his apparell, with a prevy coyte, iij*li.* vj*s.* viij*d.* In the chamber att grese headd (i.e. at the head of the stairs), thre stele capes, xij*s.*' Three side-saddles occur.

Books were few and far between. Thomas Coghill, mentioned above, gave all his books to his son, ' and if he shall die, then they to remayne to my next heire ' ; John Lockwood had ' a bouke of Crownacles.'

Horses and dogs too are rarely mentioned. John Fitz-Thomas of Bilton Park (1541) gives ' to my lorde of Combrelande, one crose of golde, with one cople of houndes and ther lyomes (leashes) and one blake begill and his lyome and his coller.' Another testator has a colt called ' Bay Tunstall.'

Many names of cows and oxen may be found in this volume, e.g. : 'Alblacke,' 'Brodehead,' 'Byrkell,' 'Defte,' 'Dowglas,' 'Flowrill,' 'Gallande,' 'Gareland,' 'Grenehorne,' 'Lowley,' 'Lyllye,' 'Marrigold,' 'Mother Like,' 'Scubeld,' 'Sether,' 'Sperehorne,' 'Spinkeld,' 'Taggeld' and 'Toppin.'

Of curious christian names only one calls for note, viz. : 'Agapite,' son of Thomas Beckwith of Clint, 1517.

Space will not allow of any more extracts. May we, in conclusion, call the attention of Dr. Collins and the Surtees Society to the urgent need of a glossary ? An excellent examination paper could be made of the archaic and obsolete words. Few people, we imagine, would be able offhand to explain the following terms : 'one bolster with a codware,' 'one dishbinke,' 'one reckand,' 'one great 'kymling,' 'one broling iron,' 'sousekittes,' 'a vergious brake,' 'a garded twentye whye,' 'one umble ewe,' 'happins,' 'iiij par of herden,' 'ij of the best whisynges,' 'vij chymies,' or 'two wombles, one of them a scoring womble, the other a harde womble.'

The second volume[1] to be noticed is edited by Mr. J. W. Clay, F.S.A., than whom there is no greater authority on Yorkshire genealogy. It contains 239 wills, between 1516 and 1551, principally those of great landowners and members of Visitation families. Here we are moving throughout among people of position : peers, knights, squires, gentlemen, city magnates, and their wives and daughters. In some ways therefore, though not in others, this volume is of greater interest than the last. We read of jewellery and plate, tapestries and dresses that would be of fabulous value in these days of the millionaire collector, but we miss in a large measure some of those charming little touches of human nature which we found among the smaller folk.

There are some interesting directions as to burials and tombs, but not so many as might have been expected.

Sir Thomas Johnson of Lindley (1542) directs—

that myne executours do cause a stone to be laide upon me, an ymage of the Nativitie of oure Lorde sett opon the same, and an ymage of my self maide knelinge under, with myne armes in foure corners of the same stone to be likewise sett for a remembrance.

[1] Surtees Society, vol. 106.

Sir William Gascoigne of Gawthorp (1545) directs to be buried in the parish church of Harewood—

on the southe side where my auncesters do lye. Item, I give fortie poundes to the settinge furthe of a quere there, and to make a tomb over my grave.

Alderman Thomas Thomson of Hull :—

I will that my wif cause make upon the stone whiche I have bought to lay upone my grave, a picture of latten for myself, for ij wives, and for my children, with scriptur about it, and the iiij evangelistes, with my marchaunt marke set upon it, after the best manner.

Sir William Middleton of Stockeld (1549) directs to be buried—

in the quere of Sainct Nicolas of the south syd of the parishe churche of Ilkeley, under the stone that myne ancetoure Sir Peres Myddylton lyethe.

Sir James Strangways (1541) directs that—

my executors by the advise of the lorde Dacre, shall maike one ile of the southe side of the quere of Osmoderley, of the length of the quere, and to bestowe of the buyldinge thereof xl*li*., to th'entent that I and my wif may be buried ther.

Nicholas Bosville of Denaby (1521) orders 'a through stone to lay on my grave, withe scripture of laton of the same, xl*s*.'

Richard Willoughby, alderman of Nottingham directs (1545) :—

I will that my bodie shall be buried in the churche of Sancte ———— at Nottingeham, nighe unto the plaice where as my father was buried, and to have at my buriall thre masses withe note, that is to saie, the masse of the Holy Goste, the masse of Our Ladie, and the masse of Requiem. Item, my will and mynde is to be buried under stole.

In 1541, John Mering of Mering makes most elaborate provision for his funeral and obit ; the services, the number and weight of the tapers, the alms, the bedesmen and their gowns, and many other matters are set out in great detail.

There are two interesting statements of the motives which led to the making of the will at a particular time.

Ralph Gascoigne of Wheldale (1522) makes his will because he is 'intendyng to go to the Kinge's warres when it shall please his grace.'

Walter Paslew of Riddlesden (1544) makes his will because he is—

entendinge, by the gracie of God, according to the kinges comaundement, by his letters to me directed, shortelie to take my jorney towarde the Scottes, for the defence of the realme of Englande.

The lists of plate are so numerous that it is difficult to make a selection ; a few of the more important ones follow.

Katherine, Countess of Northumberland (1542) :—

A standinge cope doble gilte, with a cover pounced and paris worke ; a pounsett goblett gilte with a cover ; a cope of assey with a cressande sett on the bodome ; a spoone with an acorne, doble gilte ; my gret silver crose with oure ladie and Sancte John, with a foot of silver and gilte to sett the crose in over the altare ; a silver foote gilte, to putt in reliques, with three wiers of silver to stande on ; a spone with Sancte Katheryne doble gilte ; a cope of assay with a cresande ; a longe silver spone for sokett ; a longe forke of silver for sokett ; a pix of silver set in burralles for the sacrament ; a hollie watter fatte, with a cover of silver and a swenkyll of silver to the same [etc.].

John Neville, Lord Latimer (1542), mentions :—

Towe of my best gilte standinge cuppes with covers, towe gilte goblettes with one cover, my best basinge and ewer of silver, my towe silver flaggons.

Sir William Middleton of Stockeld (1549) :—

I will one goblett with the cover of silver and doble gilte, weing twenty and eghte ownces or ther abouts, to remayne at my howse at Stockelde as an herelome from heire to heyre, in recompence of suche heyrlomes as I put away for the lone to the Kinges Majesty, and that my heyres frome one to an other shall have the occupancy and possession of the said goblet.

Sir Marmaduke Constable of Everingham (1541) leaves to his son Robert—

a basyne with ewer of silver, havinge myne armes and my wife's, a pare of standinge pottes, marke with lions, the King of Skotte's armes, to remayne as airlomes to his here after hyme.

Dame Elizabeth Savile (1541) :—

One goblet of silver without a cover ; one silver goblet with a cover ; a silver salte gilte, with a cover ; one silver goblet ; ij gret silver saltes, parcell gilte, with a cover ; a paire of beades with gawdes of golde ; one paire of corall beades.

Dame Jane Constable of Wassand (1540) :—

Two basins and ewers of silver ; 'a dussen silver spoones with th'appostles gilted of ther endes ; a litle standinge pece with a cover doble gilte ; a gret salte with a cover, parcell gilte ; a litle salte with a cover, parcell gilte ; a gret salte, parcell gilte, without cover ; a litle silver canne with a cover' ; besides numerous spoons, some gilt.

Christopher Stapleton of Wighill (1537) mentions the following silver :—

'A salte of silver, covered, percell gilte,' 'a goblet of silver and gilte, without a cover,' 'a long spone for grene gynger,' 'xij silver spones of Sancte

John,' ' too spones sylver and gylte,' ' one silver cuppe gilte, of th'olde facione,' ' a litle silver flagon for rose water,' ' a gilte cuppe with a cover, called a peyre, and a noder cuppe of the facyone of an nutte, called grypeege,' ' the seale of my armes in sylver, and a rynge called a sygnet, with a Sarasyn heide graven in it,' ' a basen and one ewer of silver, too bolles and a cover therunto of antyke worke, one grete holoe boole gilte, with a cover, one odre litle flatte cuppe of silver with a cover ' ; ' one cuppe of silver called a peyre.'

Robert Creyke of Beverley (1538) :—

Thre booles of sylver, chaiste and gilte, withe a cover ; a basynge with a newer of sylver, percell gilte ; a standinge cupe of sylver and gilte withe a cover, with my armes in the toppe ; a sylver pott gilted, wythe a cover, with my armes in them ; a standinge cupe of sylver gilte with a cover, and the image of Sanct John the Baptiste in the knope of the cover ; a pott of sylver gilte with a cover, and a colobyne in the toppe ; sex spones of silver and gilten knoppys, and roses in the knoppes ; ij spones of sylver slipped at the endes ; a white pot of sylver withe a cover, not gilte ; a goblet of sylver percell gilte, without a cover ; one whit sylver pott, withoute a cover ; a goblet of sylver percell gilt, withe a cover ; a whit pott of sylver, withoute a cover.

Another interesting will is that of Katherine Nandike, late Prioress of Wickham (1541). She bequeaths—

' to my laidie counties of Northumberlande one silver crosse, ij standinge maser and a corporax ; to eght of my susters that was professide in Wikham Abbay, to every one of theme vjs. viijd.' ; to a god-daughter 'a pair of awmer bedes,' and to a niece ' one rabande of ij yerdes of silke, and ij silver aglettes.'

Isabel Swales, a sister of the hospital at Killingwoldgrove (1536), bequeaths—

to the House of Killyngraves my greatest maser, to bee an heyrelome in the House, and not to be taken frome it, but to bee in the kepyng of the eldest Broder, orels th'eldest Suster, and thaye to bring it forthe at there being in the haule.

Roger Tochetts of Guisbrough (1536) gives to his son and heir ' one salte of sylver and vj sylver spones with madyn hedes of ther ends.'

We also find ' a whit sylver goblet that I use to ett pottage,' ' a writhyne rynge of golde,' other rings set with ' a stone of turkas,' a ' turquays ' or ' a Turkie stone ' (turquois), a ' cornell,' a ' nemerald,' and a ' camewe ' ; ' a pare of jeatt beades with silver gawdies,' ' one paire of almer (amber) beades with silver gawdies,' a silver whistle, and ' a silver spoyne with a forke to eate suckett withe.'

The best will for jewellery is that of Thomasine Bussey of Newstead (1545). She bequeaths—

H

ij rynges, one havinge a dyamond, the other a rubie ; a rynge with a saphire ; a crosse of golde with a diamonde and a cheyne of golde ; a Sancte Andros crose of golde with iiij rubyes and ij perles and a cheyne ; a crose of golde with fyve diamondes and thre pendant perles ; a flower of golde, diverslie enamelyde, with a rubie, a saphire, lupe and a perle ; a pomander of golde, sett with thre diamondes, ij rubyes, vj perles, hanginge at a chayne of golde ; a Sancte Anthony's crose of golde, with a bell ; a corse of golde wire with a grett buckill and a pendant ; a litle chayne of golde with towe agglettes of golde ; the secunde corse, with buckell and pendante ; a floure of golde, with a rubie, a saphire and a perle ; the third corse, with buckill and pendant.

Margaret Newby of Kirkfenton (1531) leaves 'one pare of corall beades with sylver gawdies.'

Thomas Thomson, alderman of Hull (1540), mentions some interesting items :—

My brasyne morter with the pestell, whiche morter haithe my marchaunte marke set upon it ; my golde ringe with the greatest saffure beinge in it ; a golde ringe with an other saffoure set therin ; my best bedes of silver and gilte, contenynge in nombre vij^{xx} and x, besides the gawdes ; a great candle-stike of latten with xv floures or lightes therto belonginge.

Katherine, Countess of Northumberland (1542), mentions the following tapestries :—

ij peces of arrayes with the xij apostles and xij proffettes ; a hanginge of rede and grene say, paynted with a border of the birth of Christe ; a grene hanginge playne, with a border of antike warke ; iiij peces of newe arras of the storie of Venus ; thre peces of tapstrie werke of Alexander ; a hanginge paynted red and yolowe, with a border of the passion ; a coverynge of a bede oversee warke, with birdes and beasts on it ; thre quishinges [cushions], wherof towe of carpett warke, the thirde tapstre warke with pounde garnettes [pomegranates], etc.

Mrs. Isabel Craike (1548) :—

The chamber hinginges of fullarie worke payntid, with one bed of cremisen satten and white, and the curtanes of reade sarcenet and blewe ; one coverying of a bed of ymagerie worke unlyned, whiche cost me five pounde ; iiij quishinges with popingaes of them ; a diaper borde clothe withe birde eyes ; one coverynge withe the hanginge of grene sae paynted ; a teaster for a bed maide of my lorde Cardinall armes ; vj quishinges of tufftes, withe birdes in them ; my best carpet of parke warke.

Leonard Percehay of Ryton, esq. (1516), directs—

that my best gowne be given to the use of my chauntry in Kirkeby Mysperton to maike a vestement of, to pay for my soull and myn ancestres.

Robert Creyke of Beverley mentions—

the parlour hanginges and the chawmer hanginges of tappistre warke ; a gowne of blake atten furred withe budge ; a gowne of blake damaske furred with coney ; a gowne of chamlet furred with funes ; a gowne of browne blewe furred with coney ; a tawney velvet jacket ; a gowne of blake clothe, lyned withe blake satten and garded withe blake velvet ; a gowne of russett clothe furred with buge ; my best dublett of tawney satten.

Jane Hammerton (1537) bequeaths—

my mariage gowne of russet damaske, with the sleves turneupe with russet velvet, and a plagard to the same, a kyrtle of tawny saten and a square patled of white saten and golde, a paire of sleves of cremysyn satten, one velvet bonet blake with a white frontelet of satten with golde, ij edges of silke womens worke of gold.

As might be expected, we find some valuable lists of arms and armour.

Sir Brian Stapleton of Burton Joyce (1545) bequeaths to his son Richard—

all my harnes that is other (either) in my armye chamber or other placies, that is to say, jackes, sallettes, splentes, almen revettes, legges harnesses, and all my bowes, arrowes, or sheffe of arrowes, haylles, standerdes, and any other manner of harness that belongithe to warre.

Christopher Wilberfoss (1533) gives a sword and buckler to his son Roger ; a baslard to each of his sons John, Robert and Henry ; to his son William, 'a jacke, a salett, vij chymies, a gorgett of male, and a halbart' ; to his son Roger, 'a salett, a halbarte, a corsett of whit harnes, a fold of male, and a pare of splentes' ; to his son John, 'a litle jacke' ; to his son Robert 'a pare of briganders, with the reversion of a fold of male, and an olde gorgett.'

John Bassett of Fledborough, esq. (1542), mentions 'all my harnes and all other my weapens mett and convenyent fore warre.'

As regards individual objects of rarity, we may mention first of all two clocks.

Richard Byngham of Carcolston (1531), desires that—

my cloke with the bell, the side borde in the haull with the tristillis set in the ground, and a pare of yrn galos in the chymnaye, doe remayne as heireloomes.

James Conyers of Whitby (1541) gives to the parish church—

one payre of orgayns and one clocke, and one goodlie chales of silver, doble gilte with golde, for to mynistre my maker withall.

Two other organs occur in addition to the one just mentioned.

Christopher Stapleton of Wighill (1537) gives—

to the parishe churche of Wighall a paire of organes that standeth in the hye quere of the churche.

Christopher Wilberfoss (1533) leaves 4*s.* for 'the mendyng of the organes for the mayneteynyng of God's service.'

The only other musical instrument, except hunting-horns, occurs in the will of Thomas Brigham (1542). He bequeaths to his son Ralph, 'my chamlett gowne, my long night gowne, both my chamlett jackets, and a paire of virginals.' He also left to his brother-in-law his 'great hawke,' from which it might appear that he was something of a sportsman as well as a musician.

Lancelot Stapleton of Wath was better equipped for the chase. He mentions—

all my houndes ; my best crosse bowe : my bygest horne flowede withe sylver ; all my longe bowes and my quyver ; my quaile nett and my flight nett ; my partrike nettes called a tonnell, and my towe partrike horse.

We may quote here a quaint bequest made by Ralph Bigod of Seaton (1545). He gives—

to my nawnte Warrayn the graie horse whiche I had of her, if he goo streght, and if he goo not streyghte, then she to have the white amblinge mere whiche I had of Maister Baites, and she to give to myn executores my ringe of golde, enambeled with blacke letters.

John Neville, Lord Latimer (1542), directs—

that after my decesse the Master and Vicare [of Well] shall take all the rentes of the parsonedge of Sancte Georgie Churche in Yorke, for the terme of fortie yeres, and therwith to fynde a scole maister at Well for kepinge a scole and techinge of gramer ther, and to pray for me and them that I am most bounden to pray for.

This school is still in existence.

Books, as in the previous volume, occur but rarely.

Walter Clifton of Gray's Inn (1540) bequeaths to Christofer Holme of Paull Holme—

Feherber bridgementes, with other moo bookes of the lawe, so that he do continewe and studie the lawes of this realme at London, at one of the Innes of the Courte or of the Chancerie, by the spacie of iij or iiij yeres.

Fitzherbert's *Abridgment* was first printed in 1514, and again in 1516. Other books mentioned are *The flower of the ten commandementes, Rationale Divinorum et Summa Angelica, Casus decretalium et doctorum, Chawcer,* and a *Booke of Merie Conceytes.* All these belonged to Edmund Kingston, vicar of Southwell in 1549. He also possessed 'a bed steade of foure postes carved,' 'a paynnted clothe of the pictour of the King opon it,' 'a pictour of Marie Maglene,' and 'a paynnted clothe havyng three doctours opon it.'

William Molyneux (1541) explains a well known expression:—

A holl garnyshe of pewther vessell newe, that is to say, xij platers, xij dishes, xij sawcers, xij potedgers.

Among miscellaneous articles we may mention a 'flanders chiste with a rounde lid,' 'my lambecke (alembic) and my bras pott to sett it on'; another 'lymbeke of tin'; and a 'stillitorie,' or distilling apparatus.

James Conyers of Whitby (1541) gives

to the repayringe of the bridge xxs., with shoppes of the briges, whiche I buyldide of my proper costes and chardges, I give to the brige for ever.

It appears from this that the old bridge at Whitby had, like so many others, a row or rows of shops along it.

Isabel Swales (1536) bequeaths 'to the Godeslove beddes at Beverlay yaites in Hull, a paire of sheites.' Tanner mentions a hospital at Hull, called 'God's House,' which is probably the one here referred to.

Henry Clifford, Earl of Cumberland, generally known as the 'Shepherd Lord,' makes a curious provision for an unmarried daughter :—

I will that the laydie Elizabeth, my doughter, shall have for her mariage a thousande poundes sterlinge, if she be maried to a man of honoure, beinge an erle or an erle's sone and heyre or heire apparaunte, his lands beinge unherited ; and if she be maried to a barrone or a barron's sone and heyre or heyre apparaunte, a thousand markes sterlinge ; and if she be maried unto a knyghte havinge his landes unheryted, eight hundreth markes.

An editorial note states that Elizabeth married Sir Christopher Metcalfe of Nappa, so that presumably she had to be content with £533 6s. 8d. instead of £1,000. 'Unherited' appears to mean 'not settled,' so that the intended husband would be free to make a settlement on his wife.

Thomas Fenton (1547) gives—

to my ladie Nevill one olde riall, evermore desiringe her to be good ladie to my litle meyde, her god doughter, as my trust is in her so to be.

Edmund Clifton (1547) gives—

to Sir Gervys Clifton, knyght, the standinge cuppe of silver and gilte and a goblett parcel gilte, which hee hath all redie in his custodie, opon condicion that he helpe and assiste my wif, and do not enforce her nor be abowte here to take any husbande but suche as she shall willinglie be pleased and contented with, nor be abowte to do here any other displeasour, neyther by worde nor dede ; and if he do any thinge contrarie to this condicion, then this bequeste to be voide.

A liberal minded husband, this !

Richard Plumpton of York (1544) seems to have anticipated that his death would not be unwelcome to some of his relatives, and to have been quite resigned to the fact. He gives—

to Mr. William Plompton and his childer twoo hoggesheades of wyne to maike merie withall.

Edmund Clifton (1547) gives 40s. to Jane Mering—

of this condicion, that she shall professe and knowlege hereself not to have [done] here dewtie to me and to my wif, before Mr. parson and iiij or fyve of the honester men in the parishe.

One wonders what poor Jane had done that she should be pilloried in this way, but no further light is thrown on her delinquencies.

Miss Thorpe was clearly another obstreperous damsel, for her father, John Thorpe of Thorpe (1533), bequeaths—

to Issabell my doughtor to hir mariage xl marcs, if she be rulede aftre my feoffes, or els never a pennye.

The will of Stephen Tempest of Broughton (1549) contains the following very enigmatic sentence :—

I will that my said wif have and enyoe (enjoy) quyetelie suche lodgyng as is benethe the floore of the haull, duryng her widdoheade.

At first sight this reads like a pious wish that Mrs. Tempest should be interred under the hall, the very opposite to the desire of Christopher Tancred of Whixley, an eccentric Yorkshireman who, two centuries later, directed that his coffin should be suspended from the hall rafters ; but as it is open to another construction, the testator should have the benefit of the doubt.

These extracts must close with an equally obscure quotation from the will of Thomas Nevill of Sancton, 1531 :—

Item, I will that they that hath my lande in the towne of Santon kepe it.

Mr. Clay's book, like the previous one, would have been improved by a glossary, but this is all that the most carping critic can say in its dispraise.

OUR OLDEST FAMILIES

V. THE LEIGHTONS

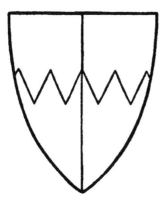

THE old house of Leighton of Shropshire may easily find place amongst those few English families which can point to a twelfth-century forefather. Needless to say that round a landed house of which records carry back the story to a date within a century of Domesday, the early pedigree makers busied themselves with their wonted success. The longer the pedigree given into their hands the more anxious were they to tag to it some ancestor who should wander in the misty places beyond the conquest-year, giving thereby to the family record the grace which would be added to Berkeley Castle by an Anglo-Saxon tower under the hand of a Victorian jerry-builder.

To the credit of the College of Arms be it said that Tresswell and Vincent, visiting the county in 1622, were content to begin their table with the true ancestor of Leighton, although cloaking him with the unlikely name of 'Titus de Leighton, miles,' and marrying him, whom Eyton sets down as a contemporary of Henry I., to a sister of the Valence Earl of Pembroke who was to be born some hundred years later. But those who followed Somerset and Rouge Croix were less restrained, and in Wotton's *English Baronetage*, that casket of spurious legend, we find Leighton in England ' long before the Conquest and of noble extraction, as appears by Doomsday-book,' which venerable record, as may be guessed, is innocent of such false witnessing. As in the case of Sewal, founder of the ancient house of Shirley of Ettington, the unfamiliar Christian name of the patriarch of the Leightons has been used as an argument for his Anglo-Saxon origin. And here to our wonder the learned Eyton may be called to warrant the guesses of Wotton and his fellows, for the historian of feudal Shropshire, puzzled by the name of Tihel, hazards the opinion that Tihel must have been an Anglo-Saxon. When we have shown that Tihel is outlandish and Breton to boot, the case for the old English origin of Leighton falls to the ground, and this is shown clearly by the description of the Domesday holder of Bumpstead in Essex as 'Tihel the Breton.'[1] Doubtless when

William de Coningsby
Came out of Brittany
With his wife Tiffany
And his maid Manfas
And his dog Hardigras

his neighbour Tihel of Leighton made the passage of the Channel with that famous and joyous family party.

Tihel's son Richard appears as Richard Fitz Tiel in the *cartæ* of 1166, holding a knight's fee of old feoffment in the barony of William FitzAlan. His trespass in the forest and his giving of false evidence reveal him as living in 1177 and 1178, and he may have been the Richard de Letton, a plaintiff in a suit of 1194. He is succeeded by his son, another Richard, who, by a deed yet existing at Leighton, had confirmation from William FitzAlan in 1200 or 1201 of his ancestor's estate of 'Lecton.'

Since the days when Tihel founded the house of Leighton his descendants have for the most part been content to add little to the history of the country. Writing themselves knights and esquires, sheriffs, justices of the peace and custodes rotulorum, colonels of the militia and members of the court of the Welsh Marches, they have done their duty in Shropshire. Themis of the quarter sessions has called them blessed, and the muse of medieval history, who goes clad in scarlet, has passed them by to their enduring good fortune. For families eager to meddle with the affairs of state, whose swords are ready to whip out for a red or white rose, take, as a rule, light root in their lands, and the Leightons are still

---

[1] See 'Helion of Helions Bumpstead,' by J. H. Round, M.A., in the *Transactions of the Essex Archæological Society* for 1901.

lords of their Shropshire manors. A Leighton of Stretton-in-the-Dale was steward in Montgomery for Richard of York, but like a wise steward he saw from afar the turn of the tide, and he was Henry VII.'s man before ever the crown was picked out the hawthorn bush. His descendant, Edward Leighton of Wattlesborough, displayed no less cautious prescience when he joined the grave council board of the Whig plotters in the interest of William of Orange, to whom at the Hague Edward's brother, Captain Baldwin Leighton, carried their resolutions. A Williamite baronetcy given in 1693 rewarded the family loyalty to the new sovereigns. Daniel Leighton, son of Sir Edward the first baronet, was a lieutenant-colonel of horse and fought at Fontenoy and elsewhere, whilst his brother, the second baronet, made family history by changing his seat at Wattlesborough for Loton. The sixth baronet, a general of King George's forces, was wounded in America and saw the opening of the Peninsular war. More noteworthy in the story of the Leightons is the truly remarkable parliamentary record of a family which may be said to have made the representation of Shropshire in parliament hereditary in their line since the mother of parliaments began. On another page of this present number of *The Ancestor* will be found a memorial of this record as it has been traced for us by Mr. J. H. Round, who has arranged for the first time the story of this family's parliamentary history. It will be noted that the Leightons, keen Whigs under William III., have now gone the road of many other Whig houses in refusing to translate old Whig as new Liberal.

Such a family seated firmly upon the land in God's peace and the king's might be trusted to advance itself by its marriages. With Ankaret Burgh, a coheir of the lords of Mawddwy, John the Lancastrian-Yorkist had Wattlesborough, Cardeston and Loton, all lordships in Salop, which are still in the hands of the family. Stretton had come by a match with Cambray, and the heir of the Leicester Warrens of Tabley was wife of the eighth baronet.

The ninth baronet, Sir Bryan Baldwin Mawddwy Leighton, is now of Loton and has sons to follow him, so that after eight centuries the line of Tihel of Leighton endures and flourishes in the county of Shropshire.

The arms of Leighton would seem to point to some early connection by blood or tenure with the house of FitzWarin.

The shield as now borne is *quarterly gold ana gues inaentea*. This shield with a baston over it appears first upon the seal in white wax of Sir Richard Leighton, lord of Leighton, appended to a charter dated at Leighton 13 July, 1315, and the coat with the baston is likewise found upon the effigy in Leighton church, which is attributed to this same Sir Richard.

O. B.

Sir Richard de Leighton, Kt., of Leighton,
Shropshire, M.P. for Shropshire in six
Parliaments, 1313, 1314, 1316, 1318 [1]

John de Leighton

John Leighton, esq.

Edward Leighton, esq.

John Leighton, esq. M.P. for Shropshire 1472, 1478

William Leighton of   Sir Thomas Leighton, Kt.
Plash, Shropshire

William Leighton of Plash   John Leighton, esq.

William Leighton, M.P. for
Much Wenlock, 1601

Sir Edward Leighton, Kt.   Sir Thomas Leighton,
M.P. for Shropshire 1553,   Kt. M.P. for Worces-
1563   tershire 1601

Thomas Leighton, esq.

Robert Leighton, esq.

Edward Leighton, esq.

Robert Leighton, esq. M.P. for Shrewsbury 1661–78

Sir Edward Leighton, 1st Bart., contested Shropshire 1695,
M.P. for Shropshire 1698, and for Shrewsbury 1708

Sir Edward Leighton,   General Daniel Leighton,
2nd Bart.   M.P. for Hereford 1747

Sir Charlton Leighton,   Baldwin Leighton, esq.
3rd Bart.

Sir Charlton Leighton,   Sir Baldwin Leighton,
4th Bart. M.P. for   6th Bart.
Shrewsbury 1774 (un-
seated), 1780–90

Sir Baldwin Leighton, 7th
Bart., M.P. for South
Shropshire 1859–65

Sir Baldwin Leighton,   Stanley Leighton, esq., of
8th Bart., M.P. for   Sweeney Hall, Shropshire,
South Shropshire 1877–85   M.P. for North Shropshire
d. 1897   1874–85, and for West
                             Shropshire 1885–1901, d. 1901

[1] See Eyton's *Shropshire*, vii. 333–4. But the number is there given as five, because the
1316 return had not then come to light. Three of these Parliaments were in 1313.—
J.H.R.

NOTES ON SOME ARMORIAL GLASS IN
SALISBURY CATHEDRAL

ABOUT fifty years ago, in the course of a careful account of the stained glass then existing at Salisbury, Mr. Charles Winston published in the Salisbury volume of the Archæological Institute some valuable hints as to the probable ownership and date of the remarkable series of escutcheons which are so conspicuous at the base of the great west window in the nave of the cathedral.

The present writer does not claim to have done very much more. All that is attempted in these notes is to carry the investigation a little further, and to offer one or two suggestions in the hope of throwing a little more light on this interesting subject.

So far as the writer is aware these shields have never been separately illustrated, although two of them and part of two others, one of which no longer exists, are outlined in the 79th plate in Carter's *Ancient Architecture*. They are however of such exceeding interest, and are so completely representative of English heraldic art of the second half of the thirteenth century that they have been drawn accurately to scale, with the leads marked and coloured in water colour, so as to show as nearly as possible the appearance which they present.

The glass of which they are fashioned is exceedingly thick and heavy, and the colouring is perfectly luminous and well preserved. The capricious lines of the lead-work, which are very noticeable in some of the shields, and the broken colour, which makes them so splendidly decorative, are doubtless due to the costliness of ancient glass, which reached the craftsman in quite small pieces, so that even the smallest fragments if satisfactory in colour would be treasured and worked into the design as occasion served without regard to their shape.

These shields are all of the same size—17 inches along the line of the chief and 21 inches from chief to foot—being somewhat narrower and longer in appearance than the contemporary shields carved on the walls of Westminster Abbey.

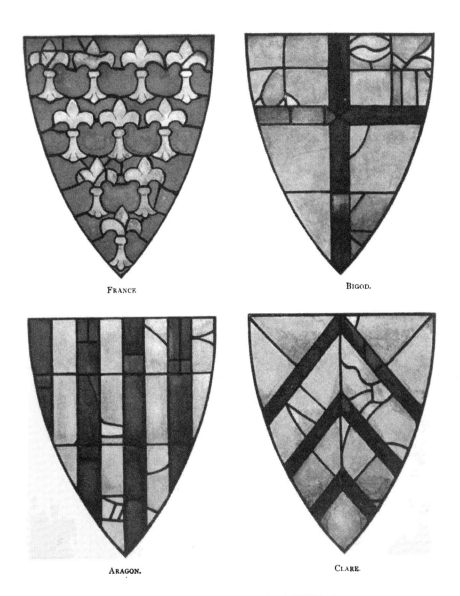

FRANCE.

BIGOD.

ARAGON.

CLARE.

STAINED GLASS IN SALISBURY CATHEDRAL.

There are six of these fine escutcheons, and one other which, although so obviously a piece of patchwork that no drawing has been made of it, must not be passed without mention. They are arranged in the window in the following order : (1) gold three cheverons gules ; (2) paly gules and gold of eight pieces ; (3) azure powdered with golden fleur-de-lis ; (4) gules three leopards gold ; (5) silver a lion gules crowned gold and a border sable bezanty ; (6) gold a cross gules— but this enumeration will not be followed in the consideration of these armorials. The shield which has disappeared seems to have been chequered.

It is natural to speak first of the shield of England (fig. 1), which is believed to refer to Henry III. The colour of the field is a gorgeous carmine. The leopards are of a beautiful golden hue with the shading and outline of their features and claws still perfectly distinct. It will be observed that the original head of the uppermost has been lost, and that its place is filled with a piece of white glass which shows traces of having been painted yellow.

The shape of the beasts, which bear a close resemblance to those of Henry III.'s sculptured shield in Westminster Abbey, is completely characteristic of the date to which they have been assigned. It is not perhaps the most pleasing type. There is but little of that striking conventionalism and spirited drawing which makes the heraldic animals of fifty or sixty years later so delightful to behold ; but the draughts-manship has strong individuality, and his bold lines would serve to determine the approximate period of this shield even if there were no other indication of date.

The second coat to be described (fig. 2) is a not uncommon variant of the arms of the Arragonese Counts of Provence, who employed the undifferenced *gold four pales gules* of Arra-gon. This was the paternal coat-armour of Eleanor, Queen of Henry III. She was the second daughter of Raymond Berenger IV., Count of Provence, and there can be but little doubt that our shield commemorates her. Much of the red glass of it has become almost black in course of time.

The next escutcheon (fig. 3) demands more than a cursory mention. It can only be intended for a representation of that earlier form of the arms of France which was carried by the French kings from the first quarter of the thirteenth century till 1376, when Charles V., desiring to differentiate his own arms of France from those assumed by Edward III. nearly forty years earlier, ordained that the number of lilies in his coat was to be three '*pour symboliser la Sainte-Trinité.*'

The field, of an exquisitely pure and rich blue, is in our example simply charged with ten golden fleur-de-lis, which, it may be remarked, are of unusually fine and massive form. Matthew Paris' MS.[1] gives an even simpler type of shield to the French king—'scutum azureum vi gladioli flores aurei '—and these flowers are of almost exactly the same shape as those in the shield at Salisbury.

The counterseal of Philip III. (1270–85) bears a shield charged with ten lilies arranged in the same way as those in fig. 3. On the other hand his grandfather, Louis VIII. (1223–26), who was the first king to use the complete escutcheon of France powdered with lilies on his counterseal, employed a shield of the round-headed shape charged with eleven whole lilies and parts of four others.

Our escutcheon is ascribed to Louis IX. (1226–70), the brother-in-law and staunch friend of Henry III. He died during the eighth (his second) crusade, and was canonized by Boniface VIII. in 1297.

It is scarcely probable that this shield refers to Margaret of France, who became Edward I.'s wife in 1299 after the death of Eleanor of Castile. If that were the case the arms of England would be for Edward I., and the only apparent reason for the Arragon shield would be its insertion as a memorial to his mother. There are however other indications which point to a date earlier than 1299 as that to which the shields of England, France and Arragon must be referred.

The next in order of dignity is charged with the well-known arms of Richard of Cornwall (fig. 4). The field is of a lovely silvery white, and the border, which at the distance of a very few feet appears to be quite black, is really of very dark purple glass. The striking form of the rampant lion, stiff and restrained yet thoroughly vigorous in drawing, is again markedly characteristic of the latter half of the thirteenth century ; and there can be little question that this coat is rightly attributed to Richard, second son of King John, created Earl of Cornwall and Poitiers by his brother Henry in 1225, and elected King of the Romans in 1256. He was

---

[1] Cotton MS. Nero. D. i.

thrice married, first to Isabel Marshal, the widow of Gilbert de Clare, first Earl of Gloucester and Hertford, and after her death to Sancia of Provence, the youngest of Raymond's daughters. He died a few months before his brother King Henry, and his third wife, Beatrice von Falkenstein, survived him.

The drawing of his arms by Matthew Paris is almost precisely similar in style and feeling to the shield at Salisbury. The lion is however somewhat less stiff, and there are fewer besants in the border.

A word may be said here with regard to the patchwork shield which finds a place among these armorials. This is an escutcheon of the same size and shape as the rest of the series, displaying a field of silvery glass with a green demon and a blue border charged with besant-like disks of yellow glass. Of these materials the white and the yellow have all the appearance of thirteenth-century glass, the demon seems to be sixteenth-century work, and the blue glass of the border is certainly modern. It is possible that the white glass and yellow disks are parts of another coat of arms which once belonged to this group, perhaps a second escutcheon of Cornwall, referring to Henry, first surviving son of the King of the Romans. After fighting on the king's side at Lewes, where he was taken prisoner, Prince Henry took the cross in 1268, and while on his way home from the crusade was murdered by the sons of Simon de Montfort at Viterbo in 1271. It is hardly likely that a second Cornwall shield, if these fragments be really part of those arms, would refer to Edmund of Almaine, the second son of Richard's second marriage, since he does not emerge from obscurity till 1272, when he succeeded his father as Earl of Cornwall at the age of twenty-two.

The Clare shield (fig. 5) has suffered somewhat from the effects of more than 600 years of weathering, and the tinctures though perfectly distinct are darker than those of the other coats-of-arms. A striking feature in this escutcheon is the extreme narrowness of the cheverons characteristic of the period, the red glass which is exposed between the edges of the leads being only just three-quarters of an inch in width. In spite of this the elegant angle of the sharply-pointed cheverons enables them to fill the field in a really beautiful manner.

There is no reason to question the assignment of this
shield to Gilbert de Clare, who succeeded his father Richard
as third Earl of Cornwall and Hertford in 1262. Five years
earlier Gilbert had married Alice de Lusignan, daughter of
the king's half-brother Guy, Count of Cognac, whose aunt
and namesake became the wife of another great English noble,
John de Warenne, Earl of Surrey, in 1247.

The last shield of this collection which survives remains
to be considered (fig. 6). It is noteworthy that the cross is of
the same remarkable narrowness that has been observed in the
cheverons of de Clare, so that instead of occupying one-fifth of
the escutcheon, which the pedants define as the proper width
for an uncharged cross, it is in this example little more than
one-eighth of the field. This coat is believed to be that of
Roger le Bigod, fourth Earl of Norfolk (1225–70).

There was at least one other shield belonging to this
group, for a part of a checky shield, intended doubtless for
the arms of Warenne, is shown in Carter's plate of the Chapter House windows; but the present writer has no knowledge
of its ever having appeared with the rest in the west window
of the nave.

If the date which has been suggested for these coats be
correct, namely a few years before 1272, this lost shield would
refer to John de Warenne, Earl of Surrey (1240–1305), who
married the elder Alice de Lusignan, aunt of Gilbert de Clare's
countess.

The relationships between the various bearers of these
shields of arms is shown in the accompanying table, where the
names of those to whom the arms are believed to refer are
given in capital letters. But a desire to record a number of
not very closely connected matches seems hardly reason
enough to account for so remarkable a 'levy of shields,'
though it may have had something to do with the matter.
Some important event was probably the occasion for the
painting of this collection of armorial bearings, and it would
seem that such an event must be sought for between 1262,
the date of Gilbert de Clare's succession to his earldoms, and
1270, the year in which St. Louis died.

May it not be possible that the year 1268, when the cross
was raised for the eighth time, supplies the required date ?
It was the crusade of *Louis*. *Henry III.* and *Eleanor* were on
the throne of England. Their son together with their nephew

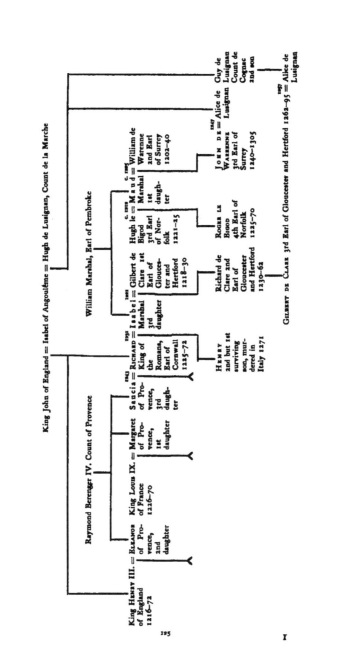

King John of England == Isabel of Angoulême == Hugh de Lusignan, Count de la Marche

Raymond Berenger IV. Count of Provence

William Marshal, Earl of Pembroke

King Henry III. == Eleanor of Provence, 2nd daughter, of England 1216–72

King Louis IX. == Margaret of Provence, 1st daughter, of France 1226–70

Richard == Sancia of Provence, 3rd daughter, King of the Romans, Earl of Cornwall 1225–72

Isabel == Gilbert de Clare 1st Earl of Gloucester and Hertford 1218–30, Marshal 3rd daughter

Hugh le == Maud Marshal 1st daughter == William de Warenne 2nd Earl of Surrey 1202–40, Bigod 3rd Earl of Norfolk 1211–25

Guy de Lusignan Count de Cognac 2nd son == Alice de Lusignan

John de Warenne 3rd Earl of Surrey 1240–1305 == Alice de Lusignan

Henry 2nd but 1st surviving son, murdered in Italy 1271

Richard de Clare 2nd Earl of Gloucester and Hertford 1230–62

Roger le Bigod 4th Earl of Norfolk 1225–70

Gilbert de Clare 3rd Earl of Gloucester and Hertford 1262–95 == Alice de Lusignan

125

I

Henry, son of *Richard of Cornwall,* took the cross ; and the example set by these princes was followed by the Earls of Surrey and Gloucester, *John de Warenne* and *Gilbert de Clare.* And if the arms of *Roger le Bigod* were not included for the same reason, he was, in virtue of his office of Marshal, a personage of such high importance, and he had been so lately reconciled to King Henry, that in some such reasons as these may be found the motive for the honour which was thereby shown him.

One last question—why were these shields placed in Salisbury Chapter House ?—is, it is to be feared, unanswerable. It is however almost certain—provided that the conclusions as to proprietorship and date here arrived at are correct—that they were not originally made for that position, for the building of the Chapter House was not begun till the reign of Edward I. was well advanced. But by whose orders the escutcheons were made, why and by whom they were given to Salisbury Cathedral, and when they were first placed in the position which they occupied till they were removed in 1828 to the great triple lancet in the nave, are riddles which still await their solution.

E. E. DORLING.

A GENEALOGIST'S KALENDAR OF CHANCERY SUITS OF THE TIME OF CHARLES I.

DENT v. HEARD and another

D$\frac{7}{18}$ Bill (2 June 1641) of Thomas Dent of Newcastle-on-Tyne, gent., complainant against Robert Heard of Newcastle and Anthony Norman.

Concerning a bond dated 7 April 10 Car. I. whereby the complainant became bound with John Redhead of Newcastle, yeoman, since deceased, to the defendant, Robert Heard. The defendant Norman is described as a scrivener 'and one who hath conceived causeles spleene' against the complainant.

DAYE v. BUBB and others

D$\frac{7}{11}$ Bill (29 June 1631) of Joseph Daye of the city of London, clerk.

Answer (10 Oct. 1631) of Forster Elmes of Henley, co. Oxford, and Thomas Harvey *alias* Ellis of Strowd, co. Gloucester, defendants with William Bubb and John Holliday, both of Strowd, William Barnard of Henley and Austin Knappe of Henley.

Richard Daye, clerk, who about 10 years since settled lands in Strowd upon the marriage of his son John. He died about two years since
=

John Daye, son and heir=Elizabeth Porter, died about one year since, dau. of Patrick without issue | Porter of Tewxbury. Married about ten years since

Joseph Daye of London, clerk, compt., heir of his brother

DENE v. HEXT

D$\frac{1}{17}$ Bill (27 Oct. 1631) of Richard Dene of Newton St. Petrocke, co. Devon, esquire.

Answer (at St. Ives, co. Cornwall, 20 Jan. 163$\frac{1}{2}$) of Richard Hext, gent.

Concerning a bond for 20*l.* (dated 7 July 22 Jac. I.) given by the complainant to the defendant, which sum was, according to the complainant, to be paid only in the event of his recovering lands in Upper Loders, co. Dorset, for which he has maintained suits at law for the space of seven years. The lands are claimed in respect of the compt.'s wife Phillippe, who was sister and heir to Thomas Hele, esquire, who died without issue. Arthur Hext, brother to the defendant, was an ancient servant and a kinsman to the said Thomas Hele. The defendant states that Thomas Hele bore no great affection to his brother-in-law, and by will gave legacies to the said Arthur, for the preferment of him and of his wife and children, and to one Mary Champernon, now lately dead.

EARL OF DANBYE v. BERRYE and another

D $\frac{7}{16}$ Replication (Mich. 6 Car. I.) of Henry, Earl of Danbye, to the answers of Richard Berrye, M.D., and Robert Bladen, gent., defendants.

Concerning the sales of certain fee-farms.

DAYE v. DAYE

D $\frac{11}{10}$ Replication (Easter 7 Car. I.) of Humphrey Daye, Richard Daye, James Daye and Henry Daye, infants, by Henry Martyn and Elizabeth his wife, their guardians, to the answers of Frances Daye, widow, and Francis Daye, gent., the defendants.

Concerning the lands late of John Daye, deceased.

DEAVE v. TOMPKINS

D $\frac{3}{11}$ Replication (   ) of John Deave, complainant, to the answer of John Tompkins, the defendant.

Maintaining the bill of complaint.

DAINTY v. ROOKES

D $\frac{1}{11}$ Bill (23 April 1645) of Thomas Dainty of London, stationer, executor of the will of Robert Milborne, late of London, stationer.

Demurrer and answer (8 May 1645) of John Rookes of Wickhambrooke, co. Suffolk, gentleman, defendant, with Margaret Webster, relict and extrix. of Edward Webster of Hadley, co. Suffolk, notary public.

Concerning the debts of near 600l. of the said Robert Milborne to Thomas Goade, D.D., rector of Hadley, who died about four or five years since, to which debt the complainant hath since paid to the Doctor's executors.

DADE v. TOOPE and others

D $\frac{1}{11}$ Bill (13 May 1646) of John Dade, citizen and merchant taylor of London.

Answers (21 and 22 May 1646) of Henry Toope, Anthony Fryer and Henry Wilson.

> Concerning pipes of Canary shipped in the *George and Anthony* of London, whereof Henry Toope was master, the other defendants being his co-partners in the ship.

DAVYS *v.* JERVIS

D $\frac{1}{14}$ Bill (. . . June 1646) of William Davys of Woodford, co. Wilts, gentleman.

Answer (23 Oct. 1646) of Thomas Jervis of Wilford, co. Wilts, yeoman.

> Concerning a lease of a farm and lands in Woodford, assigned by the defendant to the complainant.

DENT *v.* SCARBOROUGH

D $\frac{1}{14}$ Bill (17 July 1641) of Marmaduke Dent of Karkyn, co. York, and James Dent his son and heir apparent, compts. against Robert Scarborough of Forcet, co. York.

> Concerning leases of closes of land called the Quarrells in Karkyn.

DAWSON *v.* DAWSON and another

D $\frac{1}{14}$ Bill (9 Feb. 164 $\frac{1}{2}$) of Joan Dawson (relict of Myles Dawson of Crostwaite, co. Westmerland, yeoman, lately deceased), complainant against Robert Dawson and his wife and John Hodgson of Cartmell fell, co. Lancaster.

> Concerning the mortgage of a copyhold messuage and lands at Dawson Fold made 31 Jan. 162$\frac{1}{2}$ by Robert Dawson of Dawson Fold in the Lithe, co. Westmerland, yeoman, to the said Myles, for the payment of 200*l.* Myles Dawson died about three years since.

DOD *v.* YARD

D $\frac{1}{14}$ Bill (20 May 1642) of Timothy Dod, clerk, and Jane his wife, late wife and extrix. of Richard Combe of London, haberdasher, deceased.

Answer (4 June 1642) of Philip Yard of London, haberdasher.

> Concerning the alleged 'unfaithfull dealinge' of the defendant with the said Richard Combe, who late was partner with him in selling hatbands at the sign of the Angel in Watling Street. Richard Combe died about three years since.

DE LA BARR *v.* WITHRINGS

D$\frac{1}{15}$ Answer, plea and demurrer (28 April 1646) of Thomas Withrings, esquire, defendant to the bill of complaint of John de la Barr.

The defendant has alleged that the complainant promised the defendant one third part of the profits of the office of postmaster for foreign parts for his using influence with the Earl of Portland, Lord Cottington and other friends at Court to procure him a restitution to the said place. The complainant also alleges that the defendant beat and wounded him whereby he fell into a fever, and was forced to keep his bed for eighteen weeks, to his damage to the amount of 1500*l.*, besides the expenses of his cure, which amounted to 220*l.* The complainant has also alleged that the defendant offered to make good these losses if the complainant would but forgive the injury 'and not publish it, especiallie to Secretary Cooke.'

DELLAWOOD *v.* HICKMAN and others

D$\frac{1}{15}$ Bill (28 Nov. 1645) of Nicholas Dellawood of London, gent.

Answers (27 Jan. 1645) of Leonard Hickman (defendant with Samuel Forrest, Nicholas Burnell, cit. and haberdasher of London, John North, Thomas Collins, Grace Slade, John Howard, Richard Smithe and Austen, widow).

Concerning the alleged sale by Nicholas Condall, late of Westminster, gent., deceased, to Samuel Forrest of London, gent., of seven messuages in Knightsbridge and Kensington, co. Middx. By indenture dated 10 June 5 Car. I. the said Condall and Forrest sold their interest in the premises to Nicholas Burnell, who was a debtor of the complainant.

DELLABARRE *v.* POWELL

D$\frac{1}{10}$ Bill (25 June 1646) of John Dellabarre of London, merchant.

Answer (6 Feb. 164$\frac{4}{5}$) of Sir Edward Powell of Fulham, co. Middx., baronet.

Concerning a capital messuage in Fenchurch Street, whereof the defendant is seised in right of his wife Dame Mary, dau. of Sir Peter Vanlore, deceased.

DEARLING *v.* BOOKER and another

D$\frac{1}{11}$ Bill (27 Nov. 1641) of John Dearling of Horsham, co. Sussex, sawyer, on behalf of himself and of John, Richard, Margaret and Hannah, his poor children.

Answers (at Lewes 7 Jan. 164$\frac{1}{2}$) of William Booker and William Alcocke of Lewes, gent., defendants.

Concerning the will dated 15 Jan. 162$\frac{1}{2}$ of John Booker of St. Johns in Lewes, co. Sussex, yeoman. By this will legacies were given to

Margaret, Mary and Elizabeth Booker, daus. of Roger Booker, brother of the testator. The testator made William Booker, his brother, his exor. William Alcocke was an overseer of the will. The said Mary and Elizabeth died young and unmarried within two or three years of their uncle's death, and the said Margaret, wife of the complainant, administered their goods.

DOWNER *v.* VECCAR

D.¹⁵₁₅ Bill (12 Nov. 1645) of George Downer of St. Katherine's Tower, London, cordwainer, and Ann his wife, complainants against Richard Veccar the elder and Richard Veccar the younger.

Concerning the estate of William Browne, deceased, late of Otford, co. Kent, father of the complainant Ann.

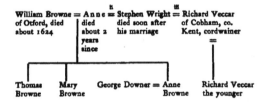

DICKENS *v.* WINDLE

D.¹⁵₁₅ Bill (5 Sep. 1645) of Walter Dickens of London, girdler.
Answer (13 Sep. 1645) of Thomas Windle of Dublin, merchant.

Concerning a sale in 1639 to the defendant of the household stuff which the complainant had in Dublin, the said complainant being about to settle in London amongst his friends and acquaintances.

DYNHAM *v.* BATHURST

D.¹⁵₁₅ Bill (6 June 1645) of Edward Dynham of London, Doctor of Physic.

Third and further answer (22 May 23 Car. I.) of George Bathurst, esquire, defendant.

Concerning the estate of Jane, the mother of the complainant, for whom and for whose six younger children the defendant was a trustee. As Jane Dynham, widow, she had a lease of land in Oakley, co. Bucks, 22 April 9 Car. I. Before 16 June 11 Car. I., she was wife of Ezekiel Pownall of Wraxall, co. Somerset, clerk. The complainant's uncle, William Dynham, is named. The defendant married a sister of the said Jane.

Dallender v. Woodman and others

D¹¹⁄₁₁ Bill (22 June 1631) of Ralph Dallender of Buckland, co. Surrey, gent.

Answer (11 Oct. 1631) of John Woodman and Edward Lawe (defendants with John Killicke of Doggets, yeoman, and Robert Woodman of Horley, yeoman).

Concerning the custom of the complainant's manor of Buckland.

Duckmanton v. Bowman

D¹⁄₁₅ Answer (26 Apr. 1620) of Isaac Bowman, defendant, to the bill of William Duckmanton.

Concerning the complainant's employment by the defendant as his 'drey clearke,' the defendant being a brewer.

Earl of Dover v. Hilton

D¹⁄₃₇ Answer (9 July, 1631) of Mary Hilton, wife of Henry Hilton, one of the defendants to the bill of Henry, Earl of Dover.

Concerning the debts of Edward Carrell, gent., deceased. The defendant was living about 8 years since in the house in Aldersgate Street of the Earl of Devonshire, her father-in-law. She is styled the Lady Hilton in a receipt dated 3 June 1624.

Delahay v. Winston

D¹⁄₁₅ Answer (26 Nov. 1631) of William Winston and Eleanor Winston, defendants to the bill of John Delahay.

Concerning the manor of Trewynt, co. Hereford, of which Robert Winston, great grandfather of the defendants, made a settlement by indenture 2 Jan. 34 Hen. VIII. before the marriage of his son Watkin with Joane Baskervile. A writing is mentioned as dated 5 Ric. II. purporting to be an entail of certain lands in Winston to Walter, the son of John Winston and the heirs of his body.

Robert Winston who was seised of the
manor of Trewyn, co. Hereford, and
by indenture 2 Jan. 34 Hen. VIII.
covenanted with Thomas Baskevile,
esq., to settle the moiety thereof upon
the marriage of his son and heir with
Jane Baskevile, and the other moiety
to the use of himself and his wife
Maude with remr. to the said Watkin
and Joan==

Watkin Winston==Joane Baskervile
son and heir   dau. of Thomas Baskervile,
                    esquire

Thomas Winston, son and heir,
died about 19 years since
==

William Winston,   Eleanor Winston,
son and heir, a   a compt.
compt.

DEWELL v. KNIGHT and others

D⁺⁺   Answers (24 June 1644) of Thomas Knight, Anne his wife, and Elizabeth Taylor *alias* Rogers to the bill of Henry Dewell, complainant.

Concerning a messuage and copyhold land in Walton-on-Thames. The said Elizabeth is relict of one Samuel Taylor, a tenant of the house.

DANIELL v. PIGOTT

D⁺⁺   Answer (21 Aug. 1646) of Richard Pigott, gent., defendant (with Richard Pigott, grocer) to the bill of John Daniell, citizen and merchant of London.

Concerning a lease to the compt. made by the defendant, who was servant to Mr. Daniel Harvy of London, merchant.

DONNE v. KINGSTON and another

D⁺⁺   Bill (10 June 1646) of Roger Donne of London, citizen and fletcher, and Jane his wife.

Answer (19 June 1646) and further answer (6 Nov. 1646) of Sarah Kingston and Samuel Snow, the defendants.

Concerning the estate of William Woofe, fletcher, deceased, whose servant the complainant was for many years. The said William by his indenture dated in August 1625 settled a rent charge out of his houses in Grub Street in St. Giles without Cripplegate upon the complainants, who were then about to be married.

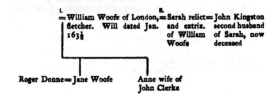

DEIRSLEY v. HAMOND and another

D.⅛ Bill (18 Feb. 164⅘) of Richard Deirsley and Thomas Deirsley his son, both of Colchester, maltsters, and John Gower of the same, brewer.

Answer (4 May 1646) of Thomas Hamond of Great Wallingfield, co. Suffolk, yeoman.

Answer (8 May 1646) of Nicholas Harsenett of Upminster, gent.

Concerning a debt of the defendant Hamond for which the complainants were sureties.

DARY v. CAREW and others

D.⅛ Bill (19 June 1646) of William Dary, Mary Dary, Katherine Dary, Mary Dary, Jane Dary and Dorcas Dary (all infants within the age of 12 years, being the six children of John Dary of Shalford, co. Surrey, husbandman, by Mary his wife, daughter and heir of John Awsten, late of Godalmyn, co. Surrey, deceased, eldest brother to William Awsten, late of Beddington, co. Surrey, yeoman) by John Dary their father and guardian.

Demurrer (   ) of William Lock, gent. (defendant with Sir Francis Carewe and his wife, Joshua Tucker, Thomas Darknoll, Gabriel Butler and Chapman).

Concerning the estate of William Awsten, deceased, who died at Beddington in January last. He had been a servant to the Carew family.

DOWNE v. RICE and others

D.⅛ Bill (8 July 1641) of John Downe of Pilton, co. Devon, gent., complainant against Philip Rice, Roger Boucher, Richard Rice.

Concerning a loan for which the complainant was surety with Hugh Dallin of Pilton, yeoman.

Downes v. Adams and another

D.$\frac{1}{11}$ Bill (14 Feb. 1644½) of John Downes, citizen and haberdasher of London.

Answers (23 Feb. 1644½) of William Adams and (14 April 1646) of Richard Freeman, son of Robert Freeman of London, esquire, deceased.

Concerning the dealings in silk of Robert Freeman and Thomas Chapman, both deceased.

Drury v. Taylor

D.$\frac{1}{16}$ Bill (8 Feb. 1644½) of William Drury of March in Ely, son and heir of Jeremy Drury late of London, grocer, deceased, complainant against Arthur Taylor.

Concerning a capital messuage or farm house with lands in Wisbich St. Maryes in Ely, whereof the complainant's father was seised, which Jeremy Drury leased the same to Arthur Taylor of Wisbich, gent., the defendant.

Dixon v. Tirrell and others

D.$\frac{1}{17}$ Bill (27 Nov. 1646) of George Dixon of Mellise, co. Suffolk, gent.

Answer (1 May 1647) of John Woods and Richard Cooper (defendants with James Tirrell of Mendham, co. Suffolk, esquire or gent.

Concerning a mortgage of copyholds in Mellis made by the complainant to the said Tirrell, as security for a loan of money which he needed to discharge parliament rates and other assessments. The complainant opens his case by declaring that he is known to be a man ' very well affected to the proceedings of this present parliament.' The complainant was heir to copyholds in the manors of Mellis, St. John's and Burgate, on the death of Nicholas Fanner, clerk, who was his uncle.

Dewies v. Allport and others

D.$\frac{1}{18}$ Bill (11 May 1646) of Isaac Dewies of Norton Mandevile, co. Essex, yeoman.

Answer (22 May 1646) of William Lock and Joseph Allport.

Concerning lands called Mayletts <i>etc.</i> in Norton Mandevile, whereof John Meade of Thaxted, gent., was seised for life as tenant by courtesy with reversion to Thomas Meade his son, son and heir of Grace Meade, late wife of the said John. The said John Meade is said to have made some estate to one Lawrence Norcott.

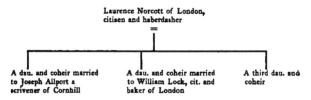

Danby and another *v.* Mawde and others

D$\frac{1}{2}\frac{1}{6}$ Bill (1 Feb. 164$\frac{3}{4}$) of Sir Thomas Danby of Farneley, co. York, knight, and Ralph Hopton of Armeley, esq., complainants against Robert Mawde of Skelton, esq., William Steile, Dorothy Smith and Mary Smith.

Concerning the prebend of Gevendale in the cathedral church of Ripon, for the purchase of which the complainant Sir Thomas Danby dealt with the said Mawde, who pretended to have a good estate of the same in fee simple.

Day and another *v.* Poynett and another

D$\frac{1}{5}\frac{1}{6}$ Bill (5 May 1646) of Thomas Day of Maighfeild, co. Sussex, yeoman, and William Hickmot the elder of Cranbrook, co. Kent, butcher.

Answer (8 May 1646) of William Poynett of Staplehurst, co. Kent, innkeeper, and Richard Brickenden of Cranbrooke, yeoman.

Concerning a suit in Nov. 1646 in the ecclesiastical court at Canterbury touching the will of Thomas Munn of Cranbrooke, butcher, deceased, admon. of whose goods was granted *pendente lite* to Dorothy his relict, who afterwards married the complainant Thomas Day, and who is now dead. Richard Brickenden was a party to the admon. bond dated 26 Sept. 20 Car. I.

Dunke *v.* Baylie

D$\frac{1}{2}\frac{1}{1}$ Bill (Feb. 164$\frac{3}{4}$) of William Dunke of Benenden, co. Kent, clothier.

Answer (30 April 1647) of Thomas Baylie of Frittenden, co. Kent, and Thomas Baylie the younger (defendants with)

Concerning a piece of marshland of the complainants in Ivychurch in Romney Marsh, and the customs of the marsh as relating to the scouring of ditches.

Dash *v.* Wheeler and others

D$\frac{1}{1}\frac{1}{1}$ Bill (9 May 1646) of John Dash of Chichester, co. Sussex weaver.

Answer (28 May 1646) of Richard Wheeler, John Hancocke, John Harding and Mary his wife, all of Newport, and Bartholomew Harris or Havant and Anne his wife.

Concerning the will dated 21 Nov. 1646 of John Hancocke late of Chichester, weaver, deceased, who was seised of a garden plot in Newport in the Isle of Wight. The said John came to be a soldier in the garrison of Chichester and was quartered in the complainant's house for a year before he died. By his will he gave the garden plot to the complainant, with remainder to Mary Dash, aged seven years, the complainant's daughter, with remainder to Nicholas Dash, complainant's son, then aged five years, with remainder to his own right heirs. The said Mary Harding alleges that John Hancocke of Newport, yeoman, father of the deceased, made a lease 27 April 1616 of the said plot for 51 years to Richard Wheeler of Newport, weaver, the said Mary's

former husband.   The said Mary is extrix. of her said former husband
and married John Harding ten years since.   The lease was given by
John Harding and his wife to Anne Wheeler, dau. of the said Mary,
who died two years after the gift, upon which the plot was given to
Richard Wheeler, eldest son of the said Richard Wheeler, deceased, by
the said Anne.   The said Anne Harris says that she is of kin to John
Hancocke the son, who about two years since left in her hands certain
writings, she being then a widow living at Havant.   The defendant
John Hancocke, eldest son known to be living of John Hancocke who
granted the lease to Richard Wheeler, hath in his custody a deed whereby
Richard Hancocke his grandfather purchased the garden plot.   This
defendant does not know whether his elder brother Richard Hancocke,
whose abode is of late beyond sea, be dead or no.

DOCTON and others v. LANGFORD

D┐   Bill (18 June 1632) of John Docton, Peter Sander, Hugh Nicholl
the elder, Hugh Nicholl the younger, Hugh Nicholl, Thomas Prist, William
Churton, John Vine, and Justinian May.
Answer (2 Oct. 1632) of Emanuel Langford, esquire, and (5 Oct. 1632)
of Elizabeth, Priscilla and Grace Langford and likewise of Mary and Julyan
Langford (defendants with Dorothy, Katherine and Amy Langford).
Concerning the will of Katherine Cary of Clovelley, co. Devon,
widow, deceased (relict of George Carie, deceased), who had four
children, viz. Henry, Mary, Alice and Julyan.   She married the said
Mary to John Arundel of Trerise, esquire, the said Alice to Emanuel
Langford, gent., and the said Julyan to Thomas Arundel, esquire
(brother of John).   She is alleged by the complainants to have made
a will 30 Dec. last past, making the said Henry Carie (who hath lived
many years in London) and John Arundel her exors. to whom she
gave all her goods.   The complainants were purchasers of part of the
goods.   The said Alice Langford hath by Emanuel Langford fifteen
children.   The said Katherine had often suits at law with William
Cary, esq., her son-in-law.   She died on New Year's Day last.   Henry
Cary her son 'for some unkind cariage and behaviour conceived by his
said mother towardes her' had not been for many years admitted to
her presence.   The defendant Langford says that the widow Cary
gave by deed of gift nearly all of her goods to eight of his daughters—
Elizabeth, Priscilla, Grace, Mary, Julyan, Dorothy, Catherine and
Amy Langford.

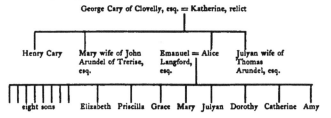

George Cary of Clovelly, esq. = Katherine, relict

Henry Cary   Mary wife of John   Emanuel = Alice   Julyan wife of
              Arundel of Trerise,   Langford,   Thomas
              esq.   esq.   Arundel, esq.

eight sons   Elizabeth Priscilla Grace Mary Julyan Dorothy Catherine Amy

DAVIES v. DAVIES and another

D$\frac{1}{16}$ Bill (24 May 1641) of Hugh Davies of Wrexham, co. Denbigh, gent.

Answer (25 June 1641) of Gwen Davies, widow, and Humfrey Lloyd, gent.

> Concerning a settlement of messuages and lands in Wrexham, made by the complainant's father David ap John Robert of Wrexham, co. Denbigh, gent. By indenture dated 2 June 13 Car. I. made between (i) the said David ap John Robert, (ii) John Everton of Chester, merchant, and Edward Nicholas of Wrexham, (iii) Bartholomew Davies (second son of David ap John Robert), (iv) Philip Davis (third son), and (v) John Davies (fourth son), the said David ap John Robert settled a messuage and lands etc. in Wrexham to the use of the said Bartholomew and Gwen his wife, after the death of the said David and Elizabeth his wife, with rem' to the heirs of the body of the said Bartholomew, with rem' to the complainant. The said Bartholomew survived his parents and died in November last past without issue.

DAVIES v. DOULBEN and others

D$\frac{1}{16}$ Bill (28 May 1641) of John Davies the elder, citizen and clothworker of London, and John Davies and Henry Davies, infants under the age of 18 years, children of the aforesaid John Davies by Margaret his wife.

Answer (7 July 1641) of William Doulben, esquire (a defendant with John Doulben and Henry Lloyd, gentlemen).

> Concerning the will of David Doulben, Lord Bishop of Bangor, dated 22 Nov. 1632 by which he gave 20l. to each descendant of his father and mother who should be living at the time of his death. The defendants are executors of this will with its codicil. The complainant's wife Margaret was one of the daughters of Henry Doulben, one of the sons of the said Robert Winn Doulben and Jane. The defendants assert that there is not enough money at present in their hands to discharge the legacies to the complainant's two sons. William Doulben the defendant is a brother, and his fellow executors nephews of the said Bishop of Bangor. They have paid 20l. legacies to Jane, Katherine, David, Elizabeth, Luce, Margaret and Jane Doulben, to Jane and Katherine Lloyd, to Jane Hughes and Hugh Peirs, to one of Morris Lloyd's children and to Hugh and Robert Doulben. The like sum is yet to be paid to Hugh, William and Jane Stoddard, Hugh Lloyd, Mary Hughes, Dorothy Hughes, Jane Doulben, John Doulben, Luce Doulben, David Doulben, Jane Doulben, Mary Doulben, Emme Doulben, John Doulben, David Doulben, Richard Doulben, Humphrey Doulben, William Doulben, John Doulben, William Doulben, David Doulben, Richard Doulben, Henry Davies and John Davies, Henry Lloyd, and to two of John Conway's children.

DUTTON v. LLOYD and another

D$\frac{1}{16}$ Bill (30 June 1631) of Sr Ralph Dutton of Standish, co. Glouc., knight.

Answer (5 Oct. 1631) of Thomas Lloyd of Wheatenhurst *alias* Whittnister, co. Glouc., gent., and of Thomas Beard, yeoman.

Concerning the complainant's water mills in Moreton Valence and in Sawle in the parish of Standish.

DYER *v.* ANDROWE and others

D⅟₇ Bill (12 May 1632) of John Dyer of Probus, co. Cornwall, yeoman.

Answer (2 Oct. 1632) of John Androwe and Philippe his wife, and Robert Bone and Jane his wife.

Concerning a tenement called Trewyns in Probus parcel of the manor of Wolvedon, which tenement, according to the complainant's case, Francis Trogyan, esquire, since deceased, by his deed indented in Jan. 14 Elizab., leased to the complainant, together with Richard Dyer his elder brother and one Joan Score, Richard's servant, for their three lives. The said Joan afterwards matched herself without her master's consent with one William Ferrys and had issue a daughter, and although only a lessee in trust, entered with her husband upon her part of the tenement, thereby oppressing the complainant and his said brother. Not content with this, about July 22 Elizab. she with her husband and daughter took a new lease in reversion of the said tenement from Sir George Cary, knight. After this the said Richard Dyer died, the complainant being then young and within years. When the complainant entered upon the tenement he was beaten and wounded by the said William Ferrys, and being vexed by suits at law was afterwards forced to submit the matter to the arbitrament of two men 'mostly of his the said Ferris owne choyse.' The defendants allege that Joan Score married with the good liking of Richard Dyer.

```
William Ferrys  ═  Joan Shore relict
whose will is   │   and extrix. died in
dated in July   │   June 1628
1607

John Androwe  ═  Philippe Ferrys, only child,
              │   extrix. of her mother's will

Robert Bone  ═  Jane Androwe
```

DYKE and another *v.* DYKE

D⅟₇ Bill (27 June 1631) of Jeremy Dyke and John Dodson, executors of William Dyke, late of London, clerk, deceased.

Answer (23 July 1631) of John Dyke of London, merchant.

Concerning the will, dated 2 July 1618, of Mary Dyke, wife of the said William Dyke, clerk, and formerly wife of John Waddis, whereby she gave to the defendant for the good of William Dyke her husband her leasehold dwelling house in Aldgate, charged with an annuity to Katherine Jackson her sister. The said William Dyke made a will 27 July 1619, whereof his son Jeremy and the said John Dodson who had married his daughter Elizabeth were executors with John Waddis and Roger Harris. The said William's other sons are named— Zachary, Nathaniel and Joseph Dyke, of whom the said Joseph is now dead.

DELL v. SHACKLEY

D$\frac{1}{13}$ Bill (20 Nov. 1632) of Joshua Dell of Saltash, co. Cornwall, merchant.

Answer (29 Nov. 1632) ot Andrew Shackley of Saltash, merchant.

Concerning certain dealings in cloves.

DYOS v. KYNASTON and others

D$\frac{1}{10}$ Bill (14 June 1631) of Richard Dyos, cousin and heir of Nicholas Dyos, deceased.

Answer (26 Sep. 1631 at Ruyton, co. Salop) of Thomas Kynaston, gent., Gilbert Fownes, gent., bailiff to the Lord Craven of the manor of Ruyton, and Edward Davies *alias* Butcher.

Concerning matters arising out of the suit which the said Nicholas Dyos brought in this court against Jeffrey Davyes, John Meyres and others touching a burgage in Ruyton, co. Salop, which the said Nicholas claimed by descent from Richard Dyos his father. The said Nicholas was uncle to the complainant, and died without issue about seven years past. The defendant Thomas Kynaston is son and heir of Richard Kynaston, deceased, and alleges that Richard Dyos the grandfather conveyed the burgage on 16 April 39 Elizabeth to his younger son George Dyos, who was then about to marry Elizabeth Hall, which Elizabeth having died without issue, the said George conveyed the burgage 20 July 44 Elizabeth to the said Richard Kynaston. The defendant Kynaston names his uncle Thomas Kynaston.

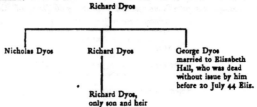

Richard Dyos

Nicholas Dyos   Richard Dyos   George Dyos married to Elizabeth Hall, who was dead without issue by him before 20 July 44 Eliz.

Richard Dyos, only son and heir

DAMMERELL v. HOLT

D$\frac{1}{61}$ Bill (11 Oct. 1631) of James Dammerell *alias* Dammeron ot Lymehouse in Stepney, mariner.

Answer (19 Oct. 1631) of Lawrence Holt, citizen and clothworker of London.

Concerning a tenement and land in Packfield, part of the estate ot Elizabeth Cox of Great Yarmouth, widow, who died seised of lands in Packfield, Kirklie, Gysland, Carlton and Covell, co. Suffolk, leaving a will dated in Nov. 44 Eliza, which was proved in the Commissary Court of Norwich by the exors. who were her son Arthur and her son-in-law John Felton, uncle in law to the complainant. The said Felton was brother to Daniel Felton, citizen and grocer of London.

```
            I.                    II.
... Dammerell = Elizabeth, who = ... Cox
alias Dammeron | survived both her
of Great Yar-  | husbands
mouth, mariner |
               |
        Arthur Dammerell = ... died soon after
        alias Dammeron   |  her husband
                         |
              James Dammerell alias
              Dammeron of Lymehouse,
              mariner
```

DOLBEN v. MIDDLETON

D$\frac{1}{8\frac{1}{3}}$ Bill (5 Nov. 1631) of Elizabeth Dolben, relict and extrix. of William Dolben, D.D., deceased.

Answer (22 Nov. 1631) of Sir Thomas Middleton, knight (defendant with John Chambers and Anne his wife).

> Concerning a bill in Chancery exhibited by the said William Dolben in Easter term last against the present defendants. The said Dolben was executor of the will and codicil of William Middleton, a merchant of London, which William, together with Sir Thomas Middleton, knight and alderman of London, lent 2000l. unto Pryamus Lloyde of Marrington, co. Salop, esquire, who with his son and heir apparent Richard Lloyde, by indenture dat. 14 March 5 Car. I. mortgaged lands in Marrington to the Middletons. The said Anne is alleged by her husband to be sister and next heir of William Middleton, deceased. The defendant Sir Thomas is son and heir of the said Sir Thomas the alderman, who is now dead.

DODINGTON v. DODINGTON

D$\frac{1}{11}$ Bill (13 Feb. 164$\frac{4}{5}$) of Anne Dodington, widow, relict of John Dodington of Breamore, co. Southampton, esquire, deceased.

Answer (2 May 1645) of Edward Dodington, esquire, younger brother of the said John.

> The complainant recites that in a treaty of marriage between herself and her late husband in Feb. 19 Car. I. in consideration of her portion of 4000l. the said John agreed to assure to her for life for her jointure manors and lands of the value of 800l. yearly, and also the said John agreed to leave her, if she survived him, either his dwelling house in the close of Sarum, or some other house fit for her quality, with its goods and household stuff. John Dodington died 5 Sept. 1644. The defendant says that the complainant, who was dau. of Sir Henry Wallopp, knight, deceased, and sister to Robert Wallopp, esquire, was married to his brother 14 March 164$\frac{4}{5}$. The said John left a will dated 1 July 1644. The defendant denies that the promised jointure was of the amount of 800l. yearly, or that his brother promised to leave his widow the house in the close of Sarum. The said John gave the said house by will to his only child Anne Dodington. The defendant names Sir William Dodington, knight,

K

deceased, as father of himself and the said John. He also names Mr. Hoby, Mr. [? John] Buckley and Mr. Hanham, as brothers-in-law of himself and the said John.

Douglas v. Norwood and others

D$\frac{1}{2\frac{1}{5}}$ Bill (4 Nov. 1645) of William Douglas of London, merchant, using the trade of a merchant to Virginia and elsewhere.

Answer and demurrer (11 Nov. 1645) of William Thompson and William Webster (defendants with Thomas Norwood and Nicholas Wallis).

Concerning the debts of the said Norwood to the complainant.

Davenport v. Franke

D$\frac{1}{2\frac{1}{5}}$ Bill (12 May 1645) of James Davenport of St. Martins in the fields, esquire, executor of the will of Joan Wells, widow, deceased.

Answer (16 May 1645) of Sir Leventhorpe Franke, knight.

Concerning a mortgage by the defendant and Dame Lucy his wife of copyholds in the manor of Hallingbury Bourchiers in Essex to the said Joan Wells, of whom the defendant had taken up 500l. at interest.

Dunn v. Howland and others

D$\frac{1}{2\frac{1}{5}}$ Bill (11 Nov. 1645) of Edward Dunn of St. George's, Southwark, co. Surrey, combmaker, and Martha his wife.

Answer (19 Nov. 1645) of Sir John Howland, knight (defendant with George Duncombe, esquire, and other unnamed).

Concerning messuages and lands in Streatham, copyholds of the manor of Totingbecke, co. Surrey, whereof Martin Cann, citizen and cloth-worker of London, was seised.

A FAMILY OF LAWYERS

To face page 142

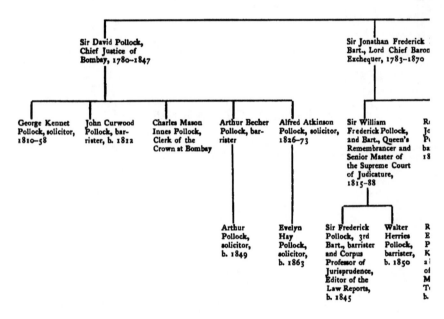

Davi
d. 1

Sir David Pollock,
Chief Justice of
Bombay, 1780–1847

Sir Jonathan Frederick
Bart., Lord Chief Baron
Exchequer, 1783–1870

George Kennet
Pollock, solicitor,
1810–58

John Curwood
Pollock, bar-
rister, b. 1812

Charles Mason
Innes Pollock,
Clerk of the
Crown at Bombay

Arthur Becher
Pollock, bar-
rister

Alfred Atkinson
Pollock, solicitor,
1826–73

Sir William
Frederick Pollock,
2nd Bart., Queen's
Remembrancer and
Senior Master of
the Supreme Court
of Judicature,
1815–88

R
Jo
Po
ba
18

Arthur
Pollock,
solicitor,
b. 1849

Evelyn
Hay
Pollock,
solicitor,
b. 1863

Sir Frederick
Pollock, 3rd
Bart., barrister
and Corpus
Professor of
Jurisprudence,
Editor of the
Law Reports,
b. 1845

Walter
Herries
Pollock,
barrister,
b. 1850

R
E
P
K
a
o
M
T
b.

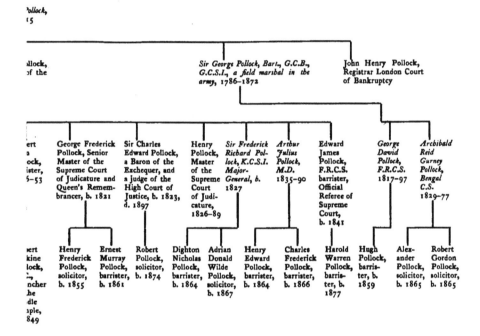

Pollock,
15

llock,
of the

Sir George Pollock, Bart., G.C.B., G.C.S.I., a field marshal in the army, 1786–1872

John Henry Pollock, Registrar London Court of Bankruptcy

ert
a
ock,
ister,
5–53

George Frederick Pollock, Senior Master of the Supreme Court of Judicature and Queen's Remembrancer, b. 1821

Sir Charles Edward Pollock, a Baron of the Exchequer, and a judge of the High Court of Justice, b. 1823, d. 1897

Henry Pollock, Master of the Supreme Court of Judicature, 1826–89

Sir Frederick Richard Pollock, K.C.S.I. Major-General, b. 1827

Arthur Julius Pollock, M.D. 1835–90

Edward James Pollock, F.R.C.S. barrister, Official Referee of Supreme Court, b. 1841

George David Pollock, F.R.C.S. 1817–97

Archibald Reid Gurney Pollock, Bengal C.S. 1829–77

ert
kine
lock,
—,
ncher
he
dle
ple,
849

Henry Frederick Pollock, solicitor, b. 1855

Ernest Murray Pollock, barrister, b. 1861

Robert Pollock, solicitor, b. 1874

Dighton Nicholas Pollock, barrister, b. 1864

Adrian Donald Wilde Pollock, solicitor, b. 1867

Henry Edward Pollock, barrister, b. 1864

Charles Frederick Pollock, barrister, b. 1866

Harold Warren Pollock, barrister, b. 1877

Hugh Pollock, barrister, b. 1859

Alexander Pollock, solicitor, b. 1865

Robert Gordon Pollock, solicitor, b. 1865

SEAL OF RICHARD NEVILL, EARL OF WARWICK.

SEAL OF RICHARD NEVILL, EARL OF WARWICK.

THE ARMS OF THE KING-MAKER

THE seal of Richard, Earl of Warwick, better known as the King-maker, of which an illustration is given opposite, is believed to be the only impression of which the existence is known. It is attached to a document of no intrinsic importance, which bears the autograph of the earl, 'R. Warrewyk,' and of which the date is Feb. 1, 1465 (4 Edw. IV.)[1] This document, with its seal, was known to the great Camden, which suggests that even in his day it was deemed remarkable and rare. It appears to have been lost sight of subsequently till re-discovered by myself in a loft above the stables at Birch Hall, the residence of the Right Hon. James Round, who has allowed it to be photographed for *The Ancestor*. It may be remembered that among the documents similarly found at Belvoir in a loft over the stables, by Sir Henry Maxwell-Lyte, was one which similarly bore the King-maker's autograph. The impression, fortunately, is a very fine one, every link in the chain of the muzzled bear of Warwick being clearly visible, as is also the ermine of the Newburgh chevron and the differencing of the label on the coat of Nevill. Mr. St. John Hope has drawn my attention to the fact that Drummond's *Noble Families* contains a poor engraving of the seal apparently from another impression, but the photograph of it which is here given is taken from a cast specially made to secure exactitude of illustration.

A short chart pedigree is needed to explain the description which follows.

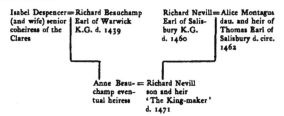

Isabel Despencer = Richard Beauchamp
(2nd wife) senior | Earl of Warwick
coheiress of the | K.G. d. 1439
Clares

Richard Nevill = Alice Montagu
Earl of Salis- | dau. and heir of
bury K.G. | Thomas Earl of
d. 1460 | Salisbury d. circ.
| 1462

Anne Beau- = Richard Nevill
champ even- | son and heir
tual heiress | 'The King-maker'
| d. 1471

[1] It thus belongs to the close of his period of greatest power, during which he was 'much more prominent than the King,' while 'foreign observers looked on him as the real ruler of England.'

The special interest of this fine seal consists in its combination, in marshalling, crests, and supporters, of the King-maker's paternal earldom of Salisbury with his wife's earldom of Warwick. The muzzled bear of Warwick forms the dexter supporter, the griffin of Salisbury the sinister, unless this griffin is the sinister supporter shown on the seal of his wife's father's arms facing the muzzled bear. So also with the crests. In the last volume of *The Ancestor* illustrations were given (pp. 170, 174) of the garter-plates, from Mr. St. John Hope's book, of the earl's father Richard (Nevill), Earl of Salisbury, and of his wife's father Richard (Beauchamp), Earl of Warwick, and their seals are here reproduced, by Mr. Hope's permission, from the same source. It will be observed that both their crests figure on the King-maker's seal—on the dexter side the swan's head, the crest of the Earl of Warwick, on the sinister the sitting griffin of the Earl of Salisbury.

The marshalling of the arms is more complicated. The earl's father Richard Nevill, who was a younger son, having married the heiress of the Earls of Salisbury, and becoming, in consequence, Earl of Salisbury himself, placed her arms (Montague quartering Monthermer) in the first and fourth quarters of his shield, relegating his own paternal coat, Nevill differenced with a label gobony, to the second and third. But on one of his two seals here illustrated his paternal coat is also shown on a separate escutcheon on the dexter side, and that of Longespée, Earl of Salisbury (of an entirely distinct line), on the sinister.

But his contemporary the Earl of Warwick, father of the King-maker's wife, adopted another principle. In accordance with modern practice he placed on his own shield, which was Beauchamp quartering Newburgh (the arms of the earldom of Warwick[1]), an escutcheon of pretence with the arms of his second wife, the sole heiress of the Despencers, who were senior coheirs of the Clares, Earls of Gloucester. It should be noted that in her case the chevrons of Clare take precedence in the first quarter of her paternal coat of Despencer.

It was probably because she brought to her husband land only that her arms are merely placed on an escutcheon of pretence, instead of being incorporated as the first quarter of

---

[1] The earldom of Warwick descended from Newburgh [Neufbourg] to Beauchamp through Mauduit. I describe the above coat as 'the arms of the Earldom of Warwick' because it is variously attributed (see Papworth, p. 374).

the shield, as would doubtless have been done if she had
brought him an earldom. The escutcheon of pretence is
similarly seen on the shield of the earl's contemporary, Lord
Montague, a younger brother of the King-maker, who so
dealt with the arms of his wife, an Ingoldsthorpe heiress.

Now, how were all these coats, seven in number, to be
marshalled on the King-maker's seal? His equestrian seal, of
which the *matrix*, taken, it is said, from his body when he fell
at Barnet field, is now in the British Museum, displays a
peculiar arrangement. The photograph of it here given, from
a cast taken for the purpose, shows the arms of Nevill (differenced) alone on his shield, and the crest of Beauchamp alone
on his helm, while the trappers of his horse display in front
the arms of the earldom of Salisbury and those of the earldom
of Warwick behind. But on the heraldic seal we see that he
has, broadly speaking, adopted the same principle as his father;
that is to say, he has given to his wife's arms the place of
honour in the first and fourth quarters, while relegating his
own to the second and third. But instead of placing the
whole of his own in each of these quarters he has placed in
the second his mother's arms, those of the earldom of Salisbury,
and in the third his father's, namely Nevill differenced. I doubt
if there was any reason for this beyond the obvious difficulty,
indeed the impossibility, of engraving his mother's quarterly
coat in what would have been not a fourth but a sixteenth
part of the shield. When we turn to the arrangement of his
wife's arms we are confronted by a difficulty of another kind.
According at least to our modern notions, the quarterly coat
of her father and the quarterly coat of her mother should have
been combined in a quarter showing the four coats. But this
simple arrangement was not adopted. Two of the coats were
marshalled quarterly in the first quarter, and the other two
quarterly in the fourth. But instead of keeping to the right
combinations, Beauchamp quartering Newburgh, which was her
father's coat, and Clare quartering Despencer, which was her
mother's coat, Beauchamp was unnaturally made to quarter the
arms of the Clares, and Newburgh, still more unnaturally, to
quarter those of the Despencers, a house with which the
Newburghs had nothing to do.

The interest of all this is that it shows us the designer
feeling his way, as it seems to me, towards a system of
quartering. He wished to assign to the wife's arms the first

and fourth quarters as the place of honour, but he could not adopt what to our minds was the simplest way of doing so. So he picked out for his first quarter the first quarter of her father's coat and the first quarter of her mother's, as being the most important, and relegated the others to the fourth quarter. The result, heraldically, made nonsense, but at least it is more interesting nonsense than the fearful monstrosities of later days in which families have vied with one another in constructing a kind of heraldic 'crazy quilt.' For every one of the coats quartered by Richard Nevill was that of a family actually represented either by himself or by his wife.

But even as 'the last of the barons' was the first, it has been well said, who possessed a train of artillery, so we trace even in his seal a falling off from the heraldic art, still medieval in spirit, seen in those of the previous generation here illustrated. And in his arms as given on the Rows Roll we note a sharper fall; the new heraldry is already rudely displacing the old.

The picture from the Rows Roll, made in the time of Richard III., shows a lamentable falling off from the armory of the seals, an armory speaking of facts, of lordships and high seigniories in the grasp of the great earls. The arms upon the Rows Roll show the coat of Montagu, quartered in one case with Monthermer and Nevill and in the other with Monthermer, Nevill and Francis, impaling a welter of coats in which quarters for 'the Erles Warrewyk in the Britons dayes' and 'Syr Guy at the batell of Wynchester,' when he smote the giant Dane, find themselves shouldering the actualities of Beauchamp, Tony, Despenser and Clare.

At the lady's feet lies the bear of Beauchamp, at her lord's the Nevill bull with the Monthermer eagle perched on his quarters. It will be noted that although heraldry as a silly science is beginning to feel its way, the good Rows who had seen many a knight in his plates does not attempt to fill the shield upon the earl's arm with more quarters than those of Montagu and Monthermer.[1]

One more point. In the legend of this seal there is but one addition to the style 'Earl of Warwick,' and that is 'dominus de Bergevveny.'[2] The latter was a territorial title,

---

[1] These two paragraphs describing the illustration from the Roll are contributed by the Editor.

[2] This is distinctly the reading in the legend, but it is perhaps an engraver's error, for in the document the form of the name is 'Bergevenny.'

THE ROWS ROLL.

SEAL OF RICHARD BEAUCHAMP, EARL OF WARWICK

SEAL OF RICHARD NEVILL, EARL OF SALISBURY.

SEAL OF JOHN NEVILL, LORD MONTAGUE.

the earl's wife having succeeded her father and brother in the possession of Abergavenny under a family entail. On his equestrian seal the secondary title is 'domini Glamorgancie et Morgan',' Glamorgan having descended from the Clares through his wife's ancestors the Despencers, the arms of both which families are so prominent on his seals. The same double style is found on a seal of his father-in-law Richard, Earl of Warwick (1436), in right of his wife Isabel Despencer, whose ancestor Edward, Lord Despencer, had styled himself Lord of Glamorgan and Morgannock in his will (1375). Neither in the heraldic nor in the equestrian seal is the earl styled Earl of Salisbury, although in the document to which the former is attached he adopts the quasi-regal style ' *Nos Ricardum Neville Comitem Warrewici et Sar'.*' He had succeeded to the latter dignity some five years before, at his father's death, in 1460.

J. HORACE ROUND.

FAMILY HISTORY IN THE PUBLIC RECORDS

IN our first number we spoke of the value for family history of the information which is steadily being brought to light in the noble Calendars of Rolls now being issued by the Public Record Office. The latest volume of the Close Rolls Calendar (1279-88) contains the abstract of the following interesting deed :—

> Enrolment of grant by Stephen de Grandon, brother and heir of Ralph de Grandon, to Laura, daughter of Laurence de Scaccario, whom Ralph married at St. Botulph's church, Colchester, on the morrow of the Epiphany 6 Edward (7 Jan. 1277/8), of all the manor of Levelaund, co. Kent, and all the manor of Bolemere, co. Essex, with which manors Ralph dowered Laura at the door of the church when he married her : to have for life in dower in accordance with Ralph's deed.

On turning to the standard County Histories, Hasted's Kent and Morant's Essex, we can find no mention of the Grandon family under either of the places named. But when we examine closely Morant's account of Bulmer, we find that one of its manors was named Grandon-hall, though he could neither explain its name, or tell us anything about its early history. This was clearly the manor referred to in the deed above. So too, though Hasted's account appears to preclude any connexion between the Grandon family and Leveland, the *Archæologia Cantiana* (xii. 218) contains a list of the 'Holders of Fees in Kent, 38 Henry III.' (1253–4), in which we read that Ralph de 'Crendone' holds one fee in Levelonde of the Archbishop (of Canterbury).

Laurence 'de Scaccario' was sheriff of Essex from the 4th to the 7th Edward I., and died 12 Edward I. (1283-4) seised of the manor of Twinsted, which parish is adjacent to Bulmer. St. Botolph's church, at the door of which, in accordance with the practice of the time, the dower was granted, belonged to the Augustinian Priory of St. Botolph, and its ruins are now among the sights of Colchester. It is of course extremely rare to find the place and date of a marriage in this class of life recorded at so early a date.

J. HORACE ROUND.

THE RECORDS OF COLCHESTER [1]

A MONG our great collections of local records still await-
ing exploration that of the Borough of Colchester occupies
a leading place.   But an admirable start has been made in the
volume which is the subject of this notice, and for which we
are indebted to the industry and the enterprise of Mr. Gurney
Benham, who has himself filled the mayor's chair in the ancient
borough on the Colne.   The miscellaneous documents entered
on the folios of the *Red Paper Book* illustrate not only municipal institutions, but the social life of the old world from the
days of Henry III. to those of Edward VI.   Colchester was
in no sense one of those towns which owed its origin to a
religious house, but the great Benedictine Abbey of St. John,
on the rising ground to the south beyond the Roman walls,
looms large throughout the pages of the *Red Paper Book*.   For
town and abbey were ever at strife, wrangling most as to juris-
diction, racing even to hold inquests on corpses found on
disputed ground.   To the accident of a burglarious entry
effected through the refectory window in 1345 we are indebted for a knowledge of the fact that the monks were not
content with wooden mazers only, for ten silver cups and
twenty-five silver spoons formed part of the booty.   St. John's
was not the only religious house at Colchester, as we are
reminded by a record which is of interest to the genealogist.
This is a list of the inhabitants of Colchester who took the
oath under the Act of Succession in 1534, an oath which was
made an instrument for testing the loyalty of the nation.   In
each parish the rector's name is followed by those of his parishioners, which gives a useful clue for searching parish registers.
At the end of this list are the names of the canons of St.
Botolph's Priory and the monks of St. John's who took the
oath, a matter, we may explain, of some consequence, for it
involved the rejection of the Pope's authority.

The genealogist will also welcome the long list of burgesses

---

[1] *The Red Paper Book of Colchester.*   By W. Gurney Benham (privately
published).

admitted to the freedom of the borough in the fifteenth century, and such documents as the wills of John Elys (1485) and Matthew Rede (1517). The former directs that three images, those of St. Helen, St. Margaret, and St. John the Baptist (his own name was John, and his wife's Margaret, while St. Helen was the patron saint of the town), should be placed on the east gate ; and the latter is a long document mentioning testator's children, among whom are 'Margarete Aleyn' and 'yonge Margarete.' Of special interest is the long account of the dispute as to the will of William Bury in 1492. 'John Dixwell gentylman and Kateryne his wiffe, doughter and heir of William Bury of Colchester gentilman,' complained to the bailiffs that they were wronged in the matter of this will. Their witnesses deposed that, about twenty years before, they were present by William's deathbed when the man of law arrived in the person of 'oone Benett Popy, a lettrid man, and being in singlier favour with the said William Bury,' who came bringing 'pen, ynke, and papier with hym.' But William appears to have died before he had done more than bequeath his body to be buried in St. John's Abbey 'besid the grave of his secound wiffe,' and it was alleged that his will which was entered on the court rolls of the borough was not genuine. Hence the complaints of his daughter and her husband as 'like to suffre wrongfull disheritauns of maners, lands and tenements.' Among the documents here printed are some which prove clearly that the freedom of the borough could be claimed, in the fifteenth century, by any man born and baptized within its borders. In case of dispute evidence as to the christening was called for, and the godfathers questioned.

The passion for litigation in Tudor times and the mischief it often wrought receive curious illustration in the tale of Nicholas Moore and his doings (1548). This man was a scrivener, who practised with his clients to stir up 'very many old and blynd titles and suytes,' trusting to champerty for his gains. So effectually did he set the whole town by the ears that its 'ruyne' could only be averted by 'the infinit mercy of God,' and by promptly expelling Nicholas from the borough, a measure resolved on at a special assembly of the whole Council. Mr. Benham's task has been no easy one, for the volume, though now well cared for, has suffered much in the past, and the text is in a bad state. But his patience has

triumphed over many difficulties, and he has further earned
our gratitude by a copious index to the names of places and
persons. We trust that this volume, of which only seventy-
five copies have been issued, may be followed by others
dealing with the contents of the borough record-room.

J. HORACE ROUND.

EARLY LANCASHIRE RECORDS[1]

The north-western counties of Cumberland, Westmorland and Lancashire present to the historian greater difficulty in
their early history than any others.   For it was not till well on
into the twelfth century that they assumed their present forms
and definitely became counties.   A further complication is introduced in the case of Lancashire by the difference between
the county as a geographical expression and the great fief
named after it owing to community of feudal tenure.   Even
to-day this complication is roughly represented by the co-exist-
ence of the County of Lancashire and the sovereign's Duchy
of Lancaster.

Mr. Farrer, whose work on Lancashire fines and whose
edition of the Cockersand Cartulary have already proved him a
notable recruit to that band of workers who have done so much
for the history of the north of England, has set himself here
to show us what it is possible to learn from the sure evidence
of records as to Lancashire lords and lands for some hundred
and fifty years after the date of Domesday.   The larger portion
of the volume consists of the text of the Pipe Rolls, with Mr.
Farrer's notes on them ; for instead of publishing the bare text
as Mr. Hodgson did for Northumberland, and Mr. Hodgson
Hinde for Cumberland and Westmorland, he has added elaborate annotations.   Stapleton did this for the early Rolls of
Normandy, but made his work a distracting one to use by
separating the introduction from the Rolls.   Mr. Farrer has
wisely appended his notes to the roll of each year, so that they

---

[1] *The Lancashire Pipe Rolls of* 1130 *and* 1155–1216, *the Latin text extended and
notes added ; also early Lancashire charters of the period from the reign of William
Rufus to that of King John.* By William Farrer (Liverpool : Young & Sons).

are given in a form most convenient to the student. But the second portion of the volume is the most novel in conception. Eyton, it is true, did something of the kind for the William Salt Society in his ' Staffordshire Chartulary,' but it is doubtful if so remarkable a collection of charters as this has been made for any county. Having worked in the same field myself I rejoice to see the importance and illustrative value of these documents for county history recognized, and am glad to find that Mr. Farrer has followed the method I adopted in my *Early Charters* (1888).[1]

In a brief introduction to the volume Mr. Farrer sketches for his readers the history of the county down to the reign of Henry III. ; and an appendix at the end of the Pipe Rolls contains an analysis of the manors constituting the Honour, with their issues and their fate. From the striking coloured map which forms the frontispiece to the volume, and depicts the feudal tenures of the county in 1212, to the noble index at its close, the contents are a very treasure-house for the topographer and the genealogist.

The history of the present county in early times is briefly recapitulated in Mr. Farrer's introduction. On the eve of the Norman Conquest it was divided into two portions, of which the southern was known as the land ' between Mersey and Ribble,' while the northern extended from the Ribble to the Duddon (which was then the boundary of Cumbria), and included what was afterwards to become, as the barony of Kendal, a part of Westmorland. This northern portion had been attached to the kingdom of Northumbria, was held by Harold's brother, Earl Tostig of Northumberland, and is surveyed in Domesday Book under Yorkshire. An exceedingly difficult problem is presented to the Domesday student by the vast fief of Roger ' the Poitevin' and its tenure at the time of the Survey. Mr. Farrer's conclusions on this subject are as follows :—

Upon the subjugation of the north by the Conqueror, all Lancashire from the Mersey to the Duddon was bestowed upon Roger, son of Roger de Montgomery, commonly called ' the Poitevin,' who also received Bowland and a large estate in Craven, in the county of York. Count Roger was probably put in possession in the year 1068. Within a few years he was dispossessed, on account of his participation in the rebellious acts of Duke Robert of Normandy during

[1] In the Pipe Roll Society's publications, namely that of printing at the foot of each charter notes on its contents, its witnesses, and its probable date.

the period 1077–8. Subsequently William Rufus returned to him his estates in Lancashire, or the greater part of them. . . . In 1102 he again adhered to Duke Robert . . . with the result that he and his father's house were finally banished from the kingdom and his estates confiscated.

Domesday, however, speaks of a portion of his vast estates as if they were still in his possession, while another portion is entered as having formerly been his. Mr. Farrer holds that ' it was during the twelve years which followed the Count's final expulsion that Henry I. incorporated the Honour of Lancaster,' but this statement and the others by which it is immediately followed appear to me to be open to some question. Let us take them in order.

[1] In 1114–6 the newly incorporated Honour with a quota of service to the military host of some sixty odd knights, was bestowed by King Henry upon his nephew Stephen who had already succeeded to the Comtes of Boulogne and Mortain.

Here we touch national history, to say nothing of the de-volution of mighty fiefs. Yet what is our sole evidence ? Merely the Lindsey Survey, which proves that Stephen was, at its date, already in possession of the lands which Roger had held in that district. It does not tell us at what date Henry bestowed them on him, and its own date is matter of question ; for though Mr. Eyton and Mr. Chester Waters had estab-lished it to their satisfaction as 1114–6, it would be more correct to assign it to 1115–8.[1] Moreover, Stephen had certainly not succeeded at that early date to the *comté* of Bou-logne (the heiress of which he married) ; and this correction affects, we shall find, the date of one at least of Mr. Farrer's documents. To continue :—

[2] Count Stephen, thus holding the Honour by his uncle's gift, continued in possession after his accession to the Crown in 1135, until the troublous period of 1138–1141. In the former year he gave all Lancashire north of the Ribble to David King of Scots, as part of the price of peace, after the latter's victorious campaign, undertaken in pursuit of his alleged title to Cumberland and Northumberland (see pp. 274 and 297). In the latter year as a result of his defeat and capture at the battle of Lincoln he gave the whole Honour of Lancaster—with the exception of the Montbegon fee—and Lancashire between the Ribble and the Mersey to Ranulf, Earl of Chester, under circumstances which are fully detailed in the following pages (see pp. 368 *et seq.*).

I must venture to point out, in the first place, that the cam-paign which ended in David's rout at ' the Battle of the Standard '

---

[1] *Feudal England*, p. 189.

on Cowton Moor can hardly be described as ' victorious ' ; in
the second, that the treaty with David took place, not in 1138,
but in April 1139 ; in the third, that this treaty mentions
only the earldom of Northumberland, and says nothing of
Lancashire ; in the fourth, that Mr. Farrer here contradicts
himself, for the two interesting charters (pp. 274–5) to which
he refers us as belonging to the period of David's dominion in
Lancashire are both dated by him as ' *circa* 1136–8,' that is, as
belonging to the period previous to the treaty which put
David, he holds, in possession of north Lancashire. The
point is one of considerable interest, for David's acquisition
of this region, established by Mr. Farrer's charters, appears to
have been hitherto overlooked. An additional reason for not
assigning that acquisition to the treaty of 1139 is that the
earldom of Northumberland was demanded throughout, and
obtained, not for David, but for Henry his son, who issued
charters as its earl.

Next, as to the grant to Ranulf, Earl of Chester, Mr. Farrer
here again, I fear, contradicts himself. On referring to the
page cited we find the grant in question dated December 1140
(pp. 367–8), while the Battle of Lincoln, as Mr. Farrer knows
(p. 369), did not take place till 1141. Moreover, on page 4 we
find the charter similarly assigned to 'early in December,
1140.' This, it will be seen, upsets the whole argument.
Lastly, the language used in this grant to the earl requires
to be exactly given on account of its important bearing on
the status of the county and the Honour at the time. The
words are :—

(1) Et totam terram Rogeri Pictavis a Northampton' usque in Scotiam,
excepta terra Rogeri de Monte Begonis in Lincolnshire (*sic*). Dedit eciam
idem Rex eidem Comiti hereditarie (2) honorem de Lancastre cum perti-
nentiis suis et (3) totam terram deinter Ribliam et Mersam, etc., etc. (p. 368).

It appears to me that in the passage quoted above from
the introduction, Mr. Farrer has rolled up three grants into
two, although they are separate in the charter. What was
here the ' honor de Lancastre,' the subject of the second clause ?
Was it not that ' honor Lancastriæ ' which David speaks of in
both his charters, and which represents, Mr. Farrer holds,
Lancashire north of the Ribble, the sphere of David's dominion ? As he has himself clearly explained in his notes to the
Pipe Roll of 1182 (p. 47), the Northern Circuit arranged in
1179 comprised, with other counties, (1) the land ' Inter Rible

et Mersesee,' and (2) 'Loncastre.' On this he observes that 'the nomenclature and divisions of the Domesday Survey were still in use.' It appears to me that they were similarly in use at the intervening period when Stephen made the above grant to Earl Ranulf, and that, consequently, the district north of the Ribble was included in that grant. It is only 'after 1182' that the two portions into which was divided the Lancashire of to-day begin to be 'described as a shire,' and 'it may be said that in 1182 the two ancient divisions, viz. "the land between the Ribble and the Mersey" and "Lancaster," were finally united in name under the style of "Lancashire"' (p. xvii.), the river Lyme being adopted as the boundary of the county.

If Mr. Farrer had done no more than continue the printing of the Pipe Rolls beyond 1175, the limit of the Pipe Roll Society's publications, to the close of John's reign, he would have earned our gratitude, but his notes add greatly to their interest and value. Particularly useful, it seems to me, is the list of outlying manors in other counties farmed with the Honour of Lancaster under Henry II. While treating of this portion one may question whether the status of the thegns was 'distinctly servile in character.' Certain customary services were due from their lands, but these were not technically of a 'servile' character. The 'Radchenistri' on the Welsh border were liable to similar work.

It is when we turn to the collection of charters that the value of the evidence here printed for local family history becomes most apparent. The pedigree, for instance, of the Hoghtons of Hoghton is here carried back through Adam de Hocton to his grandfather 'Hamo Pincerna', who received a moiety of Heaton in Lonsdale in frank marriage with the daughter of Warine Bussel, who lived in the early years of the twelfth century. Indeed a single charter gives us three generations of the Hoghtons in that century. Here we have an excellent instance of what *The Ancestor* hopes to achieve namely, not mere destruction but the substitution of truth for error. I had to show in a paper on 'The Companions of the Conqueror,'[1] that the account of the origin of this family which found its way into *Burke's Peerage* in 1900 was not only wildly wrong, but could actually be shown to relate to

[1] *Monthly Review*, June, 1901, p. 109.

a family of another name, not in Lancashire, but in Norfolk. Now Mr. Farrer's work enables us to give the true origin and to show how ancient it is.

Exactly similar is the case of Molyneux. In the article of which I have spoken I dealt with the Battle 'roll,' and cited from *Burke's Peerage* this amazing passage :—

William de Molines, one of the Norman nobles in the train of the Conqueror, stands in the eighteenth order upon the roll of Battle Abbey.[1]

The surname of 'Molines' is wanting as a fact, according to the late Duchess of Cleveland, in all the copies of the roll ; and even if it had been there, it would have been worthless as evidence. Nor, as Mr. Farrer points out, is the name of 'Molyneux' the same. The latter is derived not from Moulins, but from Moulineaux. But if we cannot take the house back to the battle of Hastings, Mr. Farrer holds that we can trace its pedigree, and even its possession of that Sefton from which the title of its earldom is derived, to the days of William Rufus, when its founder received from Roger of Poitou the moiety of a knight's fee.

The earliest charter, it appears, in which the name is found is that of Stephen, here printed, by which he grants to Robert de 'Moliness' and 'his heir' his land in Down Litherland for fourteen shillings a year. Mr. Farrer dates this charter '*circa* 1114–1116,' but this date involves a double fallacy. It is based on the assumptions that Stephen, who makes this grant as Count of Boulogne and Mortain, obtained the Honour of Lancaster in 1114, and that he already possessed those styles at that date. I have shown above that these are errors ; and as Stephen seems to be first styled Count of Boulogne in 1125, I think that this charter cannot be of earlier date. Mr. Farrer rightly hesitates to accept a 'Vivian de Mulinaus' as the first feoffee of Sefton (*temp.* William Rufus), pointing out that the incorrect pedigree drawn up by William Dethick, Garter, 20 July, 1589, makes him father of an Adam who released land to Cockersand Abbey, that abbey not being founded till about 1184. But in any case it is clear that Molyneux of Sefton is among the oldest of our Norman houses.

On a famous Lancashire name, that of the Lathoms of

[1] *Monthly Review*, June, 1901, p. 96. This passage is duly repeated in the 1902 edition of 'Burke.'

Lathom, Mr. Farrer has something to say. He finds their founder, Robert son of Henry, occurring on the Pipe Roll of 1169. The Singleton family can be traced, it seems, a little further back ; for a charter of *circa* 1155, here printed, confirms to their ancestor Uchtred son of Huck eight bovates in Broughton in Amounderness for eight shillings a year. One of the witnesses of this charter is Roger son of Ravenkil, to whom Mr. Farrer is 'inclined to attribute a Scandinavian origin, as the descendant of one of the Norse invaders who descended upon the coast of Lancashire in the tenth century.' He is here identified as son of a Raghanald, thegn of Lytham, Bootle and Woodplumpton, and as father of the Richard who founded Lytham Priory and lived under Henry II. and Richard I. Another ancient local family now represented in the peerage is that of Pennington, of which the founder Gamel, living about the middle of the twelfth century, bore one of the interesting names found in this district among thegns of native origin.

When we turn to a well-known baronial house of alien extraction, Mr. Farrer's work appears to me not quite so satisfactory. He cannot tell us whether the Montbegons' fief of Hornby was 'created by Roger the Poictevin, by Henry I. or by Count Stephen after he received the Honour of Lancaster'; nor, as I understand, does he carry back that family beyond the Lindsey survey, in which it is found about the middle of the reign of Henry I. holding lands in Lincolnshire. Yet Roger de Montbegon and his wife were already holding lands 'between Ribble and Mersey' under William Rufus, and although no one, it would seem, has observed the fact, Robert de Montbegon occurs in Domesday Book. Again, we read, on page 146, of Roger de Montbegon giving the enormous sum of £500 (should it not be 500 marcs ?) in 1199, for ' Olive, the widow of Robert de St. John, with her estate in co. York,' but there is no mention of the fact that she was an heiress in her own right and of exceptionally interesting origin.[1]

In glancing through these pages one cannot help observing a certain number of such slips as are apt to creep into a work dealing with so many facts, names and dates. The important charter of Richard I. to Gilbert Fitz Reinfred was renewed,

[1] See my *Studies in Peerage and Family History*, pp. vii. 127.

according to Mr. Farrer, 'at Châlus, on March 5th in the
10th year, 1199, exactly one month before his death from
a wound sustained in the siege of that town' (p. 398). This,
if accurate, would overthrow the statements of all the chroniclers. But 'Castrum Liddi' was not Châlus ; it was Château-
du-Loir, between Tours and Le Mans, far away to the north,
and this charter is of extreme importance as evidence of
Richard's whereabouts at the date of its grant. Three pages
further on (p. 401), another renewal of a charter under
Richard's second seal is attributed (rightly, I think) by Mr.
Farrer to the same occasion, but wrongly to Châlus. And
the old belief as to the second seal coming into use in 1194
is there repeated on Dr. Stubbs' authority, although I have
admittedly disproved it in my *Feudal England*. The assertion
that 'Henry Duke of Normandy, son of the Empress Matilda,
had been elected Sovereign at Winchester on April 8th, 1141'
(p. 4), is, I must confess, startling.

Among minor points one may note that Faramus was not
a 'Norman' baron (p. 308), that on page 302 'Campuauene' is
not represented by Campagny, while 'Oisiuelini' should be
read 'Oismelini.' On page 315 John is made to speak of
Henry I. as 'his grandfather,' though the charter has 'proavi,'
and on the next page Haughley, the head of a great Honour, is
wrongly placed in Essex instead of in Suffolk. Farnham Royal
is in Bucks, not in Leicestershire (p. 297), and a difficulty
about the abbots of Evesham, in Norman times, on page 321,
has been duly dealt with by General Wrottesley and in the
Introduction to Domesday in the *Victoria History of Worcestershire*. 'Graham,' one may add, is Grantham, not Greetham,
Lincs (p. 369).

These however are but small points. What is really
serious is the error as to the charter constituting the Preston
guild merchant, of which the local festivities have reminded
us this very year. By combining an entry on the Pipe Roll
of 1175 (p. 43) with the charter of Henry II. on pages 412-3,
it becomes clear, as Mr. Farrer says, that this charter granting
to Preston the liberties enjoyed by Newcastle-under-Lyme
belongs to the autumn of that year. But, unluckily, he goes
further and prints after it, as exemplifying those liberties, the
'charter of Henry II. to the burgesses of Newcastle-under-
Lyme, creating that town a free borough with a guild
merchant and all the liberties and free customs pertaining

to such a guild,' September 18, 1173, 19 Henry II. The opening and the closing words of this charter prove at once that it was granted, not by Henry II., but by Henry III., to whose nineteenth year (1235) it belongs. I will not attempt to explain the whole mystery, but Mr. Farrer, I am sure, will be the first to admit the gravity of the error, for he modestly anticipates in his introduction even more defects in his work than the critic will be able to discover.

One may congratulate, in conclusion, not only students, but Mr. Farrer on the publication of these documents within the covers of a single volume. The number of periodicals and transactions in which such subjects are dealt with seems to be ever on the increase, and the difficulty of finding what one is in search of increases in proportion. Here, on the contrary, it is possible to consult with luxurious ease one's materials. Mr. Farrer, on his part, must be envied for having permanently associated his name with the early history of Lancashire by producing this handsome volume, while other workers have to scatter their efforts up and down among those publications which are willing to give them refuge.

J. HORACE ROUND.

THE ORIEL REGISTER [1]

Oriel now comes into line with those few colleges of the Universities of Oxford and Cambridge whose records are made accessible to the biographer and historian. It is questionable whether any single work is of more constant service in dealing with English genealogy of the post-medieval period than the eight volumes of Mr. Joseph Foster's *Alumni Oxonienses*, although in accuracy of detail they leave much to be desired. But for ample and exact particulars of the careers of Oriel men one must in future look to Dr. Shadwell's two volumes of records.

In the compilation of these Oriel *dossiers* five college books have been called to aid : the College Register, the Treasurers'

[1] *Registrum Orielense*, an account of the members of Oriel College, Oxford. Vol. i., 1500-1700 ; vol. ii., 1701-1900. Collected and arranged by Charles Lancelot Shadwell, D.C.L., late Fellow of Oriel College. (London : Henry Frowde.)

Accounts, the Caution Books, the Buttery Books, and the Benefactors' Books. From these sources we have the academical history of the student : his admission to Oriel College and his matriculation, his payments of caution money and his library fees, his degrees, and his gifts of plate—'eare goblets,' bowls and covers, salt-cellars and tankards—much of which King Charles' cruel necessities melted into shillings. Even had it survived the civil war the Oriel plate would not have been with us to glad our sale-rooms, for old and battered or worn plate was doomed without remorse to the melting-pot by Fellows for whom ancient silver pieces had none of that charm which to-day raises the price of a pint pot to its fill of guineas. A tankard may have borne name and arms of a dead and gone commoner with inscriptions in good Oriel Latin, but when rubbed or dinted it was carried away by the silversmith in exchange for a new salver or sugar-caster. The ecclesiologist will note with interest that Nathaniel Napier, a fellow-commoner of 1653-4, gave a bronze eagle for the chapel in place of the customary silver piece.

We are assured by Dr. Shadwell that every particular concerning the students has been inserted, for which the college books are the authority. But Dr. Shadwell's work has not ended here. Whenever easily obtainable, additional notes have been added of the student's career in the world or church preferment. In some few cases wills are quoted ; in others the dates of birth or baptism, death or burial have been filled in. Some students indeed appear in the pages of this register entirely by grace of researches made outside the college records, and we are reminded of this by the fact that Alexander Barclay, the author of the *Ship of Fools*, heads Dr. Shadwell's register although the books of his reputed college know him not.

The genealogist will recognise at once the two sources from which the college drew its students—the commoners and fellow-commoners who matriculate as sons of squires, knights, and lords, and the servitors or batelers who come upon the books as *fil. pleb.* or *fil. paup.* That an Oxford undergraduate should valet another, live upon his broken meats and sleep at his bed-foot is strange reading in the twentieth century, but it should be remembered that many a bateler was a tenant's son who had ridden to college with his young master, and that the industrious servitor might come in the end to sit at the high table with a silver tankard in his fist. With the eighteenth

century these poor scholars disappear, but two Bible clerks
remain, whose names and light duties recall, although to the
antiquary only, a class whose position latter-day sentiment
would not bear with. The magnificent fellow-commoner
survived the poor scholar to disappear in his turn before the
modern spirit.

Not the least interesting entries are those of students who
matriculate as *cler. fil.*, of whom the first would appear to
be William Cooke of Northamptonshire in 1586, an ex-
hibitioner of St. Anthony's Hospital. The admissions of
the sons of the clergy as commoners will add much new
material for the long wrangle over Macaulay's famous estimate
of the social position of the English clergy in the seventeenth
century.

Apart from its value to the genealogist and biographer,
our knowledge of old academic life is the richer for such a
work as this. It is good news of the awakening interest in
historical research that the impressions of Dr. Shadwell's first
volume should be already all but exhausted. The ' dignity of
the Society,' a phrase with which a famous will made us lately
familiar, is enhanced by these two volumes which will occupy
an honoured place among the Oriel bookshelves. At the
thought we turn to the entry in 1873 of ' Rhodes, Cecil John
—matr. Oriel, 13 Oct. 1873, fil. 4ᵘˢ Francisci Will. de Bishops
Stortford, Herts, cler., 20,' and contrast the record of the
famous premier of Cape Colony with that of his fellow admitted
upon the same day, of whose career since taking a bachelor's
degree Dr. Shadwell has but to say that he is ' believed to be
no longer living.'

ARMORIAL KALENDARS.[1]

The St. George's Kalendar, whose first number was issued
as long ago as the first year of this present century, has now
to welcome two other armorial kalendars, newcomers in these
islands. For many years the admirably produced and most
interesting work of Otto Hupp of Munich has come oversea
to an increasing number of Englishmen who find his yearly

[1] *The Scottish Heraldic Kalendar* for the year 1903 ; Herbert H. Flower
(editor) ; L. Ingleby Wood (artist) ; Otto Schulze, Edinburgh. *The
Imperial Heraldic Kalendar*, 1903 ; Otto Schulze, Edinburgh.

revival of the art of the old German shield rolls beautiful and suggestive, and it is not strange that, once the experiment was ventured upon, more than one attempt should be made to nationalize with us the idea which he originated.

The first of these kalendars is entitled *The Scottish Heraldic Kalendar*. It was not to be imagined that the Scot, in London or in Edinburgh, would waste two saxpences upon a kalendar such as the *St. George's*, which finds in the English homefield enough armory for its purpose. *The Scottish Heraldic Kalendar* then has its welcome assured from Edinburgh to New Zealand, to say nothing of that city of London in which the prophecy of the stone of Scone is often ruefully remembered by the race which carried that fatal fetish southward.

Six plates only are afforded by this first issue of *The Scottish Kalendar*, a number which should be increased by the popularity which such a venture should earn. The plates of arms are of the armorial ensigns of the Prince of Wales as Prince and Great Steward of Scotland, of Robert Bruce, and of four of his supporters : Sir Walter the Steward, the good Sir James of Douglas, Sir Christopher Seton, and Randolph, Earl of Moray. The arms are boldly drawn in colours, the helmets and mantles taking inspiration somewhat directly from the Münchener kalendar, a fact which sometimes throws the crests and shields somewhat out of the picture.

An accompanying kalendar affords the names and feasts of ancient Scottish saints, to which have been added those commemorated in Archbishop Laud's Scottish Prayer-book, with dates of great events of Scottish history. A too rapid glance at these would suggest that the occasions of Scottish rejoicing are afforded in the main by such anniversaries as the murder of Lord Darnley, the assassination of the Regent Moray, the assassination of King James I. and the beheading or bloody deaths of many others who have figured upon the perilous stage of Scottish history. These reminiscences of the scaffold should have warned our editor against such dangerous items in his kalendars as the commemorations of the deaths of certain Kings of Scotland, James VIII. Charles III. and Henry IX., and if fear of the axe could not stay his hand, good Scottish logic might have served. For if Henry IX. has lived and reigned who then is King Edward VII. whose 'ascension' is recorded under January 22. Surely if the Act of Settlement prevail upon January 22, it must be respected even upon January 31, and the gentleman who died upon the latter date must be content with a humbler title.

With the description of the arms of the 'Duke of Rothesay' we begin to differ with our editor in the matter of blazonry. *The Ancestor* has from the first protested against the tangle of words in mishandled French tripping over unnecessary commas which the post-medieval heraldry books have inveigled too many antiquaries into adopting. But when the heraldry book system is adopted its intricacies should be followed with due care. There is no reason or ancient precedent whatever for describing the lion of the Scottish royal crest as aught but a sitting lion, crowned and holding a sword and sceptre in his paws, but if the later form of blazon be followed some more possible jargon might be found for the beast's position than *serjant effronte*. *Lozendy* is, we presume, a misprint in the case of the Teck escutcheon, but we would point out that the *lions passant* of the blazon are *lions passant gardant* or 'leopards' in the picture. We cannot complain that the dragon badge of the Prince of Wales has its decorative value destroyed by the addition of a piece of ground cut off for it to prowl upon, for this tasteless folly has been ordered by the officials who have set forth the prince's achievement, but we may suggest that the dragon has no need of a label about his neck, for the prince is the lord and not the heir apparent in his principality of Wales. At the early date of the arms chosen for illustration the finding of crests has been a difficulty for the artist. The helm of Robert Bruce has been surmounted by the most improbable crest for the period of a large turban-like red cap within a crown with a lion sitting upon the top, crowned in like fashion and bearing a sword. The whole of this composition is too briefly described in the letterpress as *a lion serjant gules*, and for authority we are referred to the crest of David II. in the *Armorial de Geire*, as the printer miscalls the book of the Gelre herald. The crest, too, violates the laws of good heraldry by sitting sidelong upon a helm which fronts us. The artist should understand that he may not serve two masters. If the customs of the debased heraldic system of our times are to be followed thus, it is useless to attempt to give the ancient manner to his picture of arms. Over the helm of Sir Walter the Steward we have a vast lion head rased, for which we imagine no authority could be produced. The blazon of the shield is again undecided. A checkered or checky fesse may be described by the book, if the blazoner prefers it, as a fesse chequé ; but when we have announced that chequé is a French word, and therefore accented it, it should bear the acute and not the grave accent which follows it here.

The achievement of Douglas strikes us as the most successful in the kalendar. The wreath from which the crest springs might in this as in other cases make more clear that it is a true twist round the brows of the helmet and not a straight and sausage-shaped object, but the whole of this composition is well balanced, and the red heart of Douglas is kept to the reasonable size which we find upon the ancient seals of the house. Sir Christopher Seton's crest of the ermine goat's head might well have been adjusted upon the helm after the fashion which it takes in Gelre's armorial, which, by the way, gives the crest of Randolph of Moray as a buck's head, and not as the antelope's head here figured.

The whole kalendar is an essay to which we wish the prosperity it will doubtless attain to in a land which holds more closely to the sweet and bitter memories of the past than, as we admit with regret, does the great kingdom to the south. Therefore we cannot quarrel with the perfervid preface in which the editor declares that no finer 'stores of National Heraldry and History exist in any country of Europe,' although the former part of the boast would be hard to sustain—for Scotland, apart from some interesting seals, is very poor in fine old examples of arms. But even the perfervid humour cannot excuse the statement that our present sovereign 'rests his title to the imperial throne on his descent from the Stuart race.' However the matter may be recorded in the rich stores of Scottish history, we read otherwise in our southern history books.

For the *Imperial Heraldic Kalendar* we have little to say. The cover bears a shield of the royal arms indifferently executed in a style which contrasts forcibly with the Garter around it. This Garter, which has been copied from the one surrounding the arms of Charles the Bold on his Garter plate at Windsor, follows that example with too little knowledge. The lower part of this famous plate having been broken away in the original, our artist here has felt himself unequal to inventing a buckle and tongue, and therefore leaves his Garter as meaningless as the edge of a soup plate with a Garter motto upon it.

In the six plates of arms nothing calls for our attention but the crest of the Duke of Devonshire, in which a hissing cobra rears its long neck in a manner which makes a more possible and effective crest than the 'nowed' snake which modern debased heraldry insists upon depicting as trundling its feeble coils after a fashion which never fails to suggest the safety bicycle. We have here Lord Salisbury's arms, with nothing done to temper the difficulties of the improbable crest with its morion floating in the air above a sheaf of arrows, Lord Rosebery's arms and Sir William Vernon-Harcourt's. The hopeless muddle of the blazon of Sir William's quartered coat shows that the editor of the kalendar is unacquainted with any known system of heraldry, and the vast peacock, perched in haphazard fashion sideways upon the fronted helm, shows an equal ignorance in the artist of armorial composition. The helms of the peers follow in each case the ridiculous custom of sitting themselves upon the red caps of the coronets. The archiepiscopal cross in the arms of the Archbishop of Canterbury is described as a 'crosier or episcopal staff,' a blunder which shows slight acquaintance with the church and the ornaments of the ministers thereof. The last achievement of arms is that of Michael Arthur Bass, Lord Burton, and many innocent folk will learn for the first time that Lord Bass has abandoned the ancient badge of the equilateral triangle gules for a newer and more complicated arrangement of demi-lions and fleurs de lys. The imperial reasons for the appearance of his arms in the *Imperial Heraldic Kalendar* are beyond our guessing. His supporters are described as *lions regardant*, and as the heraldry of the handbooks is followed in the blazon, this should mean that their heads are craned backward ; but this illustration does not show this, and the lions' feet in the picture rest upon harts' heads rased, which are 'caboshed' in the blazon. But the blazon with its mis-spellings and wandering punctuation is even less important than the pictures, which at least are printed in bright colours which take the eye. The back of the cover is adorned with shields of arms of the colonies and these shields are styled 'crests' by the editor.

THE SWORDSMAN AND THE SWORD[1]

For Mr. Chadband's 'soaring human boy' the austerities of the study of English history are mitigated by one circumstance only. The characters in the heavily constructed romances of Mr. Hume and Dr. Bright are not always devising Constitutions of Clarendon or Provisions of Oxford with the sole intent, as it appears to the embittered schoolboy, of adding more dates to the hopeless cairn of dates which must be picked over and committed to memory or to memory's secret servant, the shirt-cuff. There comes a tide in the affairs of kings when, delay the matter as the crabbed historian will, they must put on shining plates of steel and go gallantly with their knights at their backs to meet other kings over sea and rush into hewing and thrusting against other eager horsemen. The historians would hurry over these matters protesting, if of the old school, that the rise of the Whig party to power marks the spot where the Historic Muse should linger dallying, and, if of the new school, that the rise under the Tudors of the price of the three-hooped pot of ale is the toothsome kernel of all chronicles. But the schoolboy heeds them not, and reconstructing the battle of Cressy upon his desk with the aid of his collection of steel nibs passes with agreeable musings the hour which should have crammed him with indigestible facts.

The prize boy, who moves up the school term by term, to whom the Constitutions of Clarendon are familiar and whom the appearance of the Provisions of Oxford in an examination paper moves to no desperate guess at the peculiarities of some forgotten siege larder, may in time stand up a historian, although, sooth to say, few of his kind come to this end, but the boy who decorates his history book's fly-leaf with the doings of swords and battle-axes, is, although he would deny the suggestion in his wrath, an antiquary in making.

For the past time of the nation clangs like a smithy, and the antiquary who loves the past must learn to love and to know something of the white weapon which hung at the thigh of most of our forefathers whose heads had escaped the Church's razor, and even, if bishops' registers speak truth, by

[1] *The Sword and the Centuries*, by Captain Alfred Hutton, F.S.A. (London : Grant Richards).

the side of some turbulent men who should have learned the doom appointed for those who smite with the sword. The story of the arms beloved by those who came before us will not appeal to the antiquary alone, for the Englishman who sees an old sword hung upon a wall without a passing desire to take it in his hands is a poor soul, for whom the men of Cressy and Agincourt have died in vain.

In Captain Hutton's *The Sword ana the Centuries* we have a big book with a peculiar value. It may be said of Captain Hutton that he is become an antiquary for love of the sword and its ancestry. With due respect for the letters which follow his name his book is a book of the archæology of the sword written by a swordsman, rather than a book of old swordsman-ship written by an antiquary, and here lies its essential interest. Others will follow him who will explain to us in more learned detail the development of the art and craft of sword smithing and history of ornament as applied to the weapon, and the signs whereby we may set dates to the few specimens which time may cast up. But in Captain Hutton we have a master of fence, a stark man of his hands, whose fingers well know the poise and balance of all weapons, whose wits have set them-selves to learn how best may be delivered the crashing stroke of the battle-axe, the whirling 'hauke' of the two-hand sword, and the subtle thrust of the colichemarde.

When such a man sets himself to fight over again for us some scores of the famous combats of history, from fifteenth-century axe work to nineteenth-century backswording, no antiquary or historian can afford to lose a seat in his class. Although Captain Hutton's stories are for the well-read man old stories retold, they are retold with a purpose and spirit which compels interest.

As in other collections of this nature the earlier period is but slightly represented. Olivier de la Marche's account of the fight on foot and on horseback of the Lord of Ternant with a Spanish squire, and the story of Jacques de Lalain's battle-axe combat with one Thomas Qué of England, who was doubtless a Kay from the north country, these two, with the savage medley of two tailors of Valenciennes, carry us to the end of the middle ages. Indeed, we might have spared Mahuot and Jacotin from a book carrying so knightly a title. Mahuot, who prefaces his club attack with a dash of sand in his adversary's eyes, and Jacotin, who tears Mahuot's own two eyes from their sockets before flinging him over the barricade to the waiting hangman, were, as Alice said of the Walrus and his friend, 'both very unpleasant characters,' and the gallows pitched outside the lists might in such cases have been licensed to carry two. Captain Hutton's note on such combats of the baser sort becomes strangely inexact when he quotes the drawing in the margin of a fourteenth-century plea roll of the judicial duel between Hamon le Stare and Walter Blowberne, which drawing he can never have examined with any care. It is quoted to support the assertion of Vulson de la Colombière that in England and France common men in these cases 'were armed with the club only, as the shield, being that part of the armour on which its owner's heraldic devices were painted, was considered doubly noble, and it must in no way be contaminated with the touch of plebeian hands.' Of the drawing in question our author says that the combatants are 'armed with a peculiar kind of club, and are 'without shields.' As Hamon, who is depicted in the background of the drawing as suffering the fate of his namesake, the son of Hammedatha, and Walter his vanquisher, both appear with large shields and armed with beaked axes or martels, it would be better that Captain Hutton should see such matters with his own sharp eyes rather than with those of the good M. Vulson.

With the coming of the sixteenth century Captain Hutton is more at ease. The swords and daggers, rapiers and rapier-foils which so admirably illustrate his margins are for the most part familiar blades from his own armoury, and blades used after fashions of which he is perhaps the best known of living exponents. We have the glorious combat in which Bayard overthrew a Spaniard whose treachery would have satisfied an Elizabethan playhouse, and the combat which the Baron of Vienne le Chastel waged in his lady's quarrel. The famous duel of Jarnac and Chastaigneraie, so interesting in its detail to the swordsman, is of course given us at length, and another attempt is made to clear the *coup de Jarnac* from the infamy which a misapplied proverb would fix to it. Many stories are added of those days of King Francis, and Brantôme is picked over again for his tales of noble cutthroats and assassins, in which he is able for the most part to show how the scripture was fulfilled upon the bodies of those who smote with the rapier, the estoc and the dagger. Indeed, the reader may remark with high satisfaction that, in the days of King Louis XIII. and of the Grand Monarque, the headsman was sometimes permitted to improve upon the promise of the gospel. The famous duel of the Mignons is here well told, and we may again rejoice over the tale of how, at a single joyous meeting in a horse market, no less than four of the gentlemen who perfumed the court of Henry III. with their presence were sent to precede their royal master in the path down which the dagger of a deserving but as yet unbeatified ecclesiastic was soon to hurry him.

The era of the colichemarde and small sword follows that of the rapier and dagger. Captain Hutton might with advantage have given the general reader the curious etymology of the former word. We have the adventure of the Regent Orleans and of the Chevalier d'Eon de Beaumont, with many other such stories. The Duke of Hamilton is killed by a mysterious sword-thrust after having rid the world of my Lord Mohun. Major Oneby runs Mr. Gower through and through behind a locked door in a tavern room, and in the seclusion of his Newgate cell saves the hangman his black job. In another tavern room my Lord Byron slays his neighbour, Mr. Chaworth. We are reminded that little more than a century ago privilege of peerage could save a peer from the ungentlemanly penalties of manslaughter. With the period of Sheridan's two duels with Captain Matthews, the day of the sword is ending in England. The pistol supplanted the sword, and the deadliness of the pistol in the hands of Captain Gronow and his friends and its absurdity in the shaking fingers of Mr. Winkle and his friends put an end for ever to the duel in England, a matter for a dozen congratulations on the part of all sensible people, and for a half-hearted regret on the part of a few who have found that the policeman and the magistrate cannot on all occasions protect a private man's honour.

Captain Hutton's chapters on schools of fence are carried as late as M. Pierre Vigny's essays in the *escrime* of the walking stick, but in the space which he leaves himself his account of the school of St. George and the Angelos is of necessity slight and anecdotal.

A somewhat inconsequent account of the headsman Sanson might have been allowed to make way for more useful matter. So also the legends of the prowess of Rob Roy, which add nothing to our knowledge of the claymore and dirk. Even good Sir Walter, as his famous notes to *Rob Roy* will show, had more than suspicion of the heroic doings of this braggart Highland cattle thief. We would willingly have seen such pages filled with more tales of the doings of George Silver of the ' grips and closes,' of Toby Silver his worthy brother, and of that Austin Badger who made so many tall frays with those most English weapons, the broadsword and round target—

> All in the open manly way
> Of honest gentlemen,

for, truth to tell, Captain Hutton's stories of oversea rapier and dagger men leave an ill taste in the mouth, and it is not good that the white weapon should be tarnished by scandals.

Were another name than Captain Hutton's set to *The Sword and the Centuries* we should be querulous at such chapter openings as

> ' Our former gallant scene is played, and the curtain down. Ring up again, Mr. Prompter, and now what meets our eye ? '

and we might express a distaste for such colloquialisms as meet us in the account of Major Oneby's duel. ' Young and old they all wore wigs in those days. Wasn't it a funny fashion ? ' But seeing that it is Captain Hutton with whom we have to deal, Captain Hutton, who could meet us like George Silver, his spiritual ancestor, with Single Rapier, Rapier and Dagger, the Single Dagger, the Sword and Target, the Sword and Buckler, and two-hand Sword, the Staffe, Battell Axe or Morris Pike, we will be discreet and content ourselves for an ending with hearty commendation of this great Swordsman's book of Swordsmanship.

O. B.

SUSSEX MARRIAGE LICENSES, 1586–1643[1]

The latest addition to the list of county record societies is that of Sussex, a county already distinguished for the excellence of the volumes issued by its Archæological Society. The honorary secretary of the latter, Mr. Michell Whitley, occupies the same position in the newly-formed society, and is to be congratulated on obtaining the support of a very fair number of members at the outset.

[1] *Sussex Marriage Licenses* (Lewes : Sussex Record Society, 1902).

For the readers of *The Ancestor* it is needless to dwell on the value or interest of marriage licenses. These which are here printed are of the Archdeaconry of Lewes, and cover 'the whole of East Sussex with the exception of eleven parishes in the Deanery of South Malling, all of which were peculiars of the Archbishop of Canterbury, and of the parish of Battle, a peculiar of the Dean of Battle.' Mr. Dunkin, a member of the society's council, who has edited the volume, has executed his task with great care, and the indexes of persons and of places deserve special commendation. The places are indexed on the sound system adopted by the Public Record Office, namely that of giving first the modern name, followed by its variants within parentheses. The proportion of 'yeomen' in these entries appears to be very large. Here and there are scattered a few Christian names which would have delighted the author of *Hudibras*. One notes 'Zealous Fuller' as a surety of 'Obedient Fuller' (1607), and 'Morefruit Luffe' of Heathfield, brother of 'Preserve Luffe' (1626), a combination which suggests the existence of a Realjam Luffe completing the trio. Among the brides are 'Fearegod' and 'Rejoyce' Harman, maidens, and 'Ephanuell' Dyne, widow. The prize, however, should perhaps be awarded to 'Performethyvowes Seires' (1632), a Maresfield carrier. Such record societies as that which has issued this volume ought to appeal to those whose ancestors were long settled in a county as being almost certain to supply them with useful genealogical information.

J. H. R.

A LITTLE PEERAGE[1]

In 1734 began the first work which could serve as an annual directory of the Peerage. Of the first impression one copy remains, which was found in the British Museum bound up with a Goldsmith's almanac for 1735. This tiny little book is now republished in fac-simile with an introduction by Mr. A. C. Fox-Davies. To the 'exact list of the Lords Spiritual and Temporal' is added the 'exact list of the House of Commons,' which is perhaps more interesting than the list of the Lords.

[1] *An Exact List of the Lords Spiritual and Temporal* (Elliot Stock, 1902).

Mr. Fox-Davies's figures show us the present numbers of our crowded upper house for comparison with those of 1734, when lords were few in the land, although no less than thirty-one dukes sat in that house of 1734. Beyond the scantiness of the list these lords of King George II.'s house offer few points for comment. Their London addresses show us the movement of fashion. No duke lives now in Soho Square as did the Duke of Cleveland, nor do the neighbouring mazes of Soho shelter to-day the group of earls who threaded their way home to them from Westminster with link-boys before and running footmen beside. Mr. Fox-Davies's editorial remarks in the matter of these dwellings show no great familiarity with London topography. Dirty Lane, where lived the Earl of Abingdon, was a tolerably important West End street, despite its humble name; but Mr. Fox-Davies interjects, 'wherever that neighbourhood may have been,' and his comment on Lord Orrery's address of 'Petty France' leaves us doubting whether he realizes that 'Petty France' was in London. The residence of Earl Rivers at Liège needs, we are told, 'no further explanation,' but to those who do not remember that the then Lord Rivers was a canon at Liège an explanation might be needed. Lord Denbigh's name is, it is true, here spelled as Fielding, but to say that 'this would seem to discount the celebrated anecdote' of Henry Fielding's jest founded upon the spelling of Feilding is surely attaching too much value to the authority of this little book. The Feildings have for centuries favoured the present spelling of their name, and Mr. Fox-Davies would hardly have us believe, also on the word of the Complete List, that Lord Haversham spelled his name Thopmson.

The commoners, as we have said, give a more interesting view to one glancing down their list. Here in this very un-reformed Parliament of 1734 are the old county families sitting for the old boroughs. The carpet-bagger as we know him was not. When in 1734 a stranger came to a strange borough, he came with a bag of guineas for the electors to drink his health with, and safely disposed in his saddle bags he carried my lord's *congé d'élire* to the free and independent electors. But opposite this list of names a genealogist might set the names of the counties which sent these members up, and be right in most cases. Here be three Walpoles from Norfolk, with Sir Robert at the head of them, and three Onslows from

Surrey. Devonshire sends Courtenay, Arscot, Chichester, Fortescue and Rolle ; Shropshire three Kynastons and a Corbet ; Staffordshire a Bagot and a Chetwynd ; whilst five Finches and four Lowthers sit in this parliament.

Bound in its trim cover of linen boards, counterfeiting old leather with some success, this little book will tempt many who keep a modern Burke or Debrett upon their reference shelves to set beside it this little ancestor of theirs.

SCROPE OF DANBY[1]

By the generosity of Mr. John Henry Metcalfe *The Ancestor* has received one of the six presentation copies of his book on the Scrope earldom of Wiltes. This sumptuous work hardly takes its place as a work of genealogy, although a great chart pedigree of the Scropes of Danby has been added to it. It is rather to be regarded as a memorial and a plea—a memorial of the noble Yorkshire house of Scrope and a plea for the recognition of the present head of the name as Earl of Wiltes according to the terms of the creation of that earldom.

The name of Scrope, so famous in our history, is one of those strange epithet names which the Normans flung at one another in their gibing speech. Giffard the chubby-cheek and Pauncefote the paunch-face may be set beside Scrope the crab, a name which, aimed at a pair of grasping ancestral hands or the sidelong walk of a bow-legged forefather, has in the course of splendid generations come to have a noble ring in it. The name is found soon after the conquest of England, but the pedigree of the right line of Scrope may begin safely with Sir William le Scrope of Bolton, the bailiff of Richmondshire, who fought at Falkirk field. The son of this William came to be Chief Justice of England, so that Scrope had for a firm foundation, even as the most of the old names in the peerage, the fee-book of a successful lawyer. From the loins of the chief justice came a race of warriors. His eldest son died of wounds taken at the siege of Morlaix ; the youngest was at Nevill's Cross, Calais and Najara, and was summoned to parliament as Lord Scrope of Bolton in 44

---

[1] A great historic peerage, *The Earldom of Wiltes*, by John Henry Metcalfe.

M

Edward III. He it was who challenged the right of the
Grosvenors to his blue shield with the golden bend in the
famous suit which lasted five years and ended in a judgment
for the Scrope, who was then of such standing that a simple
Cheshire knight could hardly have hoped for another issue.
Readers of *The Ancestor* do not need to be reminded that to
them has been given the first critical and illuminating study
of the evidence in the great case of Scrope against Grosvenor.

The next bearer of the golden bend was Sir William le
Scrope, a Knight of the Garter, who brought the fortunes of
Scrope to their highest point. He was a soldier under John
of Gaunt, and seneschal of Aquitaine, and many governments
and honours were given him as the years passed, he being a
singular favourite of King Richard II. He bought the Isle of
Man with its little kingship of the Salisburys in 1393, and in
1396 he became Lord Chamberlain. In 1397 he was created
Earl of Wiltshire, with remainder to his heirs male for ever.
The list of his succeeding dignities is a long one, extending
to the year 1399, which year saw him Lord Treasurer of
England and guardian of the realm during the king's absence
in Ireland. But with honours came lands and riches, for
the earl was chief amongst those painted hoods and long
sleeves of Richard's wasteful court, and lords and commons counted his rewards with jealous anger. The same year
which saw a Scrope at the helm of the kingdom saw his
head packed with two others in a white basket and sent up
from the west country as an agreeable present to the good
commonalty of London. Since the attainder which followed
no Scrope has been called to the Lords as Earl of Wiltshire,
although Mr. Scrope of Danby claimed the honour in 1859
as heir male of the earl.[1] The attainder has been challenged
as invalid, but it was confirmed by another parliament summoned when Henry of Bolingbroke's seat upon the throne
was assured, and there is no doubt but that the forfeiture
was acquiesced in by the family of Scrope. The earl died
without issue, and the modern claim to his earldom came
from the descendant of his next brother Roger, who succeeded
his father in 1403 as Lord Scrope of Bolton. This claim was
based upon the language of the creation of 1397, *heredibus suis
masculis in perpetuum*, and concerning the vexed question of this
earldom we have nothing useful to say. For us at least, as

[1] *Ancestor*, i. 117.

ror the Scropes for the best part of five centuries, it is *chose jugée*, although the unfortunate decision in the parallel case of the earldom of Devon has given the Scrope claim a vitality which it would otherwise have lacked. Nor have we, for Mr. Scrope's sake, any desire that the Crown should exercise its prerogative and revive the earldom of Wiltshire in his person. It is associated with but two years of the story of the Scropes. The romance of history is in this case with the name and not with the dignity. In these days of cheapened titles it surely carries more distinction to a Yorkshire squire to be the un-titled chief of a historic name than to be raised to the lords on a title which has little interest and few associations for any one but a peerage lawyer.

Three interesting illustrations are given us by Mr. Metcalfe. The first is a print from the original copper plate of the huge bookplate of Simon Scrope of Danby, dated 1698, showing the Scrope coat with twenty-six others quar-tered 'by right of Descent from Heirs General,' which include the usual proportion of heralds' fantasies—Mac-Morogh, King of Leinster ; Lupus, Earl of Chester ; Leofric, Earl of Mercia— and the like. It is a good specimen of armory of a dull and inept period. The crown from which come the feathers of the crest bears no relation to the helm it surmounts, and the meagre supporters stand on ribbon edges in the approved manner. A far choicer piece of armory is the seal of William Scrope as Lord of Man and the Isles appended to a document dated 1395 in the national archives of France. The shield bears the three legs of Man, differenced with a label for a reason which is not apparent, seeing that, although his father was alive, William Scrope was not heir of Man but its lord by his own purchase. The earl's portrait is the third of the illustrations. Mr. Metcalfe hazards that it 'may have been copied from an older painting,' but he is evidently unwilling to say more for this shameless 'portrait of an ancestor,' the very type of the Jacobean Romano-Gothic confections of whose existence he admits himself to be aware.

It gives an especial interest to this book that it is the work of a Metcalfe, of a family near of kin and of ancient alliance with their neighbours the Scropes. We could wish that Mr. Metcalfe had given us in the volume some specimens of the great skill in armory which has given him so high a place amongst those who during the last half century have striven

to raise the quality of our heraldic work. He has however
favoured us with some copies of his bookplates designed for
members of the house of Scrope, and these, although the
simplicity of the charges give little scope for the fantastic
beauty which distinguished so much of his earlier work, at
least show that the hand of one who must be regarded as the
doyen of English armorial art has lost none of its sureness.

THE BEGINNING OF THE BEWLEYS

Sir Edmund Bewley, whose notices of the Irish Lowthers we reviewed in a former number of *The Ancestor*,
has now completed a volume of the history of his own
family.[1]   The book is a good example of modern genealogical
work.   With its 158 pages of text, its six chart pedigrees,
and its efficient indices, it goes to make one more brick in
the building up of the history of the old English people.
Criticism will concern itself with the second chapter of the
book, which deals with the remote original of the Cumberland
Bewleys. The misty field beyond the earliest probable ancestor
is as fascinating to the eyes of the genealogist as were the wild
seas and waste places at the edge of the round world to the
medieval geographer, and both genealogist and geographer are
in the same danger. For as the old makers of world maps
sprinkled the wonders of headless men and six-handed
monsters on the lands beyond their kenning, even so the
genealogist is tempted to set at the head of his charts names
which he will never be able to connect by an honest drop
line to the name of his first forefather.
Let it not be imagined that Sir Edmund attempts any
violence upon recorded fact in order to stretch his pedigree to
greater length. He is content to derive from Thomas de
Beaulieu of Thistlethwaite, in Castle Sowerby, who is found
living there in 1332, which allows his decendants a span of
pedigree which most of Sir Edmund's fellow genealogists will
strive after in vain. But Sir Edmund although professing
himself clean of the popular belief that a common surname

[1] *The Bewleys of Cumberland and their Irish and other descendants, with full
pedigrees of the family from* 1332 *to the present day*, by Sir Edmund Thomas
Bewley, M.A., LL.D. (Dublin : William McGee, 1902).

points to a common ancestry, is yet willing to write us a chapter concerning the doings of the Beaulieus of Hainault, from whom he would persuade himself that the Cumberland Beaulieus sprang.

His argument would seem to be as follows, if we do him no injustice.

There was a château and village of Beaulieu near Havré in Hainault. Rivers, as we know, flow by Macedon and Monmouth, and other Beaulieus are scattered about France. So far we are little advanced.

A gentle family took its name from this Hainault Beaulieu, holding of the counts of Hainault. Even so the other Beaulieus were giving names to other seigneurs.

A Hainault squire, an able man-at-arms, was serving the English king in France in 1379, according to one version of Froissart's Chronicles, or according to another version, was serving the French king. Here we are still far from Thistlethwaite in Cumberland, and the proofs that a Messire Richard de Beaulieu, apparently a French knight, fell at Poitiers, do not help the cumulative argument, for the existence of oversea Beaulieus is not in debate.

We come then to meet the last charge of Sir Edmund's massed contentions.

In 1326, John of Hainault, brother of the count, landed with Queen Isabel of England at Harwich, and joined in the enterprise which deposed Edward II. and made his son king in his place. A few months afterwards the same John came again from Hainault and set out with the boy king in his first ride against the Scots, the Hainaulters fighting in the streets of York with the English archers who marched with them. Sir Edmund argues that as the Sire de Havré followed John of Hainault in this last journey, the house of Beaulieu, which held of Havré, may have sent a horseman with their lord. But as John's Hainaulters quitted the country, and that in ill odour with the English, we are no nearer to Thistlethwaite.

In 1328 King Edward III. was married to Philippe of Hainault, a girl of fourteen years. In 1338 Gilbert de Beaulieu is named amongst the following of Queen Philippe when she goes over sea, and Sir Edmund assumes that this Gilbert was a Hainaulter who had come with her ten years earlier. We will not quarrel with the assumption, it is a probability supported by no evidence. The same Gilbert de

Beaulieu is given for life by letters patent in 1339 the bailiwick of the forestership of Okedene, in Knaresborough Forest, being named in the letters as 'dilectus valettus' of the queen, that is to say, he was a gentleman of the queen's household.

The queen's confessor, Robert of Eglesfeld, was a Cumberland man from Eglesfeld in Brigham. A John of Eglesfeld of this family died in 1354, and the wardship and marriage of the heir was granted to Richard de Beaulieu and Margaret his wife, by letters patent of 1355, which Richard was son of Thomas of Thistlethwaithe. Sir Edmund hastens to record his comment on the transaction. Robert, the queen's confessor, may have advised the queen that his cousin's death will be a good occasion for rewarding one of her Hainaulters, or rather one of their descendants, a piece of advice which sounds curiously unlike what we should look for from a Cumberland man, layman or clerk. The occurrence of Richard's wife in the grant is held to suggest 'that she as well as Richard de Beaulieu, stood well in the favour' of the queen.

'There would seem,' says Sir Edmund Bewley in summing up (and Sir Edmund has sat upon the judicial bench), 'to be good grounds for attributing a Hainault origin to the de Beaulieus of Cumberland.'

The facts so impartially laid before us by Sir Edmund compel us to record our belief that there exist no grounds for such an attribution.

What does this Hainault story amount to? We put aside the unnecessary matter. We concede that there were Seigneurs of Beaulieu in Hainault, although little be known of them. A Beaulieu may have followed John of Hainault in his two rides in England, but the evidence that John settled any of his men-at-arms in England during his short visits is still to seek, and the riot at York makes such a suggestion a highly unlikely one. Queen Philippe makes a grant to a Beaulieu in 1338, which Beaulieu, being of her household, was possibly a Hainaulter, although she, having been ten years queen of England, to which high place she came at fourteen years of age, might be expected to have more Englishmen round her than Hainaulters.

From the Eglesfeld business we gain nothing. A Cumberland man dies, and a Cumberland neighbour and his wife buy the wardship and marriage of his heir. The dead tenant was of some kinship to the queen's confessor, and the queen, who does not appear in the transaction, came thirty years before from Hainault. Therefore Beaulieu, who had the wardship of young Eglesfeld, is probably a descendant of a Hainaulter, and his wife, thus shown to be a favourite of the queen, a Hainaulter into the bargain!

Turning to Cumberland, we find that in 1332 we have already two landowners named Beaulieu, Thomas of Thistlethwaite and Roger of Blencarne, who are brothers according to Sir Edmund Bewley, although no evidence appears for the guess. These two men, settled and landed in 1332, we are asked to accept as probable sons for a Gilbert de Beaulieu, of whom all that we know is that he is a follower of Queen Philippe, a grantee of a bailiwick in Yorkshire in 1339, and that he *might* have come over with the queen in 1328, only three or four years before the date at which we find two landed houses of the name in Cumberland. Such an argument addressed to Sir Edmund on the bench would have fared ill, however seductively set forth.

The heraldic evidence, such as it is, helps nothing in the Hainault contention. The Beaulieus of Cumberland bore at an early date a shield with a cheveron between three birds' heads —arms unlike the Hainault shield of Beaulieu in charge and colour.

Sir Edmund goes too far in his eagerness to set aside the heraldic evidence when we find him saying that 'if the de Beaulieus came from Hainault in the time of Edward III. there is no necessary presumption that after they had settled in England their old arms would be retained.' On the contrary, there is, in default of evidence of a change by reason of inheritance or otherwise, a very strong presumption in favour of such retention.

It is significant of Sir Edmund Bewley's good faith as a genealogist, that in spite of his inclination towards a shadowy race-father from Hainault, he does not conceal from us his knowledge that in Bewley Castle, near Appleby, he has a place-name which might yield a more probable ancestor than the tenant of the lord of Havré. Sir Edmund is of opinion that Bewley, or Beaulieu Castle and manor, being held by the Bishops of Carlisle, had their name bestowed upon them by Hugh, Bishop of Carlisle, who had been Abbot of Beaulieu in Hampshire.

Now we dare hazard that in a single page of Sir Edmund's own book lies the key to the pedigree of Bewley. Here we have a mention of Roger Bewley (of Blencarne), which, Sir Edmund assures us, is the earliest finding of the name in Cumberland. And in what company do we find him ? He is a defendant against the prior of Carlisle, who pleads that his goods and chattels at Dalston have been carried away, to the value of £100, by the said Roger, with Richard le Wayte and others, *together with John, Bishop of Carlisle,* and others. Roger, then, we see first as the man of the bishop, who was the lord of Beaulieu Castle and manor. Let Roger but be his bailiff or tenant at the castle, and his name is accounted for more easily than by supposing that a Hainaulter who *may* have come to London in 1328 had within three or four years settled two sons as heads of north country households.

The mere mention of Dalston in this plea provides Roger, thus associated with that place, with a possible ancestry, for the earliest versions of the arms of Beaulieu give us naught but the well known arms of Dalston of Dalston, the black cheveron between three daws' heads playing upon the name of that house, which Beaulieu differences in the case of a fourteenth century William de Beaulieu by dancing the cheveron. Here again Sir Edmund notes the ' striking resemblance ' of the arms of Dalston and Bewley, and gives us the opinion that one of the great barons ' may have granted originally the arms of both Dalstons and Bewleys.' But such a grant is in the case of Dalston, at least, more than improbable, for the Dalston coat being a punning one with no meaning or importance beyond the play upon a word, was undoubtedly assumed by the family without need of grant from a feudal lord. Sir Edmund does not understand that the grant of William, baron of Graystock, to Adam of Blencowe in 1355, which he quotes, stands upon a different footing, it being a grant of a version of the arms of Graystock, to which Adam, without the grant, would have had no right. In the case of nearly all ancient grants of arms, it will be found that their effect is the convey-ance by A to B of the whole arms of A, or some portion of them. In the case of B assuming a new shield for himself no grant would be needed.

In Sir Edmund's carefully arranged pedigrees, which bear upon their faces the stamp of accuracy and clear arrangement, we follow the fortune of an ancient and interesting family of

northern gentry and their descendants in Ireland.   Beginning
with Thomas of Thistlethwaite, who pays a subsidy in 1332,
and Richard, presumably his son, who succeeds him at Thistlethwaite, we come in the third generation to another Richard,
who is a knight of the shire in 1385.   The next generation
shows William, the son and heir, as a man of growing
importance, a knight of the shire as his father was, a com-
missioner to Scotland in 1429, and the king's escheator for
Cumberland and Westmorland.   He dies in 1434, leaving
daughters only, so the Bewleys never come to the rank of
a knightly house, and the line is carried on from William's
brother, a burgess of Carlisle, whose son is probably the first
Bewley of Hesket, a manor which his descendant, Thomas
Bewley of Hesket, sold in 1630 to William Lawson of Isell,
husband of his aunt Judith, and an ancestor of the beer-
contemning baronet of our own day.

From Matthew Bewley, a younger son living at Woodhall
in the earlier half of the sixteenth century, comes our
author, Sir Edmund Bewley.   The descendants of Matthew
would seem to be of the class of yeomen and husbandmen
and are found at Woodhall until the nineteenth century, when
the children and grandchildren of George Bewley of Woodhall,
headmaster of Kendal school, begin to take the old name of
Bewley far afield to Canada, Philadelphia and South Australia.
In the time of Thomas Bewley of Haltcliffe Hall and
Woodhall, great-grandson of Matthew Bewley, a new element
is brought into the family history.   The descendants of the
hard-riding border gentry are taken with the fantastic creed of
George Fox, and go meekly one by one to Carlisle jail for
non-payment of tithes.   Mungo Bewley, a younger son of
Woodhall, and a Quaker minister, settles at Edenderry in
King's County, where he dies in 1747.   Through him a clan
of Bewleys in Ireland and New Zealand, in the United States
and in British India, are able to trace their clear descent from
Thomas de Bewley of 1332, by grace, so far as the latter
generations are concerned, to the wonderful registers of births,
deaths and marriages which are the pride of the Quaker sect.

Sir Edmund's book is adorned with a most interesting
photogravure of the picture now at Brayton, of Judith Bewley,
wife of William Lawson of Isell, whose husband bought
Hesket of the last Bewley of the direct line.   In high
crowned hat, great ruff and wide sleeved bodice, this thin-

lipped, thin-faced woman makes a 'portrait of an ancestress,' which calls up at once the long and low rooms and panelled walls of a northern hall. The other illustration calling for a word is a picture of Sir Edmund's arms and crest, and this we notice but to remark that the crest is so displayed as to have no artistic or structural relation with the helmet which should support it. Concerning this crest of Bewley we shall have more to say in another number of *The Ancestor*.

O. B.

WHAT IS BELIEVED

Under this heading The Ancestor *will call the attention of press and public to much curious lore concerning genealogy, heraldry and the like with which our magazines, our reviews and newspapers from time to time delight us. It is a sign of awakening interest in such matters that the subjects with which* The Ancestor *sets itself to deal are becoming less and less the sealed garden of a few workers. But upon what strange food the growing appetite for popular archæology must feed will be shown in the columns before us. Our press, the best-informed and the most widely sympathetic in the world, which watches its record of science, art and literature with a jealous eye, still permits itself, in this little corner of things, to be victimized by the most recklessly furnished information, and it would seem that no story is too wildly improbable to find the widest currency. It is no criticism for attacking's sake that we shall offer, and we have but to beg the distinguished journals from which we shall draw our texts for comment to take in good part what is offered in good faith and good humour.*

WHEN our learned contemporary the *Ex Libris Journal* would carry its interest in armory beyond the limits of those fascinating book labels concerning which it is the acknowledged guide and authority, more than one of its writers may be followed with some pleasure and profit by the seeker for material which should fall under the heading of these paragraphs. The Rise of Heraldry is there found a pleasant text for the harmless speculations of those to whom a desire for exact evidence as a base for speculation is a tiresome pedantry. We draw a passage at hazard :—

I am among those who hold that heraldry, as now understood, first arose in the wearing of ' coats of arms ' or surcoats of silk or other light material, at the time of the crusades, and that these were worn above the war harness or vesture and thus incorporated the sash or shield suspender as the Bend, the military girdle as the Fess, beside other ornaments and portions of apparel of the nobles, knights and priests. Of this fact traces are to be found throughout heraldry as well as among many early writers, and even in the very name of a ' coat of arms ' ; and yet there are but few modern treatises on heraldry—however learned the authors—which do not start with the positive statement that *coats of arms* were first represented *on shields*! The tabards of our heralds represent the original ' coat of arms.'

Arms borne upon a coat are then older than arms upon shields—but for the support of such a theory we shall need certain evidences. First let us seek for our earliest examples of European armory and note whether they be borne upon coats or upon shields. Secondly, if we attach importance in this regard to the phrase of 'coat of arms' let us ascertain whether it be older in language than 'shield of arms.' The absurdity of the belt and scarf theory is surely obvious when we consider its full force. Every knight, let us say, has 'a sash or shield suspender' ; every knight has a 'military girdle.' Therefore every knight begins his armorial career equipped already with a coat of arms which bears a fesse and a bend, to say nothing of the additional charges supplied by his 'other ornaments and portions of apparel.' And as we who are familiar with the earliest armory know that it begins in western Europe with an abundant brood of fierce lions ramping in all the colours of the rainbow, we may well ask whereabouts in his costume the knight wore his lion, if it be not where the Spartan boy wore the fox cub.

* * *

A fresh paragraph brings us to a quotation of the late Mr. Smith Ellis, who 'gave particular emphasis to the fact that in the tenth century Henry I., Emperor of Germany, called Henry the Fowler, issued a code of tournament laws called "Leges Hasti-ludiales," which afford unequivocal proofs of the long established usage of family ensigns or symbols, of the existence of heralds to register and regulate them, and evidence of their being regarded as marks of honour and the especial privilege of the nobly born.'

* * *

We venture to correct Mr. W. Cecil Wade. If the laws of Henry the Fowler indeed show that the Imperial College of Heralds were keeping an armorial register some five hundred years before our own officers had entered upon their duties, to what purpose are bewildered English antiquaries groping in the twelfth century for the origins of armory ? But doubtless Mr. Wade has been since informed by his editor that the famous Leges Hasti-ludiales are the forged decretals of heraldry, and that Mr. W. Cecil Wade remains the one orthodox believer in their authenticity, although the ingenious Georg Rüxner, Jerusalem Herald, and true author and begetter of the Leges Hasti-ludiales, once had a larger audience.

* * *

A more modern legend is as eagerly swallowed by Mr. Wade. It is the legend of the crusaders' swords which came hewing at poor Tommy when Fuzzy Wuzzy rushed at the British square. 'I have the highest military authority for stating that the Emirs told our officers that the great cross-hilted swords which were captured from them in the recent Soudan battles were originally possessed by the Crusaders.' Now one of these 'great cross-hilted swords' may be readily bought in a London sale-room or pawnbroker's shop for a pound or so. A sword which an expert will vouch for as a sword of the days of the Crusaders may label itself at many times its weight in silver and be sure of finding a purchaser. These be facts for which any dealer in curiosities will be our witness, and before them the legend of the crusaders' swords may reconsider itself. An old sword blade has turned up at rare intervals in the desert to which so many odd matters find their way, but nothing goes to show that the Mahdi's predecessors were such large purchasers of cast war material at the end of the crusades as the legend would have us believe.

* * *

We can spare the *Ex Libris Journal* one more note, as the *Ex Libris Journal* is important from the point of view of this column in that it is a well-known magazine for antiquaries, or at least for those interested in antiquarian matters. The origin of armory is still puzzling its writers and correspondents, one of whom urges us to consider seriously whether certain arms did not give rise to certain surnames, as for example the wolf's head shield to the name of Lupus, and the corbie-crow shield to the name of Corbet. That such speculations should be possible in our day shows only too clearly how far the intelligent study of armory which the work of Planché and Perceval should have set on foot has degenerated to intellectual pottering. By this time the very sucklings of the modern archæological spirit should be protesting against such aimless guesses finding their way into print. For Corbet, is it not enough to say that this ancient house begins with the ' Roger son of

Corbet' of the Domesday Survey? If the name then be derived from the arms, those arms must have existed before the conquest of England, and the Leges Hasti-ludiales are our sole authority for pre-conquest heraldry. For the Lupus shield we may say that no one in England was ever called Lupus to our knowledge but the late Duke of Westminster. Hugh of Avranches, with whom the duke's family was connected by a genealogical myth, was certainly called Lupus by certain chroniclers who wrote of him after his death, but this for the reason that they were writing in Latin. Hugh therefore was not surnamed Lupus or the Wolf in his lifetime, and as he died in 1101 he could have borne no arms. The wolf's-head shield is a fantasy provided for him by the later heralds, which has served as an additional quartering for the many score of gentlemen persuaded that they were the representatives of Hugh the Fat.

* * *

From *Flamstead, its Church and History*, by its vicar, the Rev. I. Vincent Bullard, we cull an unusually fine specimen of a family armorial myth. Sir Edgar Sebright, head of a family long connected with Flamstead, contributes a chapter on his pedigree. It has been a tradition, it seems, in the Sebright family that they must look to Sebert, King of Essex, as their founder. This tale Sir Edgar gives with due caution as 'only a family tradition.' But he feels himself on sure ground when he relates that his ancestor Walter Sebright, who lived at 'Sebright Hall' in Essex under Henry II., quartered the arms 'azure 6 Besants or ' of his ancestors of the ancient family of Bissett. 'He married the daughter and sole heiress of Sir Henry de Ashe, Knight, and his descendants quarter the Bissett and de Ashe arms, which thus came into their family about 750 years ago. It may be of interest here to mention that the oldest conveyance of land which the British Museum contains is a settlement of some land made by Peter Sebright, grandson of Walter above mentioned, on his son Mabell Sebright and his wife Katherine, executed in the 22 year of King Edward the First.'

* * *

A family legend is of little worth unless it bestow upon the family some noble singularity. Walter Sebright in this legend, although himself living at a time when the first scanty beginnings of armory are showing themselves, was quartering the arms of Bissett some hundred and fifty years before we find the earliest English example of a quartered shield. The Bissetts were evidently bearing their shield of 'azure 6 Besants or' before armory itself began, although the claims of the family of Sir Henry de Ashe, Knight, must have come near to rivalling them in this matter.

* * *

One cannot guess at the origin of the really amazing legend of the most ancient deed. The conveyances of land in the British Museum begin with Assyrian baked bricks and Egyptian papyri. For English deeds Sir Edgar will find that there is hardly a country attorney but can tumble out of a client's muniment box a score of older deeds of land than the Sebright conveyance. A hundred such lie on the table before this present writer.

* * *

The writer of these lines once sought for the most famous Englishman of history, and found him, to his own mind, in Guy Fawkes. Countrymen of his who have forgotten Chaucer and Sir Philip Sydney remember their Guy Fawkes. Guy's attempt is remembered by those to whom the achievements of Caxton or Pitt are naught. Glorious in his failure he remains firm on his historic legs when oblivion has snatched his smouldering match and blown every member of King James's parliament out of men's minds. Yet his twilight is near. He shall receive a sudden blow, this Guy Fawkes, if his restless spirit ever encounter the daily press of a degenerate day when 'spade work' on the part of His Majesty's Opposition is a phrase carrying nothing of the meaning which his vigorous mind read into it.

* * *

A bearer of Guy's name has lately taken his place in the list of rear-admirals. It seemed good to the Admiralty that he should hoist his new pennant on the Fifth of November. Thereat a Service journal became wrath, and said in its anger that this thing should not come to pass. That a Fawkes should be bidden to hoist his pennant on the great festival of Blessed Guy was an unseemly joke, an insult to Rear-Admiral Fawkes—to the navy—to the country, a thing to hasten the Service even faster on its doomed way to the dogs. Then arose a mild morning newspaper and would with mild words have calmed the outcry of the Service paper, as with deft handkerchief the nose of the weeping child is wiped. No insult, said the morning newspaper, could have been aimed at the gallant rear-admiral. His family, the morning newspaper was assured, was of the most respectable, and settled in the north country for more than three centuries *before the arrival of Guido.*

*   *   *

There in a word we have it. Guy Fawkes is cast off and disowned of his countrymen. Yet more Fawkes was he than the good rear-admiral himself, who is Fawkes only on the distaff side. He was a Fawkes whom the admiral's family had called cousins with, although the exact place of his grandsire in the pedigree was unascertained. He was a child of Yorkshire, son and grandson of honoured citizens of York,[1] English of the English, yet for the morning newspaper he is a foreigner, one who 'arrived' as any obscure and undesirable alien might arrive, and Guy's dark lantern is gone out before his niche. Truly this matter of fame is a vaporous thing.

[1] Chance has it that in Mr. Baildon's article on Yorkshire wills in this present number of *The Ancestor* we find mention of a legacy given to the young Guy Fawkes.

N

SOME PORTRAITS AT THE SOCIETY OF ANTIQUARIES

Bartolomeo Liviano de Alviano (No. XVI)

THE charm of this portrait is impossible to convey either by description in words or by pictured reproduction. It lies partly in the colour and partly in the manner of the painting. Partly also because it is typically the portrait of an Italian of the fifteenth century, and involuntarily brings to our minds visions of all the princely youths from the picture galleries of Venice, Florence and Rome. The white shirt with broad black bands in the fashion of the Renaissance, enriched by a yellow (originally gilded) pattern of vases, dolphins, caducei and cornucopiæ, the fine golden-brown hair, some locks of which curl their way along the edge of the round black cap, the pale though warm complexion and the long contemptuous mouth combine to give that air of pride of race wedded to a scepticism of all things, of physical strength and of wealth, which we are accustomed to associate with the men of the Golden Age. Mr. Scharf infers from the style of painting that it is either the work of Antonello da Messina or Roger van der Weyden. The details are treated with a Flemish solidity of workmanship, while the exquisite colour and lightness of the touch betray Italian influence. Roger van der Weyden's residence in Italy might account for a combination of the two styles. Antonello died a year after the discovery of America, and van der Weyden pre-deceased him by thirty-two years. The panel is not of oak, but probably of poplar, a wood much used by Italians, and on the back are still traces of old writing, too much worn to decipher. The Rev. Thomas Kerrich, to whom the Society owes this work, pasted the name by which it is known on a slip at the back, and in black ink on the side of the panel is marked the date when it was acquired, thus—

T.K.
M.C.O.
1795

It is just under 1½ ft. by 1 ft. in size, and is certainly one of the most beautiful portraits the Society owns.

BARTOLOMEO LIVIANO DE ALVIANO.

HENRY V. (No. XV)

In Rapin and Tindal's *History of England* there is the following description of Henry V.'s person :—

It is certain he had all the Endowments of Body and Mind required to form a great Man. His Stature was tall and majestick, though a little too slender and long necked. His hair was black and his eyes of the same colour were exceeding lively.

The somewhat melancholy presentment of Henry V. here reproduced hardly corresponds to this description; indeed the black and lively eye is replaced by a blue one, and the majesty of the countenance has escaped the notice of the artist. But, as this picture is a copy, one of many made either contemporarily or later, the characteristics have become obliterated. The portraits in the National Gallery and the one in the royal collection at Windsor are stronger and more lifelike. The features are similar and very regular, and the close cropped brown hair is shaven behind the ears according to the old Norman fashion in all the pictures. In the engraving done by Vertue for Rapin's history quoted above, the effect is considerably altered by the introduction of a cap and crown on the head and the orb and cross in the left hand. The small vignette in Sandford's *Genealogical History of England* was also apparently taken from the picture now at Windsor, modified by the addition of a crown and a sword in the right hand. Here too the expression of the countenance is more cheerful and the lower lips more determined.

The tomb in Westminster bears the same character as the Windsor portrait; an engraving of it in Sandford (published 1707) is thus described :—

Here you have the Form of this Monument of Grey Marble, as it now remains, but of the Head of his *Effigies*, Covering of his Trunk, and his Regalia (having been all of silver, and stolen away) are supplied by this Shadow, copied from an original picture of him in the Royal Palace of White-Hall.

The picture is painted on a panel 1 ft. 4½ in. by 1 ft. 9½ in.

KING HENRY V.

MARGARET OF YORK (No. XIX)

The marriage of Margaret of York to Charles the Bold, the last Duke of Burgundy of the French line, in 1468 was celebrated with a splendour which taxed even the heralds' powers of description.[1]　It was an event of importance in European history, and Louis XI. had done his utmost to thwart it by suggesting Philibert, Prince of Savoy, as a husband.　But the alliance of Charles with Margaret was consummated, and its importance was seen when two years later Edward IV. appealed to his brother-in-law and obtained assistance to recover his throne.　Hugo van der Goes, a native of Ghent, was employed on the decorations for the wedding, and Mr. Scharf suggests that the portrait here reproduced was probably painted by him.　He says that 'his long experience and practice both as a decorator and painter of historical subjects on walls, as well in Italy as in his own country, would satisfactorily account for the force and largeness of style which distinguish the picture.'　Margaret's face is not attractive.　It is pale with bright scarlet lips, and the hair is entirely concealed by a black cap from which falls a gauze veil.　Her features are regular, though the chin recedes slightly and the eyes look oriental.　She seems to have been possessed of good business capacities, for we read of her coming over to England after she became a widow, to arrange for licences to export oxen, sheep and wool to Flanders free of customs. She was deprived of a large part of her dowry when Henry came to the throne, and to this, besides party spirit, may be ascribed her encouragement of Perkin Warbeck and Lambert Simnel.　She was thus at one time a patroness of disaffected Englishmen.　During a short period in her service Caxton acquired the art of printing books.　In 1500 she became godmother to Charles V.　He was a grandson of her husband's and named after him.

The picture is painted on an oak panel, and on the square brown frame, partly above and partly below, is the following inscription in gold letters :—

MARGAR · DE · IORO : 8 VXOR.
CAROLI · DVOIS : BOVRGON.

It has been engraved in the Paston letters by Facius and was bequeathed to the Society by the Rev. Thomas Kerrich.

[1] *Dictionary of National Biography.*

MARGARET OF YORK.

Richard III. (No. XXI)

Richard III. has been surnamed the Hunchback, and we have been told that his left shoulder was higher than the right. The tradition of his deformed appearance has always been closely followed by artists in modern times (see, for example, Abbey's picture of him as the Duke of Gloucester). But in no contemporary portrait is the defect shown distinctly, and the one here reproduced is no exception to the rule. The expression of the face is anxious, and the pale grey eyes have that look of cunning we are accustomed to associate with his character. Though he performed feats of prowess on the battlefield there is nothing warlike in his appearance. The picture is larger than the one reproduced in the last number of *The Ancestor*, being 19 in. by 14 in. The sword which is held in the right hand in front of the left shoulder is described in Mr. Scharf's catalogue as silvered half way up the blade, the rest of the blade being in shadow, giving the appearance of the sword being broken. Since the catalogue was written the picture has been cleaned, and it is now apparent that the sword is intentionally painted as broken. The shadow was a dark streak of surface paint, while the background, described as brown, is now found to be dark olive green. It is at least possible that the picture is a commemorative one, painted after the sword of York was broken at Bosworth field.

This picture was bequeathed to the Society by the Rev. Thomas Kerrich, and came into his possession in 1783.

KING RICHARD III.

Jan Schoorel, the Painter (No. XXXVIII)

[Painted by Sir Antonio More]

This portrait was a tribute from pupil to master ; it forms a link between Antonio More and Dürer.   For Jan Schoorel studied under Dürer, and Antonio Mor, or Moor, called in England Sir Antonio More, and in Spain Moro, was Schoorel's pupil.   The inscription below the portrait is as follows :—

**ANT. MORVS PHI'. HISP. REGIS PICT.
IO' SCORELIO PICTORIS
A° MDLX.**

Schoorel is a small village near Alkmaar, and the artist took his name from that, his birthplace.   He was a great traveller, and not only made a pilgrimage to Jerusalem, but went to Venice and Rome, where he painted a full length portrait of the pope, Adrian VI., who was his fellow country-man.   His best picture represents 'Christ's entry into Jerusalem,' and was painted for his patrons, the noble family of Lochorst, at Utrecht.   The two pictures by him in the National Gallery are the 'Holy Family at a fountain' and the 'Portrait of a lady,' both tender in feeling and beautiful in colour, though somewhat poor in drawing, and both presented by Queen Victoria.   More was born at Utrecht, but when he was recommended to Charles V. by Granvella, migrated to Spain and painted many members of the royal house.   He was only a short time in England when he came to paint Queen Mary before her marriage with Philip.   He was treated with great intimacy by Philip, but that familiarity was near to becoming his ruin, and he was finally obliged to flee from Spain.   He returned to the Netherlands and was there patronized by Alva.   His work shows the influence of Holbein.   The colour is warm and the drawing is forcible.   This portrait is described as much damaged, but the injuries are slight and have not materially affected its artistic beauty.   That he could do finer work the portrait of Sir Thomas Gresham at the National Portrait Gallery testifies, but he did not paint many such, and the Society is fortunate in possessing the Jan Schoorel.

The diameter of the picture is 22 in., and it is painted on a wooden panel which is not oak.   It was bequeathed to the Society by the Rev. Thomas Kerrich.

JAN SCHOOREL, THE PAINTER.

WILLIAM BURTON, THE LEICESTERSHIRE ANTIQUARY

(No. XLII)

William Burton, who was born in 1575, was a thinker,
linguist and scholar, and was the author of almost the first
attempt at County History. He was intended for the Bar
and was a member of the Inner Temple, but his delicate
health prevented him from practising and led him to devote
himself to the study of heraldry, topography and antiquities.
He had a knowledge of Spanish and Italian, and studied emblem writers, and finally occupied himself seriously with his
Description of Leicestershire.[1] From a MS. 'Valediction to the
Reader,' dated from Lindley 1641, in an interleaved copy
which he had revised and enlarged for a second edition, we
learn that as far back as 1597 the book was begun, 'not with
an intendment that it should ever come to the public view,
but for my own private use, which after it had slept a long
time, was on a sudden raised out of the dust and by the force
of a higher power drawn to the press, having scarce an
allowance of time for the furbishing and putting on a mantle'
(Nichol's *Leicestershire,* iii. xvi.). The 'higher power' was his
patron, George, Marquis of Buckingham, to whom the work
was dedicated on publication (in folio) in 1662. Almost all
the information contained in Burton's book was later em-
bodied in Nichol, and if the discursive matter had been
omitted would have formed but a slender volume; its chief
merit lay in the fact of its being one of the first of its kind.

His portrait shows us a kindly delicate face, with a clear
fair complexion, large blue eyes and short brown hair. The
face is well painted, though the reflected lights are a trifle over-
done. The hands are somewhat stiff, and the ruffle is a heavy
grey. But the coat of arms painted on one side on the background and the medallion on the other are very perfect in
execution and are clean and fresh in colour, the green of the
mantling being noticeably good. The scutcheon of his arms
has twelve quarterings and two crests and the motto 'Lux
Vita.'[2] On the tablet on the opposite side is written the
following inscription :—

[1] *Dictionary of National Biography.*
[2] The original drawing of this shield with its two crested helms may be
found in a MS. now in my own possession.—ED.

WILLIAM BURTON, THE LEICESTERSHIRE ANTIQUARY.

WILLMUS BURTON
filius natu maximus Radulfi Burton de Lindley, com.
Leic. armig. Socius Interioris Templi et Apprenti-
cius legum Angliæ, 25 Aug : 1604 An :
AT. 29.

From this tablet on the medallion with his *impresa*, namely the figure of Death seated, holding a chaplet on his knees and resting his feet on a coffin, there is inscribed, 'Hic terminus ad quem,' and on a scroll issuing out of the mouth of the figure is written, 'Mira cogalardon.'

The picture is painted on a panel 2 ft. 4½ in. by nearly 3 ft., and presented to the Society in 1837 by Robert Bigsby.

The Very Rev. Jeremiah Milles, D.D. (No. XLIV)

In the year 1768 the Very Rev. Jeremiah Milles, Dean of Exeter, became President of the Society of Antiquaries and held the office till his death. He had previously been a Fellow for twenty-seven years, and his successor in the office of President presented the portrait here reproduced to the Society. It is a copy by Miss Black from the original in the possession of the dean's family, and shows us a robust middle-aged man in a full clergyman's wig. His expression is cheerful, and he appears somewhat material for his spiritual calling. He suffered, indeed, from no lack of worldly goods, and besides having a large private fortune, inherited from his uncle, Bishop Milles, continued to hold valuable rectorships until he became Dean of Exeter in 1762. He was from early life interested in archæology. His reputation suffered by his rushing into the Chatterton dispute, of which S. T. Coleridge wrote that he ' foully calumniated Chatterton, an owl mangling a poor dead nightingale,' and that ' though only a dean he was in dulness and malignity most episcopally eminent.'

He was happy in his family, and his sons, reterred to by Miss Burney, were ' very agreeable and amiable,' appearing ' to regard their father only as an elder brother.' Richard Gough also speaks of the dean's ' domestic happiness.'

The head is life-size on a canvas 2 ft. by 2 ft. 6 in., and is painted in a smooth uninteresting style, but belongs to a good school.

THE VERY REV. JEREMIAH MILLES, D.D.

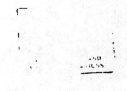

EDWARD HARLEY, SECOND EARL OF OXFORD (No. L)

To the prodigality of the second Earl of Oxford and the frugal mind of his widow the British Museum owes the enormous collection of books, prints, pamphlets and manuscripts known as the Harleian Manuscripts. The collection was begun by the first earl, the celebrated minister, and his son Edward spent a large part of his fortune in adding to it. After his death, his widow, who took no interest in literary matters, sold 50,000 printed books, 41,000 prints and 360,000 pamphlets for £13,000, or rather less than the cost of binding. This was in the year 1742, and in the year 1754 the British Museum acquired the collection, also extraordinarily below its value. The vast sums Lord Oxford had spent on his collection and on *Wimpole*, etc., were the cause of financial embarrassments, but when these reached a crisis in 1738, and he sold *Wimpole* to pay off a debt of £100,000, his position seemed little better. Of the £500,000 his wife (the only daughter and heir of the Duke of Newcastle) brought him, £400,000 is said to have been sacrificed to 'indolence, good nature and want of worldly wisdom.' Lord Oxford was a friend of wits and poets, and his library was at their disposal. He was devoted to Pope, whom his wife hated ; Swift, Samuel Palmer, Joseph Ames, Zachary Grey, and many others frequented his house. He sought to drown his cares in wine and died at the age of fifty-two.

The portrait here reproduced seems to be characteristic of the man ; it is carefully painted but is not a strong work. The crimson dressing gown with its lining of pale blue is well treated and shows feeling for colour and drapery. On the back of the canvas is written: 'The Rt. Hon^{bl.} Edward Earl of Oxford and Earl of Mortimar, the proprietor and collector of the Harlean Mus^{m.} Library. Died 1741 ; aged 52. M. Dahl. pinxit.'

It was presented to the Society by George Vertue in February 1755.

ESTELLE NATHAN.

Edward Harley, Second Earl of Oxford.

TRAFFORD HALL.

WHICKLESWICK: A LOST TOWNSHIP

THE announcement made some years ago that Trafford Park had been sold to Mr. Hooley gave rise to
many sage reflections upon the mutability of human affairs.
Heads were gravely shaken, and much good ink and paper
wasted in lamenting that the Traffords were at last severed
from the home that had been theirs from time immemorial.
I say wasted advisedly, not that I intend, with Shirley and
Mr. Round, to scoff at the family and their antiquity. On
the contrary, I believe that Sir Humphrey may with good
reason claim to be the descendant, as well as the successor in·
title, of the thegn who held Trafford ere the Norman was yet
in the land. But when last in Manchester I was informed on
excellent authority that he was still owner of Trafford; and
for aught I know he is to this day.

On the Chester road, between the park gates and Old
Trafford railway station, may be seen a range of low buildings
lying a little back from the highway behind some big thorn
trees. There is nothing in their appearance either distinguished or picturesque: they present in fact their hinder parts
to our view, while the true front is concealed by a high wall.
Though a building of brick and timber, the whole has been
covered with a coat of rough cast, so that neither date nor
character can be discerned. Modern slate roofs and sash
windows complete the disguise. But that is the Old Hall of
Trafford; and though for several generations it has ceased to
be the residence of the family, the name clings to it still.

At the time of Leland's visit, nearly 400 years ago, there
was a park at Trafford; but that is not the park we know.[1]
None of the old county maps are sufficiently accurate to determine its exact position and extent, but it probably lay
between the old road (long since diverted) and the boundary
of Manchester parish. After about 1770, when the Duke of
Bridgewater's canals had cut up that area, we find a new park
further to the west, in the loop of the Irwell, subsequently en-

---

[1] The territory of the Trafford Park Estates (limited) does, I believe, include a portion of the ancient park.

larged by the inclusion of a newly drained moss and other additions.

Marching with Manchester on that side is another large parish, taking its name of Eccles from the kirk town, and including the capital manor of Barton upon Irwell with its members. Two of these, Davyhulme and Whickleswick, as the old maps show, occupied the portion lying on the left bank of Irwell, bounded on the south by Flixton and on the east by Manchester; and it is Whickleswick that disappears to make way for Trafford Park. Its old gabled manor house yet forms an insignificant portion of the great rambling modern hall; the hamlet has been demolished to lay out a kitchen garden; and on the large scale ordnance map of to-day one of the park plantations alone preserves the ancient name. But if Whickleswick has thus been wiped off the face of the earth, and even the name has all but perished, the Traffords have made amends by preserving a series of evidences, thanks to which we can trace the history of the township from remote times.[1]

Early in the seventeenth century was drawn up 'a Pedegree with a Breviat,' or abstract of title, the former (see next page) of which may serve to introduce the narrative that follows.

Our history begins with a grant, or quitclaim, from the lord of Barton, thus abstracted in the Breviat :—

Sans date. Gilbert of Barton gave confirmed and released to Mathew the son of William Lalyng and to Margery Neece of y[e] sayd Gilbert for Marr[e] all his right and claim in the Manor of Quyckleswyk (within meeres) with th'app[n] lib'ties com'odities and easem[ts] free lands in all places in y[e] town of Barton (except Boylsnap) yielding to s[d] Gilbert and his heirs the annual rent for all services, viz. x[d]. per ann'. This is Soccage tenure & of the Lord of Barton.

The name Lalyng is quite unknown to me; and it is a rather suspicious circumstance that the grantor's brother, who

[1] I have not enjoyed the privilege of access to the Trafford muniments, but only to copies made by the late Canon Raines (Chetham Library, Raines MSS. vol. xxv.), from which the following particulars are in great part taken. Unfortunately, despite his diligence, Canon Raines' scholarship leaves much to be desired; and I have had to take his copies as I found them. Where no other reference is given, it may be assumed that the Raines MS. is my authority.

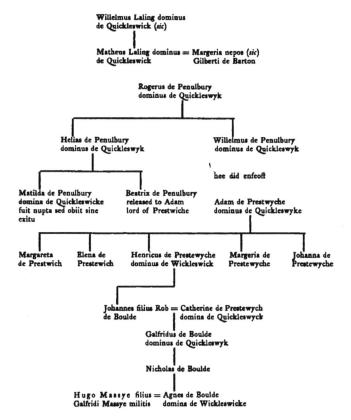

was lord of Withington, is commonly styled Matthew son of William. There are other details which suggest that the abstract is scarcely accurate; but I have found no other copy of this deed, and have no means of checking it. Gilbert succeeded his grandmother in 1222, and was living in 1255, but dead in 1260.[1]

The next tenant known to the Breviat is Roger de Penulbury, whose title is not shown, nor am I able satisfactorily to account for it. But meanwhile there are other interests arising in Whickleswick. William de Eccles, clerk, is frequently a witness of Barton charters, and it seems he had a son of the same name. Both are met with again in the Coucher Book of Whalley Abbey; indeed the two occur together, as father and son, on at least one occasion. William son of William the clerk of Eccles has a grant, or release, from Agnes daughter of Sir Gilbert de Barton of land in Barton called Crosfeld. Whether this was in Whickleswick I do not know; but the younger William had a sister Alice, who occurs as Alice de Quikleswyk in the Coucher Book,[2] and she makes a quitclaim of her right there to Roger de Penulbury; while her son Robert will be found, many years later, engaged in litigation with William son of Roger.[3]

By another charter the same Agnes grants to Elias son of Adam de Holum lands in Barton and Holm; but the copy I have is not very intelligible. In a charter of John ' son and heir ' of Sir Gilbert de Barton, Thomas son of Adam de Hulm[4] and Adam son of Thomas de Hulm are both named (along with William de Eccles, clerk, and Elias de Barton) among the principal under-tenants of Barton. Again I cannot identify these estates; but we find a John de Hulm conveying land in Whickleswick by the following charter :—

Sciant &c. ego Joh'es de Hulm dedi &c. Ade de Penulb'i pro homagio suo & servicio totam terram meam de Qkleswic et sex bovate[5] terre in feodo & hereditate, reddendo unum par calcarium de ferro ad pasch. Hiis testibus Rob' de Bur', Ad' de Heton, Rob' de Heton, Elia de Pen'lbur', Rad' de

[1] Roberts, *Excerpta e Rot. Fin.*; Fines Lanc.; Ches. Plea Roll 1, *m.* 6.
[2] Chetham Soc. p. 66.
[3] In the years 1301, 1302. See Assize Rolls 1321, *m.* 3; 418, *m.* 13.
[4] Is he the Thomas de Quikleswyk who witnesses a charter of Roger de Penhulbury in the Whalley *Coucher Book*, p. 67 ?
[5] *Sic.* Perhaps *sextam partem unius bovate*, rather than *sex bovatas*, should be read. See below.

Most', Rob'to cl'ico mamcestr', Henr' de T*fford, Ade (*sic*) de Urmston, Ric' de Schoreswrth.

Following this there is the quitclaim of Quickleswike already mentioned, made to Roger de Penelbury by Alice daughter of William the clerk, and witnessed by Sir Geoffrey de Chetham and others. Next we have a release by Elias son of Roger de Penlebury to his father, and a grant by Roger to Elias his son and heir, also witnessed by Sir Geoffrey.[1] These deeds are not included in the Breviat, nor is a quitclaim, dated in September 19 Edward I., by Adam son of Alexander de Pilkinton (whose interest in the manor came through Maud his wife) to William son of Roger de Pennilbury. The Breviat has however William's conveyance of the manor ('which he had by the death of Maud the daughter of Ellys of Penulbury his first begotten brother') to Adam of Prestewych; and a release, dated 27 Edward I., by Beatrice, also called daughter of Ellys, or Elias. Two deeds by her of that year, conveying Whickleswick to Prestwich, are found among the Trafford muniments; also a release to him by Adam de Pilkington, dated 19 Edward I., and a deed of Adam de Hulme (probably of about that date) which appears to be a release to Adam de Prestwych of his homage and a rent of 2*d.* due from him for one-sixth of the manor; but of this the copyist has made little sense. Adam de Hulme was no doubt the representative of John, and the rent, I suppose, the equivalent of the spurs in the older charter. Finally, as late as 1331, Beatrice daughter of Elias quitclaims to Henry de Prestwich.

In the pedigree of Penulbury there is much that remains obscure. Elias son of Robert, founder of the family, flourished in the reigns of Richard I. and John. Still earlier, Albert Grelle the younger, who died in 1182, had granted him Slivehal.[2] John, while Count of Mortain, gave him Pendlebury, from which he took his name, and the lucrative office of bailiff in the royal hundred of Salfordshire, confirming both these grants upon his accession.[3] In the survey of 1210 this es-

[1] The exact sequence and provisions of these two deeds would no doubt be more apparent if the originals were before us.

[2] Knights' fees ½; *Testa de Nevill.*

[3] So it is clearly stated in the Charter Roll. Mr. Farrer (*Lanc. Fines*, pp. 87 *n*, 188 *n*) says the grant was to Robert his father. Robert de Penulburi and Adam his son witness a grant of land in Stretford made by Hamon de Masci to Henry son of Robert de Trafford, if Canon Raines may be trusted. But

tate is described as nine bovates in Pendlebury and Chadeswrthe (Shoresworth ?), held in chief in thanage by the service of 12*s*., whereof Richard, Adam, Henry and Robert his nephews then held one bovate under him for 2*s*. He also held at this time one bovate in Pendleton of Jorwerth de Hulton,[1] and had previously conveyed a property called Guildhouses in Withington, held of Matthew son of William, lord of that manor, to Henry de Trafford, subject to a perpetual rent of 3*s*. or 4*s*.

In 1218 Elias was dead, and Adam his son had succeeded to his office of bailiff. A year later Adam had livery of one carucate in Pendlebury and one-fourth of a bovate in Shoresworth as his father's heir.[2] In 1216 he had been granted the wardship of the heir of Little Bolton as a reward for good service in Lancaster Castle. He is one of the witnesses to an agreement between Sir Robert de Grelle and Jorwerth de Hulton's daughter 'in the year that the king's brother was made Earl of Cornwall' (1225 ?). The conveyance to him of an estate in Whickleswick has been mentioned already.

Roger de Penulbury was, I suppose, the heir of Adam,[3] for we find him releasing to Henry de Trafford the homage and service, or rent, reserved by Elias, whereupon Trafford attorns tenant to Simon de Gousul, then lord of Withington. In 1246 he was suing Roger son of Elias (perhaps an uncle) and John son of Robert for land in Haleghton,[4] but without success; and in the same year Amice wife of Thomas de Pennelbiry recovered part of a property she claimed in Holland.[5] Roger's name is found as witness to a great number of charters between about 1240 and 1280, and he is mentioned among the principal under-tenants of Barton in a grant made by John 'son and heir' of Gilbert de Barton to Robert

for that I should be inclined to conjecture that Elias was brother, as well as contemporary and neighbour, of the lord of Trafford. In 1202 he made an abortive claim to land in Wolvemor (*Lanc. Fines*, p. 16).

[1] Knights' fees ¼ ; *Testa de Nevill*; *Lanc. Pipe Rolls*, 224, 231 ; *Red Book of the Exchequer*, p. 573.

[2] Memoranda Roll, K.R. No. 2. His relief and fine remained for some years unpaid ; see succeeding rolls. *Excerpta e Rot. Fin.* p. 38.

[3] Mr. Farrer calls him son of Adam, but cites no authority (*Lanc. Fines*, p. 188 *n*).

[4] Compare his charter in the *Coucher Book of Whalley Abbey*, p. 67, purporting to grant land in Westhalghton.' One of the witnesses is Thomas de Quikleswyk.

[5] Assize Roll No. 404, *mm*. 1, 7.

Grillee, to which he is also a witness. Elias, his son and heir, to whom (probably at his marriage) he conveyed Whickleswick, died before him, as we shall presently see. But it will be necessary at this point to have recourse to information supplied by the assize rolls.

From these we learn that in 1278 one Adam de Pennesbyry recovered the manor of Pennesbyry (except Drailesden, the Milneriding, and a moiety of the mill on Irwell) from Roger de Pennesbyry and Amabel widow of Elias son of Roger de Pennesbyry upon a writ of novel disseisin.[1] Amabel vouches Roger, her co-defendant, to warrant the dower he had assigned her. Roger pleads that the plaintiff never was so seised that disseisin was possible; but unfortunately for us neither party in counting further develops his pedigree. In 1284 Maud, the daughter and heir of Elias, recovered from Roger de Penulbury a messuage and land and the moiety of a mill in Barton, held by Alice daughter of William de Eccles, upon a writ of *mort d'ancestre*, Roger being the vouchee.[2] In 1291, upon a writ of novel disseisin, William de Penilbyri sues Adam de Pilkington and others for a messuage and one carucate of land in Barton, which we may take it means Whickleswick. It appears that Elias died thereof seised, Maud being his daughter and heir; and Pilkington's defence is that he is entitled to an estate for life by the courtesy of England, for Maud was his wife and bore him a daughter Cecily. Plaintiff's case however is that Maud's only daughter was stillborn, and he is her uncle and heir. The jury find that the said daughter was born at daybreak, being so weak that her life was despaired of, and so incontinently died; that the matrons present, seeing her condition, then and there in the chamber baptized her by the name Cecily, and after baptism she lived *per spatium itineris duarum leucarum*; but was never heard within the four walls.[3] Upon this special verdict judgment was reserved; and about the same time, as we have seen, both parties concurred in the sale of Whickleswick to Adam de Prestwich. Not long afterwards Beatrice daughter of Elias de Penulbury is found conveying to him the manor of Pendlebury also.

Now these facts are not easy to reconcile. It is clear that Roger de Penulbury was living in 1284, and survived Elias

---

[1] Assize Roll 1238, *m.* 31*d.*   [2] Ibid. 1265, *m.* 21*d.*
[3] Ibid. 1294, *m.* 8*d.*

his eldest son : that Elias left a daughter Maud, called his heir, who took under the grant of Whickleswick made by her grandfather : and that after her death William, as the eldest surviving son of Roger, was her heir. Who then were Adam and Beatrice, and whence was their title derived ? Was Adam the rightful representative of the family whom Roger had kept out of his inheritance for a generation ? Was he a son to whom Roger had conveyed the property during his own lifetime ? Or was he merely a feffoee, and the action a friendly one for the purpose of barring an entail ? Again, how was it that Beatrice did not share the inheritance of Maud ? Had Elias left a son, we might suppose Beatrice to be the daughter of a second marriage, excluded by the doctrine of the half blood ; and possibly that is the true explanation. But another Elias de Penulbury was killed in 1292 in a quarrel with one Richard de Bradbury on the road from Manchester,[1] and he may have been her father, and perhaps son and heir to the mysterious Adam, or even to William. The difficulty remains that, if Adam were heir male of the family after the death of the first Elias, and if Beatrice were his heir at law, she (and not William the uncle) would be heir also of Maud.[2]

Fresh difficulties confront us in the Prestwich pedigree, and it is worth an effort to dispose of some of them, though from this point the descent of Whickleswick is clear enough. Robert de Prestwich occurs first in the Pipe Roll of 1193–4 as implicated in John's rebellion, and again in subsequent rolls. He died about the year 1205–6, when Adam his son fined five marks for his father's lands.[3] Adam is the tenant in 1210, holding ten bovates in Prestwych and Faileswrthe in chief in thanage, with Adam de Heton (four bovates, presumably Heaton) and Gilbert de Notton (two bovates in Faileswrthe) as his undertenants ; also four bovates in Alkinton of ancient

[1] Assize Roll 409, m. 5.

[2] To complicate matters still further, the editor of the *Lancashire Fines* states (p. 188 n.) that in 1282 'Alice de Prestwich is returned as rendering 10s. yearly for Pendlebury,' and assumes that she was heiress of the family. That she clearly was not, as appears by the foregoing narrative ; and if the fact was as stated, I can only suppose that she was either widow of Adam or guardian of his heir. We shall however find that a lady of that name did hold the manor later, by a title that we can account for ; and possibly there has been some mistake about the date. In Baines' *Lancashire*, iii. 136, the date given is 10 Edward II.

[3] *Lanc. Pipe Rolls. Excerptat e Rot. Fin.*

Pedigree of Penulbury :

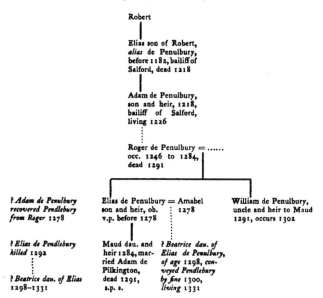

Robert

Elias son of Robert,
alias de Penulbury,
before 1182, bailiff of
Salford, dead 1218

Adam de Penulbury,
son and heir, 1218,
bailiff of Salford,
living 1226

Roger de Penulbury = ...
occ. 1246 to 1284,
dead 1291

? Adam de Penulbury
recovered Pendlebury
from Roger 1278

Elias de Penulbury = Amabel
son and heir, ob. : 1278
v.p. before 1278

William de Penulbury,
uncle and heir to Maud
1291, occurs 1302

? Elias de Pendlebury
killed 1292

Maud dau. and
heir 1284, mar-
ried Adam de
Pilkington,
dead 1291,
s.p. s.

? Beatrice dau. of
Elias de Penulbury,
of age 1298, con-
veyed Pendlebury
by fine 1300,
living 1331

? Beatrice dau. of Elias
1298–1331

tenure, under Roger de Montbegon.[1]   Between this Adam and
the later Adam who acquired Whickleswick and Pendlebury
we have nothing but the name of Thomas de Prestwich, occurring in the assize roll of 1246, and as witness to several
undated charters, though the interval of time seems rather to
require two intervening generations.

The younger Adam witnesses a number of Barton deeds,
after the death of Sir Gilbert de Barton.   He occurs in the
assize roll of 1277, and at subsequent dates down to 1313.
In the de Lacy inquisition of 1311 (4 Edward II. No. 51) he
appears as tenant of the manor of Alkrington, one-fourth part
of a knight's fee.   The various documents relating to his
purchase of Whickleswick have been already noticed.   That
manor he settled upon his son Henry by a deed thus abstracted
in the Breviat :—

A° 29 Ed. I.   Adam of Prestwyche gave the Man' of Quickleswick in
tail to Henry of Prestwych his sonn & the heires of his body, with remaind' ou'
to each of his daugters one after another & to the heirs of their bodyes
severallie, the Reversion to himself & his heyrs.

For further assurance a fine was levied in Michaelmas term
1301 (29 Edward I.), between Henry de Trafford plaintiff and
Adam de Prestwych deforciant, of one messuage 80 acres of
land, 6 of meadow, 10 of wood, and 100 of pasture in Barton,
by virtue of which Adam became tenant for life, with remainder
to his son, here called 'Henry son of Agnes de Trafford,' and
the heirs of his body, and successive remainders over to
Margaret, Ellen, Margery and Joan, sisters of Henry, as in the
Breviat.[2]   Henry de Prestwich, or de Quickeleswyke as he is
sometimes named, had a quitclaim from Beatrice de Penulbury
in 1331, and in 1346 joined with John de Trafford of New-
croft and Henry his son in a bond to Gilbert de Haydok.[3]
His heir was a daughter, Katherine, who married John de Bolde.

Henry de Prestwich however was not his father's heir.
According to several Lancashire genealogists, Prestwich and the

---

[1] Knights Fees ¼.

[2] When the editor of *Lancashire Fines* suggests (p. 196 n.), on the strength
of this fine, that Agnes held Whickleswick in her own right, he has evidently
overlooked the evidence of the fine a year earlier (p. 188).   That the suggestion is erroneous will appear sufficiently from the foregoing narrative.   A later
Henry de Trafford (son of Robert), from whom the Traffords of Garrett are
commonly but erroneously derived, is usually described in records as of
Prestwich, from 1350 onwards.

[3] Evidences of Legh of Lyme : Raines MSS. vol. xxxviii. f. 45.

bulk of Adam's property descended to a certain Alice de Wolveley, whom they supposed to be his only daughter by a former marriage, and heir of entail. Such devolution is not uncommon at that period. Sir Gilbert de Barton, for instance, had a 'daughter and heir,' Agnes, by his first wife, whose daughter Loretta (it is believed) carried Barton to the Booths ; but he also left a 'son and heir,' John, by a second wife, and other sons besides. Alice held her estate by virtue of two fines of later date, not yet printed, and these reveal her true paternity. The first was levied in Michaelmas term 5 Edward II. (1311) between Alice daughter of Richard de Pontefract and Adam de Prestwych, and by this the manor of Penulbury and certain tenements in Prestwych were settled upon Alice for life, to be held of Adam at a rose rent, remainder to Robert her son and the heirs of his body, remainder to Alice his sister similarly, remainder to Agnes another sister similarly, remainder to Adam. By the second, levied in Michaelmas term 7 Edward II. (1313) between Adam de Prestewych and Thomas de Wolveley, the manors of Prestewych, Alkerington and Pennilbury, and the advowson of Prestewych were settled upon Adam for life, remainder to Alice de Wolveley for life, remainder to Thomas her son and the heirs of his body, remainder to Robert his brother similarly, remainder successively to Alice and Agnes their sisters similarly, remainder to Roger de Prestewych. To this last fine Alice sister of John de Biroun and John son of John de Prestewych, Adam de Worlegh and Emma his wife, John and Thomas sons of Emma, all appose their claims.

In consequence of these fines, Mr. Farrer has put forward a different pedigree :—[1]

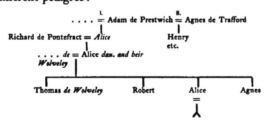

[1] *Lanc. Fines*, 196 *n.* I have had to dissent from several of Mr. Farrer's conclusions ; but it would be ungracious not to acknowledge the great assistance derived from the texts which he has printed.

But in regard to this I would observe, first, that he gives
no evidence for his assumption that de Pontefract had a wife,
and Alice de Wolveley a mother of that name. Further, that
Alice takes only an estate for life, with no remainder over to
her heirs, and the entail is on her children, to whom the name
Wolveley is never attached ; also that in the former fine neither
the name Wolveley nor any husband of Alice is mentioned,
nor does any husband of hers take a life interest under either
fine. Again, when she succeeds to her estate for life it is as
Alice *de Prestwich* ; and in that name she is returned as tenant
of Penhulbury, Prestwych and Heton, Alryngton, and property called le Brendlach in a survey of about the year 1322[1]
while later it is Thomas *de Prestewyche*, whose widow is sued
for lands in Prestwich in 1356.[2] Moreover it would seem
that Adam had sons by his first wife ; for we find a John
son of Adam de Prestwiche witnessing a Barton charter of 2
Edward II., father perhaps of the John whose claim is apposed
five years later. Finally, to leave no manner of doubt, another
survey, purporting to be of 23 Edward III., calls the tenant of
Akkeryngton *Alicia que fuit uxor Ade de Prestwyche*.[3]

We may therefore safely infer, in my opinion, that Alice de
Pontefract was the widow of Adam's son and heir apparent,
who died before 1311, in his father's lifetime, leaving the
two sons and two daughters already named ; that Adam was her
husband's name as well as his father's ; that between 1311 and
1313 she married a second husband, the Thomas de Wolveley
of the fine ; and that Thomas son of Adam de Prestewych,
who, with John son of Roger de Prestwych and others, was
indicted for a game trespass at Manchester in 1329,[4] was their
son and heir, and the person on whom Prestwich was settled
by the fine of 1313. Roger de Prestwich, next in remainder
after the children of Alice, was very probably the second
son, and the John above mentioned (whose son was left

---

[1] Lansdowne MS. 559, ff. 5*b*, 6, 6*b*, where Thomas Earl of Lancaster is
referred to as dead : ' Birch Feodary' (first part).

[2] Assize Roll, Duc. Lanc. No. 5.

[3] Lansdowne MS. 559, f. 23. In making use of these surveys, great
caution is necessary, where the original has not been traced. This MS., for
example, dates from the latter half of the fourteenth century, but (like the
Testa de Nevill) is a compilation from earlier documents ; and the copyist does
not always clearly distinguish the component parts.

[4] Coram Rege Roll, 3 Edw. III. Easter, *m.* 11*d*.

Suggested Pedigree of Prestwich :

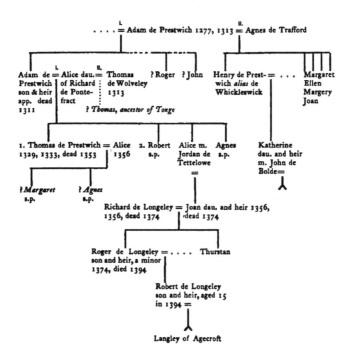

Robert de Prestwich
1194 ; died *circa* 1205

Adam de Prestwich, son
and heir 1206, 1210

Thomas de Prestwich, 1246

L
. . . . = Adam de Prestwich 1277, 1313 = Agnes de Trafford **ii.**

| Adam de Prestwich son & heir app. dead 1311 | **L** = Alice dau. of Richard de Ponte- fract **ii.** | Thomas de Wolveley 1313 | ? Roger | ? John | Henry de Prest- wich *alias* de Whickleswick | = . . . | Margaret Ellen Margery Joan |

? *Thomas, ancestor of Tonge*

1. Thomas de Prestwich = Alice   2. Robert   Alice m.   Agnes   Katherine
1329, 1333, dead 1353   1356   s.p.   Jordan de s.p.   dau. and heir
                                                 Tettelowe   m. John de
                                                                             Bolde=

? *Margaret*   ? *Agnes*
s.p.   s.p.

Richard de Longeley = Joan dau. and heir 1356,
1356, dead 1374   dead 1374

Roger de Longeley = ... Thurstan
son and heir, a minor
1374, died 1394

Robert de Longeley
son and heir, aged 15
in 1394 =

Langley of Agecroft

out of the entail) a younger son of Adam by his. first marriage.[1]

The subsequent history of the Prestwich estates, derived from various records, may be shortly summarized. Robert de Prestwich succeeded to the property settled upon him, but died without issue, and so did his sister Agnes. As to Thomas, the evidence is conflicting. He survived Robert, and died before 1353, leaving a widow ; but while some accounts say he left no issue, others state that he had two daughters, Margaret and Agnes, who were both childless.[2] The issue of the younger Alice thus became sole representatives of the elder branch of the family. She had married Jordan de Tetlow, son and heir of Adam, and had by him a daughter Joan, their heir.[3] Joan married Richard de Longeley, and from that marriage sprang the Langleys who, inheriting Pendlebury, seated themselves at Agecroft Hall, where a black and white mansion still remains, among sadly incongruous surroundings, a fine example of the domestic architecture of its period, and a lasting testimony at once to the good taste and the importance of the builders. Besides Pendlebury the Langleys held Prestwich, Alcrington, and Tetlow, all of them the inheritance of Joan de Tetlow.[4]

---

[1] From a Thomas son of Alice de Wolveley the family of Tonge claim to descend. There is abundant proof that the Thomas already spoken of left no legitimate male issue ; and most probably this Thomas was a son by her second husband.

[2] Again one account is that Margaret in 1360 took the veil at Seton, another that she married Robert de Holand. Chetham Soc. xcv. ; *Townley's Abstracts*, pp. 50 sqq.

[3] Sons named Thurstan and Robert died in infancy (*Townley's Abstracts*, l.c.).

[4] See Assize Roll, Duc. Lanc. No. 5 (The Duke *v.* Radcliffe and Prestwich ; Henry son of Henry son of Thomas *v.* same ; Radcliffe *v.* Longlegh and others) ; Assize Roll 438, m. 4*d* (Archd. of Richmond and Longley *v.* Tettelowe and others). In this suit a question is raised as to Joan's legitimacy ; but it is shown to have been certified in another action by the bishop (see also the verdict of a jury on the point, Assize Roll, Duc. Lanc. No. 2). By a singular coincidence, Jordan de Tettelowe was also heir apparent, and died in his father's lifetime, without male issue. The feoffment to younger sons made by his father illustrates what I believe to have taken place in the family of Penulbury. See also for the Tettelowes Assize Roll 1464, m. 32*d.* ; and for the descent of Prestwich, Rex *v.* Longley, on a *quare impedit*, Palat. Lanc. Plea Roll, No. 1, m. 15 (13), and *Townley's Abstracts*, cited above. The old thanage tenure of Prestwich had, in the Langleys' time, been transformed in some mysterious way into knight service.

But it is time to return to Whickleswick, where we are soon to be involved in trouble of another kind. And first I would refer to a record of 1440—the Close Roll of the Palatinate, No. 3 (56)—in which the descent of the manor is traced from Adam de Prestwich to Agnes Massey, as in the pedigree printed above, but for the omission of Bolde's surname. The Trafford evidences however, and the Breviat, tell the story more in detail. The latter continues :—

A° 4 Hen. IV. Geffrey Boulde was attainted at the Battle of Shrewsbury. This Geffrey was Son and heyr of the Body of Catherin, who was doghter and heire of the Body of Henry of Prestewiche.

John Bolde was no doubt a cadet of the well known family of that name in the adjoining Hundred of West Derby. For his father's name I have only the authority of the pedigree. In 1357 John de Bolde and Katerine his wife were, with others, indicted for a conspiracy to seize Joan Langton, and he is styled of Whikleswyk upon the same roll.[1] Next year Thomas de Gosenargh is suing Radcliffe of Ordsal, Sir Henry de Trafford, John de Bolde of Whikleswyk and his wife for a rent in Ordsal.[2] A year later they are parties to a fine at Preston,[3] with Sir Henry de Trafford plaintiff, assuring to the latter for life, at a rose rent, fourscore acres of land and four of meadow in Barton by Eccles. Here again the quantities leave little doubt that Whickleswick is meant.

Geoffrey their son had succeeded them by Michaelmas 1388 or 1389, when he makes a grant and quitclaim of his manor of Quycleswyk in the town of Barton to Henry de Trafford the younger.[4] This was, I suppose, a feoffment to uses, but we have not the reconveyance ; and when trouble had ensued after the rebellion, advantage seems to have been taken of Trafford's interest in attempting to recover the property from the Crown. The Breviat proceeds :—

A° 5 Hen. IV. It was enacted that none of the Traytors that weare against the kinge in that Battaill should forfeyt any lande wherof they were enfeoffed to the use of others, or to perform the will of such as Trusted them,

[1] Assize Roll 437, m. 11, 11d.   [2] Ibid. 438, m. 18.
[3] Monday after St. James Ap. 9 Duke Henry (Case 3, No. 69).
[4] In Canon Raines'-MS. the grant is dated Monday [before] Michaelmas 13 Richard II., the quitclaim Friday after Michaelmas 12 Richard II., but the witnesses are the same in both. I have no doubt one date or the other is wrong.

but only such as came unto them by descent of inh'tance, or by their own purchase.

By thatteynd' of Geffrey Boulde and by the colo' of ye s^d Acte, the saide Man' of Quickleswyk was seized into the kings hands, and after granted to s Geffrey by l'res patentes for terme of his lyfe, the Reversion to the King and his heirs.

By Reason hereof after the death of s^d Geffrey the Manor reverted to King Henry the vth, who died thereof seized, and from him it descended to King Henry the vj^th.

The next deed is somewhat mysterious. It is a grant by Sir Edmund de Trafford to Thomas son of John de Stanley, knight, and Thomas Spencer, vicar of Boudon, of his manor of Whikleswyk, and is dated Monday after St. Andrew, 5 Henry VI. The original seems to have borne a fine heraldic seal of Trafford's. Whether his claim was made in his own interest or in that of the Boldes does not appear; but it was based presumably upon the conveyance just mentioned, for a few months later the latter is revived in one of those quaint declarations then in vogue :—

For als myche as hit is a dede of charite in iche mat' to record a sothe, knowen be hit to all men y^t Wee S' John of Assheton S' Rauf of Longton S' Rauf of Longford S' Rauf of Radclyf knyghtes and John of Radclyf of Ordsale Esquier Weren p'sent att Mamcestr' ye Tyusday next after ye fest of ye Inuenc'on of ye holy crosse in ye yere of Henry ye sext fyft And herden Rog' Jonesson a trewe husbond A mon of sexty Wynt' and ten of age and moe Swere upon a Boke yatt he was p'sent when Geffrey of Bulde enfeoffet Henr' of Trafford ye son of Henry of Trafford knyght in ye manor of Whicleswych to hym & to hys heires for eu'more be dede of fefment & yreopon delyv^d hym seisyn and putte out one Rog' of Entessyle y^t yat tyme was tenant at wylle in ye same manor And also ye sayd S' John S Rauf [etc.] weren p'sente ye sayd daye yere and place when Thom' ye Pyp[er] a mon of sexty Wynt' and ten of age and more swere and on a boke yat he was p'sent at ye livere of seisyn yat aft' ye feofment was made to ye sayd Henr' yat ye seyd Thom' mony yeres aft' yat gederet ye rent of ye seyd Manor and payet hit to ye sayde Henry as to hym yat was lord of ye same Manor In ye witnes of y queche thynge to yese p'sentz l'res Wee have sette our seals. Writen ye day yere and place abuf seyd [May 6, 1427].

A quitclaim from Stanley and Spencer to Trafford follows in about three weeks' time.

Whatever the scheme may have been, evidently it was unsuccessful; for in 11 Henry VI. Whickleswick was still in the Crown, and a lease for twenty-one years was granted to Roger Booth, at a yearly rent of £4. 6s. 8d. A few years more and Hugh Massy and his wife present a petition of right :—

A° 18 Hen. VI. Hugh Massy and Agnes his wife, which Agnes was Dau'r and heir of the Body of Nicholas, who was Son and heir of the Body of the said Geffrey Boulde, which the Deed in tail made by Adam of Prestwyche to Henry his Sonn and the heyrs of his body, & laying down the descent in tail by s^d Agnes, and recyting all the meane proceed^gs as aboue named (except the grant of the custody), made humble suite to the kinge to consyder of their ryght and tytle & to do unto them in their behest as reason & law required, and thys for good cause & in the way of Charitee.

Upon this follows, in November, a writ referring the petition to the Chancellor of England, and in May next year a writ to the Chancellor of the Duchy to make inquisition and certify the facts. Hereupon a commission issued, and an inquisition was taken at Manchester on the Friday after Michaelmas by a jury 'who found in all things as was conteyned in the s^d petition.' Livery however was delayed, at the instance of the king's attorney, in order that search might be made for muniments in custody of the treasurer and chamberlain concerning the king's right to the manor; and when none were found, the attorney pleaded denying the form of gift in the charter of Adam de Prestwich. This issue was tried before the king's Justices at Lancaster, at the next sessions, and a verdict being returned in the petitioner's favour, they obtained a judgment in Chancery; and writs of livery issued from the Chancellor of England, on November 3, 21 Henry VI. (1442), and from the Chancellor of the Duchy on February 8. The sequel is amusing. Booth, being so discharged of the custody of the manor, ceased to pay his rent, and was sued by the Treasury for it. When he pleaded the judgment and livery made to Massy, exception was taken to his plea by the king's attorney, alleging that the manor of Whickleswyck, whereof the custody was granted him, and the manor of Quickleswicke in the town of Barton, were two distinct manors; and this issue had to be tried in the Exchequer in Hilary Term 24 Henry VI. before he was finally exonerated. 'All this,' says the Breviat, 'is proved by records and Decrees in Chancery and at Lancastre.'

Hugh Massy, who thus became possessed of Whickleswick in right of his wife, has been usually identified with a certain Hugh de Mascy from whom the Masseys of Coddington are alleged (on very insufficient evidence) to descend.[1] But the Hugh de Mascy in question appears on the scene in 12 and 13 Richard II., and was thus the contemporary of Agnes'

---

[1] Ormerod, *Cheshire* (ed. Helsby), ii. 731.

P

grandfather. William Mascy, supposed to be his son, who purchased the manor of Coddington, was fifty years old in 11 Henry VI., seven years before the date of the petition of right. There is no possible point of later contact between the two pedigrees; and while the Coddington family is still, I believe, represented in the male line, Whickleswick passed long ago to a female heir. About Hugh I have little to tell. The pedigree makes him a son of Geoffrey Massy, knight—that is, I suppose, Sir Geoffrey Massey of Tatton, who died without lawful issue in 1457, but had at any rate one natural son. According to another pedigree[1] he was son of a Richard Massy 'of Whyteswick,' and grandson of Hamon Massy of Potington.

Thomas Mascy of Whikelleswik, gentleman (grandson of Hugh), occurs in 1527 and 1533, in connection with articles for a marriage between Margaret his daughter and John Parr, son and heir apparent of Thurstan, and grandson of Hugh Parr of Cleworth, gentleman, and a receipt for her marriage portion. The will of his grandson, another Thomas Massey, who died in 1576, has been printed from Piccope's MS.[2] This will, and an inquisition taken after his death, which traces his descent from Henry de Prestwich, supply the pedigree which I have here given. After his son's death there was again an inquisition, and a second some years later, upon information that Henry de Prestwich was son and heir of Adam, and that the manor was held in chief; when a jury found that Adam died at Barton seised of the reversion of Whickleswick, which descended to Henry de Prestwich as his son and heir; that the manor was held of the queen by knight service as one tenth of a knight's fee, and that Adam held it of King Edward I. by the same service.[3] It will be evident to my readers that this jury was singularly ill-informed. They also made a blunder in their pedigree, calling the third Thomas son, and not brother, of John Massey.

[1] Harl. Soc., *Visitation of Cheshire*, 1580.
[2] *Lanc. & Ches. Wills*, Chetham Soc. [n.s.] iii. 222. The executors were his father-in-law George Lawthorne, his brother-in-law Richard Hunt, and his wife: overseers 'my Master' John Radcliff esq., and Edmund Radcliff 'my cosin.'
[3] Duc. Lanc. Inq. xii. 24; xv. 31; xvii. 85.

Massey of Whickleswick

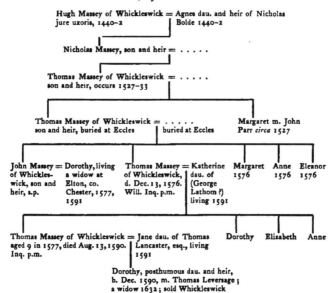

Hugh Massey of Whickleswick = Agnes dau. and heir of Nicholas
jure uxoris, 1440-2   Bolde 1440-2

Nicholas Massey, son and heir = ...

Thomas Massey of Whickleswick = ...
son and heir, occurs 1527-33

Thomas Massey of Whickleswick = ...   Margaret m. John
son and heir, buried at Eccles   buried at Eccles   Parr *circa* 1527

John Massey = Dorothy, living   Thomas Massey = Katherine   Margaret   Anne   Eleanor
of Whickle-   a widow at   of Whickleswick,   dau. of   1576   1576   1576
wick, son and   Elton, co.   d. Dec. 13, 1576.   (George
heir, s.p.   Chester, 1577,   Will. Inq. p.m.   Lathom ?)
         1591   living 1591

Thomas Massey of Whickleswick = Jane dau. of Thomas   Dorothy   Elizabeth   Anne
aged 9 in 1577, died Aug. 13, 1590.   Lancaster, esq., living
Inq. p.m.   1591

Dorothy, posthumous dau. and heir,
b. Dec. 1590, m. Thomas Leversage ;
a widow 1632 ; sold Whickleswick

In 1601 (9 October, 43 Elizabeth) Edmund Gregory, Frodary, signs a receipt for 4s., being one half year's rent of the lands late Thomas Masseyes, due to the Queen's Highness from William Leversage by reason of the wardship of his heir. The heir in question was his daughter Dorothy, who, as Dorothy Liversage of Whickleswiche widdow, by her deed of 23 April 1632, conveys the manor to Sir Cecil Trafford. The heading of the Breviat describes her as Dorothy Massy, heir general of Hugh Massy and Agnes his wife, and then wife to Thomas Leversage, gentleman, son and heir apparent of William Leversage of Northelech co. Chester,[1] esquire.

The property, of which the Traffords thus became possessed in the seventeenth century, was (to quote the conveyance) the manor of Whickleswicke *alias* Quickleswyk, a capital mansion house called Whickleswick Hall, and lands

---

[1] Northwich ? The Leversage family were in fact seated at Wheelock in that Hundred. Thomas and Dorothy had children who died apparently without issue. (Ormerod, iii. 119–21.)

containing by estimation fourscore and eighteen acres, the field names being all given at length ; also a close of 3 acres in Ordsal called the Brookes, a messuage or cottage in Whickleswick with the boat and the water passage (i.e. ferry), a parcel of land lately improved from the moss (3 acres), three other messuages with land in Whickleswick, and threescore acres of waste bounding the said manor or mansion house on one side and adjoining Whickleswick Moss on the other. Sir Cecil's father had by his first marriage acquired the capital manor of Barton, of which, as we have seen (in spite of the erroneous finding to the contrary), Whickleswick was a member ; and settled it upon Sir Cecil, though he was the son of a second wife.

From time immemorial the Traffords had been parishioners of Manchester, and had their own chapel and place of burial in the Collegiate Church. In 1701 however Humphrey Trafford was married at Eccles, and his children, Humphrey, Cecil and Mary, were there baptized. That there may be no doubt why that church was chosen, the last is called in the register daughter of 'Mr. Humphrey Trafford of Whigleswick.' Having married during his father's lifetime, he was perhaps the first of the family to reside there. In his son's time the Duke of Bridgewater's canals were made, and the old park in all probability cut up and spoilt. These canals were authorized by Acts of Parliament in 1758, 1759 and 1761. With the second edition (1769) of a pamphlet giving an account of their construction a map was published in which Whickleswick Hall is called Trafford House, and the moss Trafford Moss. Other maps twenty years later show that the waste land mentioned in the deed, between the hall and the moss, had then been converted into a park.

Meanwhile, in 1779, a younger branch of the Traffords, for four generations seated at Croston, had succeeded to the Trafford estates ; and Whickleswick, under its new name, had become the permanent home of the family ; and so it remained until the ship canal, while impairing the amenities of the place, gave the land a new value. Docks and wharves now border what was the park ; and behind them are rising warehouses, engine shops, and all the adjuncts of a thriving modern port. But it must be left to future writers to relate the history of industrial Whickleswick.

W. H. B. BIRD.

A FIFTEENTH CENTURY BOOK OF ARMS

[*Continued*]

France and England quarterly with a border of silver and azure gobony. [BEAUFORT] LE CARDYNALL DE ENGELE-TARE.

France and England quarterly. ROY HERREY THE VJ.

Gules three sheaves gold with a border gold engrailed. [KEMPE] LE CARDYNALL DE YORKE.

France and England quarterly with a label of Brittany [*iij labelys of ermyne*]. DEWKE DE CLARAUNCE.

France and England quarterly, with a label of Brittany party with France. DEWKE DE BEDFFORDE.

France and England quarterly with a border silver. DEWKE DE GLOWSESTRE.

England with *une bordwre de Fraunce*. DEWKE DE EXCESTYR.

France and England quarterly *the labelys of sylvyr* [with] *vj pelettys of gowlys.* [Nine roundels are drawn.] Dewke de Yorke.

England with *iij labelys of sylvyr.* Dewke de Northfolke.

France and England with a border (*the armys of Dewke of Glowsestyr*) quartering gold a cheveron gules (*Stafford and the Erle of Herfforde all yn one*). Dewke de Bokyngham.

France and England with a border of silver and azure gobony [Beaufort] impaled with Beauchamp and Newburgh quarterly. Duke of Somersett.

Beauchamp and Newburgh quarterly impaled with Clare and Despenser quarterly. Duke of Warwyke.

Silver three lions passant gules looking backward *an armyd w^t asewre the taylys comynge uppe bytwene the leges.* Prynce of Walys. [Sir Thomas Howe is scored out and Howell dda written in a later hand.] *Set hym by nethe the olde baronys.*[1]

Gules a leopard gold *an armyd wyth asewre.* The armys of Gyan.

Azure a fesse and three leopards' heads gold [Pole] quartering silver a bend gules with three pairs of wings of silver [Wingfield]. Duke of Sofoke.

---

[1] This and other like remarks are doubtless notes made by the compiler for the arrangement of the arms in a later book.

Sable three ostrich feathers of silver with *penys of golde*, at the foot of each is a roll of gold with the word ƕiꞓ ƕoff. *Le bages deu* ROYE.

Gold two griffons' legs rased sable lying barwise. DEWKE DE SOMERSETT [sic]. In a later hand is written *Briak du Gyan armes.*

A beryth ente asewre a chef of gowles (that is to say—parted gules and azure cheveronwise) with two leopards rampant gold armed with azure in the chief and a fleur-de-lys gold in the foot. THE BASTARDE OF CLARAUNCE.

Gules a lion gold [FITZ ALAN] quartered with sable a *frete* gold [MALTRAVERS]. COUNT DE ARRONDELL.

Gules a fesse gold between six crosslets [gold] [BEAUCHAMP] quartered with *gold and aseure ceche* [sic] *a cheveron of ermyne* [NEWBURGH]. COUNT DE WARREWYKE.

Gold a lion azure, quartered with gules *iij leweys* of silver. COUNT DE NORTHUMBERLOND.

Gules a saltire silver. COUNT DE WESTEMERLOND.

Gold three roundels gules [COURTENAY] quartered with gold a lion azure [REVIERS]. COUNT DE DOWENECHYRE.

Quarterly gules and gold with a pierced molet silver in the quarter. COUNT DE OXYNFFORD.

In the first quarter and the fourth—a lion with a border engrailed, quartered with two lions passant. In the second and third quarters—a bend between six martlets, quartered with a fret. Over all an escutcheon with a fesse between six crosslets. COUNT DE SCHROWYSBERY.

A fesse indented of three fusils for Montague quartered with gold an eagle [vert] for Monthermer — the whole

quartering gules a saltire silver with a label gobony for
Nevill. COUNT DE SALYSBERY. Below the shield is
written *Salysbery by fore chef.*

Gold a chief indented azure. COUNT DE URMOUNDE.

Gold a chief indented azure with a label *argent*.[1] COUNT DE
WYLCHYRE. BOTTELER SIR JAMYS.

Silver a saltire gules engrailed. Below this shield is written
Quartly w the armys of Salesbery.* COUNT DE WORCESTYR.
TYPTOFTE.

Azure a lion gold with the field powdered with golden fleurs
de lys [BEAUMONT] quartered with azure three *whet
chewys* or *garbys* of gold [COMYN]. LE WYSCOUNT DE
BEAUMOND.

Gules a sleeve of gold. THE OLDE KYNGE OF MAN. [This is
struck out and LORDE HASTYNGES is written below in a
later hand.]

Silver a bend sable, quartered with gules a fret gold [so
drawn]. LORD SPENSER.

Gules three *bowgys* silver. LORD ROOS.

Dor a lion gules within a border of gules engrailed [TALBOT,
the colours have been reversed], quartering gules two
lions passant [*argent* in a later hand] [STRANGE]. LORD
TALBOT.

Ermine a cheveron gules, quartering gules a fret gold. *Thys
quarter before chefe.* LORD OF AWDELEY.

Barry silver and azure with three roundels in the chief,
quartered with Hastings quartering Valence. LORD
GRAY-CODNORE.

Gold and gules ownde of vj pecys [LOVELL] quartered with azure
a *lebarde* rampant silver in a field powdered with fleurs de
lys of silver [HOLAND]. LORD LOWELL.

Gowlys a lyon of sylvyr the field powdered with *crosse croslettis
pycche of the best* [that is to say—of the colour of the
beast]. [LA WARR] quartered with azure three fleurs de
lys out of leopards heads gold [CANTELOW]. LORD DE
LAWARRE.

---

[1] It has been pointed out elsewhere that *or* and *argent* were not used by
the custom of the middle ages in English blazoning. An example here and
there of the French form being used will occur in cases such as the above,
where the artist, making his sketch in all probability from a roll of arms
written in French, lets a French word slip into his English blazon. It
will be noticed that the title of the Earl of Wiltshire, the bearer of the coat, is
itself set down in the French.

Gold a fesse between two cheverons gules. LORD FEWATER [FITZWALTER].

Sable a cross engrailed gold [WILLOUGHBY] quartered with gules a millrind cross silver [BEK]. LORD WYLBY.

Golde and asewre checche with a fesse gules. LORD CLYF-FORDE.

Gules seven voided *losengys* of gold. LORD FERRERES OF GROBY.

Gold a lion sable *armyd w^t gowlys* with a forked tail. LORD OF WELLYS.

Gules six *caloppys* of silver. LORD CALYS [SCALES].

The felde gowlys besaunte of golde with an ermine quarter. LORD SOWCH.

Silver a *gryffon of goulys armyd w^t aseure bek and fet* [BOTREAUX] quartered with barry silver and gules with three roundels of gules in the chief. LORD BOTREWSE.

Gules a cheveron silver between ten crosses formy of silver. LORD BERKELEY.

Ermine a lion gules with *a crowne of golde* within a border sable engrailed *besaunte of golde*. LORD FANHOPE.

Silver a cross gules engrailed between four *bosches of sabyll* [BOURCHIER]. A note in the margin adds *w^t lord bemond le wyscount a fore baronys*. LORD BOWCER.

Silver a saltire engrailed gules. LORD TYPTTOFTE.

Barry silver and sable with three roundels sable in the chief. LORD HUNGERFORDE.

Gules two lions passant silver *armyd w^t aseure*. LORD STRAUNGE.

Silver a chief azure and a bend or baston gules [CROMWELL] quartered with checkered gold and gules a chief ermine [TATERSHALL]. LORD CROMEWELL.

Barry gold and vert with a baston gules [POYNINGS] quartering *goulys iij lyonys of sylvre passant a bend of aseur* [FITZ PAYNE]. LORD PONYNGES.

Silver a lion sable with a crown of gold. LORD MORLAY.

Gold two lions passant azure [SOMERY] quartered with silver a cross paty azure [SUTTON]. LORD DODDLEY.

Silver a chief azure with two pierced molets gold [CLINTON] quartered with quarterly gold and gules [SAY]. LORD KLYNTON.

Gold a lion gules *armyd w^t asewre* the *tayle forche*. LORD POWES.

Paly wavy of gold and gules [MOLINES, a MAUDUIT coat] quartered with barry sable and silver with three plates in the chief [HUNGERFORD]. The colours of this last coat are muddled in the trick, which is probably meant for the more familiar coat of Hungerford with the two bars and three plates in the chief. LORD MOLAYNYS.

Gold two bends gules [SUDELEY] quartered with gules a fesse checkered *argent* and *sabyll* between six crosslets formy fitchy gold [BOTELER]. LORD SWDELEY.

Barry silver and azure with a label gules. LORD GRAYE *of Wylton.*

Fretty a chief [FITZ HUGH]. This coat is an error for the three braced cheverons with a chief, the usual coat assigned to Fitz Hugh. Here it is impaling vair a fesse gules for MARMION. LORD FEHEWE.

Barry silver and azure with three roundels gules in the chief. LORD GRAY RETHER[FELD].

Azure *iij sysefoylys sylvyr* the field powdered with *crosse crosselettys of the same* [DARCY]. LORD DARCHY.

Aseure a bende of golde [LORD SCROPE] quartered with silver a saltire gules engrailed LORD [TYPTOFTE]. LORD CROPE *of Bolton.*

Gules *iij caloppys of sylvyr* [DACRE] quartered with *golde and gowlys checche* [VAUX OF GILLESLAND]. LORD OF DAKYR.

Azure a bend gold with a label silver. LORD SCROPE *of Upsale.*

Barry silver and azure of eight pieces with *iij chaplettys of goulys yn every chapelet v rose the bouddys w'yn golde.* THE BARON OF GRAYSTOKE.

Gold a chief gules with three roundels silver [CAMOYS]. LORD CAMEWSE.

Gules a fesse gold between six crosslets gold with a crescent sable on the fesse, *quartly w' Westmerland* gules a saltire of silver [NEVILL]. LORD OF BARGEWENNE.

Sable fretty silver. LORD HERYNGETON.

Gules a saltire silver [NEVILL] quartered with gules a cross paty gold [LATIMER], impaled with BEAUCHAMP quartering with NEWBURGH. LORD LATEMER.

Goulys a lyon passaunt of sylvyr crownyd w' golde [LISLE] quartered with silver a cheveron gules [TYES]. LORD LYLE.

Silver a lion azure armyd w^t gowlys [Fauconberge] quartered with gules a saltire silver [Nevill]. Lord Fawconberge.

Golde and gowlys werre. Lord Ferreres *of Chartley.*

Gules a fesse gold between six martlets gold. Lord Beauchampe. Sr John Beachampe *of Powyk.*

Gules a cheveron gold with three *lyonsewse of sabyll* on the cheveron. Lord Cobbham.

Sable a bend gold between six fountains silver [sic] Lord Storton.

Gold a cross sable [Aton] quartered with sable a bend flowery gold [Bromflete]. Lord Wessey.

Gold fretty sable and a chief sable with three bezants thereon [St. Amand] quartered with gules a fesse between six martlets *dore* [Beauchampe]. Lord Seynt Amonde. Sr Wylyam Beauchampe.

Quarterly ermine and gules indented [Fitz Warine] quartered with silver a cross gules engrailed between four bougets sable [Bourchier]. Lord Fewarreyne [the pryore ?]. Sr Wylyam Bourcer.

An empty shield at the foot of the page. Lord of Seynt Gonys [?].

Northumbyrland armys w^t dyfference. A lion with a fleur de lys on the shoulder [Percy] quartering three luces [Lucy]. Lord Egremoyne.

Barry gules and argent with a quarter of gules and an eagle of gold on the quarter. Lord Rewers.

Sable seven pierced molets silver. Lord Bonwyle.

Quarterly gold and gules—a marginal note adds—*a bordwre of sylvyr* [Say] quartered with Azure three lions golds [Fiennes]. Lord Saye.

Gold three lions passant sable. The Baron of Carrew.

Silver two bars of azure. The Baron of Hylton.

Gules a pierced cinqfoil gold, with six *croslettys gold bottone* around it. Sir Gylberd Umferwyle *of Northumberlond.*

Silver a fesse gules between three crescents gules [Ogle] quartering gold a voided escutcheon azure [Bertram]. Sir Robarde of Ogle *of Northumberlond.*

Silver a fesse gules between three *popyngayes of grene beke and fet gowlys.* Sir Thomas Lwmley.

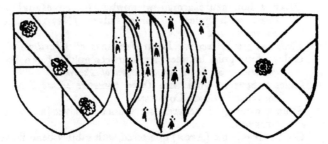

Quarterly gold and gules with a bend sable and three *caloppys of sylvyr* on the bend. Sir Wylyam Ewerys *of the byschepryke of Derham.*

Ermine three bent bows of gules. Sir Wylyam Bowys *of the byscheperyke of Derham.*

Gules a saltire silver charged with a rose. [Sir James Strangways struck out.] Nevell.

Gules a lion silver with a border engrailed silver. Sir Robarde Knollys *of North bumberland.*

Silver three cups of sable, the field crusilly fitchy. The arms would appear to take the place of an engrailed saltire originally drawn. Sir John Sorteys *of North umberlond.*

Azure a sleeve of gold. Sir John Coynyerys *of Yorkechyre.*

Silver a bend sable with three crescents of silver. Sir
   Wylyam Elmedene *of the byschoperyke of Derham.*

Gules a fesse silver between *iij orchonys* of silver.   Sir
   Robard Claxton *of the byschiperyke of Derham.*

Gules *three heronys of sylvyr, beke and fet golde.* Sir Emonde
   Heron *of North humberlond.*

Barry gold and azure [*vij pecys* is written in the margin]. Sir
   John Constabyll. *York chyre.*

Sable two lions passant *gobbone sylvyr and gowlys.* Sir Jamys
   Strangways. *Yorke chyre.*

Gules a cross paty gold with five pierced molets of gules
   [Oughtred] quartered with azure crusilly gold with *iij*
   bordonys of gold [Burdon]. Sir Robarde Owthreyght.
   Yorke chyre.

Quarterly azure and silver with a fleur de lys gold in the
   quarter. Sir Tomas Metham. *Yorke chyre.*

Gules a cheveron silver with three roses gules. Sir Robarde
   Knollys. *Yorke chyre.*

Ermine a lion azure with a golden crown. Sir Jamys Pykeringe. *Yorke chyre.*

Silver a chief sable with two pierced molets of gold. Sir
   John Salwayne. *Yorke chyre.*

Ermine three bars gules and three crescents sable. Sir
   Robarde Waterton. *Yorke chyre.*

Azure a cross paty silver voided. Sir John of Melton. *Yorke
   chyre.*

Gold a voided escutcheon of azure. Sir John Bartram. *Northumberlond.*

Silver a bend sable engrailed with three owls of silver [Savile] quartered with *goulys a chef of sylvyr iiij gymelys of the same* [Thornhill]. Sir John Saywyle. *Yorke chyre.*

Silver a fesse gules with cotises of gules with three fleurs de lys silver on the fesse. Sir Wylyam Normanwyle. *Yorke chyre.*

Gules a cheveron ermine between three lions gold [a Langton coat]. Sir John Percehaye. *Yorkechyre.* The shield has been struck through with a pen.

Sable a bend gold between six escallops gold. Sir Alysaundyr Folgham. *Derby chyre.*

Azure a fesse indented gold. Sir Harry Percy. *Yorke chyre. The olde armys.*

Silver two bends sable engrailed. SIR RAWFE RADCLYFF of *Lancaster chyre.*

Gules a fesse silver between *iij popyngays* of silver. SIR WYLYAM LUMLEY *of the byschopperyke of Derham.*

Gules three bougets ermine. SIR ROBARD ROOS *of Mydherst of Sowsex.*

Silver a cheveron gules between three lions' heads gules rased. GOY OF ROCLYFF. *York chyre.*

Gules three bars silver with three pierced molets of silver in the chief. TOMAS WESCHYNGTON *of ye byschopperyke of Derham.*

Ermine a fesse gules. WYLYAM ROMONBY. *Yorke chyre.*

Gold a lion's leg sable the shoulder issuing from the sinister side, party with sable a fesse gold. [SIR TOMAS OF STANLEY. *Lancaster chyre* struck out.]

Silver a bend *argent* [? for azure] with cotises of azure and three griffons gold passant on the bend. TOMAS GRA. *Yorke chyre.*

Azure *iij whetchevys of sylvyr.* MAYSTER JOHN MAWRSCHALL. *York chyre.*

Sable a fesse silver with *iij crosse croslettys bottone of sabyll.* JOHN OF NEWSAM. *Yorke chyre.*

Azure three crescents gold [RYTHER] quartered with a lion. SIR WYLYAM OF RYTHER *of Yorkechyre.*

Silver a fesse gules indented. SIR TOMAS BASSEWELL *of York chyre.*

Silver a fesse sable between six crosslets fitchy sable. JOHN CATTON. *Derham chyre.*

Gold three dragons' heads azure rased with tongues gules. Sir Gilberd Halsale. [*Lancaster in a later band.*]

Silver three bends gules [Byron]. Sir John Berron *of Lancaster chyre.*

Gold a cross sable with five crescents silver [Ellis] quartered with gules a lion *werre sylvyr and aseure* [Everingham]. Robarde Elys. *York chyre.*

Silver a fesse sable flowery above and below. Sir John Dawell *of York chyre.*

Sable three escallops silver. Wylyam Strykelond.

Ermine a fesse gules with three golden rings thereon [Barton] quartered with paly *argent* and *vert.* Rychard of Barton *of Lancaster chyre.*

Gold a chief azure indented with three roundels silver [Lathom] quartering silver a bend azure with three harts' heads gold [Stanley]. Sir Tomas of Stanley. *Lancaster chyre.*

Sable a fesse silver between *iij pellycanys of sylvyr* wounding themselves. Wylyam Pellesan. *Yorke chyre.*

Silver two bars gules and a quarter gules with a pierced cinqfoil of gold on the quarter. Wylyam Preston *of Lancaster chyre.*

Sable a fesse gules between three escallops silver [sic]. Wylyam Laton.

Gules three picks gold. Sir John Pygot.

Paly silver and gules and a chief azure with a leopard gold. Sir John Langford.

Azure a cheveron silver between three leaping hounds of silver. Tomas Gower.

Silver a saltire gules with five crosses paty sable. Tomas Crathorne.

Gules a fesse silver between three lambs. Sir Tomas Lambton.

Silver three bears' heads sable rased with *moselys of goulys*. Tomas Berrewyk.

Paly silver and azure with a bend gules. Sir Hewe of Anysley.

Gules a cheveron ermine between three lions gold. The lions in chief face one another after the common practice at this time when lions are depicted above a cheveron. Sir John of Langton. *York chyre*.

Azure a fesse indented gold charged with five *scaloppys* of gules. Sir Wylyam Plomton. *Yorkchyre*.

Sable a saltire gold. Sir John Clarways of Kroft. *Yorke chyre*.

Q

Sable a cheveron gold between three crescents silver. SIR
RAWF BABTHORPE. *Yorke chyre.*

Azure a lion gold. SIR EMONDE DARRELL. *Yorke chyre.*

Azure a bend gold between six golden cups. SIR RICHARD
BUTTLER. *Lancaster chyre.*

Azure a cheveron gold between three golden cups. SIR JOHN
BUTTLER. *Lancaster chyre.*

Silver a bend sable engrailed. SIR JOHN RADKLYFFE. *Lancaster chyre.*

Azure a fret silver and a border gold with *pelettys of gowlys* on
the border. SIR ALYSAUNDYR LOWNDE. *Yorke chyre.*

Silver a fesse sable. SIR JOHN KYKELEY. *Yorkechyre.*

Burelly silver and gules a quarter sable with a cross paty gold.
SIR JOHN OF ELTON. *Yorke chyre.*

Sable *iij fecys of sylvyr.* SIR RYCHARDE HAWGHTON *of Lancaster chyre.*

Silver three cheverons gules. THE BARON OF NEWTON. *Lancaster chyre.*

Silver a molet sable. [ASSHETON] SIR TOMAS AYSTON. *Lancaster chyre.* Sable *iij combys* of silver. SIR TOMAS
DWNSTALL [TUNSTALL] *of Lancaster chyre.*

Silver *iij squareleys of porpell.* Sir Emond Talbott. *Lan-caster chyre.*

Silver and gules quarterly. Sir Jafferey Massy *of Lancaster chyre.*

Silver a cheveron sable between three escallops sable with three crescents of silver on the cheveron. Sir John Sorteys. *Yorke chyre.*

Silver three boars' heads rased sable. Sir Tomas of Bowthe *of Lancaster chyre.*

Gold a dance sable. Harry Waveser [Vavasour]. *York chyre.*

Ermine a cheveron sable with three pierced cinqfoils of gold. Stewyn Haytfelde. *Yorke chyre.*

Gules a fesse silver with *iij crowys of sabyll*. JOHN OF POR-
TYNGETON. *Yorke chyre.*

Sable three running 'leverers' of silver with collars on their
necks. HOPKYNE MAWLEVERERE. *Yorke chyre.*

Silver *ij fecys fesele of sabyll*. TOMAS CONSTABYLL *of Cattys fosse,
Yorke chyre.*

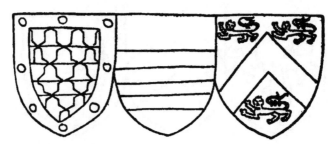

Vair a border sable with bezants. TOMAS DALAREWER. *Yorke
chyre.*

Gold two bars azure with a chief gules. ROBARDE MANERYS.
North umberlond.

Azure a cheveron silver between three leopards silver.
WYLLYSTHROPPE. *York chyre.*

Silver a cross sable engrailed. JOHN FYTZ HENRY. *Yorke chyre.*

Gules three jousting spears silver with their pennons. SCHORTHOSE. *Yorke chyre.*

Ermine a cross sable engrailed. RAWF ACCLUM. *Byschoppe ryke of Derham.* [The name was possibly corrected on a slip pasted over the name, which slip is now lost. This may be a POLLARD coat.]

Azure a fesse gold between three fleurs de lys gold. WYLYAM CHAUNCELER. *Byschoppe ryke of Derham.* In a later hand the name SKELTON is written on the shield.

Gules a sleeve of silver with an orle of *synke foylys* of silver. RAWFE ACCLUM. *York chyre.* [The name is written upon a slip pasted over another name.]

Silver a saltire sable engrailed. JAFFEREY MYDDYLTON. *Lancaster chyre.*

Silver a fesse sable between three pierced *molettys* of silver. JOHN PASLEUE. *Yorke chyre.*

Ermine a fesse gules indented. TOMAS LYYS *of the byschoppe ryke of Derham.*

Sable a cheveron gold between *iij merlettys of gold* with three pierced molets of gold upon the cheveron. JOHN MONKTON. *Northwmberland.*

Sable *iij sparehawkys of sylvyr* with their bells. TOMAS HAWKYSWORTH. *Yorke chyre.*

Azure two bars silver. HEWE OF LYGHT. *Lancaster chyre.*

A saltire silver with a fleur de lys azure. SIR JOHN NEVYLL. *Byschoperyke of Derham.*

Azure *iij flowr de lyce of ermyn.* JOHN OF BOROWE. *Yorke chyre.*

Silver three garlands gules. ROGER LASSELYS. *Yorke chyre.*

Gules six rings of gold. WYLYAM VYPOUNT *of the byschoperyke of Derham.*

Silver a fesse sable between three fleurs de lys gules with three roundels of gold on the fesse. JOHN TWHAYTYS. *Yorke chyre.*

Gules a lion *argent* with a border of *gold* and *argent* gobony. JOHN MOWBRAYE. *Northumberlond.*

Silver a bend sable engrailed with three molets of silver. NYCOLL ENTTWESYLL *of the byschoperyke of Derham.*

Gules a voided escutcheon ermine. BAYLYAFF *Lord of Barnara Castell.*

Azure three bougets gold. SIR ROBARDE ROOS *of Yngmanathorpe.*

A saltire charged with a molet [NEVILL] quartering gold a fesse indented gules quartered with silver a fesse indented gules. JOHN NEVELL. *Yorke chyre.*

Sable an escutcheon silver between six owls of silver. WATYR CALWERLEY *of Lancaster chyre.*

Silver a mill sail sable bendwise. *The olde armys of* NEWMARCHE.

Gules three horses' heads silver cut off at the neck. JOHN HORSSLEYE. *North Umberlonde.*

Azure six rings of gold. JOHN MOSGROWE. *Westmerland chyre.*

Silver three cheverons sable bezanty. COTHBERT COLVYLE. *North Umberlonde.*

Gules a cheveron silver with a green popinjay thereon. HEWE AYSTLAYE *of the byschopryk of Derham.*

Ermine a saltire gules. WYLYAM SCARGYLL. *Yorke chyre.*

Silver three rooks of the chess sable. WYLYAM ELTOFTE.

Gold billetty azure with a lion azure. SIR GYGGARD COUNT DE HON[TINGDON]. [This is the shield of Sir Guiscard d'Angle, K.G., who in 1377 was created Earl of Huntingdon for life.]

Gules a bend silver. ROBARD PRENDERGEST. *Northumberlonde.*

Barry gold and azure with a quarter silver and a garland gules on the quarter, *quartyrly wt Wastney armys.* ROBARDE HOLME. *Yorke chyre.*

Silver crusilly fitchy sable with three horse-shoes sable. ROBARDE BOWTH. *Northumberlond.*

Silver a fleur de lys sable. RYCHARDE FYSCHEBORNE *of the byschopperyke of Derham.*

Sable a lion silver with an orle of *synkefoyles of sylvyr.* SIR GERWAYS OF CLYFFTON. *Notyngham chyre.*

Silver a cheveron sable engrailed between *iij wolfe hedys of sabyll* rased. HARRY PRESTON *of Cravyn.*

Silver a bend gold and gules checky. RAWLYN VAUX. *Cumberlond chyre.*

Gules a bend sable with *iij roosys of golde.* EDWARD CLAYTON. *Lancaster chyre.*

Silver three swine sable *armyd wyth gold.* JOHN OF SWYNOWE. *Northumberlondchyre.*

Gules three cocks silver. NYCOLAS BLAUXTON *of the byschopperyke of Derham.*

Azure three crescents gold. SIR WYLYAM RYTHER *of York chyre.*

Gules two fesses indented between *iij semewys* silver. JOHN SAYER *of the byschopperyke of Deram chyre.*

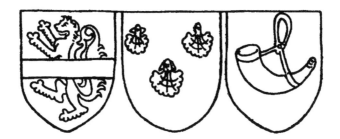

Silver a lion gules with a fesse sable athwart him. COSTANTYNE
MAHAWTE.

Sable three escallops silver. RYCHARDE ARNOLDE *of Holdyr-
nesse.*

A hunting horn. NYCOLAS BELYNGHAM. *Lancaster chyre.*

Silver a bend sable with three sheaves of silver. TOMAS
HASKETT. *Lancaster chyre.*

Gules three pillows of silver with their tassels. RYCHARDE
REDMAYNE. *Yorke chyre.*

Sabyll iij dyschys of sylvyr quartered with silver a saltire sable
and a border sable. RAWFE STANDYSCHE. *Lanc'.*

A cheveron sable between three crosses paty sable. TOMAS
MOSTON *of Howden chyre.*

Gold a cheveron gules and a chief vair. SIR ANTON' SEYNT
QWYNTYNE *of Holdernesse.*

Gold a cross gules with five escallops silver. SIR RAWFE
BIGOT.

Silver a cheveron gules between *iij hyndys hedys* rased gules.
WYLYAM FAYREFAX. *York chyre.*

Silver and gules lozengy. JOHN FETZ WYLYAM *of York chyre.*

Silver a saltire gules and a chief gules with three escallops
silver thereon. WYLYAM TAYLBOYS, *Lyncolle chyre.*

Gules a saltire silver with a molet sable. SIR ALYSAUNDYR
NEVYLL. *Yorke chyre.*

Silver a millrind cross sable with a crescent thereon for difference. SIR TOMAS FOLTHORPE. *Yorke chyre.*

Gules a lion silver with a bend azure. SIR PYERSSE TYLYALL
of Coumberlande.

Silver a fret gules and a chief azure.　Sir Cyrstoffyr Corwene *of Comberland.*

Ermine a fret gules and a chief gules.　Wylyam Thorynborowe.

Quarterly indented gules and ermine with a goat's head ermine in the quarter.　Charlys Morton.

Sable a cross silver with a cinqfoil in the quarter.　Morysby. *Westmerlande.*

Green a fret silver.　Tomas Salkell *of Comberlana.*

Silver a fret sable and a quarter sable.　Tomas Myddylton *of Yorkchyre.*

Silver a fret gules with a chief of gules.　Rychard Salkell *of Westmerland.*

Gold a bend sable with three pierced molets of silver [Hotham].　John Howton.

Silver a lion azure with an orle of crosslets gules.　Sir Wylyam Mountfort.

Sable a cheveron silver between three pots or posnets of silver. Wylyam Wystowe.

Silver an eagle sable *armyd wyth goulys.*　Rychard Wylbyrforse *of York chyre.*

Checkered gold and azure with a bend gules and three leopards gold rampant on the bend.　Harry Clyfford, *Gloucester chyre.*

Azure a cheveron ermine.　[This is a Lodbroke coat.]　Sir John Abbnall.

Silver a saltire gules.　Sir Robard Nevyll.　*York chyre of Fernley.*

Azure three roses gold.　Thomas Cyscyle.　*Yorke chyre yn Howden chyre.*

SOWTH CONTRE

Gold a cheveron gules with a border of sable engrailed. SIR UMFFREY STAFFORDE. *Dorsset chyre.*

Gold three roundels gules with a label azure. SIR PHELYPE CORTENEY. *Devynchyre.*

Azure crusilly [gold] a lion gold. SIR JOHN BREWSE *of Sowsex.*

Gules a fesse indented ermine. SIR JOHN DENHAM. *Devene chyre.*

Silver three demi-lions gules. SIR WILLIAM STORMYE *of Worcester chyre.*

Gules a soldan's head silver cut off at the neck [SOWDAN] quartering sable three pales silver wavy. SIR PERCYWALL SOWDANE *of Walys voryn'.*

Ermine a chief azure with three *lyonseuse* of silver. SIR JOHN
  LYLE. *Hampcbyre.*

Ermine three bars gules. SIR HENRY HOUSE *of Sowesx* [sic].

Silver a chief gules with two pierced molets silver. SIR JOHN
  SENGONE [ST. JOHN] *of Walys.*

Gold a fesse gules between six crosslets gules. SIR JOHN
  GREYNDER *of Glowcester cbyre.*

Silver a cheveron gules engrailed between three leopards' heads
  the lebardys hedys goulys as the cheveron ys [HALSHAM]
  quartered with paly gold and sable. [STRABOLGI] SIR
  HEWE HALSAM *of Sowsex.* [Sir Hugh Halsham died in
  1442].

Azure two cheverons gold. SIR THOMAS CHAWORTHE.
  Notyngham cbyre.

Silver a chief gules with *ij hertys hedys golae.* SIR JOHN
  POPHAM. *Hampcbyre.*

Bendy gold and azure of eight pieces with a border gules.
  SIR WILLIAM MOUNTFORT. *Warrewyk cbyre.*

Gules a cheveron silver. [The field is crusilly with crosslets
  indicated by plain crossed lines, thus, + ; the words
  the crossys sylvyr in the margin appear to have been struck
  out.] SIR MORRES OF BERKELEYE. *Cambyge cbyre.*

Azure a bend gold—a crescent for difference. CARMYNOWE.
  Devene cbyre.

Ermine a chief party gold and gules indented, with a rose
  gules on the gold. [SHOTTISBROKE] SIR RAWFE CHOTTYS-
  BROKE. *Oxynford cbyre.*

Silver a fret sable with a quarter gules. SIR RICHARD WER-
  NUN *of the Peke, Derbycbyre.*

Sable three bells of silver.   SIR WYLYAM PORTER *of Lyncolle chyre.*

Azure a cheveron gold between three leopards' heads gold. SIR HARRY FROWYKE *of Myddyllsex chyre.*

Gules a cheveron ermine between three fleurs de lys gold. SIR JOHN MWNGOMERY *of Walys.*

Sylvyr ana aseure pale a bend gules with three cinqfoils gold. SIR EDWARDE STRADLYNG *of Walys.*

Silver iij roos of purpull.   ALYXAUNDYR SPARROWE *of Myadyllsex.*

Gules a cheveron gold with *iij sterrys* of sable.   SIR RAYNALDE COBHAM *of Sowtherey chyre.*

Sable a cheveron ermine between three wings silver [NANFAN] quartering silver two wolves azure.   JOHN NANFAN *of Cornewayle.*

Azure a fesse gold between 'quatre mains' ot gold [QUATRE-MAIN] quartered with silver *ij mongrelys of goulys* [BRETON]. JOHN CATYRMAYNYS.   *Oxynford chyre.*

Sable a *faucon sylvyr armyd w[t] gola.*   TOMAS OF YEDDYNGE. *Myddylsex chyre.*

Party silver and gules with a bend countercoloured.   This is the shield of the poet.   JAFFEREY CHAWSERYS [CHAUCER]. *Oxynford chyre.*

Gold and aseure losange.   WYLYAM WARBYLTON.   *Hampchyre.*

Barry wavy of four pieces silver and gules and a bend sable with three golden crescents on the bend.   TOMAS GOLLO-FFYR.   *Oxynford chyre.*

Gules a millrind cross silver [UVEDALE] quartering azure a fret gold [SCURES].   TOMAS VEDALE.   *Hampchyre.*

Bendy gold and azure with a border of gules engrailed.   JOHN NEWBOROWE.   *Dorsset chyre.*

Sable a leopard rampant gold [BROCAS] quartered with sable two leopards silver [ROCHES].   WYLYAM BROCASE *of Hampt-chyre.*

(To be continued.)

LETTERS TO THE EDITOR

THE NOVELIST AND THE ANTIQUARY

Sir—

I observe in *The Ancestor* a paper in which the editor has
been kind enough to direct attention to my little book, *The
White Company*, and to overwhelm it with such a mass of genial
praise and ponderous irony that the impression left upon the
mind of the unfortunate author, who is alternately saluted and
belaboured, is a very mixed one. For the praise, all thanks !
For information which is new, all thanks also ! The best payment I can make for it is to return some of it in cases where,
in the most humble and respectful way possible, I may venture
to hint to this terrible specialist that he is himself misinformed.

I can assure him in the first place that I did not, as he
seems to imagine, invent my heraldic details. Such a book as
The White Company, dealing with so many special subjects as
medieval social life, monastic institutions, archery, heraldry,
land and sea warfare, etc., forbids an exhaustive study of any
one question ; but I have columns of books and sheaves of notes
to show that during a year's reading I took some pains to equip
myself for the work which has caused such trouble to the
editor's somewhat over critical spirit.

As to the question of whether the particular crest or arms
of any family quoted were exactly as described in that year, or
were so some years later, or even whether there is some in-
exactness of detail is really not of great moment. I had always
a reason for my description, but to give it in each case would
mean a considerable labour in reference. So in my detail of
actual costume, etc. The herald's dress, 'heraldic barret cap
with triple plume,' is taken not from Covent Garden, as the
editor somewhat unkindly asserts, but from a contemporary or
at least a medieval authority. I can assure him also that I had
other support than Lewis Carroll's for the assertion that heralds
blew on trumpets and wore tabards. Such criticism as this is
not helpful nor soothing.

To take a few concrete examples where the editor in

accusing me of inaccuracy has been inaccurate himself : he says that the cadency mark of crescents for the second son only came in two centuries later than the date of *The White Company*. That date is 1367. The editor will find—and it is a real pleasure to give him some information after all that he has given to me—that in a window of the Collegiate Church of St. Mary, Warwick, erected in 1361, the arms of the six sons of Thomas Beauchamp, fifteenth Earl of Warwick, appear differenced with a crescent, mullet, etc. It is probable therefore that the custom was perfectly well known to the prince's 'herald and scrivener.' That such a man should not know or speak of Saxons is absurd. Many of the oldest families in the kingdom were of pre-Norman descent, and even the most pedantic of medieval heralds could not ignore their origin.

The editor belabours me on the question of 'arms' or 'crests' upon shields or flags. Of course either arms or crests might be on either. At tournaments it was usual for the knight to exhibit two shields, one with his hereditary bearings and the other with his badge or impress. The Black Prince in his will mentions both shields. As to the flags, the arms were on the banner, and the crest might be on the standard. It is hypercriticism then to speak contemptuously of my text upon these points.

The editor quotes a blazoning and declares it to be too complex for that age. Possibly it does err upon that side. But naturally the knight would choose the most complex in testing the skill of a novice. In the blazonings mentioned in 'The Roll of Caerlaverock' (A.D. 1300) he will find some fairly complex arms. In this very number of *The Ancestor* one is given 'Azure three bars gold and a chief of gold with three pales and two gyrons of azure with an escutcheon of silver over all.' This dates from only a little later than *The White Company* and is as complex as the coat of arms in the text.

Finally, I can assure the editor that it is all right about the Cross of St. George. I have several times seen it in the course of a life which has included some long ocean voyages. There is no mistake upon my part, but just a little want of picturesque imagination upon his. The lions were the national emblem upon the English flag, St. George was the national saint. To speak of the lion of St. George was not to speak of it as a heraldic sign, but rather as the lion which is the symbol of the land of St. George. Shockingly inaccurate no doubt, but an imaginative writer demands some imaginative sympathy and response from his reader.

For all concerning Charing Cross, all thanks. I am quite mistaken about it. As to Henry's saddle, I am proud to find that I err with Dean Stanley.

Finally, let me conjure the editor to use his expert knowledge to encourage the novelist to study and to convey to his readers some of the glamour and interest of the past, instead of employing a carping and niggling style of criticism which might well discourage the writer from endeavouring to get accuracy of detail, since no man—not even the editor of *The Ancestor*—can hope to get *all* his detail accurate.

Yours faithfully,

ARTHUR CONAN DOYLE.

[Under the heading of 'Editorial Notes' we have endeavoured to defend ourselves against Sir Arthur Conan Doyle's brilliant counter-attack.]

ORIGINAL WILLS ON PARCHMENT

SIR—

In a notice in No. 2 of *The Ancestor* of a paper of mine on 'The Lowthers who held Judicial Office in Ireland in the Seventeenth Century,' the writer—not unnaturally, perhaps—expressed, or hinted, some doubt as to the accuracy of a statement that the will of Sir Gerard Lowther, one of the Justices of the Common Pleas in Ireland, dated September 24, 1624, was *on parchment*, and suggested that I might possibly have mistaken the probate copy of the will for the original.

But there has been no mistake in the matter. I was quite aware that wills on parchment were almost unknown in England, and I was familiar with the passage in Mr. Walter Rye's *Records and Record Searching* referred to by the reviewer; but as my paper was intended to be read before a meeting of the Cumberland and Westmoreland Antiquarian and Archæological Society at Durham, I thought that many of my hearers would be interested in learning that, in this case at least, a parchment will was not a creature of the imagination of a novelist.

That the document is an original will is beyond all question. It bears the signature of Sir Gerard Lowther, the testator, and the signatures of the three attesting witnesses—each in its own peculiar handwriting—and the pendant seal attached has the outline of an armorial shield, the charges on which have disappeared from pressure and rubbing.   On the back of the will is indorsed : ' Sir Gerrard Lowther his last Will and Testament ' ; and when the document was lodged for probate a further endorsement of ' *Testamentum Gerardi Lowther milis* ' was placed on it by some official of the Prerogative Court.

It was not uncommon in Ireland in the seventeenth and part of the eighteenth century that wills should be engrossed on parchment.   I have come across many of them in my own researches, and the officials of the Public Record Office in Dublin inform me, that amongst the wills proved in the Prerogative Court in Ireland, those on parchment are to be reckoned by hundreds.   Up to the present, I have not met with any will on parchment amongst those proved in the Diocesan Courts in Ireland.

The copies of wills annexed to grants of probate were on parchment, but these were not retained in the Prerogative or Consistorial Courts, and would not be found in the Public Record Office.   If for special reasons the original will was required to be kept by the executors, a transcript or exemplification of it would be made on parchment or paper, and lodged in the Court from which the probate issued.   This document, however, would express on the face of it that it was a copy, and would contain a statement as to the handing over of the original will.

This use of parchment for wills in Ireland was, no doubt, simply with a view to their better preservation.   Wills, even though dealing with personal estate as well as realty, were often left unproved, and are met with occasionally amongst the muniments of title of not inconsiderable estates.

I am, Sir, your obedient servant,

EDMUND T. BEWLEY.

40 Fitzwilliam Place, Dublin,
29 *November*, 1902.

THE GOWRIE ARMS

Dear Sir—

With reference to my note on this subject in the second number of *The Ancestor*, may I say that the armed figure on the side of the dexter supporter of the Earl of Gowrie's shield was certainly not introduced by John, third Earl, who was slain in 1600.   The figure appears in 1582, on a stone carved with the arms of William, first Earl.   The stone is now in the museum of the Scottish Antiquaries, being the gift of Lord Ruthven, to whom I am indebted for a photograph of the object.   The device left by the third Earl in Padua, and sent to King James in 1609, is another affair, and is described in my former letter.

A. LANG.

St. Andrews,
      22 *November*, 1902.

THE LANGUAGE OF HERALDRY

Sir—

The simplification of heraldry as treated in *The Ancestor* is most interesting to all to whom ancient armorial bearings are as regimental colours are to regiments in the present day.

Perhaps the following may to some extent supply additional proof, if such be required.

I have by me an original grant of differenced arms in 1540 (temp. Hen. VIII.) to Hever of Cookfield, co. Sussex, a cadet branch of Hever of Heverwood in Surrey, signed and sealed by Thomas Hawley, Clarencieux King of Arms.

The arms are thus described : ' Gules and vert quarterly on a chevron engrailed silver three sheaves gules banded betwixt three cats sauvage passant gold Upon his helm on a torse gules and vert a cat of the mountain in her proper colour, sitting holding in her mouth a goldfinch,' etc.

From this it would appear that though there is much unnecessary embroidery of language, the wording is clear compared with that of the heraldry of Elizabeth's and subsequent reigns.

For here are found silver for *argent*, sheaves for *garbs*, gold for *or*, sitting for *sejant*, and a torse of two colours instead of a colour and metal, the whole being authorized by a Tudor College of Arms.

I am, Sir, your obedient servant,

CECIL S. F. FERRERS.

Holyport, Berks,
      Oct. 29, 1902.

THE TRYONS OF HALSTEAD

Sir—

From the Parish Registers of Halstead, the following additional information relating to Sir Samuel Tryon,[1] 2nd Baronet, can be supplied :—

III. Sir Samuel Tryon of Halstead was buried 25 November 1664. His first wife Bridget, Lady Tryon, was buried at Halstead, 10 July 1654.

His widow married (ii) Timothy Thornbury and had a daughter Lois, baptised at Halstead, 20 March 166⁹⁄₀.

iii. Samuel John Tryon, eldest son of Sir Samuel by Susan Harvey, the second wife, died in infancy and was buried at Halstead, 1 November 1655.

iv. Sir Samuel John Tryon, 4th and last baronet, of Boreham, Essex, died at Boreham 24 April 1720, aged 64, and was buried at Halstead.

    1. Mary Tryon, daughter and coheir, was baptised at Boreham, 15 April 1690.

    2. Susan Tryon, daughter and coheir, married at Boreham, 13 November 1715, Barnaby Gibson of Little Stonham, Suffolk, Gent.

v. John Tryon was born at Halstead 24 Feb. 165⅞.

Sir Samuel Tryon, by his second wife Susan Harvey, had a daughter Susan baptised at Halstead, 1 February 166¾ and buried there 15th December 1669.

I can find no mention in the Halstead Register of the two sons named Moses, nor of the daughter called Anne.

        I am, Sir,

           Your obedient servant,

                C. F. D. SPERLING.

[To these valuable notes of Mr. Sperling's we have the following notes to add. Margaret, the wife of Governor Tryon, was the daughter and heir of William Wake, president and governor of Bombay. Governor Wake died at the end of Jan. 175⁹⁄₁ on his voyage from Bombay. He was son of Robert Wake of Thurning, co. Norfolk, gent. His relict Elizabeth, who was of the Norfolk family of Elwin of Thurning, died 19 June 1759, and was buried at Thurning (M.I.). He made a will 29 Sept. 1750 which, with a codicil 24 Jan. 175⁹⁄₁, was proved in the Prerogative Court of Canterbury

[1] *Ancestor*, ii. 183.

(163 *Busby*) 23 May 1751, by Peter and Joseph Godfrey, whom the testator had made his trustees and executors, power being reserved *etc.* to Elizabeth Wake, the relict and executrix.   The will names no Wake kinsfolk, and in the event of the testator's daughter dying without surviving issue, Thomas and Edward Phipps, sons of William Phipps, the late governor of Bombay, are to inherit.

The will of Sir Samuel John Tryon of Boreham in Essex, the fourth and last Tryon baronet, the date of whose death is corrected by Mr. Sperling to 24 April 1720, has been found amongst the wills proved in the Archdeaconry Court of Essex. He desired to be buried near his father's grave in the chancel of Halstead church, with an inscription : *Here lies the body of Sir Samuell John Tryon the last baronet of that Family.* He gave his plate and linen to his wife Dame Mary Tryon, his executrix.   He gave his manor of Burrells with its lands in Rawreth and Wickford to his granddaughter Mary Davy for life, with remainder to her issue, with remainder to his nephew Samuel Henderson.   If his daughter Susan Gibson died without issue the said Mary Davy was to have Gladfen Hall with its lands, with like remainders.   After his wife's death the said Mary was to have the reversion of Letches farm in Halstead, with remainder to her issue, with remainder to testator's nephew Henry Henderson.   To the said Mary Davy he gave two farms in Great and Little Maplestead, with remainder, in default of issue of her, to his two nieces Susan and Eunice Henderson.   To the said Mary Davy and her issue he gave a farm called Loveday Well and a farm in Halstead and Stisted with remainder to her issue, with remainder in default of such issue to the testator's sister Susan Henderson.   This will, dated 3 Nov. 1719, was proved 19 May 1721 by the relict, powers being reserved to Mary Davy, the other executrix, who was a minor.   Although Eleanor Tryon, half-sister of Sir Samuel John Tryon, had carried most of the Tryon estates away to the Franklyns, this will would seem to dispose of the story that the testator died in any notable poverty.]

EDITORIAL NOTES

THE controversy so happily begun in the first number
of *The Ancestor* concerning the English gentleman and
his ancient standing has not, we hope, ceased to interest our
readers. But we cannot allow this controversy to continue
as a battle over the gentility of Mr. Thomas Brassey, a matter
which, judging from the letters before us, may be said to be as
hotly in dispute as were the gentilities of Richard Barker and
William Exelby. Our correspondent the 'Learned Clerk' of
No. 2 was countered by Mr. Reade in No. 3 and we hold
back with some regret a new correspondent, 'Ap Japheth' to
wit, who would tear Mr. Reade's letter from our pages. Owd
Tom Brassey, it is allowed, could write his name, but he
wrote it with difficulty at the end of ill-spelled documents.
It is denied that in his youth he was articled to a land-surveyor,
and the ancient extraction of his family is said to have been
bluntly denied by its homely representative. The authority
of Thomas Brassey himself is again quoted us in denial of Mr.
Reade's statement that his father possessed an estate at Buerton
or elsewhere. For the discussion of these matters however
we can give little of our space. Lord Brassey himself has
declared his willingness to begin his pedigree with his famous
father, an ancestor and house-founder if ever there was one,
and in the Brassey peerage we find nothing ridiculous.

* * *

With one feature of the Brassey dispute we may concern
ourselves. We understand that Lord Brassey was officially
allowed, as of right, the ancient arms of Bressy or Bresci.
Our latest correspondent insists, and not without warmth, that
this house is long extinct in the male line, and that the arms
of Bressy passed to the Bulkeleys, descendent from a Bulkeley
marriage with the Bressy heiress. With any contention that
the 'whole coat' of a family should be the right of its head
alone and should pass in due course only to its true representatives we have every sympathy, for such was the ancient practice,
now disregarded by the heralds.
But it is well known that the 'whole coat,' by the practice

of our modern heralds, is allowed to any cadet of the house who can show a male descent from its bearer. This, we understood, Lord Brassey had shown, and if this be so, although we may blame the College of Arms for its admission of such a principle into armory, we cannot in fairness give blame for its application in a particular case. Though we are unacquainted with the rules of the College of Arms for its practice in dealing with genealogical evidences, we profess ourselves unable to believe that a pedigree based upon mere statement has in our own time been allowed to pass its examining officers.

* * *

'Ap Japheth' finds reason for taking us to task in Mr. Reade's statement that Thomas Brassey, 'though not of gentle birth, save in the technical or heraldic sense, yet came of a good yeoman stock,' and this on the ground, if we follow his argument, that the sentence contains a 'contradictory heraldic assertion.' We find no such contradiction. Mr. Reade, to our mind, refers in the first part of his sentence to the belief of certain modern writers that some unsubstantial nobility is in the blood of the remotest descendant of the bearer of a coat of arms. Such belief we hasten to repudiate for *The Ancestor*. A yeoman—and there are English counties where the class survives yet—is a yeoman to-day and would be a yeoman to-morrow, even if an antiquary should happen upon a De Banco Roll entry or Chancery Plea which should show him descended from a Domesday tenant-in-chief. It is but the other day that a genealogist showed us some evidence which would go to connect a west-country yeoman family with an ancestry which, if we read the riddle of his name aright, 'Ap Japheth' would call princely.

* * *

We owe to Mr. P. J. de Carteret, the genealogist of his ancient house, some notes in addition to the account, in our last issue, of the Carterets of St. Ouen. Mr. Carteret points out that our reference to Jane Anne Le Maistre, wife of Elias Le Maistre, is couched in a misleading form. This lady, who became Dame de St. Ouen on the death of Robert, Earl of Granville, was by birth a Dumaresq. Her great-grandson, Edward Charles Malet de Carteret, to-day the twenty-eighth Seigneur of St. Ouen, has admirably restored the ancient manor which was falling into ruin. On his adding his name to the long list of Carterets who have been elected jurats, he was granted precedence of all his fellow-jurats for that he was Seigneur of St. Ouen and representative of the Carterets. This ancient right of precedence has always been with the Seigneurs of St. Ouen, and was confirmed by several orders in council under Charles II.

* * *

A note of the greatest interest which had escaped us in our survey of the Carterets is pointed out to us by our correspondent. It is that from about 1100 to the death of Sir Charles de Carteret in 1715 the manor of St. Ouen descended without a break from father to son, a record which is surely a very remarkable one. For a case of the reverse fortune our readers have only to refer to our article on the family of Knightley of Fawsley. Since the sixteenth century at least Fawsley has hardly ever descended for more than one generation in a direct line. Again and again have direct heirs failed and cousins been called in to the inheritance, until in our own time it seems as though in a coming generation Fawsley will seek in vain for cadets of the house of Knightley.

* * *

We have received from the solicitors to Sir Lambton Loraine a letter directing our attention to a deed poll lately executed under his hand, which deed poll is addressed especially to His Majesty's officers of arms, with whom Sir Lambton Loraine would appear to have a very pretty quarrel and one of the greatest interest to students of English armorial practice.

* * *

Abandoning Whereas and Whereas Sir Lambton's case would appear to be as follows. His family of Loraine is an ancient one, seated at Kirkharle in Northumberland in the fifteenth century, matching with the gentle houses of Northumberland, being tenants in chief of the Crown, and styled squires in the inquests held after their deaths and in other records and muniments. They bore arms as of ancient right and custom, their shield being quarterly sable and silver with a cross quarterly and counter-coloured, which Sir Lambton's solicitors describe with unnecessary detail as 'sometimes represented as hung by its guige [O blessed word of the Hand-

books of Heraldry !] on its supporter a bay laurel tree couped
with two branches sprouting out proper.'

*   *   *

Of this family Robert Loraine is at home at Kirkharle
when William Flower, Norroy King of Arms, is 'visiting'
Northumberland in 1575, and his arms and lineage might well
be looked for in the visitation book of that county. But they
are neglected ' as were the pedigrees and arms of nearly all the
noble and gentle men then seated in the said county of Northumberland.' Loraine abides at Kirkharle, a squire of name
and land, and in due time comes Sir Richard St. George,
knight, Norroy King of Arms, a-visiting Northumberland,
but in his book, as in Flower's, no pedigree is set down for
the squire of Kirkharle. Tombstones and escheators' inquests
still give the family the style of their rank, their crossed shield
is still displayed by them unquestioned upon stone and brass
and wax, and in 1664 Thomas Loraine of Kirkharle is created
a baronet.

*   *   *

Before this time the heralds have moved. William Loraine,
a cadet of the house and uncle to the first baronet, at the age
of twenty-three years obtains from Sir John Borough, Garter
King of Arms, a certificate of his arms.   The arms in this
certificate are described as ' argent a pale fusilly azure in
the dexter chief point an escutcheon of the last,' a shield for
which no ancient authority may be found, and a shield very
unlike the quartered cross of Loraine. With the new shield
went a crest as new as the shield.

*   *   *

This shield with a variant of the new crest is pictured
beside the pedigree entered by Sir William Dugdale in the
visitation book of 1666, at which date the Loraines are at last
discovered by the heralds in the ancient home of Kirkharle.
But with this new coat and crest the Northumbrian Loraines,
as may be guessed, meddle not. Their old coat is good
enough for them : the first baronet seals his will with it, and
it is borne by those who follow him.   Wherefore Sir Lambton
Loraine, baronet and rear-admiral, declares in his deed poll
that he does not ' for the reasons hereinbefore given accept as
arms proper to be attached to the family pedigree of Loraine
of Kirkharle the arms designed by Sir John Borough Knight,'

and that he has used after the custom of his forefathers, and shall on all occasions in future use, the arms of those fore-fathers.

* * *

We have every sympathy with Sir Lambton Loraine, and with his desire to use the shield which his forefathers bore in the border wars rather than the shield whose story begins and ends with its being neatly tricked with pen and ink in two seventeenth-century register books. But we watch him with a fearful interest as he goes with his sailor-like reckless-ness towards his doom. Let him remain obstinate in his determination, and nothing will save him. Pitying and help-less we shall see his name written in some dictionary of Armorial Gents with his arms in all the shame of italics and himself exposed to all the social ignominy which notoriously attends the contumacious and non-armigerous gent.

* * *

Four volumes of *The Ancestor* now lie before our readers, and in face of the manifold errors and inaccuracies of these four volumes the editor is fain to acknowledge sorrowfully that the last phrase of Sir Conan Doyle's reply to us finds its mark. Infallibility is not with us. But turning to the beginning of Sir Conan's letter we must hasten to add that none of the corrections we seek for have come to us through Sir Conan Doyle.

* * *

Sir Conan bids us look in his letter for payment in kind for the information we have given him. In the humblest fashion let us assure him that he has as yet wiped out nothing of his debt.

* * *

Surely no misunderstanding of the meaning of our article on 'The Antiquary and the Novelist' is possible ! Well we know that there be ' nine and sixty ways of constructing tribal lays,' and that Sir Conan's way is one of the nine and sixty and as right as any of the others. Be it far from us that we should be suspected of a desire to teach Sir Conan how the bricks of romance should be laid. But with detail of a certain nature *The Ancestor* has its concern. Of this detail we find an abun-dance has gone to the making of *The White Company*, and after considering it gravely and with due care we find it has been in nearly every case mishandled and mistaken.

* * *

Sir Conan's answer is the answer of the Bellman : 'What I tell you three times is true,' but Sir Conan has more than the bellman's imperiousness, and what he has asserted a second time must be accepted by us.

* * *

In this matter Sir Conan has chosen to meet us as an antiquary, and as such his authority must needs be of the slightest. To the nearest Cæsar of archæology we appeal, asking whether a man to whom the cabstand monument in Charing Cross station represents a 'beautiful old stone cross' hallowed by six hundred years of memories speaks with such authority in archæological matters that his unsupported word can be taken in evidence.

* * *

Yet it is with mere assertion that Sir Conan would bear us down. We deny that our criticism can be truly described as carping and niggling. Had we used such our article would have been spun to a tedious length. It is upon the question of armory that we must first defend ourselves. Sir Conan very properly disclaims pedantic exactness for his many blazons of arms, but declares that he had always a good reason for his description. If he told us that his armory was frankly fancywork to colour the page withal he would be well within his rights as a novelist, but we may well complain of the repeated assertion that the colour is true in the main and based upon good authority. What good reason, forsooth, can be shown for the swan wings of Beauchamp or for the 'roebuck gules on a field argent' of Montague? The good reason for these, we are to believe, could be found by Sir Conan if he could afford the labour of referring to it. We deny that any such reason exists.

* * *

In the matter of costume, too, the word of Sir Conan's answer must content us. Does he describe the *salade* as the characteristic tilting helm of the days of Chandos, the brigandine as a confection of chainmail? Sir Conan points to his locked bookshelves for all reply. Sir Conan's heralds are tabarded Jacks of all trades, at once presented to us as heralds, as scriveners and as musicians or trumpeters, and to those who question the accuracy of the presentation Sir Conan replies that he has ' support for the assertion.'

* * *

Back again with our armory we find Sir Nigel Loring's companions bearing their 'crests' on their banners as well as on their shields. Naked assertion must confirm the custom. 'Of course,' says Sir Conan, 'either arms or crests might be on either.' If Sir Conan Doyle can show instances of this practice in the fourteenth century he should not delay to add to our knowledge of the armory of that period, but if he cannot show such his 'of course' is of little value. The passage which follows concerning the Black Prince's will, a document sufficiently well known to antiquaries, only serves to show that Sir Conan has not pushed his armorial studies far enough to understand the distinction between the crest and the badge. The medley of figures presented by the 'standard' in ages long after our period is not to the purpose. We are dealing with the fourteenth century and with its banners.

* * *

It is difficult, as Sir Conan Doyle is not familiar with the customs or practice of medieval armory, to make it clear to him why his Alleyne Edricson should not in the fourteenth century blazon a shield to Sir Nigel's satisfaction as 'argent a fesse azure charged with three lozenges dividing three mullets sable, over all on an escutcheon of the first a jambe gules.' We say that if Sir Conan examines this shield he will find it incompletely blazoned even by the rules of his handbook of heraldry, and may add that the fourteenth century not having as yet invented the handbook's formula for blazoning shields, Master Alleyne could hardly be asked to pass his little-go in the use of that formula under the approving eye of Sir Nigel. Sir Conan's 'argent' and his 'escutcheon of the first' are both far away from his period. As a copy of every known roll of English arms is now amongst the writer's manuscripts, it is useless to refer him for information to the Roll of Caerlaverock. Neither this nor any other roll has any support for Sir Conan, nor will any fourteenth century armorial document give the least colour to Sir Nigel's most amazing boast of the sixty-four noble quarterings of his shield, a phrase of which no Englishman of his time or near it could have guessed the meaning.

* * *

We come at last to the one and only point at which Sir Conan has an answer ready for us. Sir Conan asserted that the crescent was in the fourteenth century already an established ' difference ' for the shield of a second son and we mocked at the idea. And now Sir Conan, with ' real pleasure ' in giving us the information, tells of a window erected in 1361 in the Collegiate Church of St. Mary in Warwick, wherein the arms of the sons of Thomas Beauchamp, the Earl of Warwick, appear with these differences. Sir Conan may stint his pleasure for his information can have no foundation other than some passage in a handbook of heraldry.

* * *

No such window, we believe, exists at the present day, although the figures of the earl's sons are found in seventeenth century drawings, at which date there remained some in a window of the choir, and some in the great north window. The choir was not built in 1361, having been begun in pursuance of the will of the earl who died in 1369. After the choir was built the nave was begun, and when the great north window was finished these images of the Beauchamps were at last placed in position. But Sir Conan's date matters little. What does matter is that, although the younger sons difference their arms, as did many fourteenth-century knights, with small charges, the ' cadency mark of the descent for the second son ' is not to be found, the second son differencing with a ring. As therefore, in the only case in which Sir Conan is bold enough to quote authority, that authority crumbles on handling, the value of his other assertions suffers sympathetically.

* * *

What can we say to Sir Conan's explanation of the ' red lion of Saint George ' ? We confess that we can make nothing of it. ' To speak of the Lion of St. George was not to speak of it as a heraldic sign but rather as the Lion which is the symbol of the land of St. George. . . . The Lions were the national emblem upon the English flag.'

* * *

But Sir Conan, if he will pardon us, does speak of the

lion of St. George as a heraldic sign. Not in one but in many passages does he describe this 'red lion' as the national badge borne by every English archer. No red lion has ever appeared in an English banner, nor was any red lion ever recognized as a symbol of the land of St. George, although it appears on the banner of the king of the land of St. Andrew. Sir Conan has reason for his complaint. When we see the glorious red cross of Saint George, the ancient national emblem of our race, exchanged for a red lion without significance or historic associations, our 'imaginative sympathy' fails us altogether.

    *   *   *

We offer our hearty thanks to Sir Conan for that he has met us in fair field, and we repeat that blame for any errors in *The White Company* is with the makers of bad handbooks of archæology and not with the novelist. That Sir Conan has, as he asserts, read columns of books is but too apparent, in every page of his romance. Had he read but his Froissart, his Chaucer and his Langland, and kept his bookshelves clear of the rest, *The White Company* would have been the better book and its author beyond our criticism.

Butler & Tanner, The Selwood Printing Works, Frome, and London.

THE PASTON LETTERS

Edited by JAMES GAIRDNER

Of the Public Record Office

4 *vols.*, 21*s. net.*

THE FOURTH VOLUME CONTAINING THE INTRODUCTION AND
SUPPLEMENT MAY BE PURCHASED SEPARATELY.

Price 10*s.* 6*d. net.*

These Letters are the genuine correspondence of a family in
Norfolk during the Wars of the Roses. As such they are altogether
unique in character ; yet the language is not so antiquated as to present
any serious difficulty to the modern reader. The topics of the letters
relate partly to the private affairs of the family, and partly to the
stirring events of the time ; and the correspondence includes State
papers, love-letters, bailiffs' accounts, sentimental poems, jocular epistles,
etc.

Besides the public news of the day, such as the loss of Normandy
by the English ; the indictment and subsequent murder at sea of the
Duke of Suffolk ; and all the fluctuations of the great struggle of York
and Lancaster ; we have the story of John Paston's first introduction
to his wife ; incidental notices of severe domestic discipline, in which
his sister frequently had her head broken ; letters from Dame Elizabeth
Brews, a match-making mamma, who reminds the youngest John
Paston that Friday is 'St. Valentine's Day,' and invites him to come
and visit her family from the Thursday evening till the Monday, etc.,
etc.

Every letter has been exhaustively annotated ; and a Chronological
Table, with most copious Indices, conclude the Work.

HENRY HALLAM, *Introduction to the Literature of Europe,* i. 228. *Ed.* 1837 : ' *The
Paston Letters* are an important testimony to the progressive condition of Society, and come in
as a precious link in the chain of moral history of England which they alone in this period
supply. They stand, indeed, singly, as far as I know, in Europe ; for though it is highly
probable that in the archives of Italian families, if not in France or Germany, a series of
merely private letters equally ancient may be concealed ; I do not recollect that any have
been published. They are all written in the reigns of Henry VI. and Edward IV., except a
few that extend as far as Henry VII., by different members of a wealthy and respectable, but
not noble, family ; and are, therefore, pictures of the life of the English gentry of that age.'

THE MORNING POST : ' A reprint of Mr. James Gairdner's edition of *The Paston
Letters* with some fresh matter, including a new introduction. Originally published in
1872–75, it was reprinted in 1895, and is now again reproduced. The introductions have
been reset in larger type, and joined together in one, conveniently broken here and there by
fresh headings. The preface is practically a new one. . . . It is highly satisfactory for
readers who care about history, social or political, to have this well-printed and admirably
introduced and annotated edition of these famous letters.'

MANCHESTER GUARDIAN : ' One of the monuments of English historical scholarship that needs no commendation.'

ARCHIBALD CONSTABLE & CO LTD
2 WHITEHALL GARDENS WESTMINSTER

The Stall Plates of the Knights of the Order of the Garter 1348-1485

Consisting of a Series of 91 Full-sized Coloured Facsimiles with Descriptive Notes and Historical Introductions by

W. H. ST. JOHN HOPE, M.A., F.S.A.

Dedicated by gracious privilege during her lifetime to HER LATE MAJESTY QUEEN VICTORIA, SOVEREIGN OF THE MOST NOBLE ORDER OF THE GARTER.

The edition is strictly limited and only 500 copies of the work have been printed.

The object of the work is to illustrate the whole of the earlier Stall Plates, being the remaining memorials of the fourteenth and fifteenth century of Knights elected under the Plantagenet Sovereigns from Edward the Third, Founder of the Order, to Richard the Third, inclusive, together with three palimpsest plates and one of later date.

The Stall Plates are represented full-size and in colours on Japan vellum, in exact facsimile of the originals, in the highest style of chromolithography, from photographs of the plates themselves.

Each plate is accompanied by descriptive and explanatory notes, and the original and general characteristics of the Stall Plates are fully dealt with in an historical introduction.

There are also included numerous seals of the Knights, reproduced by photography from casts specially taken for this work.

The work may be obtained bound in half leather, gilt, price £6 net; or the plates and sheets loose in a portfolio, £5 10s. net; or without binding or portfolio, £5 net.

ATHENÆUM : 'It is pleasant to welcome the first part of a long promised and most important heraldic work, and to find nothing to say of it which is not commendatory. The present part contains ten coloured facsimiles out of the ninety plates which the work will include when completed. They reflect the greatest credit on all concerned in their production.'

MORNING POST : 'There is a fine field for antiquarian research in the splendid collection of heraldic plates attached to the stalls in the choir of St. George's Chapel, Windsor Castle, and it will be a matter of satisfaction to all who are interested in old memorials that Mr. W. H. St. John Hope has given close examination to these ancient insignia and now presents the results of his investigations, with many reproductions.'

ARCHIBALD CONSTABLE & CO LTD
2 WHITEHALL GARDENS WESTMINSTER

ENGLISH CORONATION RECORDS

Edited by

LEOPOLD G. WICKHAM LEGG, B.A.
NEW COLLEGE, OXFORD

Imperial 8vo.

Edition limited to 500 copies of which only a few remain.

Price 31s. 6d. net.

This work is an attempt to illustrate the history of the coronation of the Sovereigns of England from the earliest times to the present. Twenty-nine documents have been collected; and, so far as possible, the transcripts have been made from contemporary manuscripts.

A translation has been added to the Latin and Anglo-French documents.

Mr. W. H. St. John Hope has written a note on the 'Cap of Maintenance,' in which he has described the history and manner of the investiture of peers.

The whole work constitutes a full collection of coronation precedents.

The illustrations include a reproduction in colours of the picture of an English coronation at Corpus Christi College, Cambridge, and a photogravure of the coronation of St. Edmund in a manuscript belonging to Captain Holford; and also reproductions in collotype from the manuscript life of St. Edward in the University Library at Cambridge. The Crown of Queen Edith, which is represented from a portrait of Queen Henrietta Maria in the National Portrait Gallery, has not, it is thought, been noticed before. A feature of the illustrations will be the coronation chair which has been taken from the block cut for the late Sir Gilbert Scott's *Gleanings from Westminster Abbey*; and there are also three plates showing the coronation robes of Queen Victoria.

ATHENÆUM : ' Among the minor compensations for the prolonged delay incident to a modern act of crowning is the time that it affords for the production of such an important historical treatise as that which has just been produced by Mr. Wickham Legg. In this handsome volume we find brought together every historical document of importance that bears on the question of English coronations from that of Aidan in the sixth century to that of Victoria thirteen centuries later.'

ARCHIBALD CONSTABLE & CO Ltd
2 WHITEHALL GARDENS WESTMINSTER

THE

HOUSE OF PERCY

By GERALD BRENAN

With numerous Illustrations, and an Introduction by THE EDITOR

Dedicated by Permission to
HIS GRACE THE DUKE OF NORTHUMBERLAND

2 vols. large 8vo, price £1 1s. net

EDITION DE LUXE

Also a Large Paper Edition limited to 150 copies
£3 3s. net

The following is a list of some of the Illustrations included in in 'The House of Percy':

Alnwick Castle, Bamborough Castle, from drawing by Herbert Railton. Portrait of Henry Percy, 1st Earl of Northumberland—the 'Earl Percie' of Chevy Chase (reproduced in colours from a contemporary MS.). Portrait of Henry, 7th Earl of Northumberland. The Village of Perci in Normandy : the cradle of the race. Syon House, Northumberland House, from drawings by Herbert Railton. The full armorial bearings of the present Duke of Northumberland in colours. Various shields, signatures, and *facsimile* letters.

NEWCASTLE LEADER : ' The history is admirably illustrated with clever drawings by Herbert Railton, elaborate reproductions of the arms, crests, escutcheons, and pedigrees of the Percy family and its branches. Of course Alnwick Castle comes in for special treatment, and Mr. Railton is at his best in his sketches of that famous fortress-residence.'

ARCHIBALD CONSTABLE & CO LTD
2 WHITEHALL GARDENS WESTMINSTER

THE
POSTHUMOUS MEMOIRS
OF FRANÇOIS RENE

Vicomte de Chateaubriand

Sometime Ambassador

to England

Translated by ALEXANDER TEIXEIRA DE MATTOS

Illustrated with Contemporary Portraits. In 6 vols.

Purple cloth, gilt top, price £4 10s. net

Portrait of François René, Vicomte de Chateaubriand
(*frontispiece*). The Chateau de Combourg. Chateaubriand's
birthplace, at St. Malo. Portraits of Louis XVIII.; Marie
Antoinette; Malsherbes; Mirabeau; General Washington;
Madame de Chateaubriand, wife of the Author; the Baron de
Breteuil; the Comte de Rivarol; Frederic William II.; Pel-
tier, Editor of *Les Actes des Apôtres*; Napoleon Buonaparte;
the Comte de Montlosier; the Abbé Delille; L. M. de
Fontanes; Burke; Pitt; and George III.

This noblest of nineteenth-century biographies covers the whole eighty
years of the distinguished author's life,—his career at the court of Louis XVI.,
—his emigration to America upon the outbreak of the Revolution,—wander-
ings among the North-American Indians,—return to France,—service in the
Royalist Army,—days of poverty in London,—literary and diplomatic career
under Napoleon I.,—resignation of the Valais Legation upon the murder of
Duc d'Enghien,—journey in the East,—attacks upon Napoleon,—the history
of the First Restoration,—of Chateaubriand's Embassy to Sweden,—of the
Hundred Days which Chateaubriand spent with Louis XVIII. at Ghent.
The Second Restoration is fully described, and Chateaubriand writes of
his peerage,—of the assassination of the Duc de Berry,—of his Embassy to
Berlin and life in that capital,—of his Embassy to London,—of his relations
with George IV. and his Ministers,—of English Society at that period,—of
the suicide of Lord Londonderry,—of the death of Louis XVIII. and accession of Charles X.,—of his conduct in opposition, as Minister of Foreign
Affairs, and as Ambassador to Rome,—of Roman Society, ancient and modern;
of his interviews with Popes Leo XII. and Pius VIII., of the Papal Con-
claves. He writes in full detail of the fall of the Polignac Ministry, the
Revolution of July, and the usurpation of Louis-Philippe

ARCHIBALD CONSTABLE & CO Ltd
2 WHITEHALL GARDENS WESTMINSTER

The Old Court Suburb

(KENSINGTON)

By J. H. LEIGH HUNT

Edited, with an Introduction and Notes, by AUSTIN DOBSON

With very numerous Photogravure and other Illustrations by HERBERT
RAILTON, CLAUDE SHEPPERSON, and EDMUND J. SULLIVAN

2 vols., large square 8vo, price £1 1s. net

EDITION DE LUXE

Signed by the Artists, and limited to 150 copies, price £4 4s. net.

Kensington (the Old Court Suburb) was still, at the beginning of the
nineteenth century, in the country, and the garden of Wilberforce, who
occupied Gore House from 1808 to 1825, is described as being 'full of
lilacs and laburnums, nightingales and swallows.'

'The way to it (Kensington) is the pleasantest out of town ; you may
walk in high road, or on grass, as you please ; the fresh air salutes you from
a healthy soil, and there is not a step of the way, from its commencement at
Kensington Gore to its termination beyond Holland House, in which you
are not greeted with the face of some pleasant memory.'

ATHENÆUM : 'To produce a good old book and make it a new one without offence
is a great feat. . . . Mr. Austin Dobson was the very man to write the graceful introduction
and brief notes. . . .'

Gilbert White's Selborne

Edited by DR. R. BOWDLER SHARPE

The hitherto unpublished 'Garden Kalendar,' to which the Very
Rev. DEAN HOLE has written an Introduction, is included

Illustrated by E. J. SULLIVAN, J. G. KEULEMANS, and HERBERT RAILTON

Price, 2 vols. large 8vo, £2 2s. net.

COUNTRY LIFE : 'The Edition of "The Natural History and Antiquities of
Selborne and A Garden Kalendar," issued in two volumes, is a work so modestly beautiful,
and so precious, that the reviewer approaches it with awe. . . . The topographical pictures
by Mr. Herbert Railton of the familiar objects at Selborne—Norton Farm, the Plestor,
the Street, the Church, the Yew Tree, and so forth—are as good as can be, the very
perfection of delicate work. Birds and beasts have fallen to the lot of Mr. J. G. Keulemans, and, short of colour, I have never seen anything of the kind nearly as good as they
are. The birds are, perhaps, a trifle more perfect than the beasts. Of full-page illustrations
there are fifty ; of minor illustrations a good number. . . . Altogether this is a very complete and worthy edition, and it is destined to be the family Bible of those who follow the
cult of Gilbert White, and the number of them increases every day.'

ARCHIBALD CONSTABLE & CO LTD

2 WHITEHALL GARDENS WESTMINSTER

CONSTABLE'S

Time Table of Modern
History A.D. 400-1870

Compiled and arranged by M. MORISON.   160 pp.,
about 15 in. × 12 in.   12*s.* 6*d.* net.

CONTENTS :— Parallel Vertical Tables — Genealogical Tables — Ruling
Monarchs—General Chart of Ancient and Modern History—Index—
Maps—Europe showing the Barbarian Invasions : Europe, A.D. 451 ;
Europe, A.D. 476 ; Europe, A.D. 500 ; Europe, A.D. 768–814 ; Europe,
A.D. 962 ; Europe showing the spread of Christianity, *circa* 1000 ;
Europe, A.D. 1360 ; Europe, A.D. 1648 ; Europe, A.D. 1740 ; Central
and Eastern Europe, 1814–1863.

The work is an epitome of Modern History, 400–1870,
and constitutes a book of reference invaluable to historical
students.   Facts and dates in the history, not of Europe
alone, but also of Asia and America, are dealt with.

The tables consist of parallel vertical columns, each column
containing a history of one of the important nations of the
world during the period covered.

The work also contains a series of the more important
European Genealogical Tables, complete list of ruling
Monarchs and Popes, a chart showing a bird's-eye view of
ancient and modern history, and a full index.   Added to these
are a series of Maps showing the barbarian migrations over
Europe, the spread of Christianity and the various important
territorial changes which have taken place in Europe since the
year 400 A.D.

THE SCHOOLMASTER : 'This is a most valuable book of reference for teachers and
students of history. . . . We can heartily recommend it as a work of real usefulness.'
THE ACADEMY : 'A most valuable book, and almost deserves the adjective "monumental." It is a compendium of historical dates viewed from almost every possible aspect. No
student should think his shelves complete without this uniquely valuable book.' *THE
DAILY NEWS* : 'To the professional historian this volume will prove a convenient "ready
reckoner"; to the amateur it will come as a boon and a blessing.' *WESTMINSTER
GAZETTE* : 'The information is given in the clearest type, with ample margins, and as a
book of reference it is one of the easiest to consult with the assurance of satisfactory results'
THE GUARDIAN : 'Remarkably accurate. . . . We can conscientiously recommend the
book as a companion to the histories of Europe.'

ARCHIBALD CONSTABLE & CO Ltd
2 WHITEHALL GARDENS WESTMINSTER

THE ANCESTOR

INDEX OF NAMES

VOLUMES I.–IV.

Aa, iii. 237
Abbott, i. 271, 273 ; ii. 227
Abell, i. 274
Ablett, ii. 208, 209
Acclum, iv. 241
Acliston, ii. 142
Acton, i. 266
Adam, i. 273, 274 ; ii. 129
Adams, i. 275 ; ii. 30, 219 ; iv. 135
Adcock, i. 266 ; ii. 227
Adleston, iii. 64
Aguillon, i. 245, 246
Alabaster, i. 273
Alcocke, Alkoc, ii. 136, 153 ; iv. 130
Alcorne, ii. 208
Aleyn, iv. 150
Alford, ii. 197
Alington, ii. 210
Alkumlowe, Alcmudelowe, ii. 136, 145
Allabye, i. 266
Allanson, ii. 208
Allardice, iv. 83, 87
Allen, i. 275 ; ii. 208, 209 ; iii. 61, 126
Allison, ii. 23
Allostock, see Lostock
Alloway, ii. 211
Allport, i. 272 ; iv. 135
Alsopp, i. 164, 270
Alviano, iv. 190
Alwey, i. 241
Ambler, ii. 218
Ambrose, i. 271
Amerongen, van, iii. 238
Ames, i. 240
Amstel, iii. 237
Amy, ii. 211, 212
Amyand, i. 13
Amyes, Amies, iii. 51
Anderson, ii. 57, 209 ; iii. 115
Anderton, Andirton, Andreton, i. 273 ;
    ii. 130, 133, 135, 139, 140, 144
Andrewe, i. 273, 277 ; ii. 211
Androwes, i. 271 ; iv. 139
Anger, i. 275
Angle, iv. 243
Anguish, ii. 84
Anne, ii. 198
Annyon, i. 267
Anstis, iii. 33
Anstrudder, i. 275
Anysley, iv. 237
Ap Griffin, ii. 96
Ap John, iv. 138

Ap Rhys, iii. 118
Applebee, iii. 51
Appleton, ii. 84
Apsey, i. 268
Apsley, i. 267, 275, 277
Aquila, i. 177
Arblaster, ii. 211
Arbuthnot, iv. 84
Arderne, i. 183, 248
Argent, ii. 203
Armentirs, Armetiers, Armetières, Ar-
    meters, Armenters, Armere, Armets,
    Ermenters, Ermenteres, Ermets,
    Ermondeys, Ermycers, i. 191, 192,
    193
Armstrong, i. 267
Arnold, i. 269, 276 ; ii. 208 ; iv. 245
Arran, ii. 54
Arscot, iv. 173
Arundel, Arrondell, i. 219, 238, 273 ;
    ii. 94, 209, 210 ; iii. 121, 122, 186,
    201 ; iv. 137, 227
Ashberrye, ii. 210
Ashbie, ii. 208
Ashburnham, ii. 89
Ashe, i. 107, 109, 270 ; iv. 186
Ashley, Ascheley, i. 7 ; ii. 155
Ashton, i. 275, 276 ; ii. 29
Ashworth, i. 270
Askelok, iii. 79
Askewe, iii. 208
Askwith, i. 266 ; ii. 214
Assheton, iv. 238
Astell, i. 276
Astley, Aystlaye, ii. 84, 181 ; iv. 243
Aston, iii. 54
Atkins, i. 210, 211, 270, 276
Atkinson, ii. 208 ; iii. 104
Atlee, i. 265
Aton, iv. 231
Attrithe, ii. 211
Attwell, i. 274
Atwill, i. 268
Atwood, i. 269, 272
Aubrey, i. 274 ; ii. 79
August, i. 266
Austen, Austin, Austyn, Awsten,
    Awstin, Awstyn, i. 266, 267, 271,
    276 ; ii. 210 ; iv. 5, 130, 134
Averill, i. 274
Avery, i. 270
Avis, ii. 204a
Awcocke, ii. 210

Audley, Audelegh, Awdeley, Audleye, i. 173, 182, 270; ii. 4; iii. 54; iv. 228
Axe, ii. 201
Aylett, i. 276; ii. 210
Aylewaie, i. 269
Ayloffe, i. 141; ii. 211
Aynscombe, i. 272, 273

Baber, ii. 214
Babington, ii. 115
Babthorpe, iv. 238
Backe, ii. 216
Badger, iv. 170
Badlesmere, ii. 131; iv. 17
Baggelegh, ii. 150, 151
Bagot, i. 235; iv. 173
Baildon, i. 161, 162, 163, 164, 165
Bainbrigg, iv. 104
Baisepoole, ii. 221
Baits, Baites, ii. 23; iv. 112
Baitson, ii. 221
Baker, ii. 136, 221, 225; iv. 35, 36
Baldi, ii. 54
Baldwin, Bauldwyn, ii. 212, 222
Ball, ii. 133, 228
Ballard, ii. 115
Balliol, Bailleul, Baylyaff, ii. 1; iii. 82, 84; iv. 242
Ballon, ii. 172, 173
Balthroppe, ii. 227
Banecroft, ii. 130, 131, 133, 134
Banfield, i. 270
Banham, ii. 59
Baninge, iii. 69
Bank, iv. 103
Banks, ii. 38, 187, 188
Banton, ii. 218
Barber, ii. 24, 30, 34, 36, 37, 38, 224
Barclay, iv. 160
Bard, i. 259; iii. 79
Bardolf, iii. 211
Bargewenne, iv. 230
Barham, ii. 50
Barker, ii. 26, 27, 49, 50, 51, 52, 53, 221
Barnard, ii. 156; iv. 127
Barnardiston, ii. 214; iii. 59
Barners, iii. 68
Barnes, ii. 31
Baron, Baro, ii. 03; iii. 105, 242
Barr, iv. 130
Barrett, iii. 64
Barrow, ii. 59, 61
Barroby, iv. 104
Barry, Barri, ii. 98; iii. 242
Barrymore, iii. 242
Bartlemewe, ii. 211
Bartlett, ii. 223; iii. 68
Barton, ii. 218; iv. 206, 208, 214, 215, 236
Bartram, iv. 234
Baskervile, i. 109, 111; iv. 132

Bass, iv. 165
Basset, Bassett, i. 254, 274; ii. 3, 204 iii. 163, 166, 206; 217; iv. 13
Bassewell, iv. 235
Batell, ii. 146
Bateman, i. 267
Bates, ii. 229; iv. 105
Bathe, ii. 198
Bathurst, ii. 216; iv. 131
Battery, ii. 30
Battisford, ii. 223
Battye, i. 264a
Bayly, Baylie, ii. 25; iv. 136
Beale, ii. 225
Beales, ii. 229
Beard, iv. 139
Beauchamp, i. 248; ii. 111; iii. 170, 176; iv. 11, 27, 143, 226, 227, 231
Beaufort, Bewfort, iii. 174, 199; iv. 225, 226
Beaumont, ii. 209, 210, 228; iii. 241 iv. 169, 228
Bebbanburgh, iii. 73
Becher, ii. 175
Beck, Bec, Bek, i. 269; ii. 146; iv. 229
Beckett, i. 268
Beckwith, iv. 105, 106
Bedford, iii. 108
Bedwell, ii. 220
Beeke, Beke, ii. 225; iv. 16
Beijeren-Schagen, iii. 237
Bell, i. 266; ii. 88, 214
Bellingham, ii. 225; iv. 245
Bellwood, ii. 30
Bent, i. 275
Bentham, ii. 227
Bennet, ii. 177; 184
Benson, iv. 102
Bentinck, iii. 238
Beresford, Berisford, ii. 221, 223; iii. 242
Bergh, iii. 257
Berinton, ii. 136
Berkeley, Berkeleye, i. 113; ii. 89; iii. 56; iv. 11, 229, 248
Bernack, iv. 15
Bernard, Bernart, Bernerd, i. 264; ii. 130; iii. 1
Berners, i. 38; iii. 120
Bernunsah', ii. 142
Berrewgk, iv. 237
Berry, ii. 213, 226; iv. 128
Bertie, ii. 19, 31, 36, 181; iii. 141
Bertram, ii. 58
Best, ii. 219; iii. 68
Bethune, i. 259
Bett, iii. 70
Bettye, i. 274
Beverley, ii. 30
Bewley, Beaulieu, ii. 163; iv. 176
Bexley, iv. 36
Bexton, ii. 137

Biddulph, iv. 44
Bigod, Bigot, Bygot, ii. 111 ; iii. 202 ;
iv. 112, 120a, 124, 245
Biknor, i. 246
Binseley, ii. 37
Bircheles, ii. 138
Birkehead, ii. 215
Biroun, iv. 215
Bissell, iii. 49
Bissett, iv. 186
Blachford, ii. 225
Blackaller, ii. 224
Blackstock, iii. 51
Blackwell, ii. 228
Blade, ii. 217
Bladen, Blayden, ii. 226 ; iv. 128
Blak, i. 249
Blake, ii. 217, 228 ; iii. 55
Blakehale, iii. 74, 79
Blakenhale, iii. 190
Blangy, ii. 102
Blantyre, iv. 86
Blaux, iv. 244
Blayn, iii. 64
Blemund, ii. 61
Blencowe, iv. 180
Blount, Le Blounds, iii. 125
Blowberne, iv. 168
Bloys, iii. 210
Blythman, i. 267
Boar, Bor, ii. 130, 141, 142, 144, 153
Bodyam, iv. 3
Bogas, iii. 52
Bogelegh, i. 252, 253
Bohun, iii. 213 ; iv. 95
Bois, ii. 227
Bokenham, ii. 227
Boit, i. 32
Bolbek, Bolebec, ii. 172 ; iii. 224
Bold, Boulde, Bolde, ii. 154, 155 ; iv.
207, 214, 217, 219, 220
Bolney, iii. 1
Bolron, ii. 30
Bomper, i. 259
Bonavia, ii. 101, 102
Bond, i. 263, 269 ; iii. 63
Bone, i. 34 ; iv. 139
Bonebur', ii. 140
Bonell, ii. 139, 146
Bonetable, ii. 142, 143
Boniface, ii. 228
Bonwyle, iv. 231
Bonyon, ii. 218
Bonython, ii. 224
Booker, iv. 130
Booth, Bothe, Both, Bowth, ii. 136 ;
iii. 60 ; iv. 215, 221, 239, 243
Bordon, ii. 136
Boson, i. 55
Bossavern, iii. 102
Bosville, iii. 54 ; iv. 107
Bostock, i. 180 ; ii. 129, 130, 132, 136,
138, 140, 142

Boswell, i. 14, 15
Boteler, Botteler, i. 80 ; ii. 209 ; iv.
228, 230
Botetourt, iii. 168
Bothilton, iv. 89 note
Botrewse, iv. 229
Boucher, Bouchier, ii. 30 ; iv. 134
Boudlers, i. 248
Boughey, ii. 215
Boulogne, iii. 195
Boult, iii. 109
Bourchier, ii. 219 ; iii. 101, 187, 211 ;
iv. 231
Bourne, ii. 228 ; iii. 50
Boutall, i. 272
Boutell, i. 39, 45, 46, 48, 53, 54
Bowdoin, i. 259
Bower, ii. 228
Bowers, ii. 226, 227
Bowes, ii. 220
Bowet, iii. 208
Bowman, iv. 132
Bowndes, ii. 186
Bowys, iv. 232
Bowyer, iv. 34
Boyle, ii. 200 ; iii. 243
Boynton, ii. 36
Boyvill, Boyvil, iii. 80, 83, 84
Bracken, ii. 221, 222
Bradbury, iv. 212
Bradewalle, ii. 132
Bradford, iii. 58
Bradgate, ii. 219
Bradshaw, Bradesawe, Bradeschagh,
Bradeschawe, Bradeshawe, Brad-
shawe, Bradshagh, Bradshay, ii.
130, 134, 143, 144, 145, 146, 147,
153, 218
Brag, ii. 225
Bramall, Bramhall, ii. 147 ; iv. 83
Brampton, i. 248
Bramswy, ii. 197
Brand, ii. 213
Brandlinge, ii. 228
Braose, iii. 227
Brassey, iii. 239 ; iv. 258
Brauntone, i. 258
Braybroke, iii. 209 note
Brayton, iii. 59
Breadalbane, i. 117
Brederode, iii. 237
Bredham, ii. 228
Brereton, ii. 131, 133, 138, 141, 143
Bressy, Bresci, Breascy, ii. 133, 144 ;
iv. 258
Breton, Bretun, i. 254 ; iv. 250
Brett, i. 249 ; ii. 138 ; iii. 60
Brewse, iv. 247
Brickenden, iv. 136
Briggs, ii. 229
Bridges, Brydges, ii. 164, 227 ; iv. 5
Brienen, iii. 238
Brigham, ii. 201 ; iv. 112

Brinkerhoff, i. 259
Bristow, i. 241
Britten, ii. 215
Briwere, ii. 111
Brocas, i. 52 ; iv. 250
Brockett, i. 241
Brodnax, iv. 4
Bromflete, iv. 231
Bromhall, Bromehale, ii. 155 ; iii. 68
Bromley, i. 258 ; iv. 18
Bromsall, ii. 227
Brook, Brooke, ii. 30, 209, 215, 225 ;
    iii. 40, 56
Brooker, ii. 212
Browne, ii. 218 ; iv. 131
Browning, Browneing, ii. 187, 222
Bruce, Bruse, Brus, ii. 56, 200 ; iii.
    77 ; iv. 83, 162, 163
Bruen, Bruyn, i. 274 ; ii. 212
Brun, le, ii. 140, 153 ; iv. 92
Brunlisah', ? Gunlisah, ii. 143
Bryan, i. 108
Bryard, ii. 227
Bubb, iv. 127
Bucher, ii. 227
Buckle, ii. 223
Buckley, iv. 142
Buckmaster, ii. 217
Buckworth, iv. 34, 35
Bukkestrode, i. 246
Bulkeley, Bulkylegh, ii. 138, 140, 215,
    216 ; iv. 258
Buller, i. 108 ; ii. 224
Bulstrode, ii. 184
Burdon, i. 55 ; ii. 130, 133, 134, 135,
    137
Burford, ii. 203
Burges, ii. 229 ; iii. 59
Burgh, ii. 5, 154 ; iii. 176
Burgoyne, Burgoin, Burguin, iii. 40,
    106, 116
Burlace, ii. 213
Burley, i. 202
Burnall, ii. 226
Burnand, iv. 102, 103
Burnell, i. 258
Burnett, i. 40, 51
Burnhill, ii. 228
Burnell, iii. 168, 202 ; iv. 130
Burre, iii. 57
Burrell, iii. 53
Burrowe, ii. 221
Burt, ii. 223
Burton, ii. 220, 225 ; iv. 165, 200
Bury, ii. 224 ; iv. 150
Busby, i. 270
Bussel, iv. 155
Bussey, iv. 109
Busvargus, iii. 102
Butelier, iv. 140
Butler, Buttler, i. 275 ; ii. 215, 227 ;
    iv. 134, 238
Buttevant, iii. 243

Buxton, i. 55
Byatt, ii. 220
Byngham, iv. 111
Byron, iv. 169, 236

Cage, i. 162 ; iii. 52
Caldicott, iii. 55
Calley, iii. 61
Callow, iii. 58
Calverley, Calwerley, i. 163 ; iii. 109 ;
    iv. 242
Calvert, ii. 23, 24
Cambray, iv. 117
Cambrygge, iii. 203
Camden, i. 71, 83 ; iii. 32
Camell, iv. 40, 42
Cameron, ii. 55
Camoys, iv. 3, 230
Campagny, iv. 158
Campuavene, iv. 158
Cann, iv. 142
Canner, iii. 49
Cantelow, iii. 227 ; iv. 228
Cape, iii. 68
Capell, i. 275
Car, iv. 86
Carbonel, i. 248, 249
Carduil, iii. 74
Carent, i. 107
Carew, Carewe, ii. 200 ; iii. 35, 40, 125 ;
    iv. 134, 231
Carleton, iii. 124
Carlyle, ii. 190
Carminowe, Carmynowe, i. 168, 173 ;
    iv. 248
Carpenter, iii. 20, 49, 54
Carpiquet, ii. 103
Carr, Carre, Car, i. 259, 261 ; iii. 60 ;
    iv. 86
Carrell, iv. 132
Carrew, iv. 231
Carrick, iii. 83, 84
Carsewell, iii. 51
Carter, ii. 219
Carteret, Cartrai, Cartrett, iii. 63,
    218, 219 ; iv. 259
Cary, Carie, iii. 49, 64 ; iv. 137
Carynton, ii. 136
Cassilis, i. 115
Catcher, iii. 64
Catton, iii. 51 ; iv. 235
Cave, ii. 215, 224 ; iii. 49
Cavell, iii. 104
Cawsey, ii. 223
Caywood, ii. 211
Cecil, Cyscyle, i. 31 ; ii. 226 ; iii. 232 ;
    iv. 24, 246
Chaintrell, ii. 8
Chamberlain, Chamberlayn, Chamber-
    layne, ii. 141 ; iii. 51, 54, 59
Chambers, i. 275 ; iii. 68 ; iv. 141
Champernon, iv. 128
Champney, ii. 21, 22, 23, 24, 39

Chaplain, ii. 130
Chapman, ii. 209 ; iii. 53, 58
Chappell, ii. 213
Charders, ii. 139
Charite, ii. 117
Charles, ii. 225
Charnock, iii. 63
Chartres, iii. 82
Chastaigneraie, iv. 168
Chaucer, i. 168 ; iv. 250
Chaunceler, iv. 241
Chauncey, i. 89
Chave, iii. 55
Chaworth, iv. 169, 248
Chedle, ii. 216 ; iii. 65
Chedny, i. 246
Cheke, ii. 186
Chernok, Chornoc, i. 180 ; ii. 138
Cheswurth, ii. 146
Chetwynd, iv. 173
Chevell, i. 275
Cheyndutt, Chenduyt, i. 214
Cheyne, Cheyny, i. 246 ; iv. 63, 64
Chichele, iii. 188
Chichester, iv. 173
Child, ii. 186
Chittenden, i. 267
Cholmondeley, Cholmley, ii. 34, 138
Chonnesone, i. 252, 254
Christmas, iii. 58
Churton, iv. 137
Clare, i. 247 ; iii. 23, 60, 170, 204 ;
    iv. 120a, 144, 226
Clarke, i. 16, 270 ; ii. 31, 91 ; iii. 7,
    8, 50, 54, 55, 63
Clarways, iv. 237
Claverhouse, iv. 86
Clavering, ii. 24
Claxton, iv. 233
Clayton, iii. 5 ; iv. 33, 244
Cleland, iii. 66
Clement, iii. 1
Clench, ii. 210 ; iii. 52
Clerk, Clerke, i. 262 ; iii. 64 ; iv. 134
Cley, i. 252, 254
Clifford, Clyfford, Clyfforde, ii. 166 ;
    iii. 29 ; iv. 113, 229, 246
Clifton, ii. 200 ; iv. 33, 112, 113,
    243
Clinton, iii. 62, 218 ; iv. 229
Cloberry, iii. 57
Cloos, i. 81
Clopton, ii. 203 ; iii. 59
Clough, ii. 27
Clowes, iii. 56
Clyve, i. 259
Cobham, iv. 231, 249
Cock, ii. 85
Cockayne, i. 273 ; iii. 54
Cockburn, iii. 119
Cockett, iii. 61
Cockram, ii. 209
Cocks, see Cox

Codd, iii. 70
Coe, ii. 219 ; iii. 57
Coffin, ii. 213
Cogan, iii. 62
Coghill, iv. 105
Cole, i. 272 ; ii. 179 ; iii. 55, 56, 65
Coleman, ii. 222 ; iii. 59
Coleraine, i. 263
Collier, iii. 58, 64
Collin, iii. 68
Collingham, ii. 215
Collins, Collyn, i. 275 ; iii. 53, 56, 62 ;
    iv. 130
Collinson, ii. 220
Colonna, iii. 196
Colt, iv. 78
Colvile, Colvell, Colvyle, iv. 33, 98,
    100, 243
Combe, i. 248 ; iv. 129
Commelin, i. 259
Compton, i. 270 ; ii. 200
Comyn, ii. 112, 219 ; iii. 77 ; iv. 228
Condall, iv. 130
Constable, Constabyll, iv. 108, 233,
    240
Conway, ii. 201 ; iv. 82, 85, 138
Conyers, ii. 202 ; iv. 111, 113
Cook, ii. 50, 210 ; iii. 50, 53, 63, 161
Cooper, Cowper, i. 31 ; ii. 172 ; iv.
    135
Coopland, ii. 28
Cope, iii. 65
Coplestone, iii. 125
Coppin, iii. 59
Corbet, i. 248 ; ii. 5 ; iii. 61 ; iv. 173,
    185, 186
Corbiere, iv. 35, 36
Corbuson, iii. 225
Cordell, iv. 18
Corker, ii. 24
Cornish, iii. 53, 66
Corry, iii. 83, 84 ; iv. 94
Cortays, iii. 209
Corwene, iv. 246
Corter, i. 273
Cortetyngem, iii. 202
Cosway, i. 32
Cotes, ii. 4
Cottesbrooke, Cotesbroke, i. 259 ; iii.
    63
Cottington, iv. 130
Cotton, Coton, Cotun, i. 172 ; ii. 130,
    133, 134, 138, 141, 144, 149, 155,
    210 ; iii. 72
Coucy, iii. 213
Coules, iii. 51
Coulthart, iv. 61
Courci, Curci, i. 245
Courten, ii. 75, 178, 185
Courtenay, i. 245 ; iii. 164 ; iv. 21,
    173, 227, 247
Courtney, ii. 90
Courthope, iii. 53

Coveney, iii. 55
Coventry, ii. 211
Cowley, ii. 5
Cowper, i. 163 ; ii. 50, 172
Cowse, ii. 224
Cox, Cocks, i. 7 ; ii. 39 ; iii. 50, 67 ;
    iv. 140
Coynyerys, iv. 232
Cracroft, iii. 63
Craike, iv. 110
Crakanthorpe, iv. 98 note, 100
Cranfield, ii. 208
Cranley, iii. 56
Crathorne, iv. 237
Craven, iv. 140
Crawnach, Craunache, ii. 134, 140,
    141, 142
Crawford, i. 117
Crawley, iii. 67
Creake, iii. 60
Credewelle, i. 258
Crendone, iv. 148
Cressy, ii. 213
Crevequer, i. 191
Crewe, iv. 46
Creyke, iv. 109, 110
Crier, i. 277
Crispe, i. 277
Crocker, iii. 125
Croft, i. 258
Crofts, iii. 68
Croke, iii. 62
Crokedak, Crokedayk, iii. 78, 79, 80
    note
Crommelin, ii. 178
Cromwell, ii. 121, 164 ; iv. 24, 229
Crooke, ii. 178 ; iii. 5, 62
Cross, ii. 211 ; iii. 6
Crossman, ii. 221
Crosfielde, iii. 71
Crostwaite, iv. 129
Crowcher, iii. 62
Croxton, ii. 131, 132, 138, 139, 140,
    141, 142, 144, 147, 153
Cruse, iii. 69
Cruwys, iii. 125
Cudmoore, iii. 50
Culi, ii. 203
Cullen, ii. 179
Culpepper, iii. 59
Curnouylen, ii. 142
Curson, i. 248
Curteis, iii. 2
Cussans, i. 40, 48, 49
Cuyler, i. 259

Dacre, Dakar, iv. 104, 230
Dade, iv. 128
Dainty, iv. 128
Dalby, iii. 71
Dale, ii. 29 ; iii. 68
Dallender, iv. 132
Dallin, iv. 134

Dalyngruge, iv. 3
Dammerell, Dammeron, iv. 140
Danby, Danbye, ii. 30, 31, 36 ; iv.
    128, 136
Daniell, Danyel, Danyell, Daniers,
    Danyers, i. 168, 173, 174 ; ii. 133,
    144, 150, 154 ; iv. 133
Danyers, see Daniell
Darcy, Darchy, ii. 34, 36, 37, 38 ; iv.
    24, 26, 230
Darderne, ii. 197
Darknoll, iv. 134
Darnley, ii. 54
Darracott, iii. 72
Darrell, ii. 208 ; iv. 238
Dary, iv. 134
Dash, iv. 136
Dashinton, i. 275
D'Aubigny, ii. 200
Dauners, ii. 136
Davenport, Daueneport, Dauynport,
    ii. 145, 154, 155 ; iv. 142
David, iii. 69
Davies, Davys, Davyes, i. 81, 82, 170,
    208, 275 ; ii. 40, 46, 231 ; iii. 56 ;
    iv. 129, 138, 140
Davy, iv. 257
Dawell, iv. 236
Dawes, i. 272
Dawnay, ii. 29, 33, 34, 35, 39 ; iii. 153
Dawson, ii. 208 ; iii. 70, 71 ; iv. 129
Day, Daye, iii. 68 ; iv. 127, 128, 136
Deane, ii. 200
Dearling, iv. 130
Deave, iv. 128
Debanck, iii. 71
Deereinge, ii. 228
Deermar, Dearmar, iii. 72
Deirsley, iv. 134
De la Barr, Dellabarre, iv. 130
Delahay, iv. 132
Delariver, iv. 230
Dell, iii. 72 ; iv. 140
Dellawood, iv. 130
Dene, i. 214 ; iv. 127
Denham, iii. 70 ; iv. 247
Denman, iii. 70
Dennison, ii. 208
Denny, ii. 200
Dent, iv. 127, 129
Denum, Denoum, iii. 79, 80 note
Deponthe, iv. 37
Derby, i. 35 ; iii. 186, 189
Dereham, i. 55 ; iii. 69
Derman, ii. 58
Despencer, Despenser, Dispensator, ii.
    137, 149 ; iii. 74 note, 121, 170
Deverey, iii. 217
Devisley, iv. 134
Dewell, iv. 133
D'Ewes, iii. 59
Dewies, iv. 135
Deyncourt, iii. 211

Diaconus, ii. 91
Dickens, ii. 190 ; iv. 131
Dickinson, ii. 29
Digges, iv. 4
Dighton, iii. 116
Dillon, iv. 86
Dirricke, iii. 64
Dixon, i. 275 ; iv. 135
Dixwell, iv. 150
Dobbs, ii. 183
Dobson, iii. 70
Docton, iv. 137
Dod, ii. 12 ; iv. 129
Doddley, iv. 229
Doddridge, iii. 40a, 41 ; iv. 7
Dodefin, ii. 144
Dodington, iv. 141
Dodson, iv. 139
Dodsworth, i. 163 ; ii. 208 ; iii. 69
Dolben, Doulben, ii. 29 ; iv. 138, 141
Dongelberg, van, iii. 237
Donne, iv. 133, 134
Dorlton, ii. 57
Dotton, ii. 132
Doudney, ii. 218
Douglas, i. 203, 204, 206, 259 ; ii. 55 ;
    iv. 96, 142, 162, 164
Dounvill, ii. 136
Douriche, see Ludbrooke
Dove, ii. 79 ; iii. 72
Dowenechyre, iv. 227
Downe, iv. 134
Downer, iv. 131
Downes, i. 182 ; ii. 154, 181 ; iii. 52 ;
    iv. 135
Downhall, ii. 177
Doyett, ii. 50
D'Oyly, i. 168 note 3 ; ii. 4
Drake, ii. 220
Drakelowe, ii. 145
Draper, iii. 60, 72
Draycot, Draycote, i. 107, 109 ; iii. 65
Drayton, ii. 203, 204
Drew, i. 108, 109
Drueys, ii. 118
Drummond, i. 35
Drury, iv. 40, 42, 135
Duckmanton, iv. 132
Dudley, iv. 9
Dufford, ii. 202
Dugdale, ii. 44, 45, 46, 47
Dumaresq, iv. 259
Dunblaine, ii. 39
Duncombe, iv. 142
Dundee, iv. 86
Dundonald, i. 117
Dunheved, i. 247
Duning, iii. 69
Dunke, iv. 136
Dunn, iv. 142
Dunsmore, ii. 209
Dunstaple, i. 254, 255
Dunster, iv. 35, 36

Durburgh, ii. 197, 198
Dutton, i. 171, 172 ; ii. 136, 37, 154 ;
    iv. 138
Dyer, iv. 139
Dygon, ii. 198
Dyke, i. 264 ; iv .139
Dymoke, i. 55 ; iii. 121
Dyne, i. 267 ; iv. 171
Dynham, iv. 131
Dynington, ii. 220
Dyos, iv. 140
Dyotson, ii. 206
Dysart, i. 117

Eadsford, Edesford, ii. 24
Earle, ii. 208
Eastday, iii.
Eastland, i. 276
Eaton, ii. 215
Eccles, iv. 208, 211
Edmonds, iii. 62
Edwards, iii. 103
Egerton, Eggerton, Eggoten, ii. 133,
    139, 154
Eglesfield, iv. 178
Egmond, iii. 237, 238
Egremonde Burnell, iv. 18
Egremoyne, iv. 231
Eilrich, i. 248
Eldred, ii. 185
Ellice, ii. 145
Elliott, i. 269
Ellis, ii. 219 ; iii. 9 ; iv. 127, 236
Elly, i. 269
Elmedene, iv. 233
Elmerugge, i. 248
Elmes, iv. 127
Elphicke, ii. 211
Elsen, iii. 67
Eltofte, iv. 243
Elton, iv. 238
Elvin, i. 40, 50, 51
Elwin, iv. 256
Ely, i. 258
Elys, iv. 150
Engaine, ii. 203
England, ii. 90
Ent, i. 277
Enttwesyll, iv. 241
Erchebaud, ii. 204
Erdswicke, Erdeswyke, i. 70 ; ii. 133,
    134, 210
Ermondeys, i. 191
Errington, Earington, Erington, ii. 36,
    37, 38 ; iii. 158
Erskine, iv. 85
Esmond, i. 189
Essex, iii. 62
Estmonte, i. 189, 193
Estrées, i. 31
Etoun, ii. 155
Eure, ii. 210
Evans, iii. 65

Everard, i. 271 ; ii. 199
Everest, i. 266
Everingham, iv. 236
Everton, iv. 138
Every, Evers, ii. 23
Ewer, iv. 35, 36
Ewerys, iv. 232
Ewes, d', iii. 59
Ewster, iv. 32
Exelby, Eshelby, iii. 127, 130
Eyres, ii. 219
Eyton, ii. 146

Facye, iii. 72
Fairfax, Fayrefax, ii. 36, 221 ; iii. 5, 6 ;
    iv. 245
Falaise, i. 245
Falkenstein, iv. 123
Falthropp, i. 277 ; ii. 211
Fanhope, iv. 229
Fanner, iv. 135
Farmer, i. 273
Faryngton, ii. 137
Fauconberge, iv. 231
Fauntleroy, i. 105, 110
Fawkes, Faux, iv. 104, 187
Faysand, ii. 146
Feassey, iii. 51
Fehewe, iv. 230
Feild, ii. 35 ; iv. 142
Feilding, Fielding, iii. 26 ; iv. 172
Felbrigge, iii. 164, 168
Felton, iv. 140
Fenton, iv. 113
Fenwick, i. 47 ; ii. 24
Fermor, ii. 12
Ferne, i. 44, 78, 79, 83
Ferrers, Ferreres, ii. 10, 182 ; iii. 126,
    212, 214, 215, 217 ; iv. 229, 230
Ferrys, Ferris, iv. 139
Fewler, iii. 71
Field, iii. 71
Fiennes, iv. 15, 231
Fililed, Fililod, ii. 203
Filiol, ii. 203
Finch, ii. 160, 162 ; iv. 32, 173
Fitch, ii. 208
Fitton, iii. 55
FitzAdam, i. 258
FitzAlan, i. 219 ; ii. 108 ; iii. 186, 201 ;
    iv. 116, 227
FitzBaderon, ii. 172
Fitzgerald, Fytzgerod, i. 122, 123, 124,
    125, 126, 244, 245 ; ii. 92, 93, 94, 95,
    96, 97, 98, 194 ; iii. 8, 25, 209
FitzGilbert, ii. 110
FitzHenry, iv. 241
FitzHugh, ii. 197 ; iv. 14, 230
FitzJames, i. 105, 107
FitzLambert, iii. 16, 18
FitzMabel, ii. 172
FitzOther, i. 122, 123 ; ii. 98
FitzOurs, ii. 197, 198

FitzPayne, i. 249
FitzPeter, i. 258 ; iii. 4
FitzReinfred, iv. 157
FitzRichard, i. 246
FitzStephen, i. 189
FitzThomas, iv. 105
FitzTiel, iv. 116
FitzWalter, i. 113, 123, 124, 125   ii.
    98 ; iv. 229
FitzWarin, FitzWarine, FitzWaryn, i.
    258 ; iii. 101 ; iv. 231
Fitzwater, iv. 18
FitzWilliam, FetzWylyam, i. 163, 237 ;
    ii. 203 ; iv. 245
FitzWucke, i. 108
Flemings, i. 80
Fletcher, i. 260
Floyde, ii. 201
Fludd, iv. 142
Foalkes, ii. 210
Foix, iii. 174
Folgham, iv. 234
Folifate, iii. 130
Folthorpe, iv. 245
Fontaine, Fountaine, iii. 111, 116
Forbes, iv. 85
Forde, iii. 75, 79
Forester, i. 34
Fortibus, iii. 76
Forman, ii. 56
Forrest, ii. 226, 228 ; iii. 111, 114, 115 ;
    iv. 130
Forrett, i. 275
Fortescue, iv. 173
Forwood, i. 270
Foster, i. 207 ; ii. 164, 231
Fotherby, iii. 70
Fothergill, ii. 36
Foulishurst, ii. 138, 144
Foveis, i. 85
Fowler, i. 275
Fownes, i. 273 ; iv. 140
Fox, ii. 202, 220
Francis, ii. 228
Franke, iv. 142
Frankland, ii. 30
Franklin, Franklyn, i. 259 ; ii. 185,
    186 ; iv. 257
Fraunceys, i. 254 ; iii. 76
Freeman, iv. 135
Freeman-Mitford, iii. 243
Freke, ii. 214
Fretolphus, i. 87
Freville, ii. 24 ; iii. 121
Frodesham, ii. 154
Froggatt, iii. 53
Frost, i. 266
Frowyke, iv. 249
Fry, ii. 204
Fryer, iv. 129
Fuldgam, ii. 30
Fuller, iii. 2 ; iv. 171
Furnival, Furnivall, i. 280 ; iii. 82, 204

Furr, i. 276
Fygere, ii. 198
Fyscheborne, iv. 243

Gage, iii. 5
Gale, ii. 130
Gardner, i. 116
Gargrave, i. 163
Garlecmongere, i. 258
Garrard, ii. 199
Garrick, i. 3, 19
Gascoigne, ii. 19, 21, 30, 33, 34; iii. 137; iv. 107
Gate, i. 75
Gaunt, Gaud, i. 191
Gaveston, ii. 103
Gawney, iii. 72
Gay, iii. 58
Geary, iv. 38, 39, 41
Gee, ii. 147, 223
Geere, ii. 26
Geery, iii. 51
Gent, ii. 209
Geraldine, iii. 242
Gerard, ii. 138
Geri, ii. 203
Gernon, iii. 79, 80 note
Gernor, i. 125
Gerrard, i. 266
Geytington, ii. 204
Gherardini, iii. 25
Gibbs, iii. 49
Gibson, iv. 40, 256, 257
Giffard, Gyffard, i. 264; ii. 5 120, 172, 203, 204; iii. 37, 54, 223
Gilbye, ii. 221
Gildon, ii. 228
Gill, iv. 102
Gillam, Gilliam, iii. 37
Ginkel, iii. 238
Gladwin, i. 266
Glanfield, iii. 102
Glanvil, ii. 96
Glendonyn, iv. 76
Glendore, i. 168
Glossopp, ii. 224
Goade, iv. 128
Goake, iii. 63
Goathurst, i. 107
Goce, i. 252
Godard, i. 249
Godde, iv. 37
Goddard, iii. 112, 116
Godemon, ii. 137
Godfrey, ii. 212; iii. 50, 70; iv. 257
Godscall, ii. 176
Goffe, ii. 85 note 2
Gogney, ii. 50
Golding, iv. 26
Golgye, ii. 176
Golover, iv. 250
Goodall, ii. 215
Gooday, iii. 63

Goodchild, ii. 234
Goodriche, iv. 103
Goodwin, ii. 224
Goostrey, Goiestre, Gost', Gostre, Gorestre, ii. 140, 142, 143, 144, 153
Gore, iii. 37
Goring, iii. 6
Gorst, ii. 130, 133, 136
Gosenargh, iv. 219
Gosselin, iv. 34
Gotobed, i. 275
Gould, i. 259; ii. 213, 225
Goulding, i. 272
Gousul, iv. 210
Gower, iv. 134, 169, 237
Gowrie, ii. 54, 56; iv. 254
Graden, i. 275
Graham, ii. 32, 38; iv. 81, 83
Grandon, iv. 148
Granville, Grenville, Grenefeld, iii. 6, 100, 218, 222; iv. 259
Graunson, iii. 212
Gravenor, i. 170
Graves, iii. 113
Gray, Gra, i. 276; ii. 206, 207; iv. 83, 84, 228, 230, 235
Grayson, ii. 208
Graystock, Graystoke, iv. 180, 230
Greasley, i. 201
Greene, Grene, i. 266; ii. 139; iii. 1
Gregory, ii. 29; iii. 186, 190
Grenfell, Glanfill, Glanfield, Grenfield, iii. 100, 102
Grenville, see Granville
Grenedene, i. 258
Grenehoyt, ii. 142
Grelly, Gresli, Greslei, Greslet, Gresley, Greysseley, Grelle, Grillee, i. 197, 198, 199, 200, 200a, 201, 203; iv. 209, 210, 211
Grete, i. 249
Grevyle, ii. 198
Grey, i. 113, 281; ii. 122, 140, 141, 235; iii. 172; iv. 11, 15
Greynder, iv. 248
Griffin, i. 259; ii. 209
Griggs, ii. 218, 219
Grosvenor, de Grosso Venatore, i. 167, 169, 170, 171, 172, 173, 174, 176, 177, 178, 179, 180, 181, 182, 183, 184, 185, 187, 188; ii. 129, 130, 131, 132, 133, 134, 135, 136, 138, 139, 140, 141, 142, 143, 144, 145, 146, 151, 152, 154, 158; iv. 174
Grotewych, ii. 145
Guidott, i. 272
Guildford, i. 85
Gurnard, iii. 55
Gurdon-Rebow, iii. 241
Gyan, iv. 226
Gynes, iii. 210

Hacker, ii. 82; iv. 142

Hackett, iii. 40
Hadley, ii. 198, 199
Hakelutel, i. 248
Halen, iii. 164
Hales, ii. 201, 217
Halford, ii. 152 ; iii. 40
Haliburton, Habburton, ii. 55
Hall, i. 268, 269 ; ii. 25 ; iv. 140
Hallam, ii. 150 ; iii. 186
Halls, Halles, i. 271, 272
Halsale, iv. 236
Halsham, iv. 248
Halughton, i. 247
Hamerton, ii. 36 ; iii. 70 ; iv. 111
Hamey, iv. 33
Hamon, ii. 212
Hamond, iii. 61, 62 ; iv. 134
Hampden, ii. 12, 208
Hampton, iii. 83, 84, 200
Hancocke, iv. 136
Hand, i. 275
Handel, i. 11, 12, 13
Hanewode, i. 248
Hanham, iv. 142
Hankford, iii. 101
Hanlegh, ii. 145
Hansitt, ii. 34
Hanys, iii. 57
Harby, i. 277
Harcomb, ii. 21
Harcourt, iii. 203 ; iv. 16
Hardes, ii. 217
Harding, iv. 136
Hardman, iii. 116
Hardres, ii. 212
Hardwick, ii. 22
Hardy, Hardye, ii. 205 ; iii. 72
Harecroft, ii. 48
Hargrene, ii. 143
Harleston, ii. 226 ; iii. 221
Harley, iv. 204
Harman, ii. 212 ; iv. 171
Harper or Peragh, ii. 21
Harrewell, iii. 208
Harrington, i. 49 ; ii. 89
Harris, Harrys, i. 3, 4, 6, 7, 8, 9, 10, 11,
    12, 13, 14, 15, 16, 17, 18, 19, 20, 21,
    22, 23, 24, 25, 26 ; ii. 13, 231 ; iii.
    57 ; iv. 136, 139
Harsenett, iv. 134
Hart, i. 55, 268 ; ii. 217
Hartopp, iv. 35
Harvey, ii. 175, 185 ; iii. 72 ; iv. 127,
    133, 256
Haselwelle, ii. 131
Haskett, iv. 245
Hassall, ii. 154
Hasslefote, i. 270
Hastings, Hastynges, i. 219, 281 ; ii.
    50, 91 ; iii. 2, 172 ; iv. 81, 228
Hatton, i. 28 ; ii. 131, 141, 153, 201
Haveskercke, iii. 237
Haversham, iv. 172

Havré, iv. 177
Hawes, iii. 8
Hawghton, iv. 238
Hawkysworth, iv. 241
Haworth, ii. 31
Hayes, ii. 29, 220
Haydok, iv. 214
Haytfelde, iv. 239
Hazelrigg, iii. 5 note
Headley, ii. 28
Heard, iv. 127
Heath, iii. 64
Heatley, i. 275
Hedger, i. 271
Hedworth, ii. 235
Helde, ii. 135, 136
Hele, iv. 128
Hellam, ii. 176
Hemings, iii. 68
Hendeley, see Tomelynson
Hender, ii. 222
Henderson, iv. 257
Herbert, ii. 83, 88, 89
Hereford, iii. 119
Herierd, iii. 4
Heron, iv. 233
Hertford, iv. 27, 226
Herton, ii. 129
Heryngeton, iv. 230
Hesilrige, Heselrigge, i. 260, 261; iii. 37
Heton, iv. 212
Hever, iv. 255
Heward, i. 275
Hewes, ii. 227
Hexon, ii. 197
Hext, iv. 127
Heydon, ii. 229
Heynes, i. 263
Hickenbobbs, iii. 67
Hickman, iv. 130
Hickmot, iv. 136
Hide, i. 273 ; ii. 154
Higgenson, ii. 147
Higges, iii. 60
Higgons, i. 275
Hildred, ii. 213
Hill, Hull, i. 249 ; ii. 218 ; iii. 54, 62
Hillary, ii. 205
Hilliard, i. 28, 29, 34, 35 note
Hillsborough, ii. 183
Hilton, Hylton, iv. 132, 231
Hind, ii. 228
Hinton, ii. 177
Hobart, ii. 229
Hobbs, ii. 218
Hobson, ii. 50
Hoby, iv. 142
Hochecote, i. 259
Hodebovill, Hodebovyle, i. 254
Hodengs, i. 126
Hodgson, iv. 129
Hodson, ii. 30
Holand, ii. 107, 108, 112; iv. 218 note, 228

Holbeame, i. 41
Holbrooke, iii. 67
Holby, iv. 142
Holdenby, i. 164
Holes, ii. 130
Holford, i. 170, 171, 173, 175, 180 ; ii. 129, 134, 135, 136, 137, 138, 144, 145, 146, 147, 149, 151, 152 ; iv. 37
Holgrewe, Holgrene, ii. 137
Hollanby, ii. 204a
Holliday, iv. 127
Hollier, i. 261
Hollings, ii. 215
Holly, ii. 218
Holme, i. 37 ; ii. 34, 235 ; iii. 185 ; iv. 112
Holms, ii. 38
Holt, ii. 191 ; iv. 140
Homes, ii. 211
Hommet, ii. 110
Honywood, i. 269
Hooley, iv. 205
Hooper, i. 3, 18, 266, 268
Hopkins, i. 275
Hopton, i. 248 ; ii. 228 ; iii. 65 ; iv. 136
Hore, i. 274
Hornbye, ii. 26
Hornle, i. 254
Horsey, Horsley, i. 105, 108 ; ii. 45
Horssleye, iv. 242
Horton, i. 180 ; ii. 130, 131, 133, 138 ; iii. 12
Hoskins, i. 31
Hoste, ii. 179 ; iv. 33
Hotham, iv. 246
Houbelon, iii. 108, 109, 110
Houby, ii. 203
Houghton, Hoghton, Hoeton, ii. 35 ; iv. 155
Howard, i. 110 ; ii. 199, 200 ; ii. 54, 121 ; iv. 130
Howden, i. 131, 148
Howell, iii. 69 ; iv. 226
Howland, iv. 142
Howse, iv. 248
Huchown, ii. 159
Huddleston, ii. 37 ; iii. 8
Hudson, ii. 160, 161 ; iv. 103
Huegate, ii. 18
Huffam, iii. 49
Huggen, ii. 210
Hughes, iv. 138
Hugo, ii. 189
Hulkoc, ii. 153
Hull, ii. 131, 215
Hulme, i. 170, 172 note 4 ; ii. 140, 155 ; iv. 208, 209
Hulton, iv. 210
Humphrey, i. 33, 275
Humphreys, ii. 228
Hungerford(e), i. 263, 277 ; iii. 170 ; iv. 229, 230
Hunter, i. 215, 260, 261

Huntercombe, iii. 76
Huntley, Hunteleye, i. 111, 249
Hurryon, ii. 220
Hurst, ii. 139
Hussey, i. 105 ; iii. 170
Hustard, iv. 30
Hutchinson, i. 259, 277 ; ii. 208 ; iii. 109
Hutton, ii. 30, 223, 228
Huxley, ii. 141, 178
Hynde, i. 271

Ibbott, iii. 241
Ickworth, iii. 126
Ilberd, i. 105
Iles, i. 270 ; iii. 58
Ilger, i. 125
Ilond, ii. 198
Ingham, ii. 134
Ingilby, iv. 101
Ingrey, i. 275
Ingwardyn, ii. 4
Inman, i. 259, 260
Ireton, iii. 216, 217
Isham, ii. 1
Isles, ii. 214
Isted, i. 266

Jackson, ii. 147, 215 ; iii. 55, 109, 116 ; iv. 34, 35, 36, 37, 139
Jacob, i. 277
Jacobson, ii. 215
Jacson, ii. 147
James, ii. 218
Jarnac, iv. 168
Jarrett, ii. 215
Jaupin, iv. 31
Jay, iii. 5
Jeames, ii. 225
Jenison, ii. 24
Jenkins, i. 40
Jennings, ii. 28, 30
Jephson, iii. 5
Jervis, iv. 129
Jervoise, Jerveys, iii. 1
Jeudewyn, i. 246
Jobson, iii. 65
Joevene, i. 248
Johnson, i. 14, 15, 276 ; ii. 33, 210, 220 ; iii. 61 ; iv. 106
Jolliffe, iv. 44
Jones, i. 276 ; ii. 181, 229 ; iii. 49
Jorden, ii. 226
Josselin, iv. 22
Joyner, ii. 83, 88

Kay, Qué, iv. 167
Kegworth, i. 180 ; ii. 129
Keith, iv. 84, 85
Kelloway, i. 107, 108
Kellye, iii. 57
Kemp, ii. 84 ; iv. 225
Kempthorne, see Ley
Kendall, Kendell, ii. 34 ; iii. 53

Kenworthy, ii. 139
Keppel, iii. 238
Ker, ii. 55
Kerrick, ii. 14
Keys, i. 81
Killicke, iv. 132
Killom, i. 75
Killygrew, iii. 7
Kimble, Kenebelle, ii. 172
Kimpton, iii. 62
Kinaston, ii. 229
King, iii. 63
Kingston, iv. 113, 133, 134
Kinpont, iv. 83
Kintore, iv. 85
Kirbie, i. 162
Kirby, iii. 69
Kirkbride, iii. 79, 80, 83, 84
Kirke, i. 275
Kirkham, i. 275
Kirkpatrick, iv. 94
Knappe, iv. 127
Knatchbull, ii. 172
Knatchbull-Wyndham, i. 13
Knight, i. 273 ; iv. 1, 133
Knightley, ii. 2, 3, 4, 5, 6, 7, 8, 9, 10, 11, 12, 13, 121 ; iv. 260
Knill, ii. 172
Knollys, iii. 242 ; iv. 232, 233
Knotsford, ii. 8, 146
Knowles, ii. 227 ; iv. 63, 64
Knowlsley, iii. 65
Knyvett, iii. 64
Kykeley, iv. 238
Kyme, iii. 213
Kynaston, iv. 140, 173
Kynges, i. 248
Kyngesmyll, Kingesmille, Kyngesmell, Kyngesmulle, i. 264
Kyngeston, i. 81 ; ii. 198
Kynsy, ii. 136
Kynwoldesmersshe, ii. 178

Lache, ii. 135
Lacon, iii. 3
Lacy, i. 249
Lake, i. 269
Lalain, iv. 167
Lalyng, Laling, iv. 206
Lamb, ii. 31, 37, 50, 51, 52, 130
Lambert, iii. 15
Lambton, iv. 237
Lame, iv. 132
Lamploe, i. 265
Lancaster, iv. 223
Lanceles, iv. 94
Lane, i. 259
Langdale, ii. 32
Langford, i. 275 ; iv. 137, 237
Langleberge, i. 258
Langley, Longley, ii. 30 ; iv. 217, 218
Langton, iv. 219, 234, 237
Lasselys, iv. 241

Latham, i. 269 ; iv. 223
Lathom, iv. 156, 236
Latimer, i. 51 ; ii. 39 ; iv. 11, 112, 230
Laton, iv. 236
Latton, ii. 212
Lauderdale, i. 117
Launcelyn, ii. 51
Launde, i. 248
Lawarre, iv. 228
Lawe, iv. 132
Lawrye, i. 273
Lawson, ii. 23 ; iv. 181
Laycocke, iii. 35
Le Bretun, see Bretun
Lee, i. 80 ; ii. 30, 185 ; iii. 41, 127
Leftewich, ii. 136
Legge, ii. 89
Legh, ii. 133, 135, 137, 139, 144
Leigh, i. 41, 50 ; iii. 64
Leighton, i. 258 ; iv. 114
Leigne, ii. 224
Le Maire, ii. 175, 176, 177
Le Maistre, iii. 222 ; iv. 259
Le Neve, i. 44 ; ii. 85
Lens, i. 31
Lestley, i. 275
Letton, iv. 116
Leversage, iv. 223
Levet, ii. 29, 220
Levinge, i. 273 ; iii. 25 ; iv. 82
Levington, iii. 80
Levinton, iv. 91
Lewkenor, iv. 3, 4
Ley, ii. 222
Leycester, ii. 135, 136, 137, 146, 148, 155 ; iii. 204
Licence, iii. 58
Lightfoot, iv. 103
Lilly, ii. 226
Limburg, iii. 237
Lindsay, ii. 55 ; iii. 229, 230
Lingen, Lynegayne, i. 249
Liotard, i. 32
Lisle, l'Isle, i. 245 ; iv. 9, 11, 230
Lister, iii. 31
Litlewood, ii. 36, 37, 38
Little Over, Lettleover, Lytteloure, Parva Overe, ii. 136, 137, 142, 143, 145, 146
Littleton, ii. 24
Livingstone, i. 259
Lloyd, iv. 138, 141
Lobell, iii. 117
Lochard, i. 262
Lock, iv. 134, 135
Locke, ii. 228
Lockett, iii. 58
Lockton, iii. 110, 116
Lockwood, iv. 105
Lodbroke, iv. 246
Lodge, ii. 22, 25, 26 ; iv. 105
Loftus, ii. 220
Loges, Logys, ii. 117 ; iii. 73, 79

Long, i. 130, 248 ; iii. 61
Longueville, ii. 19, 201 ; iii. 140
Longworth, ii. 147
Loni, ii. 198
Lonsdaile, i. 273
Loraine, iv. 260
L'Orti, i. 251
Loryng, iii. 165
Lostock, Allostock, Lolstok, i. 179, 180 ; ii. 130, 131, 132, 133, 134, 135, 138, 140, 141, 142, 144, 145, 148, 149, 150, 151, 153, 154
Lound, i. 80
Louvain, Luvene, Lovein, iii. 231, 232, 236
Lovel, i. 48 ; iii. 36 ; iv. 228
Lovett, ii. 86
Lowder, ii. 30
Lowe, iii. 55
Lownde, iv. 238
Lowther, ii.163,164; iii. 65 ; iv. 173, 253
Lucas, iii. 119
Lucy, iii. 80 ; iv. 91, 94, 96, 100, 231
Ludbrooke *alias* Douriche, i. 273
Luffe, iv. 171
Luke, ii. 51, 227
Lupus, iv. 185, 186
Lumley, Lwmley, ii. 8 ; iv. 231, 235
Luscombe, iii. 66
Lusignan, iv. 124, 125
Luvetot, iii. 78, 79
Luxemburg, iii. 189
Lyght, iv. 241
Lyle, iv. 248
Lymerston, ii. 114, 115, 116
Lyngward, ii. 86
Lyntrete, ii. 130
Lyte, le Lyt, i. 104, 105, 106, 107, 108, 109, 110, 111
Lyttlebury, ii. 220
Lyys, iv. 241

MacGuffie, iv. 71, 73
Macnaught, iv. 76
Madocke, ii. 146, 221 ; iii. 55
Mahawte, iv. 245
Mahermer, iii. 174, 203
Mahias, ii. 103
Maie, iii. 67
Mainwaring, Meidnibar', Menewar', Menewaynk, Mesnilwarin, Meyngaryn, Meynwar', ii. 131, 132, 135, 137, 138, 140, 141, 142, 143, 144, 146, 155 ; iii. 67
Malmaynes, i. 55
Malpas, iv. 11
Maltebei, ii. 140
Maltravers, iii. 211 ; iv. 227
Malyn, Malym, ii. 227
Manaton, iii. 57
Mandeville, iii. 24, 27, 28, 30, 215
Manerys, iv. 240
Manley, iii. 37, 211

Manners, i. 31, 33, 34, 35
Mannynge, ii. 223
Mantoe, i. 275
Marmion, Mermyon, i. 113 ; iii. 120, 204 ; iv. 14, 230
Marshall, i. 254 ; ii. 141, 153, 217 ; iv. 123, 125
Marsham, iii. 59
Marshe, iii. 2
Marston, iii. 56
Martin, Martyn, ii. 212 ; iv. 3, 14, 128
Martindale, iv. 99
Massey, Masey, Masci, ii. 131, 132, 136, 137, 140, 141, 142, 144, 154 ; iii. 61 iv. 207, 209 note, 219, 221, 239
Massingberd, iii. 141
Matthew, Mathew, ii. 199 ; iv. 37
Matthews, iv. 169
Maude, i. 161, 163 ; iv. 136
Mauduit, iv. 144 note, 230
Maugham, iii. 104
Mauleverer, iv. 103, 240
Mauley, i. 138, 139
Maunsell, i. 274
Mawddwy, iv. 117
Maxwell-Lyte, ii. 59
May, iv. 3, 14, 137
Maynard, i. 260, 261
Meade, iv. 135
Mee, i. 34 ; ii. 147
Mell, iii. 65
Melton, ii. 33 ; iv. 233
Memburi, ii. 197
Menell, iii. 212
Merbury, Marbury, ii. 133, 134
Mere, ii. 143, 155
Merfeild, i. 161
Mering, iv. 107
Merse, ii. 141
Mershe, ii. 139
Merton, ii. 130, 134, 135, 138, 141, 142, 143, 144, 145, 146, 153, 186
Meschin, iii. 73
Metcalf, ii. 21 ; iii. 65 ; iv. 113, 175
Metham, iv. 233
Methlay, iii. 79
Mexborough, ii. 181
Meynill, ii. 37
Middleton, Myddylton, ii. 30, 181, 235 ; iii. 5 note, 26, 27 ; iv. 107, 108, 141, 241, 246
Mignon, iv. 169
Milborne, iv. 128
Mildmay, i. 80, 110 ; ii. 83, 88 note 2, 89, 89 note 2
Milles, iv. 202
Mirabeau, i. 21
Mitford, iii. 243
Modburlegh, Moberlegh, Moburlehe, Modberlegh, Modbirlegh, i. 171, 174, 181, 182 ; ii. 131, 132, 137, 138, 140, 141, 142, 143, 144, 155
Modlowe, ii. 149 note 3

Moeles, i. 172 note 2
Mohun, iv. 169
Moldeworth, ii. 140, 154
Molesworth, ii. 222
Molines, Molaynys, iv. 156, 230
Molyneux, Mulinaus, iv. 113, 156
Mompesson, iii. 58
Monchensy, iii. 213 note
Moncour, i. 249
Monfort, Mountfort, ii. 3 ; iv. 24, 248
Monhaut (de Monte Alto), ii. 138
Monk, Monck, ii. 224 ; iv. 5, 12
Monkton, iv. 241
Montague, Mountegew, iii. 174, 203 ;
    iv. 145, 227, 263
Montbegon, iv. 157
Monte Florum, i. 147
Monteagle, ii. 200
Montgomery, Mwngomery, ii. 1, 95,
    200 ; iv. 152, 249
Monthermer, Mount Hermer, iii. 213 ;
    iv. 144, 227
Moore, ii. 23 ; iii. 49, 65, 70 ; iv. 150
More, i. 275 ; iii. 1, 2, 70
Morant, ii. 92
Mordaunt, iii. 15
Moresby, iv. 98, 100
Morgan, i. 41, 106 ; iii. 69
Morgham, iii. 103
Morlay, iv. 229
Morren, iii. 56
Morriceby, Morysby, iv. 94, 246
Morris, iv. 36
Morten, iii. 212
Mortimer, i. 246, 247, 248, 249
Morton, ii. 136 ; iv. 246
Morvill, iii. 82, 83, 84
Mosgrove, iv. 243
Moston, iv. 245
Mountney, iii. 55
Mowbray, i. 219 ; ii. 30 ; iii. 202 ;
    iv. 8, 241
Mulcaster, iv. 100
Mulso, ii. 204
Multon, ii. 205, 206, 207 ; iii. 83 ; iv.
    93
Munke, ii. 177
Munn, iv. 136
Munsshull, ii. 146
Murcott, iii. 72
Murray, iii. 69
Murrowes, i. 162, 163
Muschamp, iii. 75, 76 note
Musgrave, ii. 220 ; iv. 99
Mynsmyth, i. 258

Nandike, iv. 109
Nanfan, iv. 250
Napier, Navagheer, iv. 30, 160
Napkin, iii. 38, 39
Nassau, iv. 42
Neast, iii. 61
Neile, ii. 74

Neilson, ii. 159
Netherton, ii. 141
Neville, Nevill, Nevell, Nevyll, i. 264 ;
    ii. 197, 225 ; iii. 70, 211 ; iv. 108,
    112, 114, 143, 228, 230, 231, 232,
    241, 242, 245, 246
Newburgh, Neufbourg, Newborowe,
    iv. 144, 226, 227, 230, 250
Newby, iv. 110
Newdegate, iii. 54
Newhall, Nova Aula, ii. 130, 131, 132,
    133, 134, 142, 143, 144, 149 note 3
Newmarche, iv. 242
Newport, iii. 3
Newsam, Neusom, i. 171 ; iv. 235
Newton, iv. 238
Nicholas, ii. 43 ; v. 138
Nicholl, iv. 137
Nicholson, i. 260, 261
Nicke, ii. 226
Nicolls, iii. 36
Nightingale, Neyttegale, Nictegale,
    Nightegle, Nigh the Gale, Nithgale,
    Nittegale, Nytegale, Nyttegale, ii.
    135, 141, 142, 143, 144, 145, 153 ;
    iii. 70
Nixon, i. 33
Noailles, ii. 70
Norable, i. 247
Norcote, ii. 146 ; iv. 135
Norman, i. 34 ; iii. 186 ; iv. 127
Normanwyle, iv. 234
Norris, ii. 82 ; iii. 71
North, iv. 130
Norton, ii. 30, 211 ; iii. 5
Nortwych, ii. 130, 141
Norwood, iv. 142
Nott, iii. 50
Notton, iv. 212
Nulls, i. 277
Nuthall, ii. 219

Oakley, i. 234
Oates, iii. 103
Ocle, ii. 203
O'Daly, i. 119
Oglander, ii. 212
Ogle, iii. 235 ; iv. 231
Oismelini, iv. 158
Oldeton, ii. 130
Oldfield, ii. 213
Olifard, iii. 31
Oliver, i. 30, 259
Ollynton, i. 248
Oneby, iv. 169, 170
Onslow, iv. 172
Opñdor', ii. 141
Ordsal, iv. 219
Orleans, iv. 169
Ormston, i. 260
Orreby, ii. 140
Orrery, iv. 172
Orton, iii. 40

Osbaldistone, ii. 212
Osborne, i. 276, 277 ; ii. 31, 35, 202 ;
    iii. 159
Oseville, ii. 203
O'Sullivan, iii. 25
Oughtred, iv. 233
Over, Ower, i. 275 ; iii. 49
Overton, i. 248
Oxenbridge, iii. 3

Page, ii. 139, 146 ; iii. 51
Paget, ii. 213 ; iii. 64
Palfreyman, iii. 109
Pallandt, iii. 237
Palliser, iv. 42
Palmer, i. 55, 266 ; ii. 1, 201
Pamele, iii. 237
Papillon, iv. 44
Paradyne, ii. 214
Parke, ii. 24
Parker, i. 80 ; ii. 171, 210, 226
Parkhurst, iv. 31, 32, 33
Parr, ii. 229 ; iv. 14, 222
Parrott, iii. 40
Parvyng, iii. 80
Paslew, Passelewe, ii. 61, 62 ; iv. 107, 241
Paul, ii. 55
Pauncefote, i. 248 ; ii. 193
Paunton, ii. 3
Paveley, iii. 83, 84
Paver, ii. 136
Payne, ii. 141 ; iii. 64
Paynel, iii. 78
Peacham, iii. 41
Peachey, iv. 4
Peak, i. 35 note
Peares, ii. 36, 37, 38, 39
Pecche, ii. 205
Pedden, ii. 48, 210
Peele, ii. 178
Peirs, ii. 37 ; iv. 138
Pell, iii. 36
Pellesan, iv. 236
Penn, ii. 215
Pennesbyry, iv. 211
Pennington, iv. 157
Penulbury, Pennelbiry, iv. 207, 209,
    210, 211, 212, 213, 214, 215
Pennoyer, ii. 208
Pepys, Pepis, ii. 221 ; iii. 63
Pepper, iii. 109
Percehay(e), iv. 110, 234
Perch, iii. 203
Percival, iii. 240
Percy, i. 168 ; iii. 137, 176 ; iv. 229,
    231, 234
Perkins, iii. 72
Peremort, i. 248
Perers, ii. 143
Perry, i. 268
Persed, ii. 140
Pete, iv. 32
Petit, iii. 105

Petitot, i. 31
Petre, i. 219
Pettus, ii. 84
Pevere, Parva Overe, Pever, Penere,
    Penerhe, Penerhee, Penver, ii. 130,
    131, 136, 138, 143
Peyto, ii. 5
Philip, i. 274 ; iii. 211
Philipps, Philipse, iii. 118 ; iv. 36
Phipps, iv. 257
Pickman, i. 269
Pierrepont, ii. 18
Pigott, Picgot, ii. 140, 153 ; iii. 124 ;
    iv. 133
Pike, iii. 51
Pikemere, Pikmer, Pykemere, ii. 130,
    135, 146
Pilkington, iv. 209, 211, 213
Pindar, Pinder, ii. 171 ; iii. 56
Pitchard, i. 248
Pitsligo, iv. 85
Planché, i. 36
Plantagenet, iv. 11
Plimer, i. 33
Plomer, iii. 72
Plomton, iv. 237
Plowden, i. 234 ; iii. 118
Plumpton, iv. 114
Pockley, ii. 34, 35
Podlicote, i. 144
Poer, i. 249
Poingdestre, i. 55
Pollard, iv. 241
Pole, ii. 198, 224, 226
Pollock, iii. 142a
Polsted, iii. 2
Pontefract, iv. 215, 216, 217
Poole, ii. 24, 218
Poore, ii. 211
Pope, ii. 212
Popham, iv. 248
Popy, iv. 150
Port(e), iii. 4, 60, 231
Porter, iv. 127, 249
Portyngeton, iv. 240
Potts, ii. 228
Pouldoune, ii. 197
Powell, ii. 217 ; iv. 130
Powes, iv. 229
Powlett, Poulett, iii. 3, 4, 10,
Pownall, iv. 131
Poynett, iv. 136
Poynings, iv. 229
Poyntz, ii. 213 ; iii. 109, 114, 115
Praers, Preheris, i. 170 ; ii. 152, 154
Praet, iii. 237
Pratt, ii. 210
Prendergeest, iv. 243
Prentall, i. 271
Presse, iii. 59
Preston, ii. 82 note 2, 83, 84, 85 note
    2, 86, 87, 87 note 1, 88, 88 note 1,
    89, 90 ; iv. 236, 243

Prestwich, Prestwyche, iv. 207, 209, 211, 212, 214, 215, 216, 217, 218, 219, 221, 222
Prettyman, Prittiman, iii. 113, 116
Price, iii. 68
Prince, iii. 68
Prist, iv. 137
Pryor, ii. 218, 219
Pudsey, i. 55
Pulford, i. 173, 183 ; ii. 140
Pullaine, ii. 34, 36, 37, 38, 39
Pullin, ii. 218
Purbeck, ii. 32
Purcell, i. 275
Purefoy, ii. 6 ; iii. 7, 8, 36, 37
Purly, ii. 204
Pusey, i. 55
Pycheford, ii. 118
Pykeringe, iv. 233
Pyle, ii. 228
Pym, ii. 199
Pyppard, iii. 210
Pyppyng, ii. 198

Quatremain, iv. 250
Quency, Quincy, i. 50, 259 ; ii. 111
Quilter, i. 267
Quikleswyk, iv. 207, 208

Radclyf, ii. 150 ; iv. 235, 238
Radeway, i. 262
Ramsay, i. 275 ; ii. 56
Ramsdon, ii. 39, 208
Ratheby, ii. 205
Rawald, ii. 141
Rawdon, iv. 81
Rawlinson, i. 271
Rayner, i. 275
Reade, iii. 59
Readham, ii. 224
Rebow, iii. 241
Rede, iv. 150
Redeman, i. 173
Redemore, ii. 135
Redesdale, iii. 243
Redhead, iv. 127
Redmayne, iv. 245
Redvers, i. 245 ; iv. 227
Redwood, Rideout, iii. 56
Reed, iii. 238
Reeve, iii. 67
Reimund, i. 122
Remnant, iii. 64
Renesse, iii. 237
Reresbye, ii. 228
Resce, iii. 1
Rewers, iv. 231
Reygate, iii. 79
Reyni, i. 258
Reynolds, i. 34, 35
Rhodes, iv. 161
Ribbesford, i. 248

Ribblesdale, iii. 26
Rice, iv. 134
Rich, iii. 5 ; iv. 13
Richardson, ii. 229 ; iii. 71
Richolte, ii. 176
Rider, ii. 139 ; iii. 80 ; iv. 88, 100
Ridley, iii. 3
Rivers, ii. 184 ; iii. 176 ; iv. 172
Robbinges, i. 268
Robert, iv. 138
Roberts, ii. 176, 221 ; iii. 57
Robertson, ii. 183
Robessart, Robearde, iii. 211
Robins, i. 277
Robinson, i. 16 ; ii. 65, 209, 211 ; iii. 148
Robson, i. 50
Roch, ii. 218 ; iv. 250
Roclyff, iv. 235
Rodest, ii. 140
Rodger, ii. 27
Roe, ii. 215
Rogers, iii. 54, 58 ; iv. 133
Rolfe, iii. 55, 60
Rolle, iii. 53 ; iv. 173
Rolls, iii. 24
Rommesleigh, i. 249
Romonby, iv. 235
Ronchamp, Rowenchaump, i. 171, 177 ; ii. 148
Rondes, i. 252, 253
Rons, ii. 201
Rookby, ii. 37
Rookes, iv. 128
Roos, Rous, i. 258, 259 ; iv. 11, 228, 235, 242
Rose, i. 275
Rosewell, iii. 56
Roskarrocke, ii. 222
Ross, i. 255 ; iv. 78, 83
Rothesay, iv. 163
Roulegh, ii. 145, 146
Round, iv. 143
Roundell, iv. 104
Rowed, ii. 210
Roxburgh, i. 116
Ruddeheath, i. 182
Rudyerd, ii. 201
Rumelli, iii. 29
Rumley, Rumlei, iii. 27
Rushton, ii. 21, 22, 23, 141, 142, 143, 153
Russell, i. 31, 230 ; iii. 17, 49, 66
Ruthven, ii. 57
Rychemonde, iii. 203
Rye, ii. 62
Rythe, iii. 20
Ryther, iv. 235, 244
Ryvere, i. 254
Ryves, ii. 224

St. Albans, ii. 61
St. Amand, iii. 206 ; iv. 231

St. George, iii. 32
St. Gilles, iii. 15
St. John, i. 277 ; iv. 32, 157, 231, 248
St. Lawrence, i. 230
St. Leger, iii. 101
St. Maur, ii. 203
St. Owen, i. 248
St. Paul, i. 80
St. Quentin, Seynt Qwyntyne, ii. 236 ; iv. 15
Sackville, ii. 200
Sadburye, iii. 56
Salkell, iv. 246
Salt, iii. 60
Saltaston, ii. 220
Salter, ii. 225
Salwayne, iv. 233
Sames, i. 267
Samways, ii. 37
Sandbach, Sondbache, i. 180 ; ii. 129, 132, 140, 141, 142, 144
Sander, iv. 137
Sanderson, ii. 89 ; iii. 115
Sandys, i. 263 ; iii. 50
Sanky, iii. 69
Sapcoats, ii. 209
Sarly, i. 259
Sasso Ferrato, i. 85
Saunders, i. 262, 263
Savile, ii. 180, 182 ; iii. 137 ; iv. 108, 234
Say, i. 247, 251 ; iii. 50 ; iv. 229, 231
Sayer, iv. 244
Scaccario, iv. 148
Scarborough, iv. 129
Scargyll, iv. 243
Scales, Calys, iv. 17, 229
Schagh, Shawe, ii. 134, 136
Schirburn, ii. 137
Schoorel, iv. 198
Schorthose, iv. 241
Schutz, iii. 242 ; iv. 39, 40
Schuyler, i. 259
Scollay, i. 259
Shore, Score, iv. 139
Scott, ii. 228 ; iii. 34
Scrope, i. 167 ; ii. 36, 37 ; iii. 207 ; iv. 173, 230
Scudamore, iii. 225, 227
Seman, ii. 50 ; iii. 66
Seaward, ii. 212
Sebright, iv. 186
Sefton, i. 34
Segar, iii. 32
Segrave, iv. 8
Seires, iv. 171
Selby, ii. 24
Selsey, iv. 4
Sentley, iii. 204
Senyor, i. 270
Seriant, ii. 144, 145
Serooskerke, iii. 238
Seton, iv. 162, 164

Sewal, iii. 214
Seymer, iii. 1
Seymour, i. 28 ; ii. 12, 202 ; iii. 211 ; iv. 27
Seys, i. 274
Shackley, iv. 140
Shadforth, iii. 70
Shakerley, ii. 139, 140, 147, 154
Sharpe, ii. 218, 219
Shaw, Schagh, ii. 134, 136 ; iv. 104
Sheafe, ii. 214
Shearburne, ii. 35
Shelley, i. 34
Sheridan, iv. 169
Sherley, ii. 200
Sherne, i. 4
Shipman, iii. 141
Shirley, ii. 182 ; iii. 214
Shoreswood, ii. 220
Shottisbroke, iv. 248
Shrewley, ii. 202
Shutt, iv. 105
Sibthorpe, ii. 227
Sidney, i. 111
Silver, iv. 170
Simpson, ii. 23, 79
Singleton, iv. 157
Sipling, iii. 21
Sittart, iv. 34, 36
Sitwell, i. 58 ; ii. 40, 48, 53
Skeat, i. 63 note 1
Skelton, iv. 241
Skenard, Skinerton, ii. 6, 8
Skinner, ii. 224 ; iii. 34 ; iv. 44, 45
Slade, iii. 53 ; iv. 130
Sladehurste, ii. 134, 136
Slee, iii. 108, 114, 116
Smally, ii. 209
Smalpece, ii. 50
Smelt, iii. 69
Smith, Smyth, Smithe, ii. 30, 141, 142, 169, 193, 209, 218, 224 ; iii. 53, 55, 63, 70, 109, 114, 115, 243 ; iv. 34, 40, 41, 42, 130, 136
Smith-Barry, iii. 242
Smithson, ii. 23, 170 ; iii. 235
Sneyde, ii. 147
Snow, iv. 133
Somers, i. 267
Somerset, ii. 209
Somery, iv. 229
Sorteys, iv. 232, 239
Sotheby, ii. 22, 31
Sothill, ii. 208
Sowdane, iv. 247
Spaigne, ii. 206, 207
Spany, ii. 50
Sparrowe, iv. 249
Speed, ii. 227
Spence, iv. 103, 105
Spencer, ii. 6, 7, 8, 200, 228 ; iii. 17 note, 20 ; iv. 220
Spenser, ii. 189 ; iii. 207 ; iv. 228

Spelman, i. 71, 80, 89
Spendelove, ii. 134, 144
Spicer, i. 262
Spilman, ii. 224
Sporett, iv. 103
Sporley, i. 128 ; ii. 77
Spurne, Sporne, ii. 48, 50
Staevenisse, iii. 237
Stafford, iii. 172, 206 ; iv. 226, 247 ; see also Toeni
Standysche, iv. 245
Stanfield, ii. 24
Stanford, iv. 17
Stanley, ii. 139 ; iv. 220, 235, 236
Stanyhurst, ii. 139
Stapleford, ii. 140
Stapleton, Stapilton, ii. 18, 19 ; iii. 27, 132
Stare, iv. 168
Staunton, ii. 226
Stavelegh, ii. 154, 155
Steede, iii. 50
Steele, Steile, ii. 147 ; iv. 35, 136
Stephenson, ii. 36, 37
Stepney-Cowell, ii. 56
Stevens, ii. 221
Stevenson, ii. 54
Steward, i. 35, 233 ; iv. 162, 163
Stewart, Stuart, i. 219 ; ii. 54, 166, 200 ; iv. 70, 83, 84
Stockdaile, ii. 221
Stockton, iii. 186
Stoddard, iv. 138
Stoke, ii. 131, 132, 140, 141, 142, 143
Stoker, iii. 186, 191
Stonehouse, iii. 7
Stonesbye, ii. 218, 219
Stormye, iv. 247
Stourton, Storton, i. 110 ; iv. 231
Stowe, iii. 109
Strabolgi, iii. 176 ; iv. 248
Stradlyng, iv. 249
Stræten, iii. 237
Strange, Straunge, iv. 228, 229
Strangways, iv. 107, 232, 233
Strathmore, i. 117
Stratton, ii. 223, 226
Stretton, i. 178
Stringer, ii. 221 ; iv. 5
Strode, iii. 58
Strykelond, iv. 236
Sturmy, i. 249
Stutevile, Stutevill, ii. 111 ; iv. 89 note
Stydolfe, ii. 181
Styles, iii. 65, 66
Subston, iii. 186
Sudborough, iii. 56
Sudeley, iv. 230
Sudintone, i. 258
Suthayk, iii. 83, 84
Sutton, ii. 203, 220 ; iv. 10 note, 11, 229
Swadell, ii. 218
Swaine, i. 162 ; ii. 211, 212

Swales, iv. 109, 113
Swetenham, Suetenham, Suetinham, ii. 130, 138, 140, 141
Swiney, i. 238
Sworton, ii. 146
Swynowe, iv. 244

Tabley, Tabbelegh, Taweleg, ii. 130, 133, 136, 142, 143, 149 note 3, iv. 117
Taillebois, i. 191
Talbot, i. 227, 246 ; ii. 35, 201 ; iii 54 ; iv. 11, 228, 239
Talworth, i. 272
Tamworth, iii. 217
Tancred, iv. 114
Tankard, ii. 29, 31, 36
Tatteshall, i. 246 ; iv. 229
Taylboys, iv. 245
Taylor, i. 268 ; ii. 24, 31, 34, 36, 37, 38, 221 ; iii. 59, 113, 116, 190 ; iv. 35, 133, 135
Taynter, ii. 219
Teck, iv. 163
Tekne, i. 259
Tempest, ii. 34 ; iii. 138 ; iv. 114
Temple, ii. 202
Tennyson, ii. 189
Tepper, iii. 72
Tetlow, Tettelowe, iv. 217, 218
Tettisworth, ii. 230
Tew, Le Tyu, ii. 132, 144, 146
Theakeston, iii. 136, 141
Thomas, iii. 69
Thompson, ii. 208 ; iv. 142
Thomson, ii. 229 ; iv. 107, 110
Thornburg, Thornborowe, ii. 5, 185 ; iv. 246, 256
Thorne, iii. 50
Thornhill, iv. 234
Thornhurst, i. 111
Thornton, ii. 1, 29, 35, 37, 38 ; iii. 52
Thorpe, iv. 103, 114
Throgmorton, ii. 6
Thweng, ii. 20, 28
Thynne, iii. 64, 235
Tichborne, Ticheborne, Thikeburne, Thycheburne, ii. 114,115,116, 117,118
Tilliol, iii. 80, 81 ; iv. 88
Tilsley, i. 266 ; ii. 34
Tiptoft, Typtofte, i. 109 ; iv. 228, 229, 230
Tirrell, iv. 135
Titcomb, ii. 226
Titmus, iii. 64
Tochetts, iv. 109
Toeni, i. 195, 196
Toft, Toffet, Tofit, Tooft, Tofte, Toftes, ii. 129, 130, 131, 132, 133, 135, 136, 137, 138, 140, 142, 143, 144, 149, 151
Tollemache, i. 242
Tollman, iii. 7
Tolson, i. 270

Tomkins, iii. 49 ; iv. 128
Tomlins, ii. 58
Tomlinson, Tomelynson, Thomlynson, Tumlynson, ii. 82, 137, 139, 146
Tomyns, iii. 12
Tonge, iv. 217, 218 note
Tony, iv. 146
Toope, iv. 128, 129
Topp, ii. 212
Torbocke, ii. 146
Tossell, ii. 225
Toun, ii. 136
Towler, ii. 221
Tracy, iii. 50
Trafford, ii. 150 ; iv. 205, 214, 217, 219, 220, 223, 224
Travers, ii. 139
Treadgold, ii. 228
Trebourghe, ii. 198
Trecarell, iii. 57
Tregear, iii. 103, 104
Tregosse, ii. 224
Tregyan, iv. 139
Trelawny, iii. 57
Tremayne, ii. 222
Trenehard, ii. 213
Trentham, iv. 39
Treswell, iii. 32
Trewman, ii. 220
Trigg, ii. 211
Trompe, iv. 93
Trotman, i. 272
Trowell, ii. 205
Trussel, ii. 133 ; iv. 27
Tryon, Trioen, Trion, ii. 175, 176, 177, 178, 179, 180, 181, 182, 183, 184, 185, 186 ; iv. 256
Tucker, iv. 134
Tunstall, i. 80 ; iv. 238
Turke, ii. 221
Turner, i. 272 ; ii. 155, 211 ; iv. 103
Tuyll, iii. 238
Twhaytys, iv. 241
Twissellton, ii. 32
Twynham, iii. 83, 84
Tyes, iv. 2, 230
Tylyall, iv. 245
Tyrwhitt, ii. 213
Tyther, iii. 54

Umferwyle, iv. 231
Upton, i. 38, 85, 97 note ; ii. 224 ; iv. 38
Urmounde, 228
Uvedale, iv. 250

Valence, i. 48, 256, 281 ; iii. 56, 172, 201 ; iv. 228
Vallière, i. 31
Vandeleur, iii. 117
Vandeput, iv. 29
Vane, i. 55 ; iv. 44
Vanlore, iv. 130
Vardill, i. 257

Vaude, iii. 238
Vanlour, i. 35 note
Vaughan, ii. 176, 195, 224
Vaux, iii. 242 ; iv. 230
Vavasour, ii. 30, 39 ; iv. 239
Veale, iii. 102
Veccar, iv. 131
Veen, iii. 237
Veere, iii. 237
Venables, Venablis, Wenables, i. 187 ; ii. 130, 133, 137, 138, 139, 140, 142, 143, 144. See also Grosvenor
Venator, i. 124, 185, 186, 187 ; ii. 130, 131, 133, 142, 144
Verdon, i. 230
Vere, ii. 9 ; iii. 42 ; iv. 17 note, 18
Vernon, Vernun, Wernoun, ii. 130, 131, 132, 133, 134, 135, 136, 137, 138, 140, 142, 144, 149, 150, 151, 154, 155 ; iii. 82 ; iv. 248
Vernon-Harcourt, iv. 165
Verrio, Vario, ii. 201
Vicar, iii. 12
Vienne le Chastel, iv. 168
Vierendeels, ii. 177
Vigures, ii. 224
Vine, iv. 137
Vipont, iv. 241
Voorst, iii. 238
Voudrey, ii. 135, 148
Vyell, ii. 203

Waddis, iv. 139
Wade, ii. 239
Wadham, i. 108
Wahul, i. 113
Wake, Wace, Wach, ii. 110, 111, 112, 113, 194 ; iii. 78, 203 ; iv. 94, 256
Wakefield, ii. 274
Walcot, i. 234
Waldeve, iii. 73
Waleys, i. 248
Walker, ii. 26, 27, 219 ; iii. 2, 71
Waller, ii. 208 ; iii. 4, 5, 6
Wallis, iv. 142
Wallop, iii. 3, 4, 7 ; iv. 141
Walls, iv. 42
Walmsley, ii. 32
Walpole, i. 232 ; iv. 172
Walshe, iii. 1, 12
Walsingham, i. 150 ; ii. 116
Walton, i. 108
Warburton, iii. 32
Warbylton, iv. 250
Ward, ii. 22, 144, 211
Wardeux, iv. 3
Warner, ii. 48, 49, 50, 51
Warr, iv. 228
Warren, Warragn, Warrenne, i. 263 ; iii. 24, 27, 64, 186, 200, 201 ; iv. 112, 117, 124, 125
Warwick, i. 273
Washington, iv. 235

Wassenaer, iii. 237
Wasteneys, Wasteneis, ii. 130, 137 ;
   iii. 211
Waterhouse, i. 161
Waterton, iv. 233
Watkinson, ii. 38
Watson, ii. 227 ; iii. 55
Watts, i. 259, 265 ; ii. 211
Wayte, iv. 180
Weaverham, i. 177
Webb, iii. 61 ; iv. 45
Webster, iv. 128, 142
Weekes, ii. 228
Welch, ii. 163 ; iii. 68
Wells, ii. 217 ; iv. 142
Wellington, ii. 219
Wemyss, Weems, iv. 84
Wenard, ii. 198
Wendell, i. 259
Wentworth, i. 259, 260 ; iv. 25, 26
Wenyere, ii. 179
Werberton, ii. 133, 137
Weschyngton, iv. 235
Wessey, iv. 231
West, iii. 64
Westcott, ii. 211
Weston, i. 246, 258 ; iii. 79, 80 note
Wetinhale, ii. 140
Wevere, ii. 137
Wharton, ii. 34, 200, 201 ; iv. 86
Wheeler, iv. 136
Whipple, ii. 86
Whitaker, iii. 27
Whitbye, i. 266
White, i. 262 ; iii. 54
Whitenhall, iii. 5
Whitfield, ii. 21
Whiting, iii. 114, 115
Whittmister, iv. 139
Whoode, ii. 227
Wibbenbury, i. 180 ; ii. 129
Wiche, ii. 226
Widdows, ii. 29
Widdrington, i. 261
Wightwick, ii. 11
Wigton, iii. 73
Wiham, i. 125 ; ii. 97, 98
Wilberfoss, Wylbyrforse, iv. 111, 112, 246
Wilbre, ii. 146
Wilburham, ii. 130, 140, 141, 150
Wildish, ii. 208
Wilkinson, i. 55 ; ii. 139
Willey, i. 276
Williams, ii. 124 ; iii. 49
Williamscote, i. 249
Williamson, i. 162, 222
Willoughby, iv. 16, 107, 229
Wills, iii. 59
Willymott, i. 266
Willys, iii. 72
Wilmot, iii. 5, 20
Wilson, iv. 129
Wiltshire, i. 261

Winch, i. 267
Winchcombe, iii. 54
Windham, iv. 42, 43
Windle, iv. 131
Windsor, i. 126 ; ii. 95 ; iv. 28 note.
   See also Fitzgerald
Wingfield, ii. 6, 9 ; iv. 226
Winnington, ii. 130, 131, 132, 133, 134,
   135, 136, 138, 142, 150 note 3, 153
Winston, iv. 132
Wiseman, i. 31
Withrings, iv. 130
Wodeburgh, i. 214
Wodehouse, ii. 194
Wolf, ii. 135
Wolsey, iv. 21
Wolveley, iv. 215, 216, 217, 218
Wolverton, Wlvardinton, Wolward-
   ington, ii. 202
Wood, i. 218, 266 ; iii. 52, 57
Woodman, iv. 132
Woods, ii. 231 ; iv. 40, 135
Woodward, i. 40, 51 ; iv. 4
Woofe, iv. 134
Worlegh, iv. 215
Worth, i. 109
Wortley, ii. 185, 226
Wortley-Montagu, i. 32
Wotton, ii. 54
Wrenche, ii. 137
Wrennebur, ii. 134
Wright, ii. 50, 147, 225 ; iii. 36, 62 ;
   iv. 131
Wriothesley, ii. 209
Wrottesley, iii. 3, 166
Wunhale, i. 55
Wyard, i. 249
Wyat, iii. 53
Wydvile, iii. 165, 176
Wyett, ii. 197
Wyfolde, Wywold, iii. 186
Wykeham, iii. 187
Wyllysthroppe, iv. 240
Wyn, iii. 65
Wyndham, i. 4
Wynyard, i. 264
Wystowe, iv. 246
Wythes, iv. 103
Wytyngham, iii. 77
Wyvil, Wivells, ii. 35, 224

Yarborough, Yarburgh, ii. 30, 34, 35,
   36 ; iii. 153
Yard, iv. 129
Yeadon, iv. 104
Yeddynge, iv. 250
Yenevet, i. 75
Yeo, ii. 224
Ylebrouwere, ii. 197
Yonge, i. 276

Zincke, i. 28, 31
Zouche, iv. 229

NEW SERIES.

The Magazine of Art.

1/- net.

Edited by M. H. SPIELMANN.

CONTENTS OF THE JANUARY PART.

PLATES.

'THE HAPPY VALLEY.' By George Wetherbee, R.I.
Rembrandt Photogravure. Frontispiece.

'MAIDENHOOD.' By S. Melton Fisher. In Colours, after a
Pastel.

'PORTRAIT OF A LADY.' Painted by G. F. Watts, R.A.,
at the age of 15.

THE WORK OF GEORGE WETHERBEE, R.I. By Nancy
Bell.

MODERN FURNITURE : THE WORK OF AN UNPRO-
FESSIONAL DESIGNER.—MR. FRANK BRANGWYN'S FURNITURE.
By P. G. Konody, with Eleven Illustrations.

MODERN BRITISH ETCHERS : THOMAS HOPE Mc-
LACHLAN. By A Member of the Royal Society of Painter-Etchers. With Nine
Illustrations.

BRYNHILD ON SIGURD'S FUNERAL PYRE. Poem. By
Theodore Watts-Dunton. Illustrated by Byam Shaw, R.I.

CHARLES DICKENS AS A LOVER OF ART AND ARTISTS.
—I. By His Younger Daughter. With Three Illustrations.

THE RECENT ADVANCE IN ARCHITECTURE :—I. OUR
BEST MUNICIPAL BUILDINGS. By T. Raffles Davison. With Thirteen
Illustrations by the Author.

WALDO STORY : SCULPTOR.—I. By Evelyn March
Phillipps. With Eight Illustrations.

A METAL POINT DRAUGHTSMAN : MR. ÆLFRED
FAHEY. With Five Illustrations.

THE STUDENT : THE ART OF PAINTING IN PASTEL.
By S. Melton Fisher. With Three Illustrations.

RECENT ACQUISITIONS AT OUR PUBLIC MUSEUMS
AND GALLERIES.
THE EDINBURGH MUSEUM OF SCIENCE AND ART. By D. J. Vallance.
With Ten Illustrations.

CURIOSITIES OF ART : I.—THE FIRST OIL PICTURE
OF MR. GEORGE F. WATTS, R.A.

THE CHRONICLE OF ART. JANUARY. With an Illustration.

PUBLISHED BY CASSELL & CO., LIMITED.

a

The Architectural Review

FOR JANUARY, 1903.

Edited by an Advisory Committee consisting of

R. NORMAN SHAW, R.A.
JOHN BELCHER, A.R.A., F.R.I.B.A.
FRANK T. BAGGALLAY, F.R.I.B.A.
REGINALD BLOMFIELD, M.A.
GERALD C. HORSLEY.
MERVYN MACARTNEY.
E. J. MAY.

WALTER MILLARD.
ERNEST NEWTON.
EDWARD S. PRIOR, M.A.
HALSEY RICARDO.
Professor F. M. SIMPSON.
LEONARD STOKES, F.R.I.B.A., and
D. S. MacCOLL, M.A.

The Contents of the JANUARY NUMBER include:—

ABINGDON. By REV. W. J. LOFTIE. With Map and Eighteen Illustrations.

MEDIÆVAL FIGURE - SCULPTURE IN ENGLAND. Chapter IV. FIRST GOTHIC SCULPTURE, 1160-1275. With Forty-nine Illustrations.

LITHOGRAPH PLATE: 'THE LAST OF NEWGATE.' Drawn by MUIRHEAD BONE.

ARCHITECTURE AND THE ROYAL ACADEMY: A DISCUSSION. IV. By PROFESSOR F. M. SIMPSON.

CURRENT ARCHITECTURE.

BOOKS.

6d. net.

OF ALL BOOKSTALLS AND NEWSAGENTS.

EFFINGHAM HOUSE, ARUNDEL STREET, STRAND, W.C.

First of all . .

Go to any Bookseller's

and

Buy 'From the Abyss'

Opinions of the 'Literati.'

G. K. Chesterton in the *Daily News* says:

'The only book I ever read which really impressed me with a sense of the problems of the great poor populations of London. . . . Gives any reader what he really needs—an awful, confounding, asphyxiating sense of numbers and population.'

The Pall Mall Gazette says:

'It is an essay of singular and amazing power.'

The Pilot says:

'Those who want, to know how the vast army of the poor live cannot do better than get a little book "From the Abyss." Its price is *only* one shilling, but for that small coin more can be learnt of the ways and means of the poor than from many more costly volumes'

The Dundee Advertiser says:

'A remarkable little book.'

The Sussex Daily News says:

'Open it wherever one may passages of literary beauty and reflective power leap to the eye; but "From the Abyss," should be read as a whole. To read it is a pleasure and a rare .experience.'

1/- NET R. BRIMLEY JOHNSON, NET 1/-
8 York Buildings, Adelphi, W.C.

CASTLES AND ABBEYS

PART I. Contains
(with Special Presentation Plate):
1. Windsor Castle.
2. Dunfermline Abbey.
3. Tintern Abbey.
4. Westminster Abbey.
5. Dublin Castle.

PART II. Contains
(with special Presentation Plate):
1. Dublin Castle (completion).
2. Tower of London.
3. Glastonbury Abbey.
4. Melrose Abbey.
5. Chepstow Castle.
6. Boyle Abbey.

PART III. Contains:
1. Boyle Abbey (finish of).
2. Stirling Castle.
3. Battle Abbey.
4. Warwick Castle.
5. Conway Castle.
6. Kenilworth Castle.

PART VII. Contains:
1. Tewkesbury Abbey.
   The Battle of Tewkesbury.
2. Urquhart Castle.
   The Black Cat's Secret.
3. Alnwick Castle.
   The Revolt of Harry Hotspur.

PART VIII. Contains:
1. Rochester Castle.
   Legend: The Forester's Revenge.
2. Waltham Abbey.
   Legend: The Spell of the Demon.
3. Limerick Castle.
   Legend: All for Love.

PART IX. Contains:
1. Netley Abbey.
   Legend: The Pygmalion of the Cloister.
2. Barnard Castle.
   Legends: (1) Count Jaffroy's Gift.
   (2) The Rebellion of 1569.
3. Holyrood Palace (Extracts from the Registers).
   Legend: The Faithful Wife.

OF

GREAT BRITAIN & IRELAND.

PART IV. Contains:
1. Kenilworth Castle (finish of).
   Legends: (1) Legend of Amy Robsart.
   (2) Legend of Alice Charlcot.
2. Malmesbury Abbey.
   Legend: The Silent Brother Nemo.
3. Edinburgh Castle.
   Legend: Taken by Strategy.

PART V. Contains:
1. Cardiff Castle.
   Legend: A Costly Lesson.
2. Carisbrook Castle.
   Legend: Charles I. and His Attempted Escape.
3. Roslyn Chapel and Castle.
   Legends: (1) The Rash Wager.
   (2) The Fiery Legend.

PART VI. Contains:
1. Fountains Abbey.
   Legend of Fountains Abbey.
2. Harlech Castle.
   Legends: (1) The Men of Harlech.
   (2) Curious Phenomenon at Harlech.
3. Arundel Castle.
   Legends: (1) Roundhead and Puritan.
   (2) The Legend of Syr Bevis.
   (3) The Owls of Arundel Castle.
   (4) The Surrender of a Howard on Bosworth Field.

PART X. Contains:
1. Pontefract Castle.
   Legend: How the Castle was taken from the King.
   Extract from the History of Pontefract.
2. St. Alban's Abbey.
   Legend of St. Alban.
3. Hurstmonceaux Castle.
   Legend: Maud of Ditchling.

PART XI. Contains:
1. Hastings Castle.
   Legend: The Mysterious Speculator.
2. Jedburgh Abbey.
   Legend: The Spectre at the Ball.
3. Flint Castle.
   Legend: The King of the Commons.

PART XII. Contains:
1. Berkeley Castle.
   Legend, etc., of Berkeley Castle.
2. Kelso Abbey.
   Legend of Kelso Abbey.
3. Fotheringay Castle.
   Trial and Execution of Mary Queen of Scots.

TO BE OBTAINED OF ALL BOOKSELLERS.

Or of the Publisher
JOHN DICKS, 313 Strand, London, W.C.

IN HANDSOME EMBLEMATIC COVER, 7/6
Any Single Part sent for Eightpence.

Books for the Library

LUCA AND ANDREA DELLA ROBBIA. By MAUD CRUTT-
WELL. With 150 Reproductions in Photogravure and Half-tone. 25*s*. net.

*THE STORY OF SIENA AND SAN GIMIGANO, AND
FLORENCE.* By EDMUND G. GARDNER. First Two Volumes of the 'Larger Mediæval
Town Series'; library volumes, very fully illustrated. Each 10*s*. 6*d*. net.

SONS OF FRANCIS. By ANNIE MACDONELL. Studies of Certain
of the Followers of St. Francis. With Illustrations. 12*s*. 6*d*. net.

LETTERS FROM THE EAST, 1837–57. By HENRY JAMES
Ross. Edited by his wife, JANET Ross. Illustrated. 12*s*. 6*d*. net.

THE CATHEDRALS OF GREAT BRITAIN. An Illustrated
Guide. By Rev. P. H. DITCHFIELD. With 75 Illustrations. 7*s*. 6*d*. net ; roan, 9*s*. net.

ALEXANDRE DUMAS. By HARRY A. SPURR. With 16 Illus-
trations. 12*s*. 6*d*. net. *⁎* 'The most comprehensive account in English.'—*St. James's.*

THE SPERONARA. By ALEXANDRE DUMAS. (Journey with
Dumas I.). 3*s*. 6*d*. net. *⁎* 'As fresh and brilliant as a good novel.'—*Outlook.*

MAZZINI. By BOLTON KING, M.A. First Volume of 'The
Temple Biographies,' an important new series. Illustrated. 4*s*. 6*d*. net.

BEATRICE D'ESTE, DUCHESS OF MILAN. By JULIA
Cartwright. A Study of the Renaissance. Illustrated. 15*s*. net.

FLORENTINE VILLAS. By JANET ROSS. With Photogravures
from Medals and Zache's Engravings ; also Line-drawings. £3 3*s*. net.

STORIES OF THE TUSCAN ARTISTS. By ALBINIA WHERRY.
With 8 Photogravures and 45 Half-tone Reproductions. 10*s*. 6*d*. net.

THACKERAY'S PROSE WORKS. Illustrated by C. E. BROCK.
Edited by WALTER JERROLD. In 30 vols., 15 ready. 3*s*. net per vol.

HAZLITT'S COLLECTED WORKS. Edited by A. R. WALLER
and A. GLOVER. Introduction by W. E. HENLEY. In 12 vols., 5 ready. 7*s*. 6*d*. net
per vol.

THE BREAKFAST TABLE SERIES OF O. W. HOLMES.
(Autocrat—Professor—Poet). Profusely Illustrated by H. M. BROCK. Three vols.
3*s*. 6*d*. net each. *⁎* 'All that was needed to make the charm still keener.'—
Pall Mall.

LAMB'S ESSAYS OF ELIA. Profusely Illustrated by C. E.
BROCK. Introduction by A. BIRRELL. 2 vols. 7*s*. 6*d*. net. [*Fourth Edition.*

BOSWELL'S JOHNSON. Edited by A. GLOVER. Introduction
by AUSTIN DOBSON. 150 Illustrations by H. RAILTON, and Portraits. 3 vols., 22*s*. 6*d*.
net.

⁎ *Messrs. Dent would be pleased to receive the names of BOOK
LOVERS to whom they may regularly send their List.*

J. M. Dent & Co., London

HOW TO
FURNISH SMARTLY

Either FOR CASH or
ON THE INSTALMENT PLAN.

For Cash.—Messrs. NORMAN & STACEY offer their customers the largest and most artistic selection of furniture in London at the lowest possible prices.

On the Instalment Plan.—Messrs. NORMAN & STACEY give intending purchasers the advantage of their clever scheme (endorsed by Mr. LABOUCHERE and others), which enables customers to furnish their house or flat throughout (even to the extent of Linen, Silver, Cutlery, Blinds, etc.) **out of income** by dividing the whole amount into 6, 12, or 18 monthly payments.

NORMAN & STACEY,
LIMITED,

252, 253, 254, 255, 256 TOTTENHAM COURT ROAD.

CPSIA information can be obtained
at www.ICGtesting.com
Printed in the USA
LVHW080233060420
652336LV00012B/131